THE CONSTRUCTIVE PROMISE OF SCHLEIERMACHER'S THEOLOGY

Rethinking Theologies: Constructing
Alternatives in History and Doctrine

Edited by
Marion Grau
Susannah Cornwall
Steed Davidson

Volume 4

THE CONSTRUCTIVE PROMISE OF SCHLEIERMACHER'S THEOLOGY

Shelli M. Poe

LONDON • NEW YORK • OXFORD • NEW DELHI • SYDNEY

T&T CLARK
Bloomsbury Publishing Plc
50 Bedford Square, London, WC1B 3DP, UK
1385 Broadway, New York, NY 10018, USA
29 Earlsfort Terrace, Dublin 2, Ireland

BLOOMSBURY, T&T CLARK and the T&T Clark logo are trademarks
of Bloomsbury Publishing Plc

First published in Great Britain 2021
Paperback edition published 2023

Copyright © Shelli M. Poe, 2021

Shelli M. Poe has asserted her right under the Copyright, Designs and Patents Act,
1988, to be identified as Author of this work.

For legal purposes the Acknowledgments on p. ix constitute an extension
of this copyright page.

Cover design: Terry Woodley
Cover image: Piotr Malinowski / Alamy Stock Photo

All rights reserved. No part of this publication may be reproduced or transmitted
in any form or by any means, electronic or mechanical, including photocopying,
recording, or any information storage or retrieval system, without prior permission
in writing from the publishers.

Bloomsbury Publishing Plc does not have any control over, or responsibility for, any
third-party websites referred to or in this book. All internet addresses given in this
book were correct at the time of going to press. The author and publisher regret any
inconvenience caused if addresses have changed or sites have ceased to exist, but can
accept no responsibility for any such changes.

A catalogue record for this book is available from the British Library.

Library of Congress Cataloging-in-Publication Data
Names: Poe, Shelli M., author.
Title: The constructive promise of Schleiermacher's theology / Shelli M. Poe.
Description: London; New York: T&T Clark, 2021. | Series: Rethinking theologies:
constructing alternatives in history and doctrine |
Includes bibliographical references and index. |
Identifiers: LCCN 2020044059 (print) | LCCN 2020044060 (ebook) |
ISBN 9780567691682 (hb) | ISBN 9780567691705 (epub) | ISBN 9780567691699 (epdf)
Subjects: LCSH: Schleiermacher, Friedrich, 1768–1834. | Theology, Doctrinal.
Classification: LCC BX4827.S3 P639 2021 (print) | LCC BX4827.S3 (ebook) |
DDC 230/.044–dc23
LC record available at https://lccn.loc.gov/2020044059
LC ebook record available at https://lccn.loc.gov/2020044060

ISBN: HB: 978-0-5676-9168-2
PB: 978-0-5677-0025-4
ePDF: 978-0-5676-9169-9
ePUB: 978-0-5676-9170-5

Series: Rethinking Theologies: Constructing Alternatives in History and Doctrine

Typeset by Newgen KnowledgeWorks Pvt. Ltd., Chennai, India

To find out more about our authors and books visit www.bloomsbury.com
and sign up for our newsletters.

*To Jody and Sofia,
my love and my very heart*

CONTENTS

Acknowledgments	ix
List of Abbreviations	xi
INTRODUCTION	1
Schleiermacher and Constructive Forms of Theology	2
Schleiermacher's Contributions to Constructive Conversations	2
Methods and Motivations	5
A Brief Introduction to Schleiermacher's Thought on Religion and Theology	8
Religion	10
Theology	13
The Approach of This Volume	16
Constructive Forms of Theology	16
Schleiermacher and Sexism, Colonialism, and Racism	17
Initial Motivations	26
Chapter Overview	33
Chapter 1	
TRINITY	39
Schleiermacher and the Doctrine of the Trinity	42
Problematic Features of Trinitarian Doctrine	47
Subordination, Oscillation, and Speculation	47
Sexism and Idolatry, Death-Centrism, and Kyriarchy	50
Essential Trinitarianism	53
Schleiermacher's Beginnings	53
Constructive Interpretation and Development	57
Chapter 2	
CHRIST AND REDEMPTION	79
Contemporary Challenges to Christology	82
Schleiermacher's Christology	90
Avoiding the Chalcedonian Formula	90
The Person of Christ: Divine Indwelling and the Completion of Creation	92
The Work of Christ	96
Womanist Atonement Theories and Schleiermacher's Soteriology	101
Womanist Critiques of Substitutionary Atonement	102
Engaging Schleiermacher's Soteriology: Comparison and Evaluation	108

Further Benefits of Schleiermacher's Soteriology	130
Sin	131
Body and Affect	136
Natality and Joy	138

Chapter 3
CHURCH AND SPIRIT

CHURCH AND SPIRIT	143
Joy and Laughter as Ecclesial Practices	144
Schleiermacher's Ecclesial Imagination	146
Schleiermacher's Christological Pneumatology	151
Feminist Laughter	152
Expanding the Imaginary: A Queer Community of Woman	156
Lilith	161
Eve	165
Hagar	168
Mary	172
Schleiermacher and a Queer Community of Woman	175

Chapter 4
GOD AND CREATION

GOD AND CREATION	179
Absolute Causality and Divine Sovereignty	180
Divine Aseity, Human Self-Initiated Activity, and Divine Omnipotence	182
Radical Monotheism and Sin and Evil	187
Divine Sovereignty and Prayerful Submission	194
Feminist Ecumenism and Purgative Submission	195
Incarnational Submission	202
CONCLUSION	211
Bibliography	217
Index	229

ACKNOWLEDGMENTS

A number of colleagues have devoted their time and expertise to reading drafts of some of the material that follows and/or talking with me about material for other projects that has come to shape what I have offered here. I would like to thank Paul DeHart, Andrew Dole, Christine Helmer, Cathie Kelsey, Paul Nimmo, Kevin Vander Schel, Mary Streufert, and Ed Waggoner for their invaluable suggestions, conversations, and questions. My gratitude also goes to my colleagues at Millsaps College's Works in Progress faculty cohort, especially Tamar Shirinian, Steven Smith, Elise Smith, Elizabeth Egan, and Charles S. Preston, who read and commented on early drafts of some of the book's chapters. I also want to thank Susannah Cornwall and Marion Grau, whose skillful editorial feedback on the manuscript helped bring the work to its final form. Anna Turton has been a pleasure to work with as an acquisitions editor, and I am honored that she has been as enthusiastic about my second monograph with T&T Clark as she was with the first.

It is with a heavy and full heart that I express my gratitude to the late Terrence Tice for his comments on the manuscript as well. He was in the process of reading and commenting on its chapters when he unexpectedly passed away. I am honored and grateful to have been engaged in conversation with Terry. He has influenced so many scholars' lives and work, and I am grateful to be counted among them. His legacy will live on in the Schleiermacher Digital Archive at Iliff School of Theology and in the generations of Schleiermacher scholars to come. I hope to become just half as generous and kindhearted as he was, both as a scholar and as a person.

Some of the following material was first published or presented in other venues: Chapter 3 includes material first published in "Lilith, Christianity," *Encyclopedia of the Bible and Its Reception, vol. 16*, edited by Christine Helmer (Berlin: De Gruyter, pp. 665–6). A brief version of a portion of Chapter 3 was presented to the Women, Gender, and Religion Group at the Southeastern Commission for the Study of Religion, a regional branch of the American Academy of Religion, under the title, "Expanding the Imaginary: A Queer Community for Feminist Ecumenism," in Raleigh, NC, on March 6, 2017. Thank you to those in attendance for your encouragement and questions. Chapter 4 includes revised versions of material first published in "Friedrich Schleiermacher's Theology as a Resource for Ecological Economics," *Theology Today* 73/1 (2016): 9–23 and in "Locating Prayerful Submission for Feminist Ecumenism: Holy Saturday or Incarnate Life?" *Feminist Theology* 26/2 (2018): 171–84.

Between writing early chapter drafts and bringing the manuscript to its final stage, I gave birth to a beautiful baby, Sofia Marie. Her presence has brought more depth and urgency to this book project than I could have imagined it would.

I hope that she might experience a church whose theology supports, encourages, and empowers her to know that she is loved beyond measure, and that this life is and can be beautiful. My stepchildren, Ray and Henry, keep teaching me about the courage it takes to be and to become, and about the beauty of transformation. I'm so glad we're family. To my spouse and friend, Jody, I can only say thank you for walking with me through this new season of our lives and for supporting my work, day in and day out, in innumerable ways.

ABBREVIATIONS

BO	Schleiermacher, Friedrich. *Brief Outline of the Study of Theology*. Translated by William Farrer. Eugene, OR: Wipf & Stock, 2007.
CEC	Schleiermacher, Friedrich. *Christmas Eve Celebration: A Dialogue*. Revised edition. Edited and translated by Terrence N. Tice. Eugene, OR: Cascade Books, 2010.
CF	Schleiermacher, Friedrich. *Christian Faith: A New Translation and Critical Edition*. Translated by Terrence Tice, Catherine Kelsey, and Edwina Lawyer. Edited by Catherine Kelsey and Terrence Tice. 2 Vols. Louisville, KY: Westminster John Knox, 2016.
Letters	Schleiermacher, Friedrich. "Letters on the Occasion of the Political-Theological Task and the Open Letter of Jewish Householders." In *A Debate on Jewish Emancipation and Christian Theology in Old Berlin*. Edited and translated by Richard Crouter and Julie Klassen. Indianapolis: Hackett, 2004.
OD1	Schleiermacher, Friedrich. "On the Discrepancy between the Sabellian and Athanasian Method of Representing the Doctrine of a Trinity in the Godhead (Part One)." Translated by Moses Stuart. *Biblical Repository and Quarterly Observer* 5/18 (April 1835): 265–353.
OD2	Schleiermacher, Friedrich. "On the Discrepancy between the Sabellian and Athanasian Method of Representing the Doctrine of a Trinity in the Godhead (Part Two)." Translated by Moses Stuart. *Biblical Repository and Quarterly Observer* 6/19 (July 1835): 1–116.
OR	Schleiermacher, Friedrich. *On Religion: Speeches to Its Cultured Despisers*. Cambridge Texts in the History of Philosophy. Edited by Richard Crouter. Cambridge: Cambridge University Press, 1996.
PP	Schleiermacher, Friedrich. "The Power of Prayer in Relation to Outward Circumstances." In *Selected Sermons of Schleiermacher*. Translated by Mary F. Wilson. Edited by W. Robertson Nicoll. Eugene, OR: Wipf & Stock, 2004, pp. 38–51.
SS	Schleiermacher, Friedrich. *Schleiermacher: Christmas Dialogue, the Second Speech, and Other Selections*. Edited and Translated with an Introduction by Julia A. Lamm. Mahwah, NJ: Paulist Press, 2014.

INTRODUCTION

Friedrich Schleiermacher (1768–1834) has been widely acclaimed as the progenitor of modern theology. His *Christian Faith* (1830/1) details the major loci of systematic theology in ways that trouble long-standing assumptions, offer novel analyses and constructive contributions, and encourage his readers to confront advances in modern sciences. Yet many scholars have not yet recognized how Schleiermacher's thought might continue to be relevant within contemporary efforts at doctrinal refinement and development. The main argument of this book is that Schleiermacher offers a theology that can be developed in conversation with contemporary theologians to disrupt kyriarchal ways of thinking.[1] I investigate four areas of Schleiermacher's theology in his *Christian Faith*: the doctrine of the Trinity, Christology and redemption, ecclesiology and pneumatology, and the doctrines of God and creation. In each of these areas, Schleiermacher's theology disrupts kyriarchal patterns of thought and works hand in hand with contemporary efforts aimed at constructing life-giving forms of Christian theology.

Key features of my argument include the following claims. Schleiermacher's trinitarian thought calls for readers to let go of the traditionally androcentric and arguably hierarchical doctrine of the immanent Trinity. The doctrine of the immanent Trinity can be replaced with a doctrine of the essential Trinity that I develop out of Schleiermacher's theology, which understands the divine essence in a non-gendered and non-hierarchical way. With regard to Christology and soteriology, Schleiermacher rejects the idea of the substitutionary death of the God-man, which womanist theologians have shown is especially detrimental for

---

1. Elisabeth Schüssler Fiorenza coined the term "kyriarchy," which means "the rule of the emperor/master/lord/father/husband over his subordinates" (Elisabeth Schüssler Fiorenza, *Jesus: Miriam's Child, Sophia's Prophet: Critical Issues in Feminist Christology* [New York: Continuum, 2004; originally published in 1994], p. 14). She introduced this term in response to the inadequacy of "patriarchy" to describe the exploitation of women along with those who are not "elite Western educated propertied Euro-American men" (ibid.). By adopting the word "kyriarchy," I aim to emphasize that "not all men dominate and exploit all women without difference," and that a central focus of theologies that aim at social justice should be those who live "at the bottom of the kyriarchal pyramid and who struggle against multiplicative forms of oppression" (ibid.).

those who have historically engaged in voluntary or forced surrogacy roles, and which feminists have argued is androcentric. In its place, Schleiermacher offers a pneumatologically framed Christology that foregrounds the diversity of the communities that embody Christ's Spirit and sees salvation as a historical and social process that requires resistance to systems of oppression. Schleiermacher's ecclesiology and pneumatology reject spiritual elitism and hegemonic thought, which, as mujerista and queer theologians have demonstrated, have served the interests of the ruling class. His theology inspires, instead, a celebration of joy-producing love and diversity within egalitarian Christian communities aimed at establishing social justice. Finally, Schleiermacher rejects the notion of God as a disinterested being who is or could be separate from creation and who intervenes in the world, which feminists, postcolonial, and ecological theologians have argued aligns with a problematic form of masculinity that has serious consequences for oppressed peoples and the earth itself. Schleiermacher's doctrines of God and creation focus instead on the interdependence of creaturely life, which he conceives as inseparable from divine creative activity.

Focusing on these four areas of Schleiermacher's theology, I demonstrate that critical engagement with his thought provides an important historical precedent for reconstructing the major loci of systematic theology and can bolster the work of contemporary theologians—particularly womanist, feminist, queer, ecological, and postcolonial theologians—as they rethink, reconfigure, and reconstruct various portions of Christian theology in non-kyriarchal ways. Although Schleiermacher himself could not be identified as a theologian of these types, his theological impulses and insights, updated and revised in light of current thought, beneficially contribute to contemporary theologies that work against kyriarchy.

Schleiermacher and Constructive Forms of Theology

Schleiermacher's Contributions to Constructive Conversations

The challenges that face the Christian church today include a number of key and intersecting nodes whose elimination might move the church along on the way to social justice. These are the familiar "isms" and their corollaries: racism, sexism, classism, heterosexism and heteronormativity, ecological degradation, and religious exclusivism and divisiveness. The present book joins a handful of scholarly works attempting to wrestle with the potential bearing of Schleiermacher's ideas on the "isms" that plague the contemporary church and society. In 1992, Iain G. Nicol explored Schleiermacher's relationship to one of these "isms" by editing a volume on Schleiermacher and feminism, which bore that title.[2] The volume includes essays detailing Schleiermacher's understanding of women, love, and

---

2. *Schleiermacher and Feminism: Sources, Evaluations, and Responses*, Schleiermacher: Studies and Translations, vol. 12, ed. Iain Nicol (Lewiston: Edwin Mellen, 1992).

marriage; the gender inflection of his theology; his construction of the gendered self; and Schleiermacher's feminist impulses within the context of his later work. More recently, as I discuss below, Theodore Vial's *Modern Religion, Modern Race* implicates Schleiermacher in constructing a racially inflected hierarchy of religion, despite Schleiermacher's appreciation of diversity and openness to others.[3] Other scholars have offered analyses and evaluations of Schleiermacher's relation to these and other themes, including colonialism, ecology, religious pluralism, and political engagement.[4] Joining projects such as these, I demonstrate in this book how Schleiermacher's theology is both involved in some of the "isms" that need eradication and also includes elements that can work against them. Going further, I demonstrate how Schleiermacher's thought can be developed in conversation with theologians working constructively today to disrupt kyriarchy. Because this is an area of Schleiermacher studies that has not been widely explored, one of the goals of the present book is to show that doing so is a fruitful avenue for future research.

Generally speaking, those engaged in constructive forms of theology address themselves to contemporary challenges, develop Christian doctrine within these new contexts, and draw on the insights of contemporary thinkers in so doing.[5]

---

3. Theodore Vial, *Modern Religion, Modern Race* (New York: Oxford University Press, 2016).

4. See Patricia E. Guenther-Gleason, *On Schleiermacher and Gender Politics*, Harvard Theological Studies (Harrisburg, PA: Trinity Press International, 1997); Thandeka, "Schleiermacher, Feminism, and Liberation Theologies: A Key," in *The Cambridge Companion to Friedrich Schleiermacher*, ed. Jacqueline Mariña (Cambridge: Cambridge University Press, 2005), pp. 287–305; Joerg Rieger, "Friedrich Schleiermacher," in *Empire and the Christian Tradition: New Readings of Classical Theologians* (Minneapolis, MN: Fortress, 2007), pp. 271–82; Steven R. Jungkeit, *Spaces of Modern Theology: Geography and Power in Schleiermacher's World*, New Approaches to Religion and Power (New York: Palgrave Macmillan, 2012); *Schleiermacher and Sustainability: A Theology for Ecological Living*, Columbia Series in Reformed Theology, ed. Shelli M. Poe (Louisville, KY: Westminster John Knox, 2018); Jerry Dawson, *Schleiermacher: The Evolution of a Nationalist* (Austin: University of Texas, 1996); Thomas Reynolds, "Reconsidering Schleiermacher and the Problem of Religious Diversity: Toward a Dialectical Pluralism," *Journal of the American Academy of Religion* 73/1 (March 2005): 151–81.

5. My work here is consonant with much of Jason Wyman's description of "constructive theology" insofar as this book aims to be dialogical, epistemically humble, interdisciplinary, intersectional, engaged with social justice issues, context-specific, resists divorcing theology from ethics, and is conscious of the human agency involved in doing theology. Nevertheless, I avoid the term "constructive theology" for two reasons. First, I engage with many theologians who do not self-identify as constructive theologians and may stand at some remove from the project of constructive theology. Second, while many constructive theologians are skeptical of systematic theology, I believe that the systematic theologian may aim to produce a work that is consistent and coherent while simultaneously recognizing that their theology is fallible, context-specific, and needs continual revision

Such scholars use their considerable grounding in both historical theology and contemporary theory to develop Christian doctrine in light of issues of social concern. Similarly, in this work, I show how Schleiermacher's theology can be integrated with insights from subsequent thinkers to advance conversations held at the intersection of doctrine and practice about the Trinity, Christ and redemption, the Church and Spirit, and God's relation to creation. Schleiermacher moves the conversation forward by offering critique and reconstruction of each of these doctrines in ways that have not hitherto been widely acknowledged. Although scholars have recognized Schleiermacher's rejection of particular doctrinal formulations, they have not widely attended to his constructive doctrinal moves. This book puts on display Schleiermacher's constructive vision and his relevance for contemporary theology.

Schleiermacher's call for a new Protestant treatment of trinitarian doctrine and his own understanding of God suggest a way forward that warrants attention, especially given recent work like Linn Marie Tonstad's *God and Difference*, which persuasively points out the shortcomings in a number of prominent contemporary trinitarian theologies.[6] Schleiermacher's work advances contemporary Christological and soteriological conversations by retrieving the language of divine indwelling and developing the idea of Christ's familial influence within the Christian community.[7] Schleiermacher's ecclesiology and pneumatology contribute to contemporary work by highlighting joy as a hitherto underdeveloped mark of the church. Finally, his treatment of the relationship between God and creation contributes to current conversations aiming at a noncompetitive God-world relation. By engaging with these four doctrinal loci, I present Schleiermacher as a beneficial conversation partner within a reciprocal exchange in order to uncover potential points of similarity and enrichment between his thought and contemporary constructive forms of theology.[8]

and reconstruction by many interlocutors. For a history of the term, theory, and methods of constructive theology, see Jason Wyman, *Constructing Constructive Theology: An Introductory Sketch* (Minneapolis, MN: Fortress, 2017). See also *What Is Constructive Theology? Histories, Methodologies, and Perspectives*, ed. Marion Grau and Jason Wyman (New York: Bloomsbury, 2020).

6. Linn Marie Tonstad, *God and Difference: The Trinity, Sexuality, and the Transformation of Finitude* (New York: Routledge, 2016).

7. The latter dovetails with contemporary African, Asian, and postcolonial attention to spiritual ancestors as a way of understanding the way in which Christ continues to work among Christian communities. See Kwame Bediako, *Christianity in Africa: The Renewal of a Non-Western Religion* (Maryknoll, NY: Orbis, 1995), p. 217; Kwame Bediako, *Jesus in Africa: The Christian Gospel in African History and Experience* (Selangor, Malaysia: Editions Clé and Regnum Africa, 2000), pp. 20-33; Peter C. Phan, *Christianity with an Asian Face: Asian American Theology in the Making* (Maryknoll, NY: Orbis, 2003), pp. 125-45. This avenue is promising for future research.

8. Christine Helmer's *Theology and the End of Doctrine* (Louisville, KY: Westminster John Knox, 2014) also makes the case that Schleiermacher's work can be beneficial

Methods and Motivations

In line with the multiplicative forms of oppression that characterize our world, I work intersectionally in this book, not assessing Schleiermacher's thought in relation to feminist, womanist, postcolonial, or queer theologies in isolation from one another but together as a community of advocates for social justice whose interests are overlapping in many ways. The importance of the intersectionality of these points of injustice is now coming to the fore as theorists reckon with the doubling and redoubling of oppression for certain populations, and the interconnected ideas and practices that fuel many types of oppression simultaneously. By arguing for Schleiermacher's inclusion as a conversation partner with those doing constructive forms of theology, I intend to indicate the wide appeal of his theology, his weaknesses notwithstanding, for scholars who are addressing multiple, intersecting challenges.

One aspect of Schleiermacher's appeal is that the intellectual rigor of his *Christian Faith* matches the complexity of the challenges facing the Christian church and wider society. This rigor is highlighted most poignantly, perhaps, in the systematic character of his theology, which places him alongside Thomas Aquinas. Vial adds a few other Reformed thinkers as well: "There are many fine systematic theologies, but Schleiermacher's *The Christian Faith* ranks among Thomas's *Summa Theologiae*, Calvin's *Institutes of the Christian Religion*, and Barth's *Church Dogmatics* in its profundity, comprehensiveness, and epoch-making effect."[9] Schleiermacher's epoch-making effect might be attributed to the fact that he does not constrain his Christian intellect by the dominant theological claims of previous eras. Rather, as we will see, he constructs doctrine both with fidelity to Christian traditions and scripture, and also with attention to the contexts within which particular churches and individuals find themselves. Walking the line between intellectual innovation and faithfulness to the historically significant theological convictions of previous generations is a task that every theologian who remains within a tradition while engaging constructive work undertakes, and Schleiermacher does it with confidence. As he writes in a letter to Jacobi in March 1818, "The Bible is the original interpretation of the Christian feeling, and for just this reason is so established that it might always be better understood and developed. I, as a Protestant theologian, will not let anyone deprive me of this right of development."[10] The intellectual posture that Schleiermacher's theology

---

for producing doctrine. See Chapters 4 and 5, in particular: "Language and Reality: A Theological Epistemology with Some Help from Schleiermacher" and "Acknowledging Social Construction and Moving beyond Deconstruction: Doctrine for Theology and Religious Studies."

9. Theodore Vial, *Schleiermacher: A Guide for the Perplexed*, T&T Clark (New York: Bloomsbury, 2013), p. 82.

10. Friedrich Schleiermacher, "To Jacobi. Berlin, March 30, 1818," in *Schleiermacher: Christmas Dialogue, the Second Speech, and Other Selections*, The Classics of Western Spirituality, ed., trans., and with an intro. Julia Lamm (New York: Paulist Press, 2014), p. 263.

exhibits can serve as a model for contemporary theologians who are willing to sacrifice neither systematic nor traditioned modes of thinking in efforts toward the establishment of social justice in contemporary contexts.

Be that as it may, Schleiermacher's work is not completely satisfying and the task of theology is clearly not finished with him. Theologians engaging in constructive forms of theology recognize the need to update doctrine and apply it to current challenges, and often do so by drawing on contemporaneous thinkers outside of theology. In this book, I engage with thinkers who are conversant in feminist theory, womanist ethics, leftist politics, queer theory, ecological thought, and Western philosophy. The knowledge produced in such external disciplines is often integral to the constructive theologian's ability to analyze the current context and advance the theological conversation surrounding issues of social concern. As such, this book identifies places where Schleiermacher's theology and the thought of current thinkers outside of Christian theology diverge and connect, dovetail, and go their separate ways. Doing so not only demonstrates the benefits of Schleiermacher's theology as it stands but also brings his theological impulses into the present with additions, criticisms, corrections, and advancements for the current context.

By drawing together Schleiermacher's work and contemporary theologies in this book, I am also motivated to move constructive forms of theology out of the margins of theological discourse, where possible.[11] Kathryn Tanner has articulated the procedure well in her discussion of strategies for making feminist theology, in particular, more effective:

> As many elements as possible from patriarchal discourse should be rearticulated to a feminist purpose. That is the only way to keep feminist theology from being classified as a marginal, fringe movement. The more that feminist theologians use for their own purposes the cultural elements that have been appropriated by patriarchal interest, the greater the feminist claim to theological credibility, and the harder it is for a feminist agenda to be dismissed by those committed to the dominant patriarchal organization of theological discourse. Such a procedure establishes feminists as serious participants in theological discourse; it establishes their right to be talked to rather than about. The tactic of disarticulating as many

---

11. Some forms of marginal theology are intentionally marginal and would lose their critical power were they to become "mainstream." As Lisa Isherwood and Marcella Althaus-Reid write of queer theology, "it is a theology from the margins which wants to remain at the margins. … Terrible is the fate of theologies from the margin when they want to be accepted by the centre! Queer theology strives instead for differentiation and plurality" ("Queering Theology," in *The Sexual Theologian: Essays on Sex, God, and Politics*, ed. Marcella Althaus-Reid and Lisa Isherwood [New York: T&T Clark, 2004], p. 3). By bringing Schleiermacher's work together with constructive contemporary forms of theology, I aim to amplify the theologies of those who have been marginal in Christian history while keeping their critical edge.

elements as possible from patriarchal discourse and rearticulating them for feminist purposes is also the only way to further a feminist transformation of theological and social practices.[12]

If constructive forms of theology are to become routinely engaged and grappled with in mainstream contemporary theological discourse, one strategy is to take account of standard theological topics and ways of thinking that are currently dominant, while at the same time offering creative theological thought that might move the conversation further. Kwok Pui-Lan, who also finds Tanner's approach helpful, outlines two tactics postcolonial feminist theologians could take. In the first, the theologian adopts "traditional Christian themes as a way to think through theology, such as God, Christ, atonement, church, and eschatology. The advantage," she explains, is that feminists may "contest their discursive power" and "provide alternative ways of thinking."[13] A more daring alternative is to start from a feminist analysis of a sociocultural and political situation and then "articulate theological issues and themes from such an analysis."[14] Kwok advocates a hybrid approach that incorporates elements of each of these strategies. While I primarily take the first approach, I aim to bring Schleiermacher and contemporary constructive forms of theology together to illuminate and challenge one another.

At the same time as I wish to heed Tanner's advice about linking constructive forms of theology with traditional sources, it must be acknowledged that this book engages the work of Friedrich Schleiermacher—a figure who, while he is undeniably important in the history of Western Christian thought and must be reckoned with, has also been an object of scorn. If Tanner is right that "the more traditional the material with which it works, the greater the influence of feminist theology," then I concede at the outset that my choice of "traditional" material may limit the scope of this book's effects on the theological landscape.[15] I am willing to take that risk for a number of reasons. As I have argued elsewhere, Schleiermacher's theology is more faithful to traditional sources than many of his readers have been willing to concede.[16] Further, if one wishes to engage in contemporary theology,

---

12. Kathryn Tanner, "Social Theory Concerning the 'New Social Movements' and the Practice of Feminist Theology," in *Horizons in Feminist Theology: Identity, Tradition, and Norms*, ed. Rebecca S. Chopp and Sheila Greeve Davaney (Minneapolis, MN: Fortress, 1997), pp. 189–90.

13. Kwok Pui-Lan, *Postcolonial Imagination and Feminist Theology* (Louisville, KY: Westminster John Knox, 2005), p. 147.

14. Ibid.

15. Tanner, "Social Theory," 189–90.

16. See Brian A. Gerrish, *A Prince of the Church: Schleiermacher and the Beginnings of Modern Theology* (Eugene, OR: Wipf & Stock, 2001; previously published by Augsburg Fortress, 1984); Matthias Gockel, *Barth and Schleiermacher on the Doctrine of Election: A Systematic-Theological Comparison* (Oxford: Oxford University Press, 2006); Shelli M. Poe, *Essential Trinitarianism: Schleiermacher as Trinitarian Theologian*, T&T Clark Explorations in Reformed Theology (London: Bloomsbury, 2017).

there is a certain extent to which one must grapple with Schleiermacher's efforts in moving from premodern to modern or postmodern theology while remaining faithful to Christian traditions. This is due to his stature as the founder of modern theology and the influence his work has had even on his detractors. Finally, Schleiermacher's theology is admittedly heterodox in many respects and therefore has the potential to break theological readers out of standard ways of thinking in beneficial ways. He is an appropriate theological conversation partner for those doing contemporary constructive work because even though his theology falls short at times, it nonetheless has the potential to inspire, disrupt, and create anew. Importantly, this is part of what it means to belong to a tradition. As Tanner writes, "within a political understanding of culture, the meaning of tradition expands, one could say, to include diversity and novelty as essential constituting moments."[17]

A Brief Introduction to Schleiermacher's Thought on Religion and Theology

As preparation for the chapters to follow, in which I address particular doctrinal loci within Schleiermacher's theology as presented primarily in his *Christian Faith* (1830/1), here I offer a brief overview of his theological development and framing ideas. Since there are already a number of instructive introductions to his life and work, this treatment is not meant to be comprehensive or significantly detailed.[18] It is meant, rather, as a brief introduction for the reader who is relatively unfamiliar with Schleiermacher's corpus and who is most interested in his doctrinal work.

Schleiermacher came to prominence at the turn of the nineteenth century with the appearance in 1799 of *On Religion: Speeches to Its Cultured Despisers*. That text might lead the reader to suppose that Schleiermacher grew up among Romantic and Enlightenment thinkers, so thoroughly had he become acquainted with and in many ways participated in their spirit. On the contrary, Schleiermacher was raised by devout Christian parents with Reformed clergy on both sides and schooled by pietistic Moravians during his formative years, from 1783 to 1787 in Niesky and Barby (Prussian towns now part of Germany). *On Religion* evidences Schleiermacher's break from his secondary education and seminary training, where he had been taught, for instance, to understand humanity as basically sinful and to embrace a sacrificial, vicarious understanding of atonement. In his 1799 text, we find him instead focusing on the potential goodness of humanity and the world, and on creation rather than the cross. Commenting on Gen. 2, Schleiermacher writes, "In the flesh and bone of his [i.e., Adam's] bone [i.e., Eve] he discovered humanity, and in humanity the world; from this moment on he became capable of hearing the voice of the deity and of answering it, and the most sacrilegious transgressions of its laws from now on no longer precluded him

---

17. Tanner, "Social Theory," p. 194.
18. For an excellent introduction, see Vial, *Schleiermacher: A Guide for the Perplexed*.

from association with the eternal being."[19] Here the creation of humanity in its relatedness to others is envisioned as the irrevocable establishment of a graced relationship with God. Like Athanasius, Schleiermacher emphasizes redemption as continuous with creation, foregrounding the incarnation instead of the cross.[20] Despite the striking theological differences between Schleiermacher's upbringing and the views set forth in his *On Religion*, however, he did not think of the transition from his pietistic roots to his new way of theological thinking as a total break. Rather, in 1802 he famously wrote that he had become a Moravian again, "only of a higher order."[21] Schleiermacher's mature theology does, in fact, retain a number of emphases wrought in him as a young person. The importance of relationship and communities, the centrality of Christ, and the role of affect in his theology are all prime examples.

Schleiermacher's theological development continued as he began to take on further academic and ecclesial roles, first in Stolp, then at the University of Halle, and finally in Berlin. His mature doctrinal work, *Christian Faith*, appeared for the first time in 1821/2 and in revised form in 1830/1. In this work, Schleiermacher displayed the intellectual rigor and constructiveness of his own systematic theology as he sought to speak to the newly emerging controversy over science and religion and, with it, theology's place in the modern university.[22] He also sought to unify the Lutheran and Reformed churches in Prussia and to equip clergy-in-training for church service. Just one of these aims would have set before Schleiermacher a monumental task, and many have recognized the missteps he may have made along the way in attempting to effectively address his multiple goals and audiences in his mature work. For example, in leaving his explicit treatment of the doctrine of the Trinity to the end of his *Christian Faith*, he had sought to free his readers' minds for a new construction of the doctrine, since they would have received already in the foregoing text the essential points of the doctrine without its technical formulations. In addition, they would have been set on a non-speculative track by attending to the economy of salvation throughout the *Christian Faith*. For Schleiermacher, this could satisfy the need for a relatively empirical form of theology during the rise of new scientific methods and the establishment of

---

19. Friedrich Schleiermacher, *On Religion: Speeches to Its Cultured Despisers*, Cambridge Texts in the History of Philosophy, ed. Richard Crouter (New York: Cambridge University Press, 1996), p. 37. Hereafter, cited as *OR*.

20. See Athanasius, *On the Incarnation* (Crestwood, NY: St. Vladimir's Seminary Press, 1996).

21. Friedrich Schleiermacher, "Letter to Georg Reimer (30 April 1802)," in *Aus Schleiermacher's Leben: In Briefen. I–IV*, ed. Ludwig Jonas and Wilhelm Dilthey (Berlin: Georg Reimer, 1860–3), pp. 294–5; in Richard Crouter, Introduction to *On Religion*, p. xiii.

22. On the modern university, see Zachary Purvis, *Theology and the University in Nineteenth-Century Germany* (Oxford: Oxford University Press, 2016); Johannes Zachhuber, *Theology as Science in Nineteenth-Century Germany: From F.C. Baur to Ernst Troeltsch* (Oxford: Oxford University Press, 2013).

modern universities. Yet by leaving an explicit treatment of the doctrine of the Trinity to the end of the work, he opened himself to criticism by many of his contemporaries. Even so, the work that resulted from Schleiermacher's lofty goals, whatever its controversial features and faults, earned him the reputation of being the founder of modern theology.

If one wishes to march along theological history, there is no way around Schleiermacher. Even his fiercest critics have recognized as much, and he has therefore taken his place among the giants of Christian thought. His legacy, however, is still up for debate. Some claim him as a prototypical liberal theologian, others emphasize his Reformed heritage, and yet others focus on his philosophical thought rather than his theological work, highlighting his theory of religion, hermeneutics, and/or epistemology. Because of Schleiermacher's wide-ranging interests, there is enough in his corpus for just about everyone to find something they appreciate and something they repudiate. For most of the twentieth century, the latter attitude dominated the Anglophone theological scene, since it has been heavily influenced by Barthian readings and misreadings of Schleiermacher's theology. Yet, over the past forty years, there has been a new and now steady stream of critical appreciation of his work.

Religion

Two of Schleiermacher's ideas that are relevant for this book have become especially important in Schleiermacher studies: the nature of religion and the task of theology. A basic introduction to the distinction between these two is important because it underlies my understanding of constructive forms of theology along with the intersection between doctrine and practice. Following Schleiermacher, I view theology as offering criticism and resources for refining religious doctrine and practices in the current church. Theology, however, is not the Christian religion itself.

In *On Religion*, Schleiermacher distinguishes religion from metaphysics and morals. Religion is not to be found in scholastic forms of rational Christianity, since "the spirit lets itself neither be bound in academies, nor be poured successively into eager skulls; it usually evaporates on the way from the first mouth to the first ear."[23] Likewise, religion is not to be identified as a tool for the establishment of moral life within civil society, threatening punishment in an afterlife for those who might transgress the law. Rather, for Schleiermacher, "all who have religion believe in only one world."[24] Religion's essence, Schleiermacher famously states, "is neither thinking nor acting, but intuition and feeling. It wishes to intuit the universe, wishes devoutly to overhear the universe's own manifestations and

---

23. *OR*, p. 14.

24. Ibid., p. 16. Cf. *OR*, pp. 53–4. For a more detailed treatment of Schleiermacher's view of immortality, see Shelli M. Poe, "Friedrich Schleiermacher's Theology as a Resource for Ecological Economics," *Theology Today* 73/1 (2016): 9–23.

actions, longs to be grasped and filled by the universe's immediate influences in childlike passivity."[25] Religion, for Schleiermacher, arises from a being-acted-upon by the interconnected process of nature, which produces a disposition of humility and reverence.[26] Thus, he states, "to accept everything individual as part of the whole and everything limited as a representation of the infinite is religion."[27]

Accordingly, Schleiermacher builds epistemic humility into his understanding of religion and highlights how religion incites people to the enjoyment of nature, love, and freedom. He states that a religious person "must be conscious that his religion is only a part of the whole, that regarding the same objects that affect him religiously there are views just as pious and, nevertheless, completely different from his own, and that from other elements of religion intuitions and feelings flow, the sense for which he may be completely lacking."[28] Religion, he says, is "the only sworn enemy of all pedantry and all one-sidedness."[29] Although Schleiermacher admits that religion incites feelings that can be intense, he thinks that in the end it "invites us to calm and dedicated enjoyment,"[30] especially of the laws of nature.[31] Further, the interconnectedness of natural life and the relationships that constitute human life point the religious person to love.[32] Religious love mirrors "the great, ever-continuous redemptive work of eternal love," which annihilates "blind instinct, unthinking habit, dead obedience, everything indolent and passive—all these sad symptoms of the asphyxia of freedom and humanity."[33]

Up to this point in *On Religion*, Schleiermacher's thought seems rather Romantic and Enlightened, especially considering his statement that one can be religious without espousing a belief in the existence of God.[34] By the fifth and final speech, however, his commitment to the sociality of religion takes distinctively Christian tones, and his talk of the relation of humanity and divinity comes to bear a remarkable resemblance to Christ.[35] In fact, Schleiermacher says explicitly in his last speech, "I wish to lead you, as it were, to the God who has become flesh," that is, to Christianity and its mediator.[36] Grounding his understanding of religion in actual religions, Schleiermacher writes that each religion makes "a particular intuition of the universe the center of the whole religion" and relates everything to it.[37] When a person comes to relate everything to a particular intuition of the

---

25. *OR*, p. 22. I return to "intuition and feeling" in Chapter 2.
26. See *OR*, p. 45.
27. *OR*, p. 25.
28. Ibid., p. 27.
29. Ibid., p. 29.
30. Ibid., p. 30.
31. Ibid., pp. 35–6.
32. Ibid., p. 38.
33. Ibid., p. 43.
34. Ibid., p. 51.
35. Ibid., pp. 74–5.
36. Ibid., p. 96; cf. Jn 1:14.
37. Ibid., p. 104.

universe, that person becomes a new being.[38] Without such a strong intuition of the universe around which a person's religion revolves, that person cannot have a "vigorous religious life."[39] Indeed, Schleiermacher insists that "if a religion is not supposed to be a specific one, then it is not religion at all."[40] While the essence of religion may be quite open-ended for Schleiermacher, actual religions bring this essence to specificity. The original intuition of the Christian religion, for Schleiermacher,

> is none other than the intuition of the universal straining of everything finite against the unity of the whole and of the way in which the deity handles this striving, how it reconciles the enmity directed against it and sets bounds to the ever-greater distance by scattering over the whole individual points that are at once finite and infinite, at once human and divine.[41]

In brief, Christianity intuits "the universe in religion and in its history."[42] On Schleiermacher's presentation of the Christian religion, God creates new beings from the presence and influence of Christ as mediator between the finite and the infinite. Thusly, Christianity is, for Schleiermacher, the "religion of religions."[43]

It may seem a rather obvious point, but it ought to be said that Schleiermacher is thoroughly Christian even when he is theorizing about religion. His opening discussion of religion in the first and second speeches of *On Religion*—where the essence of religion is identified as the sense and taste for the infinite within the finite, or the intuition of the interconnection of the part and the whole, or the love of humanity and the universe—bears remarkable similarity to his closing discussion of Christianity as a positive religion wherein God reconciles the finite and infinite, the part and whole, and does so through a mediator. In brief, Schleiermacher seems to identify the essence of religion by reflecting on his own religion. This would certainly be problematic for those who wish to use Schleiermacher's theory of religion as a general understanding of religious life, since it clearly prioritizes Christianity over other religions. Schleiermacher's mistake in attempting to identify the essence of religion writ large with reference to his own religion was both cultural and confessional, but his readers need not repeat the error. By reading Schleiermacher with a keen awareness of his context-specific limitations, I interpret his understanding of religion as the product of a Christian theologian who is stating the way he understands religion from the perspective of a Christian.

---

38. Ibid., p. 106.
39. Ibid., p. 108.
40. Ibid., p. 110.
41. Ibid., p. 115.
42. Ibid., p. 116.
43. Schleiermacher was a supersessionist. I critique and reconstruct this aspect of his thought in Chapter 3, and in Shelli M. Poe, "Friedrich Schleiermacher's Theology as a Resource for Ecological Economics," *Theology Today* 73/1 (2016): 9–23.

His statements are, therefore, not to be represented as "objectively" coming from nowhere but from one limited situation. Schleiermacher is a Christian theologian who cannot wrest himself from his own religious viewpoint. He is Christian, even or especially when theorizing about the essence of religion, and it is beneficial to recognize as much at the beginning.

Theology

Even though Schleiermacher remains Christian when theorizing about religion, for him, the Christian religion and Christian theology are distinct. I turn to his *Brief Outline of the Study of Theology* for a sketch of his understanding of the nature and task of Christian theology. For Schleiermacher, theology is a "positive science," as opposed to a speculative one. Here, "science" has the broad meaning of *sapientia*, or knowledge. "Positive" science is "a body of scientific elements which have connectedness of their own."[44] Scientific elements or ideas are connected insofar as they are required to solve a practical problem.[45] Christian theology, particularly, brings together the knowledge and skills without which "a harmonious guidance of the Christian Church … is not possible."[46] Without the practical task of efficiency in the guidance of the church, Schleiermacher thinks Christian theology would have to be assigned to various disciplines, for example, history, psychology, ethics, and philosophy of religion.[47] For him, practical theology is theology's summit and all forms of theology ought to be guided by the goal of church guidance.

Schleiermacher's theological ideal is a "Prince of the Church," who is both interested in the Christian religion and has a scientific spirit.[48] However, these two interests are typically separated into the roles of minister and theologian, respectively. A minister is someone who is involved in governing the church, while a theologian has knowledge relating to the Christian religion.[49] This is only a relative separation, though, since theologians should have the well-being of the church in mind and ministers should have some theological knowledge.[50] As such, apart from his initial discussion of the above distinctions, when Schleiermacher writes of the theologian in the *Brief Outline*, he has in mind both ministerial and theological tendencies.

It is important to note that the knowledge of Christianity that theologians might have, on this account, is not merely empirical.[51] It is true that the theologian sets out

---

44. Friedrich Schleiermacher, *Brief Outline of the Study of Theology*, trans. William Farrer (Eugene, OR: Wipf & Stock, 2007; previously published by T&T Clark, 1850), p. 91. Hereafter, cited as *BO*.
45. *BO*, p. 91.
46. Ibid., p. 93.
47. Ibid.
48. Ibid., p. 94.
49. Ibid.
50. Ibid., p. 95.
51. Ibid., p. 99.

empirical descriptions of various religious communities, including commonalities and differences.[52] For Schleiermacher, this is done so that the essential nature and form of Christianity might be identified, which goes beyond the empirical task.[53] Drawing out the essence of Christianity is required for the theologian to assist in identifying the conservative and progressive functions of church guidance.[54] Without knowing the essence of Christianity, the minister would not know how to steer the community's life, conserving some features and implementing other new ones. Going further, those conserving and progressive functions could not be properly fulfilled without knowledge of the whole church within its history.[55] Such historical knowledge of the church reflexively verifies or annuls what had been identified previously as the essence of Christianity.[56] Given this process, Schleiermacher gives priority to historical theology within theological study. It is connected to science, broadly construed, through the identification of the essence of Christianity. It is also connected to the Christian life through the conservative and progressive functions of church guidance. Historical theology itself, however, can be properly undertaken only after understanding the principles of history.[57]

In the *Brief Outline*, Schleiermacher discusses three types of theology: philosophical, historical, and practical. He begins with a discussion of philosophical theology, much as he did in *On Religion*, by identifying the essence of Christianity through a comparison of the differences among Christian sects.[58] Here he constricts himself explicitly to a survey of Protestant churches.[59] In the introduction to his *Christian Faith*, he identifies the essential difference between other monotheistic, teleological modes of faith and Christianity by stating that in Christianity, "everything is referred to the redemption accomplished through Jesus of Nazareth."[60] The conservative function of church government uses this essence

---

52. Ibid., p. 100. Schleiermacher calls this "Philosophy of Religion."
53. Ibid., p. 101. Schleiermacher calls this "Philosophical Theology."
54. Ibid. Schleiermacher calls this "Practical theology."
55. Ibid., p. 102. Schleiermacher calls this "Historical Theology."
56. Ibid. It is this reflexive verification and/or annulment that makes the "essentialism" involved in Schleiermacher's notion of theology similar to the "strategic essentialism" that Serene Jones offers in *Feminist Theory and Christian Theology: Cartographies of Grace* (Minneapolis, MN: Fortress, 2000). The "essence" of Christianity is open for discussion and can be continually revised and/or reconstructed.
57. *BO*, p. 103. Schleiermacher calls this "Ethics."
58. Ibid., p. 105.
59. Ibid., p. 106. This connects to Schleiermacher's intention to unify the Lutheran and Reformed churches in Berlin.
60. Friedrich Schleiermacher, *Christian Faith: A New Translation and Critical Edition*, trans. Terrence Tice, Catherine Kelsey, and Edwina Lawyer; ed. Catherine Kelsey, Terrence Tice; 2 vols (Louisville, KY: Westminster John Knox, 2016), p. 79. Hereafter, cited as *CF*. I return to the teleological character of Christianity in Chapter 2.

to know what to continue to impart within churches,[61] whereas the progressive function of church government uses it to critique the church itself.[62]

Historical theology, detailed in the second part of the *Brief Outline*, includes history of the "primitive" (i.e., the early) church,[63] its development over time,[64] and its current condition.[65] Schleiermacher describes the third type of historical theology as dogmatic: it takes up the knowledge of current doctrine in the Protestant church.[66] The development of Christianity can be divided, within each of these types, into two aspects: ecclesial life and the system of doctrine.[67] Dogmatic theology is used in church guidance "to show in how many ways, and up to what point, the principle of the current period has developed itself on every side; and how the germs of improved configurations which belong to the future are related thereto."[68]

In this process, Schleiermacher uses a distinction between orthodox and heterodox doctrines. He identifies those doctrines "constructed in the spirit of a desire to hold fast that which is already [a] matter of general acknowledgment, along with the natural inferences therefrom" as orthodox and those "constructed with a tendency to keep the system of doctrine in a state of mobility, and to make room for other modes of apprehension" as heterodox.[69] For Schleiermacher, all doctrines, orthodox and heterodox, that are included in a dogmatic theologian's work should have their scriptural roots in the New Testament and have their systematic coherence demonstrated.[70] Even so, the system of doctrine is "capable of entering into conjunction with every system of philosophy that does not, by the principles it maintains, exclude or deny the religious element."[71] Here Schleiermacher addresses some elements of current constructive forms of theology, namely, biblical resources, systematic thinking, and current philosophies, that are coherent with the Christian faith.

In the final section of his *Brief Outline*, which treats practical theology, Schleiermacher states that for the practical theologian, "interest in the welfare of the Church, and a scientific spirit" must occur together.[72] Yet practical theology takes for granted that one has understood philosophical and historical theology,

---

61. *BO*, p. 106. Schleiermacher calls this "apologetics."
62. Ibid., pp. 107–8. Schleiermacher calls this "polemics."
63. Ibid., p. 127. Schleiermacher calls this "exegetical theology."
64. Ibid., p. 128. This includes both "church history" and "dogma history," or "dogmatic theology."
65. Ibid., p. 125.
66. Ibid., p. 161.
67. Ibid., p. 151.
68. Ibid., p. 163.
69. Ibid., p. 165.
70. Ibid., p. 167.
71. Ibid., p. 169.
72. Ibid., p. 187.

and primarily addresses problems that occur in church guidance.[73] Schleiermacher divides the discipline of practical theology into church government, which applies to the whole church, and church service, which applies only to individual, local congregations.[74] With regard to church government, Schleiermacher discusses especially ecclesiastical authority. As for church service, practical theology concerns itself with the system of worship, including forms of worship in preaching and liturgy, along with catechesis, a theory of missions, and pastoral care.

Such cataloging could go on, but this much should be sufficient to show that, for Schleiermacher, theology is a complex undertaking that requires skill in, for example, history, ethics, and philosophy, with the goal of the well-being and guidance of the church. It should also be clear from Schleiermacher's understanding of Christian theology as described thus far that for him theology is inherently constructive in the sense that theologians do not simply clarify and redescribe existing theological statements in new contexts. Rather, the Christian theologian conserves, critiques, and faithfully innovates.

The Approach of This Volume

Constructive Forms of Theology

Using Schleiermacher's categories, this book is situated primarily as a work of dogmatic theology insofar as it focuses on the doctrines of and challenges to doctrines within the current church. However, it also dips its toes into the world of practical theology insofar as the welfare of the church is held in view and recommendations are made for church service. As the chapter overview that follows makes clear, these recommendations primarily regard liturgical language, religious imagery, and prayer practices.

Constructive forms of theology, as I understand them, are neither tools of conversion, nor disinterested enterprises, nor occupied by a purely descriptive task. Constructive forms of theology blend the study of religious thought with proposed theological refinements for use within it. As such, each chapter of this book begins with a description of some important critiques of, problems with, or challenges for significant Christian doctrines that have arisen within the church and are pressing at the current moment, and then meets those challenges with suggestions that draw on the work of both Schleiermacher and contemporary thinkers. My goal is to advance theological conversations around the doctrine of the Trinity, Christology and redemption, ecclesiology and pneumatology, and the doctrines of God and creation in ways that will propel the cause of social justice among Christian churches. Schleiermacher's theology, I contend, is rich with potential for those willing to enter the present context and face its challenges and

---

73. Ibid., p. 188.
74. Ibid., p. 194.

Introduction   17

opportunities with openness to innovative ideas, commitment to intellectual rigor, and doctrinal fidelity to the redemptive divine work in history.

Schleiermacher and Sexism, Colonialism, and Racism

Although I emphasize the beneficial aspects of Schleiermacher's theology, it is by no means the case that his theology is entirely beneficial or that he was exemplary in all ways within his own context. Schleiermacher's own day was one of intellectual, political, and cultural change, and he himself was complicit in a number of injustices that occurred during his time—colonialism, racism, and sexism among them. Scholars have already written book-length works on his contributions to imperialism, sexism, and racism, and many more volumes of this type are needed.

My work in this book does not dismiss such critiques but has another primary function: to investigate how Schleiermacher's insights, once wrested from their unjust uses and reconstructed with the help of current thinkers, could work hand in hand with the efforts of theologians working constructively today. In the chapters to follow, I identify areas of weakness within Schleiermacher's theology, but move swiftly to the reconstructive work that is at the heart of this book. To set those critiques and Schleiermacher's work itself further in context, I provide here a brief review of three works of critical reception vis-à-vis Schleiermacher's views of gender, his involvement in colonialism, and his complicity in the construction of modern racism. I treat Patricia Guenther-Gleason's *On Schleiermacher and Gender Politics*; Joerg Rieger's *Christ and Empire* and his chapter in *Empire and the Christian Tradition*, coedited with Don H. Compier and Kwok Pui-Lan; and Theodore Vial's *Modern Race, Modern Religion*. By engaging these sources, I acknowledge the important critical work that has been accomplished in these areas, even as the present book embarks on a more constructive project with regard to Schleiermacher's work itself.

Sexism

In *On Schleiermacher and Gender Politics*, Guenther-Gleason examines how Schleiermacher developed his understanding of religion by placing it in relation to Schiller's gender-inflected aesthetic philosophy. She argues that Schleiermacher's views are split with regard to women and "the feminine." On the one hand, he shared with his group of Berlin Romantics relatively progressive views of women. Such views may have been prepared for by Schleiermacher's adolescence within the Moravian community, which taught that Christ had an androgynous nature[75] and included women in religious roles that were exceptional for the time period.[76] Guenther-Gleason offers, as an example of his progressive perspective, Schleiermacher's (1798) "Idea for a Catechism of Noble Women," which promotes friendships between

---

75. Patricia E. Guenther-Gleason, *On Schleiermacher and Gender Politics*, Harvard Theological Studies (Harrisburg, PA: Trinity Press International, 1997), p. 328.

76. Ibid., p. 38.

women and men, criticizes idealizing persons of the other gender, rejects obedience and frivolity as descriptions of women's nature, and advocates women's education.[77] On the other hand, Schleiermacher also wrote sermons and lectures that privatized women's lives and excluded them from politics and church ministry.[78] For example, in a sermon in Eph. 5:22–31, Schleiermacher writes,

> Now it is this liberating love that the man should take as the standard for himself so that, as the head of the wife, he will increasingly liberate her, internally and externally, from all that servitude to which the female sex most easily succumbs, and will remove all restrictions from her so that the power of their common life can hold sway in her unhindered.[79]

Schleiermacher has women's liberation in view here but clearly affirms the man's position of liberator and the woman's need to be liberated by him.

Although these "early" and "late" views of Schleiermacher conflict, Guenther-Gleason identifies a common thread in his lifelong association of women with religion.[80] She argues that Schleiermacher aimed at revising common understandings of "the feminine" and "the masculine" in order to advocate feminine access to the "infinite" and to appreciate the finitude of masculinity.[81] In this effort, he sometimes used gender stereotypes for the purpose of their own transformation.[82] "Femininity" in his context referred to "all aspects of life deemed inextricably tied to nature, or the world of sense. Among those aspects were religion, beauty, art, love, the culture of the ancient Greeks, and women."[83] For Schleiermacher, because there is no need to reject finitude in order to experience the infinite, there is no need to oppose "the feminine" to "the infinite."[84]

One instance of this embrace of "the feminine," or the finite, is found in Schleiermacher's high view of the human capacity for domesticity, expressed in "On the Worth of Life."[85] By praising family life, he "subverts the accounts of the

---

77. Ibid., p. 2. Guenther-Gleason identifies scholars who are optimistic about Schleiermacher's work as a resource for feminism as including Carter Heyward, Kurt Lütni, Ruth Richardson, and Dawn DeVries (ibid., p. 4). See also Ruth Jackson Ravenscroft's assessment of Schleiermacher's "Catechism" in *The Veiled God: Friedrich Schleiermacher's Theology of Finitude* (Leiden: Brill, 2019), pp. 124–32.

78. On that account, Guenther-Gleason identifies scholars less optimistic about Schleiermacher's work as Marilyn Massey, Sheila Briggs, and Katherine Faull (ibid., p. 5).

79. Friedrich Schleiermacher, *The Christian Household: A Sermonic Treatise*, trans. Dietrich Seidel and Terrence N. Tice (Lewiston, NY: Mellen, 1991), p. 17; cited in Guenther-Gleason, *On Schleiermacher and Gender Politics*, p. 351.

80. Guenther-Gleason, *On Schleiermacher and Gender Politics*, p. 4.

81. Ibid., p. 20.

82. Ibid., p. 59.

83. Ibid., p. 58.

84. Ibid., p. 257.

85. Ibid., pp. 244–5.

progress of reason that situate the family unit in a realm of nature from which the mature person must be extricated."[86] One need not reject or move beyond family life in order to reach the realm of "freedom." For Schleiermacher, freedom is not identified with Kantian transcendental freedom, a release from necessity, but is "a release only from the constraint of objects."[87] The dependence involved in family life does not amount to being constrained by objects but offers opportunities for joy. Guenther-Gleason highlights the following passage to illustrate Schleiermacher's appreciation of family life and the interdependence it brings:

> I owe it to the total arrangement of this world that I can truly live in it with human beings. ... Human love can unite me with the millions of others who are here now, who once were here, and who will be here in the future; and that I now know that they are there and that I can rejoice in their being as in my own, and that I know how infinitely many ways my nature is modified in theirs, how they develop themselves along so many different paths and make progress toward their destiny?[88]

Here human love and lineages, such as are found in family life, are not to be left behind in the cultivation of the mature person's intellectual advancement but are occasions for reflection and gratefulness.

In fact, Schleiermacher understands the unity between sense and reason as most profoundly experienced in love, which is "grounded in the feminine."[89] For him, "activity deemed 'masculine' must be grounded in the kind of unity attributed to 'the feminine,' and ... 'the feminine,' also based on this original unity, must expand outwardly through contact with 'the masculine.'"[90] In this way, Schleiermacher draws on gender stereotypes in order to transform them, "consistently taking 'the feminine' out of the static sensuous past and the disembodied, idealized future."[91] As Guenther-Gleason describes it, "in their portrayal of this transition, Schlegel and Schleiermacher did not leave real women in the position of innocent, unconscious, merely sensuous harmony from which men must flee in pursuit of freedom, but fully expected their development as well."[92]

---

86. Ibid., p. 245.
87. Friedrich Schleiermacher, *On Freedom*, trans. and intro. Albert L. Blackwell (Lewiston, NY: Mellen, 1992); cited in Guenther-Gleason, *On Schleiermacher and Gender Politics*, p. 235.
88. Schleiermacher, *Kritische Gesamtausgabe*, vol. 1.1: *Jugendschriften 1787–96*, ed. Günter Meckenstock, 1983), p. 417. In Guenther-Gleason, *On Schleiermacher and Gender Politics*, p. 245.
89. Guenther-Gleason, *On Schleiermacher and Gender Politics*, p. 275.
90. Ibid., p. 313.
91. Ibid., p. 317.
92. Ibid., pp. 278–9.

Guenther-Gleason concludes her book by emphasizing that Schleiermacher's relationship to a sort of proto-feminism is mixed:

> If this study has demonstrated Schleiermacher's defense of the feminine against those who would deny its capacity for expressing and approaching the Infinite, it must also be admitted that the success with which he made his case left him little inclined to fight for women's direct access to structures and endeavors he has just argued are of little consequence for the value of one's inner life.[93]

Even so, Schleiermacher had familial and friendly relationships with "exceptional women, whose lives were threatened by fetters on their souls, [which] led him to associate actual women directly with the much discussed feminine, allowing him to look beyond the question of what the feminine could do for men."[94] In addition, Guenther-Gleason states that "his lifelong belief in evaluating one's principles through dialogue with others, combined with his insistence that each person develop and express all that comes from within, could well have encouraged him to reassess his manner of ensuring women's continued development to accord with more progressive views being proposed in our day."[95] In the end, Guenther-Gleason sounds a hopeful note about Schleiermacher's potential for feminist theologies even as she and others recognize the ways in which he was a product of his time.

Colonialism
In *Empire and the Christian Tradition* and *Christ and Empire*, Joerg Rieger echoes the mixed legacy that Guenther-Gleason identifies, this time in relation to imperialism. Rieger argues that some of Schleiermacher's theology parallels colonial mindsets, while other portions could be liberating in today's context. As for the former, Rieger notes Schleiermacher's interests in colonialism. While Prussia was not a colonial power and Germany was not yet a nation, Schleiermacher nonetheless participated in "German colonial fantasies" through his translation of David Collins's (1798) *Account of the English Colony in New South Wales*, which he supplemented with research culled from the reports of other explorers. Following Edward Said, Rieger

---

93. Ibid., p. 352.
94. Guenther-Gleason, *On Schleiermacher and Gender Politics*, p. 58. Schleiermacher seems to have had a horse in the race, so to speak, since many of his own traits were considered "feminine" (ibid., p. 37; see also p. 58. Guenther-Gleason has the *Speeches* and *Soliloquies* in view here). For Schleiermacher, a defense of "the feminine" was not only a defense of women but of anyone who exhibited "feminine" traits, himself included. Guenther-Gleason details Schleiermacher's relationship to Herrnhutter piety, his sister Charlotte Schleiermacher, Friederike Dohna, Frau Benike, Henriette Herz, and Eleonore Grunow. See Guenther-Gleason, *On Schleiermacher and Gender Politics*, pp. 38–59.
95. Guenther-Gleason, *On Schleiermacher and Gender Politics*, p. 353.

identifies this type of activity as "a kind of intellectual authority over the Orient within Western culture."⁹⁶ In Schleiermacher's translation of Collins's book,

> He describes the Aboriginals [in Australia] as barely human—or human at the very lowest rung of human civilization. ... The Aboriginal people are described as "completely naked"—a statement which reflects Schleiermacher's prejudice about clothes since he notes in the next passage that they wear adornment and color their skin. A country populated with such people, he concludes, was of no use to the Dutch, and thus they abandoned it.⁹⁷

Although Schleiermacher differs from other colonial thinkers insofar as he rejects the slave trade and affirms peaceful living with native peoples, Rieger identifies the motives for such attitudes as "a 'natural rule,' according to which there was simply nothing to be gained from exploitation or any other relationship. There was absolutely no use for these natives to the colonial system, not even as labor force."⁹⁸ In this way, Rieger questions even those attitudes Schleiermacher holds that seem prima facie to resist colonialist impulses. Rieger argues that by translating and supplementing travel writing of this kind, Schleiermacher participated in the formation of German identity and unity.⁹⁹ Drawing in Susanne Zantop's work, he concludes that by engaging in travel writing, Schleiermacher was participating in "a sense of moral superiority over the colonizing nations."¹⁰⁰

Rieger identifies a number of theological parallels to this kind of colonial imagination in Schleiermacher's corpus. One example he offers is Schleiermacher's description of Christ's salvific work. Although Schleiermacher "rejects interpretations of the work of Christ in terms of coercive action" and is therefore "not at work like the Spanish colonizers with fire and sword, overwhelming people by sheer force and coercing them into his kingdom," nevertheless Rieger argues that the language of "attraction" and "pervasive influence" that Schleiermacher uses has resonances with colonial powers.¹⁰¹ Returning to Schleiermacher's colonial mindset with regard to native inhabitants of Australia, Rieger draws a parallel between colonizers and Christ:

> If the colonizers are superior in relation to the colonized, and if they are representatives of the "attractive power" that is a mark of those higher up, the colonized have no choice but to "gladly submit'" to the colonizers. ... Christ's

---

96. Edward Said, *Orientalism* (New York: Vintage Books, 1979), p. 19; cited in Joerg Rieger, "Friedrich Schleiermacher," in *Empire and the Christian Tradition: New Readings of Classical Theologians* (Minneapolis, MN: Fortress, 2007), p. 272.
97. Rieger, "Friedrich Schleiermacher," p. 273.
98. Ibid., p. 274.
99. Ibid.
100. Ibid., p. 275.
101. Ibid., p. 276.

own attractive power models this superiority, and the differential between Christ and the Christian gets translated into the differential between colonized and colonizers.[102]

Here Rieger argues that while Christ's power is interpreted as attraction and influence, which might seem to resist colonial domination, in fact it is simply a more subtle form of colonizing. As the colonized are manipulated into submitting into colonizers, so too are non-Christians manipulated into submitting to Christ.

Rieger also identifies colonial parallels with Schleiermacher's use of the Reformed tradition's Christological titles of prophet, priest, and king.[103] First, as prophet, Rieger notes that Schleiermacher understands Christ's teaching to have surpassed the teachings of Jewish law.[104] Such supersessionism is clearly paralleled in colonial dominance over the religions of the colonized. This can be seen in Schleiermacher's rejection of the need for religious miracles: "in view of the great advantage in power and civilization which the Christian peoples possess over the non-Christian …, the preachers of today do not need such signs."[105] Second, Rieger describes Schleiermacher's understanding of Christ as priest, who mediates between humanity and God. Because Schleiermacher understands Christ as the exclusive mediator, "Christendom as a whole … stands to the rest of humanity in the relation in which the priests stood to the laity."[106] Rieger claims that "what kinds of power and authority over others are attributed to Christians has not only theological but also political ramifications."[107] The implication is clearly that the high priesthood of Christ might lead Christians to believe that they are to have political power to mediate among the nations. Finally, Rieger treats the kingly power of Christ, which Schleiermacher restricts to the church. He states that "Schleiermacher's Christ cannot be called a brutal colonialist. He does not rule through coercion but through attraction and love. Coercion cannot produce civilization and undermines the expansion of the Christian faith in other parts of the world." However, Rieger continues, "this distinction between coercion and attraction mirrors the other distinction between 'hard' and 'soft' imperialism."[108]

---

102. Ibid., p. 277.

103. For my interpretation of these Christological titles, see Shelli M. Poe, "Friedrich Schleiermacher's Christian Faith," in *Oxford Handbook of Reformed Theology*, ed. Michael Allen and Scott Swain (Oxford: Oxford University Press, 2020), pp. 312–27.

104. Joerg Rieger, *Christ and Empire: From Paul to Postcolonial Times* (Minneapolis, MN: Fortress, 2007), p. 209.

105. Friedrich Schleiermacher, *The Christian Faith*, ed. H. R. Mackintosh and J. S. Stewart (Edinburgh: T&T Clark, 1986), p. 450; cited in Rieger, *Christ and Empire*, p. 210.

106. Schleiermacher, *The Christian Faith*, p. 465; cited in Rieger, *Christ and Empire*, p. 212.

107. Rieger, *Christ and Empire*, p. 212.

108. Ibid., p. 213.

As we have noted above, Rieger finds the language of the power of "attraction" rife with colonial overtones.

Although Schleiermacher's theology clearly includes hierarchical thinking and a mindset of Christian superiority, Rieger also identifies examples from his work that go "beyond the limitations of the colonial mindset."[109] Among these are Schleiermacher's attention to the finite, as well as "an attention to history which introduces a self-critical moment."[110] By understanding theology as an historical enterprise, religions—including Christianity—can be examined and criticized. Moving from this insight, Rieger wonders, "What if we developed, for instance, a more historically informed view of Christ, which would appreciate factors like his Jewishness and his solidarity with the 'least of these'? We might take Schleiermacher's ambiguity about the colonial as a cue and appropriate it in a different way," asking "What if colonial Christianity is not the highest stage of religion?"[111] There are seeds of such ambiguity in Schleiermacher's own corpus, and Rieger identifies Schleiermacher's explicit rejection later in life of British and Dutch colonialism as, although not unusual for his day, still significant: "Without the use of force, Schleiermacher maintains, the 'benign tribes' to which 'one came in the fifteenth century' would have become Christian, and this is 'a disgrace for the Christian peoples.'"[112] Schleiermacher also believes in "the openness and perfectibility of Christianity and Christian language," and in this respect, Rieger finds his thought "more open than contemporary cultural-linguistic approaches in theology."[113] What is most important, for Rieger, is the emphasis Schleiermacher places on being receptive to a diversity of experiences. "The latter category," Rieger explains, "is of special interest in the resistance to empire and colonialism; it potentially pushes toward a greater sensitivity for the colonial other who, forced to live a hybrid existence that pulls together the reality of the colonizer and colonized, might well display the greatest diversity of experience of all."[114] Finally, Rieger identifies in Schleiermacher's thought a resistance to "the particular forms of slavery endured for instance by Prussian workers, introduced by capitalist modes of production. People are enslaved, he says, when they are inserted into a 'mechanism' in which they lose the ability to experience a free spiritual existence."[115] For Rieger, "Schleiermacher's rejection of the industrial enslavement of the spirit is clear, and it is based on his Christological logic: no one who is capable of communication

---

109. Rieger, "Friedrich Schleiermacher," p. 278.

110. Ibid., p. 279.

111. Ibid., pp. 279–80.

112. Rieger, *Christ and Empire*, p. 221; the quoted text is from Friedrich Schleiermacher, *Die Christliche Sitte nach den Grundsätzen der evangelischen Kirche im Zusammenhang dargestellt* (Waltrop: Spenner, 1999), pp. 288–90.

113. Rieger, *Christ and Empire*, p. 223. The quoted text is from Schleiermacher, *Die Christliche Sitte*, p. 396.

114. Rieger, *Christ and Empire*, p. 223.

115. Ibid.

with Christ—and this includes all of humanity—should be turned into a 'living machine.'"[116]

Rieger identifies yet further examples of Schleiermacher's work on both the positive and negative sides, weaving together certain forms of resistance toward colonialism with the colonial mindsets that might lie beneath them. Rieger concludes by saying that "there is a sense in which his categories can provide resistance to other incarnations of colonialism in his day and perhaps in ours as well."[117] Both Guenther-Gleason and Rieger, then, identify the mixed legacy of Schleiermacher's work and yet envision ways in which his thought could hold potential for liberative projects even today.[118]

Racism
In *Modern Religion, Modern Race*, Theodore Vial argues that while many genealogies of racism in the West end with the emergence of the Enlightenment, to achieve a fuller understanding of modern racism one must go beyond Kant. Schleiermacher is one of the Romantic thinkers Vial draws on to show how the development of an expressivist theological anthropology supplies the crucial link in race theory between the biology and culture of a people group. In addition, he uses Schleiermacher's work as an example of the kind of teleological thinking that is bound up with modernity and the study of religions, which leads to hierarchical judgments in comparative religion. Although Schleiermacher himself is much better on race than many of his contemporaries early in the nineteenth century, having a "real and admirable openness to diversity,"[119] Vial contends that his expressivist anthropology and teleological approach to comparing religions are a significant part of the genealogical story of both modern religion and modern race.

Vial explains that there was no ancient concept resembling the modern understanding of "race," and that Kant invented the category.[120] For Kant, humans are one species because of their ability to reproduce with one another, but are divided into four races: "White," "Negro," "Hunnish (Mongolish)," and "Hinduish."[121] This is a biological understanding of race, which Kant believes is put in place by the purposes of nature. It is, however, not a complete picture of the modern category, which links physical, biological features of identifiable people groups to "mental or moral characteristics."[122] Although Kant affirmed this link, he could not explain it. For that, an expressivist anthropology is needed. Vial identifies Schleiermacher as a contributor to the development of such an anthropology, which he summarizes as the notion that "what you are is essentially a question of what lies within you."[123]

---

116. Ibid.
117. Ibid., p. 225.
118. See also Ravenscroft, *The Veiled God*, pp. 132–48, 152–66.
119. Vial, *Modern Religion, Modern Race*, p. 2.
120. Ibid., p. 30.
121. Ibid., p. 33.
122. Ibid., p. 164.
123. Ibid., p. 172.

Expressivists understand humans as creative beings who need to speak and act in order to determine themselves fully as individuals[124] and exercise their agency in history.[125]

Such determination is important not only for individual flourishing but also for the group of which the individual is a member. On the one hand, for Romantics, group membership is of the utmost importance for the development of conceptual thinking, language, and culture. In fact, the group always precedes the individual historically, and so the individual is given her horizon of possible experiences from the group. Over time, individuals within a group speak, think, and act alike as they learn from the group and are influenced by it.[126] On the other hand, without the creative freedom of individuals, groups would not develop in response to the agency of those individuals within them. Thus, for Schleiermacher, group membership and individuality are mutually dependent upon one another for their own shape or determination.

In this way, Schleiermacher focuses primarily on the cultures of people groups rather than biology. However, as Vial explains, "once Kant and others convince the modern world that the human race can be divided into a few large biological groups, this anthropology gives a way of theorizing essential differences between these groups that Kant's (universal cosmopolitan) anthropology cannot."[127] It does this by explaining how groups created through biological, hereditary lines could also tend to have similar ways of speaking, acting, thinking, and feeling. An expressivist anthropology forms a link between biology and culture, which is part of the modern category of "race."

In addition to contributing to expressivist anthropology, Schleiermacher also uses teleology in his understanding of religion, which has led to hierarchical comparisons between religious traditions. Vial explains that teleology is used by many modern thinkers in order to bring some meaning and order to the chaos of reality. For Schleiermacher, the goal of history is "free sociability."[128] Free sociability is connected to an expressivist anthropology because it allows people to be and express themselves, thereby fostering the development of individuals and communities.[129] On the basis of Schleiermacher's understanding of history's purpose, he thinks some religions are better than others, namely, those that allow for free sociability.

Vial examines two particular non-Christian religions that Schleiermacher discusses, to see how they fare on this teleological way of thinking. Although "Schleiermacher, compared to other eighteenth- and nineteenth-century Europeans, is not particularly racist," in Vial's estimation, he nonetheless has a low view of both the inhabitants of Australia, which we have already encountered in

124. Ibid., p. 174.
125. Ibid., p. 12.
126. Ibid., p. 179.
127. Ibid., p. 172.
128. Ibid., p. 196.
129. Ibid., p. 201.

relation to Rieger's work, and the Jewish people of his own day.[130] Vial reproduces in full the three brief passages in Schleiermacher's work on Australians and offers three tentative conclusions about Schleiermacher's views of them. First, Schleiermacher believes the inhabitants of Australia are on the lowest tier of human religion because they view the world as chaotic. Second, he cannot accept their adornment as a legitimate form of art or tradition. Third, Schleiermacher thinks they lack the leisure for conversation and expressive activities necessary to cultivate religion.[131]

As for the Jewish community in Prussia, Schleiermacher argues against their mass conversion as a requirement of full citizenship. However, like some of his Jewish friends in Berlin, he does not appreciate the Orthodox Judaism of his day for two reasons. First, he believes it has become legalistic and ritualistic. Second, he thinks its emphasis on a political messianic figure would return the Jewish people to subjugation under a law that serves the needs of the nation.[132] In order to support the full citizenship of Jews in Prussia, Schleiermacher therefore recommended that a new group of reformed Jews would need to subordinate ceremonial laws to state laws and renounce hope for a political messiah.[133]

In these ways, even though Schleiermacher's anthropology thrives on diversity, freedom of expression, and mutual influence of individuals and society, his teleological understanding of history as moving toward free sociability allows him to hierarchically compare religious traditions. Those he thinks are closer to the ideal of free sociability fare much better than the others, and as a Christian he hopes that Christianity will one day numerically surpass the other religions of the world—not by coercion but by the power of its influence—until adherents to other religions cease to exist.

Vial's argument is that although contemporary scholars of religion do not want to compare religions in a hierarchical and racist way, race and religion share a genealogy that religious studies scholars have not yet reckoned with: "We think about difference (in general, and in religious studies) by (1) making distinctions, (2) linked to teleology, which (3) ties those distinctions to progress, thereby (4) leading to a hierarchy among the distinctions."[134] Schleiermacher is a significant contributor to understandings of both religion and race, and his legacy in this regard will also have to be reckoned with.

Initial Motivations

Notwithstanding this mixed legacy, Schleiermacher's work is worth investigating in the pursuit of constructive forms of theology today. Karen V. Guth's work on

---

130. Ibid., p. 209.
131. Ibid.
132. Ibid., p. 213.
133. Ibid., p. 215. I return to Schleiermacher's view of Judaism in Chapter 2.
134. Ibid., p. 223.

the legacy of John Howard Yoder in the aftermath of his sexual abuses of women can help us understand how to engage such an effort. Rather than dismiss Yoder's thought outright, Guth argues that feminists and womanists should engage it in an effort to tell the truth about his actions, get particular about both his context and his readers' contexts when aiming at restorative justice, and emphasize the communal practices that could provide new avenues forward.[135] Following Kathryn Tanner, Guth argues that the strategy of engaging with the work of thinkers who have tainted legacies renders their work less powerful insofar as it refuses to allow the work to become a static and enduring contribution to sinful ideologies. "The most effective response to tainted legacies on this view," she explains, "is not to refuse to engage or to bypass them through the creation of 'new' ones but to repurpose explicitly tainted organizations and articulations of Christian tradition for new political purpose."[136] By doing so, the theologian both highlights the vulnerability of the doctrinal articulations of the thinker with a tainted legacy and rearticulates their work in ways that dislodge and counteract their initial power.

Schleiermacher's case is different than Yoder's, at least insofar as Schleiermacher did not, to our knowledge, physically abuse women while advocating for their rights. Neither did he make concrete colonial advances, nor perpetrate violent acts of racism. Even so, his legacy remains tainted by the ways his work contributed to a colonial mindset, racist ideology, and the disempowerment of women. By engaging his work nonetheless, I join Tanner and Guth in emphasizing the contingency of Christian thinkers, including the "father of modern theology." Further, I carry out the task of reconstructing and repurposing his doctrinal thought for our current context. By doing so in conversation with those who have been most affected by Schleiermacher's contributions to sexism, racism, colonialism, and other evils, this study also aims to "reassess who constitutes the 'legitimate authority' and to move forward in ways that acknowledge that authority."[137]

The chapters to follow will make the case more fully, but here I raise four further motivations that may encourage contemporary theologians working constructively to think theologically along with Schleiermacher, despite the ways in which his thought has been found wanting in relation to sexism, colonialism, and racism. The space of an introductory chapter does not allow for a complete exposition of the aspects of Schleiermacher's theology to follow. What I intend to show here is that Schleiermacher's thought dovetails with what some theologians working constructively have been calling for in their recent work, particularly with

---

135. Karen V. Guth, "Doing Justice to the Complex Legacy of John Howard Yoder: Restorative Justice Resources in Witness and Feminist Ethics," *Journal of the Society of Christian Ethics* 35/2 (2015): 119–39.

136. Karen V. Guth, "Moral Injury, Feminist and Womanist Ethics, and Tainted Legacies," *Journal of the Society of Christian Ethics* 38/1 (2018): 178.

137. Ibid., p. 180.

regard to his doctrine of creation, doctrine of sin, emphasis on particularity, and the way he foregrounds life rather than death.[138]

First, Schleiermacher's doctrine of "original perfection" dovetails with Serene Jones's call for feminist theologies to affirm the goodness of created life and a gracious relationship with the divine before speaking of sinfulness.[139] Jones offers an approach to sin "from the perspective of justification and sanctification," which means "seeing sin from the eschatological perspective of the woman who knows herself as sanctified and justified in faith."[140] Although she draws on the work of John Calvin to map feminist theory onto Christian theology, many of the same mappings could be drawn using Schleiermacher's work. Following Calvin, Jones thinks of sin as "unfaithfulness," which she defines as "a way of living in which women do not flourish but instead experience (and participate in) oppressive forces. With Calvin, one can say that unfaith consists of being bereft of the double gifts of faith justification and sanctification."[141] Jones therefore sets the doctrine of sin in the context of the doctrines of justification and sanctification. That is, one cannot understand the former without first understanding the latter. As a result, when women encounter talk of sin, their "dispersed and fragmented identity is [already] pulled together and held in the 'envelope of God's grace,'" and "woman is [already] pronounced a newly born agent and is called to live in just relation with others."[142] The effect is an "inherent hopefulness of feminist knowledge of sin."[143] By speaking of sin within the logical frame of justification and sanctification, women "affirm a present-day experience of transformation and a future horizon of flourishing. This makes clear," Jones explains, "the anticipatory optimism of sin-talk in feminist perspective."[144]

While the vicissitudes of history can make such optimism seem more or less realistic, Jones is highlighting a trend in feminist thought that Schleiermacher's work affirms. His doctrine of sin, including "original sin," is set in the context of "original perfection." For him, the original perfection of the world and humanity (§§59–61), which are presented in his *Christian Faith* before original and actual sin (§§70–74), mean that God has so created and sustained the world and humanity that it is possible for redemption to occur. In his words, "the totality of finite being as it influences us … harmonizes in such a way as to make possible the continuity of religious self-consciousness within that totality."[145] Alternately

---

138. I return to and flesh out these themes where appropriate in subsequent chapters, and especially in the second chapter.
139. Serene Jones, *Feminist Theory and Christian Theology: Cartographies of Grace*, Guides to Theological Inquiry (Minneapolis, MN: Fortress, 2000).
140. Ibid., pp. 95–6.
141. Ibid., p. 113.
142. Ibid., p. 112.
143. Ibid., p. 109.
144. Ibid., p. 110.
145. *CF*, §57.1, p. 337.

described, "the expression 'original perfection' posits that inasmuch as all finite being codetermines our self-consciousness, this process can be traced back to eternal omnipotent causality."¹⁴⁶ What Schleiermacher is affirming, in rather dense and technical language, is that the world and humanity are always already in a graced state of relationship with the divine. This comes out more clearly in his doctrine of sin where he states, "this consciousness of sin is conditioned by what is good, which must precede it and which is simply a result of that original perfection."¹⁴⁷ Schleiermacher's insistence on treating the original perfection of the world and humanity as logically prior to sin and evil maps onto the hopefulness or anticipatory optimism involved in feminist sin-talk.

Second, Jones also highlights the social understanding of sin that feminist theologians, among other liberation theorists and postliberationists, have tended to emphasize. She explains,

> We are born into a nexus of oppressive social relations—institutional practices, cultural patterns, and habits of language—we can never completely escape. This nexus of relations is like a theater in which we, as women agents, perform the scripts of our lives. It is often hard to tell when we are being performed by imputed social codes and when we perform roles of our own making. So too in the case of sin, it is difficult to distinguish between an exercise of our creative agency and playing a scripted role.¹⁴⁸

This social understanding of sin, not only as an action that individuals can and should be held responsible for but also as a social structure from which it can be difficult or impossible to break free, is also found in Schleiermacher's theology. In fact, as Vial has argued above, Schleiermacher contributed significantly to modern understandings of how group membership influences, shapes, and even determines the activities of the individuals who find themselves within the group. The heavy emphasis Schleiermacher places on the role and impact of the community means that his doctrine of sin is significantly social as well. This is evident especially in his doctrine of original sin, where he explains:

> If, on the one hand, the susceptibility to sin that precedes every deed is effected in each individual by the sin and susceptibility of sin of others, but if, at the same time, it is also both propagated in others and secured in them by each individual through one's own free actions, then sinfulness is of a thoroughly collective nature. ... In each individual susceptibility to sin is the work of all, and in all individuals it is the work of each. Indeed, susceptibility to sin is to be understood rightly and fully only in this commonality.¹⁴⁹

---

146. Ibid., p. 338.
147. *CF*, §68.2, p. 410.
148. Jones, *Feminist Theory and Christian Theology*, p. 123.
149. *CF*, §71.2, pp. 428–9.

For Schleiermacher, then, individuals are responsible for their own acts of wrongdoing insofar as they choose to carry out such acts, but such individuals and their actions are always set in the context of their social formation and therefore tend toward sin because of the sin of others. He understands sin primarily in a collective way as the result of social structures and practices that influence and shape individuals. The focus, for Schleiermacher as for contemporary theologians working constructively, is on social structures that reinforce and support injustice.

A third initial motivation for examining the ways that Schleiermacher's theology could work in tandem with constructive forms of theology is that, like them, Schleiermacher pays attention to the particular, the finite, and the individual. As we have seen in the above treatment of Schleiermacher's understanding of religion and theology, he strives to describe "positive religions" in particular times and places. He states in the introduction to his *Christian Faith*, "Dogmatic theology is the science concerned with the interconnection of whatever doctrine has currency in a given social organization called a Christian church at a given time."[150] Likewise, in *On Religion*, Schleiermacher inveighs against natural religion, arguing that there is no such thing as religion in general: "if a religion is not supposed to be a specific one, then it is not religion at all, but merely loose, unrelated material."[151] He goes on to claim that "just as nothing is more irreligious than to demand uniformity in humanity generally, so nothing is more unchristian than to seek uniformity in religion."[152] For Schleiermacher, then, the study of religion is specific to various traditions, and dogmatic theology attends to the interconnected ideas within churches at particular moments in history.

This emphasis on specificity and diversity dovetails with the constructive work of theologians who have also prized particularity in theology and the study of religion. Emilie Townes states the trend in the opening chapter of *Womanist Ethics and the Cultural Production of Evil*, where she indicates that her task "is to explore the twists and turns of the communities from which we spring and have our very life and breath. It is to be very particular about the particular—and explore the vastness of it."[153] Schleiermacher, womanists like Townes, and feminists like Mary McClintock Fulkerson[154] and R. Marie Griffith[155]—to take only two examples of those who have undertaken ethnographic work in theological communities—all

150. Ibid., §19, p. 131.

151. *OR*, p. 110.

152. Ibid., p. 123. The irony here should not be lost on us, given my interpretation of Schleiermacher above as understanding all religion in light of Christianity.

153. Emilie Townes, *Womanist Ethics and the Cultural Production of Evil* (New York: Palgrave Macmillan, 2006), p. 2.

154. Mary McClintock Fulkerson, *Places of Redemption: Theology for a Worldly Church* (New York: Oxford University Press, 2007).

155. R. Marie Griffith, *God's Daughters: Evangelical Women and the Power of Submission* (Berkeley: University of California, 1997).

understand the importance of the inseparability between the finite and the infinite, sense and reason, historical communities and their ideals.

Finally, Schleiermacher's theology foregrounds a deep affirmation of life and joy, rather than a focus on death and suffering. In so doing, his theology offers something like what feminist philosopher Grace Jantzen has identified as a desirable feminist mode of religious thought, namely, a focus on natality.[156] As she understands it,

> Much of traditional philosophy of religion (and western culture generally) is preoccupied with violence, sacrifice, and death, and built upon mortality not only as a human fact but as a fundamental philosophical category. But what if we were to begin with birth, and with the hope and possibility and wonder implicit in it? How if we were to treat natality and the emergence of *this* life and *this* world with the same philosophical seriousness and respect which had traditionally been paid to mortality and the striving for other worlds?[157]

Ecological theologians have also asked such questions with the hope that a focus on this life and world—rather than on technological innovations or religious themes that would allow humanity to escape it—would assist in creating a more just relationship with the planet.[158]

Schleiermacher's focus on natality may be clearly seen in his *Christmas Dialogue* (1806), which highlights the sensuality of human life amidst a celebration of the birth of Jesus of Nazareth.[159] The story takes place in a bourgeois Prussian home, with women, children, and men gathered to give each other gifts, enjoy music together, and converse about their memories and current ideas. The tone of the work is joyful, witty, and playful. Schleiermacher's emphasis on natality can be seen in his description of the singing of the young Sophie, daughter of the hostess:

> Here she knew how to give each note its proper value. Each emerged from the previous note lovingly, as if unable to let it go, and then nevertheless was just there, by itself, with measured strength, and then again, as with a pious kiss, it gave way to the next note. Even when she practiced her singing alone, she showed such a great attentiveness to the other voices—as if they, too, could be heard. And as much as she was often quite moved, still no sort of excess destroyed the harmony of the whole. Regardless of the subject matter, one can

---

156. Grace M. Janzten, *Becoming Divine: Towards a Feminist Philosophy of Religion* (Bloomington: Indiana University Press, 1999).

157. Ibid., p. 2.

158. See, for instance, Wendell Berry, "Faustian Economics," *Harper's Magazine* (May 2008): 35–42.

159. I return to an analysis of *Christmas Eve* in Chapter 3.

hardly designate it otherwise than that she sang with devotion, and she held on to and attended each note with humble love.[160]

This passage evidences the care with which Sophie treats each moment of life (while singing) and her attunement to "other voices" even when they are not physically present.

In addition, Schleiermacher explicitly reflects on being born of a woman within the story. He has Sophie exclaim,

> Oh Mother! You could just as well be the blessed mother of the divine babe, and doesn't it pain you, that you're not? Isn't this why mothers prefer having sons? Just think of the holy women who accompanied Jesus, and everything that you've told me about them. Certainly, I, too, want to become one of them, just as you are.[161]

Sophie thinks of the sacredness of her mother's role in her life, the sexism she notices even as a child, and her own desire to be a disciple of Jesus when she grows into a woman. Her mother's considered response comes a few pages later:

> Truly, I feel that she did not say too much in one respect, when she said that I could just as well be the mother of the adored child, because I can humbly worship the pure revelation of the divine in my daughter, as Mary had in her son, without the right relationship of the child to the mother being disturbed thereby.[162]

Ernestine, Sophie's mother, approves Sophie's claim that she stands in the same relationship to her own daughter as Mary did to her son; they both see the divine in these little bundles of flesh.[163] Schleiermacher's positive attitude toward embodiment, the natural order in which humanity finds itself, and the whole of created life permeate his theological work.

These are simply four themes in Schleiermacher's oeuvre that commend themselves to theologians who are interested in further resources for their own constructive projects. His thought highlights the always already present grace of God that attends created life. He understands sin collectively and emphasizes the structural or systematic nature of sinfulness and its need for redemption. His work attends to the diverse particularity of life, rather than abstractions or

---

160. Friedrich Schleiermacher, *Schleiermacher: Christmas Dialogue, the Second Speech, and Other Selections*, ed. trans. with an intro. Julia A. Lamm (New York: Paulist Press, 2014), p. 105. Hereafter, cited as *SS*.

161. *SS*, p. 107.

162. Ibid., p. 109.

163. See also Heather Walton, *Writing Methods in Theological Education* (London: SCM Press, 2014), p. 70.

generalities. Finally, Schleiermacher's theology accentuates life and joy rather than death and suffering. I return to these themes in the chapters to follow. For now, however, I hope they will encourage readers not only to see the ways in which Schleiermacher was a person of his time but also to anticipate how he can also speak in powerful ways within current contexts.

Chapter Overview

In the first chapter, I demonstrate how my reading of Schleiermacher's theology as trinitarian in his *Christian Faith* contributes to current trinitarian reflections. I explain that Schleiermacher rejects the doctrine of the immanent Trinity because of its unhelpful oscillation between monotheism and tritheism, the monarchicalism or subordinationism involved in the relation of the Father to the Son and Spirit, and because he sees it as a speculative doctrine. I further suggest that the doctrine of the immanent Trinity can be replaced with a Schleiermacher-inspired doctrine of the "essential Trinity," which understands the divine essence as communicated by God in Christ and his Spirit as Love, Wisdom, and Universal Causality. The chapter begins with a brief historical overview of trinitarian thought to situate both Schleiermacher's discussion of the doctrine and contemporary challenges to it. I engage with Elizabeth Johnson, Grace Jantzen, and Linn Marie Tonstad's work to detail some of the problematic features of trinitarian thought for feminist and queer theologians, in particular, including its sexism and idolatry, death-centrism, and kyriarchal features. Then I present my understanding of Schleiermacher's "essential trinitarianism"[164] and detail the benefits it might hold for constructive forms of theology, correlating challenges to the doctrine with constructive responses. In short, I argue that a Schleiermacher-inspired doctrine of the Trinity allows for the use of the historical nomenclature of "Father" and "Son" when conversing with ancient biblical and early Christian witnesses, but at the heart of the divine life finds non-androcentric Universal Causality, Love, and Wisdom in relation to the world. This kind of trinitarian thought advances constructive forms of theology that wish to retain a connection with the historical church yet avoid reinscribing kyriarchy in Christian thought and practice by providing an alternative to current doctrine that applies apophasis to the divine *in se* but is not reduced to doctrinal emptiness.[165] I point out the benefits and drawbacks of essential trinitarianism by engaging with Marcella Althaus-Reid, Janet Martin Soskice, Wendy Farley, Pamela Lightsey, Elisabeth Schüssler Fiorenza, and Linn Marie Tonstad. The chapter also draws on Rachel Adler's work to include recommendations for integrating the language of essential trinitarianism into Christian liturgy, using words from the New Testament Greek lexicon: *Zoe, Agape,* and *Sophia*.

In Chapter 2, I argue that Schleiermacher's thought holds promise for constructing a pneumatologically framed Christology by which Jesus of Nazareth

---

164. For the full argument, see Poe, *Essential Trinitarianism*.
165. I address the use of radical apophaticism in Poe, *Essential Trinitarianism*, pp. 175–9.

is known to contemporary Christians through Christ's Spirit that is embodied in the church. Here the importance of receiving and interpreting the gospels is foregrounded, and the diversity of various embodiments of Christ's Spirit is celebrated. In addition, Schleiermacher's Christology offers an ontology focused on the divine indwelling of Jesus as the completion of human nature. This focus has the power to decenter traditional Christological doctrinal formulas and emphasize instead the identity of the church as the embodiment of Christ's Spirit today by which people come to know Jesus of Nazareth and the wholeness of life he lived, preached, and worked to establish. I argue that Schleiermacher's soteriology holds promise primarily because of its alignment with womanist theology, wherein substitutionary atonement is rejected and the importance of resisting injustice is highlighted. However, while I find many of Schleiermacher's soteriological insights valuable, I argue that his theory of redemption needs modification in order to make it compatible with religious pluralism. To begin, Chapter 2 takes account of the challenges in Christology and atonement theory that have been important throughout Christian history and in feminist and womanist theologies in particular. These include how one holds together the divine and human in one person, whether a male savior could be redemptive for women, and whether vicarious atonement reifies surrogacy roles that especially disempower women of color. Here Rosemary Radford Ruether, Kelly Brown Douglas, Delores Williams, Jacqueline Grant, Monica Coleman, Schüssler Fiorenza, and Judith Butler are important interlocutors. I argue that Schleiermacher's Christology can aid these theologians in emphasizing Jesus' ministry rather than his maleness, but I also suggest that the soteriological significance of his perceived maleness still needs to be addressed. I further demonstrate, in conversation with the work of Delores Williams, A. Elaine Crawford, Karen Baker-Fletcher, Traci C. West, and M. Shawn Copeland, that Schleiermacher's soteriology dovetails with feminist and womanist attempts to avoid sacrificial and substitutionary atonement theories, while emphasizing Jesus' identification with the least of these and his persistence in the face of injustice. However, drawing on Jacqueline Grant and James Cone's work, I argue that Schleiermacher's soteriology needs correction from womanist and Black theologians who rightly emphasize Jesus' Jewish particularity. I detail Schleiermacher's view of Judaism in his "Letters on the Occasion of the Political-Theological Task and the Open Letter of Jewish Householders,"[166] his understanding of Jesus' relation to Jewish messianic hope, and his tendency to downplay Jesus' Jewish particularity in his *Christian Faith*. In addition to correcting Schleiermacher's work by emphasizing Jesus' Jewish particularity, I draw in Susannah Heschel's playful understanding of the "transvestite Jesus" to illuminate the relationship of Jesus to Judaism and Christianity. The chapter then

---

166. Friedrich Schleiermacher, "Letters on the Occasion of the Political-Theological Task and the Open Letter of Jewish Householders," in *A Debate on Jewish Emancipation and Christian Theology in Old Berlin*, ed. and trans. Richard Crouter and Julie Klassen (Indianapolis: Hackett, 2004). Hereafter, cited as *Letters*.

addresses other soteriological themes that are congruent with and hold potential for theologians working constructively today who understand sin socially and systemically, emphasize the importance of the body and affect, and highlight natality and joy. Here I draw on the work of Valerie Saiving Goldstein, Serene Jones, Emilie Townes, Grace Jantzen, and Sallie McFague. Finally, I consider one important way Schleiermacher's soteriology needs revision, namely, by removing his reliance on the idea of an afterlife to make sense of the divine election of all to blessedness, and replacing that reliance with both ignorance about the ways in which divine activity might be at work in other religions and also an emphasis on the interdependence of creaturely life, including religious life.

Chapter 3 is an examination of Schleiermacher's understanding of church and Spirit primarily in relation to feminist and queer thought. It comes in two parts: a demonstration of Schleiermacher's pneumatological and ecclesial emphasis on love and joy, and my constructive imagining of a "queer" community of "Woman" that could inspire a celebration of women, diversity, and interdependence in the church's efforts toward social justice. These two portions of the chapter combine to suggest that Schleiermacher's theology is generative for the Spirit-indwelt church. In the first part of the chapter, I explore both Schleiermacher's *Christmas Eve Celebration* and *Christian Faith* to demonstrate that his ecclesiology is rich with an emphasis on joy-producing love. Coupling this aspect of his theology with Rachel Adler's feminist analysis of laughter as a response to sexism, I argue that his work could be used in churches concerned with resisting injustice while empowering and celebrating women. In the second part of the chapter, I offer a constructive response to Schleiermacher's pneumatological ecclesiology that could aid Christian imaginations in embracing women's solidarity, women's value considered apart from men and children, and the complexity of human relationships. Using Schleiermacher's organic understanding of humanity, I argue for a "queering" of the church, in which its multiplicity, community, and interdependence are celebrated. To frame the discussion, I draw on Talia Mae Bettcher, Anna Marie Jagose, Gerard Loughlin, E. Patrick Johnson, Philippa Bonwick, Elizabeth Johnson, and Eve Kosofsky. I then present four characters whose stories have been narrated in biblical or traditional texts and analyzed by feminist, womanist, mujerista, and queer theologians: Lilith, Eve, Hagar, and Mary. Drawing on the work of Raphael Patai, Judith Plaskow, Phyllis Trible, Delores Williams, and Marcella Althaus-Reid, I use these figures to represent particular differences among women: those who have been deemed religiously and socially "other"; Protestant white women; women of color who have been oppressed by racism, sexism, and classism; and Roman Catholic women. Examining the intersections and divergences of these characters, I build a queer community of "Woman," which demonstrates a non-essentialist understanding of the importance of difference and interdependence in personal relations within an ecumenical community.

Chapter 4 widens the discussion to all of creation. It focuses on the asymmetrical relationship between God and creatures with the goal of demonstrating that Schleiermacher's understanding of the relation between God and creation—his infamous emphasis on absolute dependence—beneficially contributes to ecotheologies as well as ecumenical feminist conversations. I offer the notion of "incarnational submission" as a way to encourage Christians to submit to the interdependence of life with others, which exists because of divine Wisdom and Universal Causality. First, I survey important feminist challenges to a doctrine of creation, including the contrast within theological literature between divine sovereignty, on the one hand, and human agency and democratization, on the other. My conversation partners here include Delores Williams, Wendy Farley, Catherine Keller, Ivone Gebara, and Kwok Pui-Lan. Then I present Schleiermacher's understanding of the relation of God and creation, exploring its contested and beneficial features. I address divine aseity by coupling it with Schleiermacher's understanding of the inseparability of God and creation. I also take account of divine omnipotence, which is tempered in Schleiermacher's view with a non-individualistic and non-interventionist understanding of divine power. In the second part of the chapter, I explore the same relation between God and creation from another perspective by using prayer as a case study. In this effort, I engage with Sarah Coakley's apophatic, cruciform understanding of human submission to God, in contrast with Delores Williams's understanding of Jesus' ministerial vision and the importance of active resistance to injustice. I do so in conversation with Schleiermacher's sermon "On the Power of Prayer," as well as the work of Daphne Hampson, Aristotle Papanikolaou, Carolyn Chau, Karen Baker-Fletcher, and Linn Marie Tonstad. I argue that a Schleiermacher-inspired understanding of "incarnational submission" could draw out a noncompetitive relationship between God and creatures as well as the lively interplay of creaturely life, while avoiding the oppressive features inherent within an emphasis on passivity.

As this chapter overview indicates, I selectively choose a limited number of theologians in each chapter with whom to engage as important interlocutors on the subjects at hand. These conversation partners change in various chapters according to whose thought has been most influential in my own rethinking of the doctrines at hand. In addition, my choice of conversation partners is influenced by their engagement with Schleiermacher. For example, Linn Marie Tonstad and Janet Martin Soskice, whose ideas are engaged in the first chapter on the doctrine of the Trinity, have both explicitly been influenced by Schleiermacher. At the same time, I also draw in thinkers who are not explicitly influenced by Schleiermacher. For instance, in Chapter 3 I draw on Delores Williams and Marcella Althaus-Reid, neither of whom to my knowledge are directly influenced by Schleiermacher's thought but are significant voices in rethinking the story of Hagar and Mary, respectively.

In each chapter, I show how Schleiermacher's theology could advance theological conversations around sexism, classism, racism, heterosexism, ecological degradation, and exclusivism, which are sites of injustice identified by contemporary thinkers and perpetuated in Christian churches. I argue that the four loci in systematic theology that are examined in the book—the Trinity, Christ and redemption, ecclesiology and pneumatology, and the doctrines of God and creation—could be bolstered within constructive forms of theology by careful attention to Schleiermacher's theology. What results from this study is a Christian theology that foregrounds the divine name as Love, Wisdom, and Universal Causality. The triune divine essence is communicated by God in the person and work of Jesus Christ and his Spirit in the church, which illuminates divine activity in creation. Jesus is presented as the one in whom the triune God dwells and as Christians' brother. His life and ministry of love and his resistance to injustice continue within Christian communities that embody his Spirit. The Spirit of Christ so steeps Christians in love that it produces a joyful community that avoids harming those who stand in opposition to it and celebrates the differences among its members. The theology presented in this book also lifts up creation as the great matrix within which humanity finds itself by divine grace, and humanity is understood as an active and limited part of the whole of creation.

The theological choices made here have been influenced as much by Schleiermacher's mature theology as by contemporary constructive work. Schleiermacher's theology coheres with current forms of theology that are concerned with social justice, thereby enriching the collection of resources theologians working constructively might have at their disposal as they carry out their task. At the same time, it points out some of the weaknesses in Schleiermacher's work, furthering the work of Schleiermacher studies in assessing his legacy and continuing relevance for the field of Christian theology. By critically engaging with Schleiermacher, constructive forms of theology today may benefit both from his stature in the history of Christian thought and also from the new insights his thought can generate that move the conversation further in the direction of justice, truth, and beauty.

Chapter 1

TRINITY

As expressed in most liturgical settings, the doctrine of the Trinity concentrates on the Father, Son, and Holy Spirit. For some, repeated recitations and reproductions of this formula within the church have made the doctrine a site of contention.[1] It has been difficult to imagine how Christians might understand and speak of the Trinity without weaving kyriarchy into the fabric of Christian thought and life. As Janet Martin Soskice notes, "The Trinity appears still hierarchical, still male—maleness, indeed, seems enshrined in God's eternity."[2] Indeed, the doctrine of the Trinity seems particularly kyriocentric, since it includes hierarchy, patriarchy, and androcentrism. Schleiermacher also points out that it is difficult to explain the doctrine without succumbing to subordinationism, an unhealthy oscillation between undifferentiated monotheism and tritheism, and engaging in theological speculation. Adding the challenges of kyriarchy to these logical and theological problems makes the strong case that for both contemporary theologians in general and many theologians who take an interest in social justice in particular, the doctrine of the Trinity needs rethinking. Not only does the ecclesial doctrine lead to logical and theological difficulties, it also supports oppressive forms of church and society. For these reasons, Schleiermacher's call for a reformulation of the doctrine becomes increasingly compelling.

Some theologians have taken steps to constructively address the androcentric and patriarchal aspects of the doctrine of the Trinity. A particularly early attempt is found in Julian of Norwich's *Revelations of Divine Love*, which describes the Motherhood of God revealed in Christ. She uses various threefold descriptions of the Trinity, including Nature, Mercy, and Grace; and Father, Mother, and Lord.[3] More recently, Elizabeth Johnson's *She Who Is* reconceives of the Trinity as Spirit-Sophia, Jesus-Sophia, and Mother-Sophia.[4] In addition, Sarah Coakley

---

1. See Mary Daly, *Beyond God the Father: Toward a Philosophy of Women's Liberation* (Boston, MA: Beacon, 1973); Daphne Hampson, *Theology and Feminism* (Cambridge, MA: Blackwell, 1990).

2. Janet Martin Soskice, *The Kindness of God: Metaphor, Gender, and Religious Language* (Oxford: Oxford University Press, 2007), p. 111.

3. Julian of Norwich, *Revelations of Divine Love*, trans. Grace Warrack, ch. 58.

4. Elizabeth A. Johnson, *She Who Is: The Mystery of God in Feminist Theological Discourse*, 10th anniversary ed. (New York: Crossroad, 2002).

reexamines the trinitarian work of Gregory of Nyssa, for whom "the names 'father' and 'mother' are effectively the same in meaning, granted that we know that there is really 'neither male nor female' (see Gal. 3:28) in God."[5] Coakley explains:

> The message Gregory evidently wishes to convey is that gender stereotypes must be reversed, undermined, and transcended if the soul is to advance to supreme intimacy with the trinitarian God; and that the language of sexuality and gender, far from being an optional aside or mere rhetorical flourish in the process, is somehow necessary to and intrinsic to the epistemological deepening that Gregory seeks to describe.[6]

Further, in *God and Difference*, Linn Marie Tonstad argues for a radical revisioning of trinitarian thought that avoids relations of origin within the doctrine of the immanent Trinity, which reinforce gender norms and hierarchy.[7] She suggests that theologians should treat all three persons of the Trinity as they have treated the Spirit: not as an independent center of rational consciousness but as underdetermined, such that the primary characteristic of the persons is incommunicability.[8] Radically simplifying for the sake of summary, Tonstad argues for understanding the immanent divine life as the Power of God, the Glory of God, and Love or the Name of God.[9] Among these and other attempts at rethinking the Trinity, some commonalities emerge, including increased attention to the Spirit, a reclamation of the Sophia/wisdom tradition, and the proliferation of divine names.[10] Although many have experimented with new ways of imagining the Trinity, no single formulation has yet taken hold. Even the most common inclusive liturgical formula, "Creator, Redeemer, Sustainer," has not widely satisfied academic theologians because of its separation of the perichoretic (interdependent) activity of the Godhead.[11]

---

5. Sarah Coakley, *Powers and Submissions: Spirituality, Philosophy and Gender* (Malden, MA: Blackwell, 2002), p. 128.

6. Ibid.

7. By doing so, Tonstad is following Schleiermacher's critique of intra-trinitarian relations in the doctrine of the immanent Trinity.

8. Linn Marie Tonstad, *God and Difference: The Trinity, Sexuality, and the Transformation of Finitude* (New York: Routledge, 2016), p. 227.

9. Ibid., p. 231.

10. See also Sallie McFague, *Models of God: Theology for an Ecological, Nuclear Age* (Philadelphia, PA: Fortress, 1987); Kathryn Tanner, *Jesus, Humanity, and the Trinity: A Brief Systematic Theology* (Minneapolis, MN: Fortress, 2001); Kathryn Tanner, *Christ the Key* (Cambridge: Cambridge University Press, 2010).

11. Katherine Sonderegger surveys some feminist and "inclusive" formulations of the divine name in "On the Holy Name of God," *Theology Today* 58/3 (October 2001): 384–98. She concludes that Christians of all stripes should call God "Father" because this name was revealed by Jesus (pp. 397–8). However, she also thinks that Christians could someday sparingly use "her" alongside the divine name because it is in the wisdom literature and

In this chapter, I offer a doctrine of the Trinity that does not weave kyriarchy into Christian thought and life. To do so, I build on some of Schleiermacher's trinitarian commitments and doctrinal moves. Schleiermacher clearly articulates weaknesses of the traditional doctrine, calls for a rethinking of this doctrine, and takes preliminary steps toward such a reformulation in part by reinterpreting and reconsidering the much-maligned work of Sabellius. While Schleiermacher does not go all the way in offering a clear presentation of a new form of trinitarian doctrine, his thought is suggestive of and could be developed into what I refer to as a doctrine of the essential Trinity. This doctrine is more than a mere espousal of a doctrine of the economic Trinity but also does not go so far as to embrace a doctrine of the immanent Trinity. Instead, it stands midway between these options as a way to speak about the heart of the divine life on the basis of divine self-communication in and through Christ, without entering into speculation about counterfactuals regarding what God would be like apart from creation. The doctrine of the essential Trinity, as I develop it out of Schleiermacher's theology, retains many helpful elements of the traditional doctrine while avoiding its kyriarchal liabilities.

I begin by situating Schleiermacher's criticism and call for renewal of trinitarian doctrine in his ecclesial and modern context. Second, I highlight three problematic features of trinitarian doctrine as Schleiermacher identified them, namely, subordinationism, an unhelpful oscillation between monotheism and tritheism, and its speculative quality. I then take account of three aspects of the doctrine that are particularly concerning for some contemporary theologians working constructively. Following the work of Elizabeth Johnson, Grace Janzten, and Linn Tonstad, I highlight the androcentrism and sexism, death-centrism, and kyriarchy that are involved in the doctrine of the immanent Trinity. Third, I present my constructive interpretation of Schleiermacher's doctrine of the Trinity in his *Christian Faith* (first published in 1820/1, revised edition published in 1830/1) and in his treatise on Sabellianism (1822).[12] I argue that a doctrine of

mystical tradition, though she thinks the warrants for such use remain to be brought out of the tradition (396). As examples of inclusive formulations of the Triune name, Sonderegger cites Ruth C. Duck and Patricia Wilson-Kastner, *Praising God: The Trinity in Christian Worship* (Louisville, KY: Westminster John Knox, 1999); Patricia Wilson-Kastner, *Imagery for Preaching* (Minneapolis, MN: Fortress, 1989); Ruth C. Duck and Maren C. Tirabassi, eds., *Touch Holiness: Resources for Worship* (New York: Pilgrim, 1990); Ruth C. Duck, *Flames of the Spirit: Resources for Worship* (New York: Pilgrim, 1985); McFague, *Models of God*; *The New Companion to the Breviary with Seasonal Supplement* (Indianapolis, IN: Carmelites of Indianapolis, 1988); Hoyt L. Hickman, *Holy Communion: A Service Book for Use by the Minister* (Nashville, TN: Abingdon, 1987); The Anglican Church in Aotearoa, New Zealand, and Polynesia, *A New Zealand Prayer Book / He Karakai Mihinare o Aotearoa* (San Francisco, CA: Harper and Row, 1989, 1997); Elizabeth A. Johnson, *She Who Is: The Mystery of God in Feminist Theological Discourse* (New York: Crossroad, 2002).

12. *Friedrich Schleiermacher und die Trinitätslehre*, ed. Martin Tezt, Texte zur Kirchen- und Theologiegeschichte, vol. XI (Gütersloh: Gütersloher Verlagshaus Gerd Mohn, 1969).

the essential Trinity can be drawn out of his theology, which places Love, Wisdom, and Universal Causality at the heart of the divine life. This doctrine retains many of the traditional features of the doctrine of the immanent Trinity, including perichoresis and coequality, but avoids the problems both Schleiermacher and contemporary theologians have identified above. Finally, I analyze the drawbacks and benefits of my development of Schleiermacher's trinitarian thought for contemporary theologies, engaging current constructive work on love, liturgical language, and the preexistent Logos in the process. I offer *Agape* (Love), *Sophia* (Wisdom), and *Zoe* (Life) as liturgical language that might be used by those who wish to practice a Schleiermacher-inspired doctrine of the Trinity in an ecclesial context. The chapter concludes with an account of the benefits of a doctrine of the essential Trinity, emphasizing the ways in which it supports gender justice. Overall, this chapter argues that a doctrine of the essential Trinity that is derived from and inspired by Schleiermacher's work—which affirms Love, Wisdom, and Causality as the triune, perichoretic contours of the divine being that ground divine activity in the economy of salvation—can provide a non-androcentric and non-hierarchical alternative to the doctrine of the immanent Trinity and, in so doing, contribute to the ongoing scholarly work of reconstructing trinitarian doctrine in non-kyriarchal ways.

Schleiermacher and the Doctrine of the Trinity

Within many histories of the development of trinitarian doctrine, Schleiermacher's place has been marginal, at best.[13] For example, although Declan Marmion and Rik Van Nieuwenhove acknowledge that Schleiermacher's "status as a 'classic' author is beyond dispute,"[14] they claim that he had "an impoverished theological imagination when dealing with the traditional doctrine of the Trinity."[15] This comment is representative of much scholarship on the history of

---

This text was translated into English in two parts: Friedrich Schleiermacher, "On the Discrepancy between the Sabellian and Athanasian Method of Representing the Doctrine of a Trinity in the Godhead (Part One)," trans. Moses Stuart, *Biblical Repository and Quarterly Observer* 5/18 (April 1835): 265–353; and "On the Discrepancy between the Sabellian and Athanasian Method of Representing the Doctrine of a Trinity in the Godhead (Part Two)," *Biblical Repository and Quarterly Observer* 6/19 (July 1835): 1–116. Hereafter, these works will be cited as *OD1* and *OD2*, respectively.

13. For a review of the scholarship on Schleiermacher's doctrine of the Trinity, see Shelli M. Poe, "Trinitarian Thought," in *The Oxford Handbook of Schleiermacher* (Oxford: Oxford University Press, forthcoming). For an example of the treatment of Schleiermacher in the history of trinitarian thought, see Paul M. Collins, *The Trinity: A Guide for the Perplexed* (London: Bloomsbury T&T Clark, 2008).

14. Declan Marmion and Rik Van Nieuwenhove, *An Introduction to the Trinity* (Cambridge: Cambridge University Press, 2011), p. 148.

15. Ibid., p. 146.

the doctrine, following the assessment of Karl Barth.[16] Even those who interpret Schleiermacher's thought more charitably find his understanding of the doctrine inadequate. Samuel M. Powell, for example, identifies Schleiermacher's attitude toward the ecclesial doctrine as "utterly critical" when he traces the doctrine of the Trinity within German thought.[17] However, he significantly recognizes, in ways that most scholars do not, that Schleiermacher made preliminary steps toward the reconstruction of a doctrine of the Trinity.[18] Powell identifies those steps as Schleiermacher's move from talk about the divine "nature" to the divine "activity," and his identification of love and wisdom with the divine essence.[19] Yet Powell states that Schleiermacher's "lack of a substantial doctrine of the Father is a glaring omission that mars the architectural balance of his work and fails to address one of the fundamental topics of theology."[20] Many astute scholars of modern theology have not found Schleiermacher's thought substantively influential or generative for the construction of the doctrine of the Trinity.[21]

A brief consideration of the context of Schleiermacher's work can assist in understanding such claims. To begin, it is important to recall that Schleiermacher was a Reformed theologian, who served as the Reformed chaplain at Berlin's Charité Hospital from 1796 to 1802 and as the Reformed pastor of Trinity Church (*Dreifaltigkeitskirche*) in Berlin from 1809 to 1834. He was heavily engaged in church life, and, as we have already seen, he had been formed in his early years through education within the Moravian community at Herrnhut.[22] In accordance with both the Reformed tradition and Moravian piety, Schleiermacher's mature theology refers to scripture along with historical creeds and confessions, and highlights Christian affections, community, and heartfelt piety. Out of this

---

16. Karl Barth, *The Theology of Schleiermacher: Lectures at Göttingen, Winter Semester of 1923-24* (Grand Rapids, MI: Eerdmans, 1982). See also Van A. Harvey, "A Word in Defense of Schleiermacher's Theological Method," *The Journal of Religion* 42/3 (1962): 151–70.

17. Samuel M. Powell, *The Trinity in German Thought* (Cambridge: Cambridge University Press, 2001), p. 87.

18. Others who have recognized some constructive work in Schleiermacher's comments on the doctrine of the Trinity include Francis Schüssler Fiorenza and Paul DeHart. See Francis Schüssler Fiorenza, "Understanding God as Triune," in *The Cambridge Companion to Friedrich Schleiermacher*, ed. Jacqueline Mariña (Cambridge: Cambridge University, 2005), pp. 171–88; Paul DeHart, "Ter mundus accipit infinitum: The Dogmatic Coordinates of Schleiermacher's Trinitarian Treatise," *Neue Zeitschrift für Systematische Theologie und Religionsphilosophie* 52 (2010): 17–39.

19. Powell, *The Trinity in German Thought*, pp. 96, 100.

20. Ibid., p. 101.

21. Powell understands Schleiermacher's work historically as a culminating point of the critical Enlightenment and a bridge to German idealism (ibid., p. 102).

22. For my treatment of Schleiermacher's *Christian Faith* as part of his Reformed tradition, see Shelli M. Poe, "Schleiermacher's *Christian Faith*," in *Oxford Handbook of Reformed Theology* (Oxford: Oxford University Press, 2020).

ecclesial context emerges Schleiermacher's commitment to doctrines that arise out of genuine Christian piety. However, as we will see below, he does not think that the doctrine of the Trinity as it is expressed in the historic creeds is directly related to Christian piety. This is a primary motivation for his call for a reformulation and renewal of the doctrine of the Trinity.

Schleiermacher's view that the doctrine of the immanent Trinity is at a remove from genuine Christian piety dovetails with his "empirical" attitude toward the modern field of theology, which he envisions as documenting and engaging with the living piety of Christian communities throughout history. In his academic context, he explains that "dogmatic theology is the science concerned with the interconnection of whatever doctrine has currency in a given social organization called a Christian church at a given time."[23] His *Christian Faith*, therefore, aims to describe the "Christian religious states of mind and heart" of Protestants in Prussia as he observes them.[24] Because Schleiermacher conceives of theology in part as an historical and empirical enterprise and because he does not think that the doctrine of the immanent Trinity directly arises from Christian piety but is a speculative doctrine that considers God as God would have been had creation never existed, his theology does not have a place for the doctrine of the immanent Trinity. Moreover, Schleiermacher's commitment to a descriptive form of theology notwithstanding, he also maintains the importance of critique and intellectual development within Christian theology. He addresses the modification of Christian doctrine in §19.3, where he says that persons may step forward "in particular matters by way of deliberately correcting customary statements. Thus," he explains, "already on this account, our definition in no way excludes improvements and new developments in Christian doctrine."[25] As such, within his *Christian Faith*, Schleiermacher points out the weaknesses of arguments that are not valid or sound, that are not genuinely Christian,[26] or that would have ethically spurious implications,[27] and he offers

---

23. *CF*, §19, p. 131.
24. Ibid., §15, p. 116.
25. Ibid., §19.3, p. 136.
26. *CF*, §21: "In order to realize a structured body of doctrines of faith, it is necessary, first of all, to excise everything heretical from the totality of dogmatic material and to retain only what has ecclesial merit" (p. 142).
27. Schleiermacher presents Christian faith and Christian ethics separately, but he maintains in §26.2 that "only these two disciplines, taken together, present the whole reality of Christian life" (p. 164). In addition, he thinks Christian ethics "could always be described by way of a postscript in presentations of faith-doctrine too, viewed as natural outcomes of the very states that are described there" (p. 165). Faith doctrines could also be fitted into a presentation to Christian ethics, "for the reason that the articulation of self-consciousness is also a moral activity" (p. 165). An example of the way that ethical implications can condition faith doctrine is Schleiermacher's argument against eternal damnation (*CF*, §163, pp. 997–8), since Christians—being morally upright—could not feel blessed in communion with God in Christ if they knew that a portion of humanity was being simultaneously eternally damned.

points of theological correction. Schleiermacher's commitment to the critical reception of doctrine and openness to doctrinal development does not exclude the doctrine of the Trinity. He critiques the doctrine of the immanent Trinity and calls for development in this important area of Christian doctrine not only because of its speculative remove from Christian piety but also because of the intellectual confusion it breeds, which I describe below.

Finally, Schleiermacher's treatment of the doctrine of the Trinity is influenced by his respect for the newly emerging discipline of historical criticism as a legitimate interpretive method to be applied to scripture. For example, he argues that the importance of scripture for the life of the Christian community does not depend on the truth of traditional claims regarding the identity of the author of a scriptural work. Instead, "since we know that in the church all errors and imperfections can be uncovered and removed only gradually by the efficacious action of the Holy Spirit … all activity that is directed to correct exposure of authorship or to the genuine or spurious character of individual passages must be able to progress undisturbed."[28] More generally, Schleiermacher writes that "we must not admit anything misleading into exercise of the purest hermeneutical procedures possible or, as it were, knowingly prefer artfully to elaborate in our interpretation rather than to set forth a result that could disclose a conception of Christian faith less pure."[29] A particularly important example of Schleiermacher's commitment to "the purest hermeneutical procedures" is found in his refusal to read Christian beliefs anachronistically back into the stories and prophecies of Hebrew scripture. He states that "the history of Christian theology also shows plainly enough how much these efforts to find our Christian faith in the Old Testament has, in part redounded to the detriment of our application of interpretive art."[30] Partially for this reason, Schleiermacher does not identify the Holy Spirit in his own trinitarian thought with the Spirit that indwelt the prophets or the Spirit that hovered over the waters of creation. For him, doing so would be anachronistic and detrimental to proper hermeneutical methods.[31]

These features of Schleiermacher's intellectual context can help readers understand why at times his work seems "utterly critical"[32] of the ecclesial doctrine

---

28. *CF*, §131.1, p. 850.

29. Ibid.

30. *CF*, §132.2, p. 855. I return to Schleiermacher's understanding of the relationship of Judaism to Christianity in Chapter 2.

31. Karen Baker-Fletcher responds to this sort of argument by acknowledging that when Christians "see" the Trinity in the Hebrew Bible, they are engaging in "eisegesis—reading into the text, rather than exegesis or reading out of the text. Eisegesis," she claims, "is a problem when we are not honest about doing it." She advocates for honestly calling the practice eisegesis and honoring it as a type of midrash (Karen Baker-Fletcher, *Dancing with God: The Trinity from a Womanist Perspective* [St. Louis, MO: Chalice, 2006], p. 69).

32. Powell, *The Trinity in German Thought*, p. 87.

of the immanent Trinity.[33] He is committed to historical criticism of the Bible, critique and development within theology, offering descriptions of the religious states of mind and heart of Christians rather than speculative notions, and to the idea that doctrines should arise from genuine Christian piety. For these reasons, Schleiermacher criticizes certain aspects of the doctrine of the Trinity that he finds speculative, incoherent, founded on improper readings of scripture, and not grounded in genuine Christian piety. However, it is by no means the case that he lacks a robust theological imagination with regard to the doctrine of the Trinity.

---

33. It is also important to note here that although Schleiermacher has been criticized widely for his treatment of the doctrine of the Trinity, he is not the only theologian to have questioned, challenged, or criticized it. A brief survey of some of the major points of interest in the history of the doctrine illustrates its centrality, complexity, and ongoing development. Its creedal history begins in the fourth century with the Council of Nicaea, the work of the Cappadocians, and Athanasius, as they attempted to bring some consistency to experimentations and diversity in trinitarian thought during the centuries that preceded them. At the turn of the fifth century, Augustine's *De Trinitate* employed a psychological form of analogical reasoning to think through the doctrine, even as he denied the human mind's ability to grasp the reality of the Trinity. In the eleventh century, the *filioque* clause ("and the Son") within the doctrine was a significant part of the dispute between Eastern and Western Christianity that eventually led to their schism. Two centuries later, Thomas Aquinas developed the doctrine of the Trinity in the scholastic period by reversing the order of missions and processions from Augustine's formulation. In *De Trinitate*, after setting out the equality of the three divine persons, Augustine begins with the missions of the economy of salvation in Books II–IV. In the closing chapter of Book IV, he states that the temporal missions reveal the eternal processions of the divine persons. In the *Summa Theologiae*, however, after setting forth the unity of God, Thomas Aquinas begins his treatise on the Trinity in question twenty-seven with the persons of the immanent Trinity. Only later, in question forty-three, does he treat the missions of the divine persons in the economy of salvation. During the sixteenth century, Protestant Reformers went on to question the doctrine's scriptural foundations. Three centuries later, Schleiermacher called for a Protestant renewal of the doctrine. In the twentieth century, the doctrine received attention from theological giants in both Protestantism and Roman Catholicism. Karl Barth unfolded a new articulation of the doctrine at the beginning of his massive *Church Dogmatics*, while Karl Rahner unveiled his famous axiom that "the 'economic' Trinity is the 'immanent' Trinity and the 'immanent' Trinity is the 'economic' Trinity" (Karl Rahner, *The Trinity*, trans. Catherine Mowry LaCugna (New York: Crossroad, 2005), p. 22. Original edition: "Der dreifaltige Gott als tranzendeter Urgrund der Heilsgeschichte," in *Die Heilsgeschichte vor Christus*, vol. 2 of *Mysterium Salutis, Grundriss heilsgeschichtlicher Dogmatik*.) In the twenty-first century, Christian thought also saw the development of "social trinitarianism." (For an explication of the movement, see Collins, *The Trinity*.) Although this is admittedly an extremely brief walk-through of key points in trinitarian history, it nonetheless makes clear that the doctrine has not been untouched over the centuries but has continually been a site of controversy and development.

Before explicating Schleiermacher's own preliminary steps toward a reformation of the doctrine of the Trinity, I turn to its problematic features, as Schleiermacher identified them: subordinationism, an unhelpful oscillation between monotheism and tritheism, and its speculative character.[34] I then highlight challenges to the doctrine from contemporary theological quarters, including the charges of sexism and idolatry, death-centrism, and kyriarchy. This overview of the problematic features of trinitarian doctrine sets the stage for a demonstration of how Schleiermacher's theology could address those problems and contribute to an advancement of the doctrine of the Trinity.

Problematic Features of Trinitarian Doctrine

Subordination, Oscillation, and Speculation

In the traditional form of the doctrine of the immanent Trinity, relations of origin are the proper way to distinguish between the Father, Son, and Holy Spirit. As in the Athanasian Creed, "The Father is made of none: neither created, nor begotten. The Son is of the Father alone: not made, nor created: but begotten. The Holy Ghost is of the Father and of the Son: neither made, nor created, nor begotten, but proceeding."[35] The Father is unbegotten, begets the Son, and spirates the Spirit. To this order, the Western tradition further distinguishes between the Son and Spirit by indicating that the Spirit's procession originates from both the Father and the Son. Schleiermacher argues that because the persons of the immanent Trinity are distinguished by such relations of origin, the doctrine does not avoid inequalities among the persons except by theological fiat.[36] In other words, it is exceedingly difficult to square these relations of origin with the claim that the three persons are coequal.[37] If the Son and Spirit depend on the Father for their existence, then the Father seems to enjoy powers—begetting and spirating—that are exclusive to him and that make the Son and Spirit inferior to him. Schleiermacher describes it this way:

---

34. For a recent account of such issues in a wide range of theologies, see *Rethinking Trinitarian Theology*, eds. Robert J. Wozniak and Giulio Maspero (New York: T&T Clark, 2012).

35. *The Creeds of Christendom: With a History and Critical Notes, Vol. III: The Greek and Latin Creeds with Translations*, ed. Philip Schaff, rev. David S. Schaff (Grand Rapids, MI: Baker, 2007), pp. 67–8.

36. Schleiermacher offers his reading of the trinitarian and Christological controversies as they relate to subordination in *OD2*, pp. 74–9.

37. For an account of the ways in which some medieval theologians attempted to avoid subordinationism and tritheism, see Richard Cross, "Medieval Trinitarianism and Modern Theology," *Rethinking Trinitarian Theology*, ed. Robert J. Wozniak and Giulio Maspero (New York: T&T Clark, 2012), pp. 26–43.

Suppose that might has indwelt the Father from eternity to beget the Son as second divine person, but no such might indwelt the Son and yet no relationship of dependence in which the Father would stand to the Son could be adduced as a counterweight. It is then undeniable that the might of the Father would be greater than that of the Son and that the glory that the begetter has in relation to the begotten would have to be greater than the glory the begotten has in relation to the begetter.[38]

The same could be said for the relation between the Father and Son to the Holy Spirit. Although it is easy to *say*, it is difficult to *conceive* how the Father, Son, and Holy Spirit are coequal while at the same time maintaining that they are distinguished by relations of origin or dependence.

A second contentious point Schleiermacher identifies within the doctrine of the Trinity is the arguably unclear relationship between the one divine essence (*ousia*) and the three divine persons (*prosopa*). Theologians have been careful to stipulate that the divine essence is not a fourth person in addition to the Father, Son, and Holy Spirit. However, positively explaining how the essence and persons relate is difficult and tends Christian thinking toward either undifferentiated monotheism by emphasizing the one divine essence, or tritheism by emphasizing the three divine persons. Schleiermacher thinks the analogy of species to individuals is the most helpful when attempting to coherently hold these two emphases together. On such an analogy, the divine essence is likened to the species, while the divine persons are likened to individuals that make up the species. Schleiermacher claims, "we have no closer typus by which to represent a relationship such as is advanced here than that of the concept of a species and of the individual entities included under it, for the concept of a species is likewise present wholly and undivided in the individual entities that belong to it but is not present anywhere outside them."[39] Unfortunately, the analogy breaks down rather quickly in the attempt to avoid tritheism, leaving Christians without the ability "to conceive anything definite on the subject."[40] The result, in Schleiermacher's assessment, is an unhelpful oscillation between the one divine being and the three divine persons.

Third, Schleiermacher argues that the doctrine of the immanent Trinity as it has been developed in ecclesial history is not directly related to Christian piety. As he sees it, Christian piety concerns the reception of divine self-communication

---

38. *CF*, §171.2, p. 1026. Cf. *OD2*, p. 71: "Here Sabellius might come in and with as good a right say, that the assertions of his opponents are blasphemy against the Son and Spirit; yea, against the Trinity itself; inasmuch as they make two members of the Trinity have a part in the divine Unity, only through the causality of the other member."

39. *CF*, §171.3, p. 1027.

40. Ibid., p. 1028. Gregory of Nyssa already famously interrogated this analogy in "Concerning We Should Think of Saying That There Are Not Three Gods, to Ablabius," in *The Trinitarian Controversy*, ed. and trans. William G. Rusch (Philadelphia, PA: Fortress, 1980), pp. 149–61. He chalks the tendency toward tritheism up to a misuse of language.

in and through the person and work of Christ and his Spirit. The doctrine of the immanent Trinity, however, which includes three-fold distinctions among eternal divine hypostases, speculates about what God would be like apart from creation and redemption. It is, therefore, "not to be understood as if the orthodox doctrine of the Trinity were to be viewed as an immediate, or even one at all necessary, combination of expressions regarding self-consciousness."[41] As an example of the esoteric nature of the Athanasian doctrine, Schleiermacher writes,

> Sabellius might well have asked, how he who prayed to the Son, could pray to a Godhead that was begotten; and he who prayed to the Spirit, could pray to a divine nature proceeding in an indescribable manner from the Father; and yet the petitioner at the same time be able to separate the one from the other ..., when at the very same time also he was required to consider the generation of the Son as unlike to anything human, which of course made it inconceivable and indescribable to him.[42]

Because such distinctions in the doctrine of the immanent Trinity are inconceivable and indescribable, Schleiermacher maintains that Christians could reject that doctrine and their faith would be unaffected. Rather, "our faith in Christ and our living communion with him would be the same even if we had no knowledge of this transcendent fact or if this fact were different."[43] On Schleiermacher's account, the doctrine of the immanent Trinity is not a direct, authentic expression of Christian piety.[44]

These concerning features of the ecclesial doctrine of the Trinity are not adiaphora but strike at the heart of the doctrine itself. Subordinationism would render the efficacy of redemption suspect, since it puts the full divinity of the Son and Spirit into question. As Schleiermacher writes, the doctrine

> was established only in defense of the view, first, that nothing less than the divine nature was in Christ and indwells the Christian church as its common spirit. Second, in these expressions we intend neither a diminished nor a totally figurative meaning, not wanting to have anything to do with exceptional higher beings—conceived, as it were, as subordinate deities—in Christ and in the Holy Spirit.[45]

---

41. *CF*, §170.3, p. 1023.
42. *OD2*, p. 72.
43. *CF*, §170.3, p. 1023.
44. Social trinitarians have also recognized this critique and have attempted to make the doctrine relevant to Christian faith by understanding the three persons as a model of human community. See, for instance, Catherine Mowry LaCugna, *God for Us: The Trinity and Christian Life* (New York: HarperOne, 1991), and Linn Tonstad's critique of it in *God and Difference*, pp. 12–17.
45. *CF*, §170.1, p. 1020.

Further, an uneasy oscillation between undifferentiated monotheism and tritheism threatens the very identity of Christianity as a differentiated monotheistic faith. Finally, the idea that the ecclesial doctrine of the Trinity is disconnected from Christian piety implies the irrelevance of trinitarian Christian worship, which has been central to Christian practice for centuries. Whether all of Schleiermacher's criticisms of trinitarian doctrine are entirely convincing when applied to any particular theologian's work is somewhat beside the point. It remains that the questions he raises here have been continual sites of contention within the history of trinitarian doctrine, and trinitarian theories need to either address them or construct their trinitarian theologies in such a way that these questions do not arise. What most concerns me is that how theologians deal with the logical problems Schleiermacher identifies within trinitarian doctrine, especially the charge of subordinationism and speculation, often contributes to the problems that theologians concerned with sex and gender justice highlight.

Sexism and Idolatry, Death-Centrism, and Kyriarchy

I survey here just three aspects of the doctrine of the Trinity that are particularly problematic for contemporary theologians concerned about social justice: sexism and idolatry, death-centrism, and kyriarchy. In the 1990s, Elizabeth Johnson highlighted trinitarian doctrine's androcentric character and clearly explained how its exclusive use is both sexist and idolatrous. Drawing on Paul Ricoeur, Johnson emphasizes that the "symbol of God functions."[46] Whether Christians have intentionally developed views of the divine as male or masculine, repeated use of exclusively or predominantly male or masculine references to the divine functions to produce androcentrism and sexism. Johnson explains that "the way in which a faith community shapes language about God implicitly represents what it takes to be the highest good, the profoundest truth, the most appealing beauty," and this speaking "powerfully molds the corporate identity of the community and directs its praxis."[47] Intentions aside, the way Christians speak of the divine has concrete effects on the church and wider society. Oppression occurs as "speech functions effectively to legitimate structures and theories that grant a theomorphic character to men who rule but that relegate women, children, and other men to the deficient margins."[48] In addition, exclusively or predominantly masculine speech about God is idolatrous insofar as it "absolutizes a single set of metaphors."[49]

46. Johnson, *She Who Is*, p. 4.
47. Ibid.
48. Ibid., p. 18.
49. Ibid. Within the Jewish context, Rachel Adler explains that the "exclusively masculine language with which we currently refer to God is a metaphoric language that has been totalized. That is, selected metaphors have been taken to represent the totality of the God toward whom they point. Such an understanding is, at the least, inadequate and distortive." Rachel Adler, *Engendering Judaism: An Inclusive Theology and Ethics* (Boston, MA: Beacon Press, 1998), p. 66.

Johnson argues that using exclusively masculine language obscures the majority Christian view that the divine, as Creator rather than creature, cannot be captured by one metaphor. Rather, multiple metaphors, images, and stories are required to get a sense of the divine. When male or masculine metaphors for God are used exclusively, literally, and patriarchally, Johnson argues that the results are problematic for all those who seek to be faithful worshippers of the Creator rather than the creature.[50]

Moving to a second challenge, Grace Jantzen has persuasively argued that many twentieth- and twenty-first-century accounts of the doctrine of the Trinity are death-centric. This is problematic because focusing on death is implicitly androcentric and sexist. Jantzen makes clear the link between sexism and the death-centrism found in the Western imagination:

> Western civilization, dominated by masculinist structures, has had both a fascination with and a dread of death. Perhaps the most vivid illustration of this is its continuous involvement with war: waging wars, planning wars, building ever more sophisticated equipment for war, writing history as though wars were the most important events, even conducting philosophical arguments on the model of attack and defence. ... The preoccupation with death is matched by a fascination with other worlds, some other form of reality beyond the uncertainties of this present life, bound up as it is with the material body. ... When this is coupled with the age-old linkage of the female with the material and the male with the rational spirit, the sexist nature of the desire to master and ultimately to escape from matter is evident. ... If humans are to find meaning in a life which moves inexorably towards death, one strategy for dealing with anxiety is to postulate immortality and a God who guarantees it, especially ... if that God also authorizes mastery over that which reminds of mortality: women, bodiliness, and the earth to which we all return.[51]

In contrast to an emphasis on death, the means of death, escape from death, and mastery over all those who are associated with death, Jantzen argues for a feminist emphasis on natality, or being born of a woman and alive within a set of relationships. If Jantzen is right that death-centrism is androcentric and sexist, then death-centric theological accounts of the Trinity would be clearly problematic for theologians concerned with avoiding androcentrism and sexism.

Tonstad argues that such problematic death-centrism is exactly what is found in the trinitarian work of theologians like Hans Urs von Balthasar and Graham Ward. By making the cross central to Jesus' identity and closely aligning Jesus

---

50. For a recent treatment of the need for inclusive language, see also Tanya Van Wyk, "An Unfinished Reformation: The Persistence of Gender-Exclusive Language in Theology and the Maintenance of a Patriarchal Church Culture," *Verbum et Ecclesia* 39/1 (2018): 7 pages.

51. Grace M. Jantzen, *Becoming Divine: Towards a Feminist Philosophy of Religion* (Bloomington: Indiana University Press, 1999), pp. 129–30.

with the second person in the doctrine of the immanent Trinity, these theologians understand obedience unto death as a defining feature of the Son. "The implication," Tonstad argues, "is that the cross is the revelation of the Son's intra-trinitarian obedience and the appropriateness of suffering and death to his divine person."[52] In short, accounts of the Son's obedience to the Father fold suffering and death into the very being of God. Tonstad explains the trinitarian train of thought at work here:

> Such Christologies (kenotic in one sense of the term) emphasize that Jesus' self-emptying nature, as the Son who eternally receives the Father's generous sharing of his divinity, makes possible his obedient and self-sacrificial death. The Son's eternal reception (giftedness) of "self" from the Father becomes that in the divine life of which the cross is an image. The Son's road to death, the death of God, becomes the crux and fulcrum of all revelation—not primarily because it shows that God-for-us overcomes death but because the intra-trinitarian drama of the cross is the clearest narrative exposition of relations among Father, Son, and Spirit.[53]

If the Son's obedience to the Father is a defining feature of his person and this is rooted in Jesus' self-sacrificial death, then it should be clear that the doctrine of the Trinity, conceived in this way, is not likely to contribute to Jantzen's hoped-for shift in the Western "imaginary of death" toward natality, that is, being born of a woman.[54] Rather, such a death-centric doctrine of the Trinity is likely to enhance the Western imagination's emphasis on death and the passive obedience that is required by the subordinate party in a relationship of dependence.

In a third, related, challenge, Tonstad demonstrates how a cruciform understanding of the Trinity illuminates "the unexpected ways divine difference gets gendered and sexed, grounding the ultimacy of heterosexuality in the Christian imaginary."[55] In short, Christians construct a constellation of relationships that are analogous to that of the Trinity's Father and the Son: "Father-Son, God-man, Christ-church, Yahweh-Israel, and Adam-Eve."[56] This constellation makes dominant–submissive cisgender heterosexual relations ultimate. It also reinforces patriarchy on a wider scale by applying the obedience of the Son in relation to the Father to women in relation to men. Deeply connected to the problem of subordinationism discussed above, the result is the obedience, submission, and subordination of women and non-ruling people to ruling men. In this way, Tonstad argues that identifying obedience as the Son's distinct activity or role legitimates

---

52. Tonstad, *God and Difference*, p. 10.
53. Ibid., p. 11. I return to the notion of *kenosis* in Chapter 4.
54. Jantzen, *Becoming Divine*, p. 141.
55. Tonstad, *God and Difference*, p. 11.
56. Ibid., p. 136.

and even commands women's obedience to men. The result is a reinforcement of kyriarchal relations of dominance and submission.

If these problematic features of current trinitarian doctrine are to be removed, the doctrine will have to be reimagined in new ways. Together, Schleiermacher and contemporary theologians are now calling for a rethinking and reformulation of trinitarian doctrine that avoids subordinationism, grounds the doctrine of the trinity in the economy of salvation, and avoids sexism and idolatry, death-centrism, and kyriarchy. Schleiermacher's own trinitarian thought can serve as a catalyst in this effort.

Essential Trinitarianism

Schleiermacher's Beginnings

Schleiermacher's treatment of the doctrine of the Trinity is located in the conclusion of his *Christian Faith* and in a sequel to that conclusion, which was originally published in 1822 and translated into English thirteen years later under the title, "On the Discrepancy Between the Sabellian and Athanasian Method of Representing the Doctrine of a Trinity in the Godhead."[57] Much of the conclusion to Schleiermacher's *Christian Faith* is taken up with an explication of his criticism of the ecclesial doctrine, which has already been presented above. What remains is to investigate Schleiermacher's preliminary steps toward a reformulation of trinitarian doctrine and to evaluate them in light of constructive forms of theology concerned with social justice. I begin with "On the Discrepancy" and then turn to his *Christian Faith*.

In "On the Discrepancy," Schleiermacher traces the doctrine of the Trinity as it was developed in the first few centuries of the Common Era. Therein, he sets forth his understanding of the doctrine of the Trinity as developed by Sabellius, a third-century theologian well-known for being declared heretical by the prevailing authorities but who Schleiermacher thinks has been misinterpreted and deserves another look. The text begins with a nautical metaphor describing how Christian theologians have attempted to steer the Christian ship between two shoals: (1) Judaism, which understood God to be one and external to creation, and (2) Gentile polytheism, which understood the divine nature as divided among many individuals. Christianity was to maintain a middle way, wherein God dwells in humanity (*pace* Judaism), one and undivided (*pace* "paganism" or polytheism).[58] Schleiermacher understands Sabellius as developing a form of trinitarian doctrine

---

57. Schleiermacher writes of the essay that it is designed "to compare the relations of certain particulars to each other, that stand connected with what is said in my *Doctrines of the Creed*, or *Doctrines worthy of Belief* (*Glaubenslehre*, §190), and near the close of it, respecting the subject of the Trinity" (*OD1*, p. 329).

58. *OD1*, p. 331. In the course of his essay, Schleiermacher identifies and analyzes the work of a number of theologians whom he places on either side of the debate. He identifies Artemon, Praxeas, Noetus, and Beryll as steering their ships closer to Judaism. Nearer to

that maintains this middle way and believes that his view was unwisely dispensed with by the Athanasian party and the church thereafter. Schleiermacher states that "to the Sabellian views we cannot refuse at least to yield our testimony, that they are the result of originality of thought and independence of mind."[59] I hasten to note that Schleiermacher's account of Sabellianism is different than its usual presentation. For him, Sabellianism is not the view that there is no difference between the Son and the Father. Rather than a crude form of modalism that would describe the Father, Son, and Holy Spirit as temporary distinctions that are absorbed back into the Godhead after they have run their course,[60] Schleiermacher describes Sabellianism as the view that the Father, Son, and Holy Spirit are three enduring ways that God reveals Godself.[61] For our purposes, it is less important whether Schleiermacher interprets Sabellius correctly, and more important how he positions his own thought in relation to his understanding of Sabellius.

For Sabellius, as Schleiermacher understands him, the unity of the divine essence is unrevealed, but the revealed God is differentiated as Father, Son, and Holy Spirit. Schleiermacher writes that according to Sabellius, "the whole Trinity is God revealed; but the divine Being as he is in and of himself and in his simple unity, is God concealed or unrevealed."[62] The doctrine of the Trinity points to the divine union with different objects, which in turn leads to different divine offices or works.[63] The Father is the union of the divine essence with creation.[64] His office is to create, preserve, and give the law and wisdom. The Son is the union of the divine essence with humanity in Christ, and his work is redemption. The Son's union is not derived from the Father, though it depends on the arrangement of the world made by the Father. The Holy Spirit is the union of the divine essence with the church as a whole. Like the underived union of the Son, the union of the Spirit is not derived from the Father or Son, though it is dependent on the Father's arrangement of the world and the Son's work in his original community. The Spirit's work is to sanctify, that is, to operate in the community of Christians.[65]

---

tritheism are Tertullian, Hippolytus, and Origen. Schleiermacher identifies Sabellius as standing near the middle.

59. *OD2*, p. 80.

60. *OD2*, pp. 52–4. Schleiermacher states that "the supposition, that Christ made only a transitory development out of himself, which, being dependent on and arising from the will of God, might again change and cease" would "by no means satisfy the demands of Christian faith; for his regal dignity and governing power as Son, must endure at least until that undefined period, when all enemies shall be put under his feet. This much cannot be dispensed with" (*OD2*, p. 14). Particularly with regard to Sabellius, he writes, "That Sabellius did not hold the Trinity to be only a transitory development, is plain from the imagery which he employed in relation to this subject" (*OD2*, p. 53).

61. *OD2*, p. 61.

62. Ibid.

63. *OD2*, p. 68.

64. Ibid., p. 60.

65. Ibid., p. 58.

1. Trinity

The Father, Son, and Holy Spirit, for Schleiermacher's Sabellius, are not names for eternal hypostases conceived apart from creation. Neither are they simply different names for one eternal monad. As Schleiermacher writes, "The Son was not, in his view, the same as the Father, because he was united with something different from that with which the Father was united, and acted in a different sphere. ... But the real Godhead in the Father and in the Son was, in his view, one and the same."[66] For Sabellius, the Father, Son, and Holy Spirit are names for the three enduring unions and activities of God with creation, Christ, and church: "In governing the world in all its various operations on finite beings, the Godhead is Father. As redeeming, by special operations in the person of Christ and through him, it is Son. As sanctifying, and in all its operations on the community of believers, and as a Unity in the same, the Godhead is Spirit."[67]

Schleiermacher thinks this presentation of the doctrine of the Trinity is to be praised for the connections it makes between the three persons of the Trinity and the economy of salvation, which render it directly relevant for Christian piety, and for its avoidance of relations of origin to distinguish the persons, which free it from subordinationism. Yet he does not wholeheartedly adopt Sabellianism, even as he sympathetically understands it. There are at least two differences between Schleiermacher and Sabellius's views of the Trinity. First, Schleiermacher designates the Holy Spirit as the common spirit of Christ, or the common love of Christ in the church.[68] For him, the Holy Spirit only unites with the church that loves Jesus Christ as the Redeemer. It is an open question, however, whether Sabellius thought the Holy Spirit existed before Christ. "Whether Sabellius held the Spirit of the Old Testament to be the same το πνεύμα το άγιον [Holy Spirit]," Schleiermacher explains, "depended on the fact whether he acknowledged a true church under the Old Testament."[69] In contrast, Schleiermacher closely links the Spirit and the church, understood specifically as Christ's church, which did not exist before the death of Jesus of Nazareth. For Schleiermacher, the Holy Spirit

---

66. Ibid., p. 67.

67. Ibid., p. 70.

68. In my *Essential Trinitarianism*, two mistakes are included on pages 77 to 79, which relate to Schleiermacher's view of Sabellianism. The first is a footnoting error. Footnote number 95 on page 77 refers not to Schleiermacher's "On the Discrepancy" but to Francis Schüssler Fiorenza's interpretation of Schleiermacher's trinitarian thought in his "Understanding God as Triune," in *The Cambridge Companion to Friedrich Schleiermacher*, pp. 171–88. The second is an underdeveloped idea, relating to the way Schleiermacher goes beyond Sabellianism. I indicate on pages 78 to 79 that Schleiermacher's difference from Sabellianism is Schleiermacher's insistence that the Spirit attaches to the Church while Sabellius did not. This is an underdeveloped thought insofar as I did not make clear the difference between Schleiermacher's view of the church as only coming into existence after Christ, and Sabellius's underdetermined view by which he could have held the notion that the church existed prior to the existence of Christ.

69. *OD2*, p. 59.

is continuous with Christ as his Spirit. The two unions of the divine essence with human nature—one in Christ and one in the church—are distinguished from one another insofar as the indwelling of God in Christ is person-forming, and the indwelling of God in the church does not create one individual person. Second, Schleiermacher's view is different from his understanding of Sabellianism insofar as Schleiermacher does not think the unity of the divine essence is unrevealed, whereas the revealed God is differentiated as Father, Son, and Holy Spirit. Instead, as we will see in the next section, Schleiermacher identifies love and wisdom with the divine essence, which is communicated through the economy of salvation.

To further understand Schleiermacher's view, we turn to his preliminary steps toward a reformulation of the doctrine of the Trinity as outlined in his *Christian Faith*. First, he identifies the indispensable portion of the ecclesial doctrine of the Trinity. For Schleiermacher, that is the equal divinity of Christ and the Spirit, and the equal divinity of Christ and the Spirit with the divine being as such. He writes, "We also regard this equal status of the divine in each of these two unions with the divine in the other, and then also of the two with the divine nature as such, to be what is essential in the doctrine of the Trinity."[70] Because of this, Schleiermacher wants to retain the ecclesial view that it is the self-same God who creates and governs the world, redeems in and through Christ, and sanctifies in and through the Spirit in the Church. This, for Schleiermacher, is the indispensable core of the doctrine of the Trinity. It is, likewise, that without which the entire edifice of Schleiermacher's own *Christian Faith* crumbles. As he explains, "In this [Second] Part the doctrine of the uniting of the divine nature with human nature, both through the individual person of Christ and through the common spirit of the church, is essential to our presentation, and the whole conception of Christianity in our ecclesial doctrines stands or falls with this Part."[71] It is clear that Schleiermacher does not wish to throw out the whole doctrine of the Trinity but to retain what he identifies as its essence.

As a second step, Schleiermacher recommends a constriction of trinitarian thought to God's relation to the world. In accord with his interpretation of Sabellianism, Schleiermacher calls for theologians to refrain from speculating about the eternal being of God as it would be apart from creation. As he writes, "we would also like to stop with this affirmation [of the indispensable portions of the doctrine], however, not being able to assign the same importance to the additional formation of this dogma."[72] For him as for John Calvin, though now in a modern context, ecclesial doctrines should be related to the piety of Christians, which is focused on their redemption by God in and through Christ and his Spirit. For Schleiermacher, any set of eternal relations of divine persons that would be the same whether redemption by God in Christ and his Spirit existed or never came to pass would be unrelated to Christian piety because it would be unrelated

---

70. *CF*, §170.1, p. 1021.
71. Ibid., p. 1020.
72. *CF*, §170.2, p. 1021.

to redemption by God in Christ and his Spirit. Schleiermacher asks, "Who would venture to assert that the thought of such an eternal separateness would be implied in the impression made by the divine in Christ as the basis of that impression?"[73] Drawing on his Reformed heritage and modern understanding of the field of theology, Schleiermacher maintains that Christians are not obliged to affirm eternal distinctions in God based on their reception of redemption in Christ. Because Schleiermacher also maintains that the doctrine of the immanent Trinity has significant logical and theological problems, he eschews that doctrine, stating that "our faith in Christ and our living communion with him would be the same even if we had no knowledge of this transcendent fact or if this fact were different."[74]

In a third preliminary step toward reformulating the doctrine of the Trinity, Schleiermacher develops an account of God's relation to the world in the economy of salvation. He does this over the course of his entire *Christian Faith*. The main outlines of the doctrine consist in (1) God's creation and preservation of the *Naturzusammenhang* (the interconnected process of nature) with its natural and social laws, which prepare for the union of the divine essence with human nature; (2) the union of the divine essence with human nature in the person of Jesus of Nazareth; and (3) the union of the divine essence with human nature in the common love of Christ in the church, which is the sanctifying presence of Christ's Spirit. As in Schleiermacher's interpretation of Sabellianism, these three phases in the economy of salvation go hand in hand with three divine offices—creation, redemption, and sanctification. In Schleiermacher's thought, however, these three are better understood as the temporal unfolding of the one divine activity of creation: God creates the world, God brings creation to completion in Christ, and God expands the scope of completed creation in the church.[75]

What we have so far in Schleiermacher's trinitarian thought, then, is a rejection of speculation about the divine being considered apart from the world, along with an affirmation of a temporal threefold development of God's activity of creation. We have also seen Schleiermacher's commitment to the equal divinity of the divine being with the Son and Holy Spirit and the notion that the Holy Spirit is the Spirit of Christ. I have further indicated but not explained how for Schleiermacher the divine essence is not unrevealed but is identified with love and wisdom. To that notion we now turn.

Constructive Interpretation and Development

Divine Love, Wisdom, and Causality
Without a clear description of what motivates divine action in the economy of salvation, Christians would be left wondering why God creates-redeems at all through natural and social law, Jesus of Nazareth, and the Spirit of Christ in the

---

73. Ibid., p. 1022.
74. *CF*, §170.3, p. 1023.
75. I return to the notion of the completion of creation in Chapter 2.

church. Schleiermacher finds the motive for divine activity in the claim that "God is love," which he treats at the end of Part Two of the *Glaubenslehre*, just before the conclusion within which he treats the doctrine of the Trinity.[76] He writes, "if the pivotal point of the divine government of the world is redemption and the establishment of God's reign, whereby union of divine being with human nature is what is occurring, the underlying disposition in that process can be represented only as love."[77] Schleiermacher notes that without this affirmation, all other divine attributes are indefinite. For example, "even if we declare 'omnipotent' to be the attribute by virtue of which all that is finite exists by God's agency, precisely as it does exist, we have posited this entire divine act, to be sure, but without assigning a motive. Thus, we have posited it as an action that is absolutely undetermined."[78] For Schleiermacher, God creates because God loves creation, and God loves creation simply because it is the divine good-pleasure. There is no discernable reason other than the divine being itself. As such, Schleiermacher claims that "love" is an expression "for the very being of God."[79]

Schleiermacher derives this affirmation of the divine essence as love from the economy of salvation in Christ.[80] He defines love as "the orientation of wanting to unite with others and wanting to be in the other."[81] This love is the "divine factor" in Christ.[82] "In Christ himself," Schleiermacher explains, "the original divine

76. *CF*, §167, p. 1007.
77. Ibid., §165.1, p. 1004.
78. Ibid., §167.2, p. 1008.
79. Ibid., p. 1009.
80. Schleiermacher cites 1 Jn 4:16 when he introduces the doctrinal proposition that God is love: "So we know and believe the love God has for us. God is love, and those who abide in love abide in God, and God abides in them." He cites Acts 17:24–28 in his discussion of divine wisdom:

> The God who made the world and everything in it, he who is Lord of heaven and earth, does not live in shrines made by human hands, nor is he served by human hands, as though he needed anything, since he himself gives to all mortals life and breath and all things. From one ancestor he made all nations to inhabit the whole earth, and he allotted the times of their existence and the boundaries of the places where they would live, so that they would search for God and perhaps grope for him and find him—though indeed he is not far from each one of us. For "In him we live and move and have our being"; as even some of your own poets have said, "For we too are his offspring."

Schleiermacher links wisdom to the church in §169, where he notes "the world can be conceived as a complete revelation of divine wisdom only insofar as the Holy Spirit gains recognition as the ultimate world-forming power from the Christian church outward" (p. 1017).

81. *CF*, §165.1, p. 1004.
82. Ibid., §97.3, p. 601.

activity of taking up what is human and the divine activity during the being united are not distinguishable."[83] Divine love is both the means and the content of the divine indwelling in Christ. In this way, the divine orientation of wanting to unite with others becomes indistinguishable from what God in Christ actually does. Christ then redeems others by bringing them into union with himself, which is a reiteration of divine love:

> Now, if all activity in Christ proceeds from the being of God in him, and if we know of no divine activity other than the creating activity in which the preserving activity is encompassed ... then we will also have to view the efficacious action of Christ in the same way. ... Christ's activity of taking us up into community with him is thus a creative engendering of the desire-to-take-him-up-into-oneself. Or it is, rather, a creative engendering simply of an acquiescence to the working of his communicating activity, for this desire is simply a receptivity to his activity in the process of his communication.[84]

We will return to Christ and the church in the next two chapters. For now, it is important to note that Schleiermacher derives his identification of love as the essence of the divine being from the being and redeeming work of Christ in the economy of salvation. When divine love appears at the end of the *Glaubenslehre*'s second part, it is not an afterthought but the culmination of Schleiermacher's understanding of God and redemption. The claim that "God is love" is integral to his entire dogmatic work up until that point: "as the attribute by virtue of which the divine being communicates itself, divine love is recognized in the work of redemption."[85] In the union of the divine with humanity in Jesus of Nazareth, the divine disposition is communicated as "wanting to unite with others and wanting to be in the other."[86] For this reason, "love is being equated with the being or nature of God" such that it "could be substituted for the name 'God' itself."[87]

Schleiermacher then connects love to wisdom, defining wisdom as the perfect fulfillment of love. If "love" is the answer to Christians' questions about why God is the Creator-Redeemer, "wisdom" is the answer to Christians' questions about how love could be carried out perfectly in relation to the divine activity of creation-redemption. As such, love and wisdom are perichoretically related for Schleiermacher: "These two attributes are not divorced, not in any way whatsoever, but are so totally one that one can also view each attribute as already contained in the other one."[88] Divine love and wisdom are coinhering, with the result that "divine wisdom is not suited to determine any arrangement of things

---

83. Ibid., p. 603.
84. *CF*, §100.2, p. 623.
85. Ibid., §166, p. 1005.
86. Ibid., §165, p. 1004.
87. Ibid., §167, p. 1008.
88. Ibid., §165.2, p. 1004.

and any other ordering of their course than that wherein divine love is realized most fully; no more is divine love suited to self-communications in which it would not satisfy itself completely and thus would not appear as wisdom absolutely."[89] For Schleiermacher, love is given preference as proceeding directly from the self-communication of Christ. Wisdom comes into consciousness "only when we extend our self-consciousness, definitely our personal consciousness but even more our species-consciousness, to the point of relating every element of experience to each other."[90] He cautions that "if we think of God as wisdom, love would not also be so completely contained in it as wisdom would be if we think of God as love, for where omnipotent love is present, there absolute wisdom must be as well."[91] Even so, for Schleiermacher, "the two attributes cannot be thought to be divorced from each other."[92] Wisdom comes after love simply because "for us, in its temporal progressions God's communication moves more and more toward a complete presentation of God's omnipotent love."[93]

Although Schleiermacher prioritizes love over wisdom because of the temporal unfolding of divine self-communication, that prioritization falls away when the self-communication of God in the Spirit of the church and divine self-communication's illumination of creation are equally taken into account. As we have seen above, divine love communicates itself to humanity by creating and indwelling the person of Jesus. Love then motivates Jesus' redemptive work, which consists in bringing others into his life through his self-communication. The church is constituted by a shared love of Christ, and its work, in turn, is to re-present Christ in word and deed through the indwelling of Christ's Spirit. While love stands at the center of the union of the divine with humanity in Jesus, wisdom takes center stage when the union of the divine with humanity in the church continues the union of the divine with humanity in Jesus, and when one considers all that had previously prepared for the union of the divine with humanity in Jesus and the church. For this reason, Schleiermacher claims, "we cannot possibly regard the totality of finite being in its relation to our God-consciousness other than as comprising the absolutely harmonious divine work of art."[94] Thus, even though there is a temporal unfolding of Christian consciousness of the divine being wherein wisdom comes after love, wisdom and love both equally ground the economy of salvation: love motivates while wisdom orders. For this reason, although Schleiermacher gives love preference because of its centrality in the self-communication of God in and through Jesus, if the communication of God in and through the Holy Spirit of Christ in the church is equally emphasized along with the preparations for the unions of the divine with humanity, then wisdom

---

89. Ibid., §165.2, p. 1004.
90. Ibid., §167.2, pp. 1009–10.
91. Ibid., p. 1010.
92. Ibid., p. 1010.
93. *CF*, §168.1, p. 1011.
94. Ibid.

also takes its rightful place as coequal with love within the triune divine name. With this in view, Schleiermacher can say that "divine wisdom is the ground by virtue of which the world, viewed as the theater of redemption, is also the absolute revelation of Supreme Being."[95] These two attributes of God, taken together, are the only attributes Schleiermacher identifies as being expressions of the very being of God.[96] As such, elsewhere I have called these the "contours" or "structural features" of the divine life, to set them off from attributes that would be misleading if they were used as divine names.[97]

95. *CF*, §169, p. 1013.

96. Schleiermacher's description of these attributes as expressions of the being of God stands in prima facie tension with his procedure in the *Glaubenslehre* up to paragraph 167. As he acknowledges when he begins to discuss the proposition that God is love, "repeatedly it has been asserted that in God no distinction can exist between essence and attributes, and precisely on this account the concept 'attribute' is not really suitable for presentation of the divine being" (§167.1, p. 107). As such, he continues, "insofar as something true is said of God in what we posit as a divine attribute, the same must also be an expression for the divine nature itself" (§167.1, pp. 1007–8). Nonetheless, Schleiermacher maintains that divine love is exceptional because it, as opposed to other attributes, "could be substituted for the name 'God' itself" (§167.1, p. 1008). I discuss this tension and its resolution in *Essential Trinitarianism*, chapter six. In short, I see the negative divine attributes that Schleiermacher discusses in the first part of the *Glaubenslehre* (eternity, omnipresence, omnipotence, and omniscience) as establishing divine alterity. Although each of these attributes emphasizes something different about God, they all mean basically the same thing: God is unconditioned by creation, and God conditions all of creation. These negative attributes gain content only when they are joined to the divine attributes considered in the second part of the *Glaubenslehre*. This being the case, although it may seem as though Schleiermacher is overstepping his own theological boundaries by claiming that "only love and wisdom thus retain the claim of being, at the same time, expressions for the very being of God" (§167.2, p. 1009), where these distinctions indicate something "real" in God, in fact Schleiermacher is simply spelling out—albeit belatedly—exactly what he thinks the Christian reception of redemption in Christ and Christ's Spirit, which illuminates creation as a whole, means for a Christian understanding of divine activity. Here Schleiermacher finally indicates that divine causality, which is another name for "God" as the "Whence" of existence, is also Love and Wisdom. If this portion of his *Glaubenslehre* is kept in mind throughout a rereading of the work, the tension between parts one and two dissipates. God, who is the Unconditioned Conditioner of creation, is Love and Wisdom; the God of creation is the God of grace.

97. See Poe, *Essential Trinitarianism*, Chapter 4. I primarily use the terms "contour" or "structural feature" to describe the triune divine life for two reasons. First, following Schleiermacher, I am keen to avoid the language of personhood within trinitarian doctrine because such language raises the specter of tritheism. No matter how many times a theologian might indicate that trinitarian "persons" are not really persons at all, the contemporary theological imagination cannot use the word while evacuating it of all meaning in trinitarian contexts and simultaneously use the same word with full and robust

As I read Schleiermacher's systematic theology, however, there is yet one more basic description of the divine life that runs throughout the text. "Divine causality" is the ubiquitous phrase Schleiermacher uses in his *Christian Faith* when discussing God and/or divine attributes. "Divine causality" refers not to particular causes and effects within the world but to "absolute" causality or "universal" causality. That is, it refers to God's unconditioned responsibility for the existence of everything that is, considered as a whole.[98] This is the divine referent that corresponds to Christians' immediate consciousness of absolute dependence. As Schleiermacher states,

> in our proposition "absolute dependence" and "being in relation with God" are made equivalent. This affirmation is to be understood in such a way that precisely the whence coposited in this self-consciousness, the whence of our receptive and self-initiated active existence, is to be designated by the term "God," and for us "whence" holds the truly primary meaning of the term "God."[99]

Schleiermacher describes absolute causality this way: "on the one hand, it would be distinguished from the causality that is contained within the interconnected process of nature and would thus be in contrast to that causality, and, on the other hand, it would be equated with such causality in terms of its compass."[100] "Absolute" or "universal causality" is shorthand, then, for the notion that God creates the interdependent process of nature as a whole without being conditioned in any way by creation. Because this notion is equivalent to the idea that God is the "whence" of creation, "universal causality" is also a basic designation for "God."

We have already seen that Schleiermacher takes love and wisdom to be perichoretically related designations of the very essence of the divine being. Given the basic way Schleiermacher uses "universal causality" in his *Christian Faith*, it seems to me that this attribute could be added to that perichoretic relationship. By making this claim, I am going beyond Schleiermacher's own explicitly stated understanding of the divine essence in the final paragraphs of the second part of his *Christian Faith*. I do so because Schleiermacher uses all three of these names—Love, Wisdom, and Universal Causality—in the most basic way to refer

meanings in the doctrine of God and theological anthropology. Second, I want to emphasize that the triune God is considered triune not simply because three names are particularly adequate for pointing to the divine being (though it does mean that) but because the very being of God includes three distinctions. The metaphorical language of "contours" or "structural features" is useful for indicating that the divine One is not monolithic. To say that the divine life is triunely contoured means that the divine being is only adequately described in a threefold way.

98. *CF*, §164.3, p. 1001.
99. Ibid., §4.4, p. 24.
100. Ibid., §51, p. 289.

to God.¹⁰¹ Moreover, these three are conceptually related to one another. If Love is the "why" of divine activity and Wisdom is the "how" of divine activity, Universal Causality is the "what" of divine activity. Love motivates Universal Causality; Universal Causality actualizes Wisdom's plans; Wisdom orders or determines the arrangement of things so that Love can be fully realized. Put another way, Love is oriented toward union with creation; Wisdom orders creation in order to ensure the perfect realization of Love; Universal Causality creates-preserves-redeems creation for Love and by Wisdom. These three names for God are basic in the sense that they describe the very essence of God as Christians conceive of the divine on the basis of divine self-communication in Christ and the Spirit of Christ in the church, which illuminates creation.

Other divine attributes are not counted among the structural features of the divine life because they are more likely to mislead Christians about the divine being. Schleiermacher gives the example of omnipotence, which could mislead by not assigning a motive to the divine activity. At best, that lack of motive could lead to understanding God as a dead force, while at worst it could lead to understanding God as a capricious tyrant.¹⁰² Omnipotence, Schleiermacher cautions, must be understood in the sense of "almighty love."¹⁰³ Other attributes of this kind can be treated similarly:

> Indeed, as a whole set they [the divine attributes detailed in the First Part of *Christian Faith*] have been derived in abstraction from the distinct feeling content of our God-consciousness. Thus, if we do not think of them in connection with the attributes of God that do derive from our reflection on this feeling content—as is the case in the formulations "God is almighty love" and "God is eternal love"—but hold to them by themselves, faith in God as "almighty" and "eternal" is but a shadow of faith, such as the devils too can have.¹⁰⁴

101. Following Schleiermacher, I seek to avoid personification or undue anthropomorphization of the three contours of divine life in trinitarian doctrine. Capitalization here is used in order to alert readers that I am using love, wisdom, and universal causality as proper nouns rather than as general concepts or categories. Love (as opposed to love) refers not simply to any loving activity but to loving activity as defined by divine self-communication in Christ and Christ's Spirit, which illuminates creation. Likewise, Wisdom (as opposed to wisdom) does not refer to any saying or action we might deem wise but to wise activity as defined by divine self-communication in Christ and Christ's Spirit, which illuminates creation. Capitalization is chiefly used rather than saying "divine love," "divine wisdom," or "divine causality" in order to remind the reader that these three attributes are more than attributes but are indications of the very divine essence and could be substituted for the name "God."

102. I return to the notion of divine sovereignty in Chapter 4.

103. For my treatment of Schleiermacher's notions of eternity, omnipresence, omnipotence, and omniscience in relation to divine love and wisdom, see Poe, *Essential Trinitarianism*, pp. 137–50.

104. *CF*, §167.2, pp. 1008–9.

The same goes for the divine attributes treated in Aspect One of Part Two, namely, divine justice and holiness. Schleiermacher explains, "For us, those two attributes then come to be divine love, in turn, but viewed only in its preparatory expressions; and divine love is holy and just love only inasmuch as it essentially begins with these preparations, just as it is also omnipotent and eternal love."[105]

Elsewhere, I have referred to the triune name of God as Love, Wisdom, and Universal Causality, as it can be drawn out of Schleiermacher's dogmatics and constructively interpreted, as the doctrine of the essential Trinity.[106] It is meant as an alternative to the doctrine of the immanent Trinity, standing midway between the doctrine of the economic Trinity and the doctrine of the immanent Trinity. It goes further than the doctrine of the economic Trinity but does not go so far as to speculate about God as God would be apart from the world. The doctrine of the essential Trinity avoids the speculation involved in the doctrine of the immanent Trinity but nonetheless speaks of the divine essence on the basis of the economy of salvation. By standing between the doctrine of the immanent Trinity and the doctrine of the economic Trinity, the doctrine of the essential Trinity holds out another trinitarian possibility that has the potential to disrupt kyriarchal ways of thinking.

On the left side of the ledger, essential trinitarianism avoids the problems Schleiermacher identified within the doctrine of the immanent Trinity. Subordinationism does not appear because of the perichoretic character of the three divine names and the lack of relations of origin between them. Since Love, Wisdom, and Universal Causality are related conceptually and are not hypostasized *prosopa*, relations of origin do not exist between these contours of the divine life. The equality of the three contours of the one divine life therefore depends on their conceptual interdependence in light of the economy of salvation. Essential trinitarianism also mitigates an unhealthy oscillation between tritheism and undifferentiated monotheism by avoiding an affirmation of three "persons" within the divine essence. The doctrine of the essential Trinity describes the threefold, coinhering, and coequal contours of the one divine life. In this way, both the specter of tritheism and of undifferentiated monotheism are circumvented. Finally, the doctrine of the essential Trinity is directly relevant to Christian piety because it rejects speculation about God as God would be apart from the world and speaks only of the divine essence in relation to creation-redemption. The doctrine of the essential Trinity also avoids the problems that contemporary theologians concerned with gender justice have identified: it does not inscribe hierarchy and androcentrism into the divine being, it does not focus on Jesus' obedience unto death and then reinscribe such obedience into the eternal divine being, and it does not play into the patterns of heterosexism that are repeated in traditional

---

105. Ibid., p. 1009.

106. I have adopted and revised this terminology from Claude Welch, *In This Name: The Doctrine of the Trinity in Contemporary Theology* (New York: Charles Scribner's, 1925), p. 294. For the full exposition, see Poe, *Essential Trinitarianism*, pp. 81–114.

trinitarian doctrine. Even so, many of the traditional features of the doctrine of the immanent Trinity are retained. At the most basic level, the doctrine of the essential Trinity retains a focus on the three-in-one that is a hallmark of Christian thought. It also maintains the coequality and coinherence of the three structural features of the divine life. For these reasons, Schleiermacher's preliminary steps toward a reformulation of the doctrine of the Trinity, taken with my own constructive interpretation of his work as offering a doctrine of the essential Trinity, can generate further conversation and refinement of trinitarian doctrine.

Shoring Up Schleiermacher's Treatment of Love in Christian Faith
On the other side of the ledger, the sketch outlined above offers a rather underdeveloped notion of love as it is found in Schleiermacher's *Christian Faith*. As we have seen, he describes love as the desire to be in and with the other. Love is a creative activity of union brought about through self-communication. This means that God unites with human nature as God creates and dwells within the person of Jesus of Nazareth. The divine indwelling of Jesus is exhibited through his message and acts of love. The effect of this divine indwelling is that Christ influences his followers, being spontaneously imitated by them in terms of their ideas, values, speech patterns, gestures, and so forth.[107] Beyond these rather basic descriptions of love and its effects, however, the concept is left undeveloped in Schleiermacher's *Christian Faith*.

On the one hand, this underdevelopment of the concept of love is appropriate since any divine names serve their proper function only by pointing to the divine. They do not define God, in the sense of mastering or grasping or capturing the divine within concepts.[108] On the other hand, an underdeveloped notion of love could allow for invocations of the divine name that do not make clear the relation of theology to ethics. If "love" remains underdeveloped, then its very invocation could be used to avoid acting in accordance with love. James Cone and others have therefore rightly criticized theologians who "often invoked 'soft' discussions of love to the exclusion of wider structural and systemic explanations of racial injustice in America."[109] If Love is to be understood as the very essence of divine being, theologians working constructively will want to develop the notion more fully by critically attending to the gospels and specifying the kinds of policies and structures that may be connected to it in particular circumstances. After all, whether specific applications of love are truly beneficent is open to interpretation, and there can be no doubt that well-meaning people who genuinely believe that their words or actions are benefiting others are, in fact, harming them. Wendy

---

107. See Kevin Hector, *Theology without Metaphysics: God, Language, and the Spirit of Recognition* (Cambridge: Cambridge University Press, 2011), pp. 73–102.

108. See Elizabeth Johnson, "The Living God in Women's Voices," *Sewannee Theological Review* 48/3 (2005): 287–300.

109. Keri Day, "Doctrine of God in African American Theology," in *The Oxford Handbook of African American Theology*, ed. Anthony B. Pinn and Katie G. Cannon (Oxford: Oxford University Press, 2014), p. 142.

Farley, for example, writes as a queer theologian about "a church that bludgeons people like me with Scripture to insist we are not fully human and the goods of society and church should not belong to us."[110] Likewise, Marcella Althaus-Reid writes, "For many people (including myself) who have suffered the experience of being locked out of a church, for whatever reason, that image of the Christ Woman crying with the excluded woman at the door of the church represents exactly what they suffered then."[111] Notwithstanding the antinormative strands of queer theology (which I return to below), many mujerista, feminist, and queer theologians alike may be especially aware of the need to specify what love looks like in action, coupled with an openness to correcting those specifics as time goes on, contexts change, and further perspectives are brought to bear on a situation.[112] Looking to the gospels for guidance, one might name particular benefits to others that are in line with Love. For example, caring for children, advocating for women, acting on behalf of poor people, healing people who are ill, assisting people who are disabled, feeding people who are hungry, visiting those in prison, forgiving people's debts, and so on—done in systemic and local ways that would not simply treat the effects of a problematic way of life, but would address that problematic way of life itself. Schleiermacher's understanding of Love could take on more definite, context-specific content from a critical reception of the concrete activity of Christ that furthers the life and well-being of others.

The danger in fleshing out a concept of love in this way is that the ethical normativity involved could lead to oppressive conditions because of unintended conceptual mistakes and/or their practical consequences. For this reason, queer theorists have been among the most consistent in resisting prescriptive norms. Indeed, antinormativity has been at the heart of queer theory. However, thinkers like Marcella Althaus-Reid and Lisa Isherwood also recognize, as Susannah Cornwall explains, "that queer theology *cannot* set out to be totally non-normative—*even*

---

110. Wendy Farley, *Gathering Those Driven Away* (Louisville, KY: Westminster John Knox, 2011), p. 13.

111. Marcella Althaus-Reid, *Indecent Theology* (New York: Routledge, 2000), p. 116.

112. Recalling Joerg Rieger's work, Schleiermacher's own hope for the full expansion of the Christian community within the human race is an example of the way that Schleiermacher's words themselves, for example, could be harmful to potentially colonized persons, in both political and religious spheres. Schleiermacher writes in the 1833 Epiphany sermon, for example, "If only this serving love would rise up and branch out more and more, how soon we would see even one territory applying it to others, and one Christian communion to others; and we would see it handed down from one age to another" (Schleiermacher, "Our Community," p. 225). Here the language of "territory" would sound alarm bells for postcolonial theologians, ecumenical, and ecotheologians alike who appreciate diversity and recognize the need for limitations on behavior such that one individual or subgroup does not dominate the rest. For a response to the antiecological implications of such an idea, see Shelli M. Poe, "Friedrich Schleiermacher's Theology as a Resource for Ecological Economics," *Theology Today* 73/1 (2016): 9–23.

where normativity as a rule is regarded with suspicion—since this would be to close off an area of possibility and render it irredeemable."[113] Rejecting ethical values and norms in toto could be viewed as a dualistic move that "negates queer's capacity to be transformative even of this."[114] Cornwall highlights that for those like Claudia Schippert, "norms need *not* automatically become normativities."[115] The crucial difference is between ethical prescriptions and exclusionary positions. Thus, although no one can foreclose the possibility that their well-intended norms might turn out to have been exclusionary, by inviting interrogation of ethical prescriptions and remaining open to dynamic changes in response to new or newly unearthed situations, queer theologians who are suspicious of norms could nonetheless participate in the project of developing a Christological and trinitarian concept of Love and its implications for Christian action. Indeed, they could do so with clarity and vigor.

To contribute to the development of a more robust understanding of Love, Schleiermacher's account in his *Christian Faith* might be supplemented in part by his other works. In an 1833 Epiphany sermon entitled, "Our Community: Founded and Preserved through the Redeemer's Love," for example, Schleiermacher maintains that the Christian community exists through Christ's love, and that "his Kingdom consists in this love alone."[116] Through a comparison of Christ's love and the love Christians ought to exhibit, Schleiermacher develops a Christological understanding of the notion of love. Turning to Jn 6:67–68, he identifies the disciples' love of Christ as issuing specifically from Christ's communicating the

---

113. Cornwall, *Controversies in Queer Theology*, p. 230. See also Linn Marie Tonstad, "Ambivalent Loves: Christian Theologies, Queer Theologies," *Literature & Theology* 31/4 (December 2017): 472–89 (emphasis original). In a special issue of *differences: A Journal of Feminist Cultural Studies*, the editors seek "to show that norms are more dynamic and more politically engaging than queer critique has usually allowed" (Robyn Wiegman and Elizabeth A. Wilson, "Introduction: Antinormativity's Queer Conventions," *differences* 26/1 [2015], 2). They "dispute two of the most widely touted characteristics of a norm: that it is restrictive and that it excludes" (12). They conclude that antinormativity "turns systemic play (differentiations, comparisons, valuations, attenuations, skirmishes) into unforgiving rules and regulations and so converts the complexity of moving athwart into the much more anodyne notion of moving against" (18). See also Hannah McCann and Whitney Monaghan, *Queer Theory Now: From Foundations to Futures* (Macmillan International and Red Globe Press, 2020), pp. 14–16. They note that if queer theory becomes synonymous with the anti-normative, then "queer theory might lose its critical edge in deconstructing identities/boundaries" (14).

114. Cornwall, *Controversies in Queer Theology*, p. 230.

115. Ibid., p. 227. See Claudia Schippert, "Too Much Trouble? Negotiating Feminist and Queer Approaches in Religion," *Theology and Sexuality* 11 (1999): 44–63.

116. Friedrich Schleiermacher, "Our Community: Founded and Preserved through the Redeemer's Love," in *Servant of the Word: Selected Sermons of Friedrich Schleiermacher*, trans. Dawn DeVries (Philadelphia, PA: Fortress, 1987), p. 216.

words of eternal life, "which nourishes and strengthens human souls."[117] The Christian community is united, in Schleiermacher's view, by their common love for the redeemer, whereby they "keep those words [of Christ] alive ... whether through words or deeds, through audible, public means or through the silent influence of one heart compelled by the Spirit of love upon another."[118] Communicating love, therefore, need not be verbal but may also include actions and relationships. Almost immediately, Schleiermacher links love and wisdom in the sermon, and it is here that he offers more content: "We recognize here the proper art and wisdom in the communications of love: one must communicate only what can be taken in and truly received."[119] The criterion at work in Schleiermacher's thought regarding how to know whether something will be "truly received" is whether the communicator's objective is to benefit the other person:

> If we ask ourselves why so much well-meant communication among us is in vain, why is it that often what was meant to bring about good actually has the opposite effect, why what was meant to unite hearts in love and to sustain them in peace only gives occasion for new strife, the answer is sure: because in our communicating love we fail to achieve the measure of the Redeemer's wisdom. And why do we fail? Because we are more worried about ourselves than those to whom we would give, because it is more important to us to have our own way than simply to benefit them.[120]

Love ordered by Wisdom has in mind the benefit another will receive, rather than being motivated by one's own vanity, ambition, and/or complacency.[121] Schleiermacher fills out this notion of love as benefiting others when he describes the second necessary portion of Christian love, namely, that it is "a serving love."[122] Service means "to note the need of an individual to whom we are directed, and to satisfy this need, once noticed, with every effort in our power," and to "do it from the heart" with joy.[123] Such serving love, according to Schleiermacher, "creates so much good, even in outward things, and makes human life easier."[124] Finally, Schleiermacher links Christ's love and wisdom to one more "essential component," which reminds us of Universal Causality: Christ's love is, for Schleiermacher, not set upon individual persons but on "the whole human race."[125] Love's activity is expansive in scope.[126] In this account, Love is that which (a) benefits (b) the whole

117. Ibid., p. 217.
118. Ibid., p. 219.
119. Ibid., p. 220.
120. Ibid.
121. Ibid.
122. Ibid., p. 223.
123. Ibid.
124. Ibid.
125. Ibid., p. 226.
126. Ibid., p. 227.

of humanity (c) by making its life easier (d) through inward and outward acts that (e) fulfill human needs. This notion of love does not focus on the feelings of the lover toward the beloved, for example, but focuses on providing benefits to the beloved. It also views humanity as a whole rather than attending to individual human persons. By doing so, this notion of love prioritizes activities that take into consideration the structures within which humanity lives rather than occasional events that would benefit particular individuals without considering the effects of those actions on others.[127] This concept also focuses on fulfilling human needs, which could be specified with attention to access to food, water, sleep, social bonds, shelter, clothing, safety, health care, education, work, and so on. In these ways, this 1833 sermon provides a Christological account of love that could supplement Schleiermacher's underdeveloped account in his *Christian Faith*. Incidentally, it also reiterates the doctrine of the essential Trinity I have constructed from Schleiermacher's mature work. Here, too, we have Love, Wisdom, and Universal Causality linked together and at work in the economy of salvation.

Challenges for Essential Trinitarianism
There are at least two differences between the doctrine of the immanent Trinity and the doctrine of the essential Trinity that may elicit challenges for those considering essential trinitarianism. First, because the doctrine of the essential Trinity does not posit eternal divine hypostases within the divine being considered apart from creation and therefore also rejects the genetic relations of dependence between the persons, theologians working constructively will not be able to use the preexistence of the Logos to link the wisdom tradition to Jesus. For such theologians, the Logos has provided a way to infuse the feminine "Sophia" into the very being of God.[128] While jettisoning the doctrine of the immanent Trinity may be a loss in this regard, those constructing theologies could attend to the work of feminists and many before them who have cultivated a rich tradition of apophaticism in relation to the being of God in Godself. Here, I am using "the being of God in Godself" to refer to whatever or whoever God would be if God had not created. Soskice identifies such apophaticism in Augustine and Aquinas's thought. "Far from being able to 'glimpse God's inmost nature,'" she explains, "for Augustine what God is in Godself we will never know."[129] As we have seen, Schleiermacher says something very similar, in a modern context, with regard to the doctrine of the immanent Trinity.

---

127. I return to this feature of Universal Causality in Chapter 4.

128. For historical examples of this way of proceeding, see Elisabeth Schüssler Fiorenza, *Jesus: Miriam's Child, Sophia's Prophet: Critical Issues in Feminist Christology* (New York: Continuum, 1994), pp. 131–62. See also the work of George Tinker, who infuses the feminine mythic Corn Mother from Native traditions to Jesus by using the Logos tradition, in "Jesus, Corn Mother, and Conquest: Christology and Colonialism," in *Native American Religious Identity: Unforgotten Gods*, ed. Jace Weaver (Maryknoll, NY: Orbis, 1998).

129. Janet Martin Soskice, "Being and Love: Schleiermacher, Aquinas and Augustine," *Modern Theology* 34/3 (2018): 487.

One cannot pierce the Kantian veil and see God as God would be considered apart from creation. There is no way to get around the fact that humanity knows God only through the economy of salvation by which God communicates Godself in creation-redemption. Those are the limits of theological knowledge. Essential trinitarianism adheres to those limits by maintaining that we cannot conceive of the God we know as God without us, because we only know God as God-with-and-for-us. To conceive of God as God without us is to conceive of a different God than the God who has communicated Godself to us as Love, Wisdom, and Universal Causality in Christ, his Spirit, and creation. As such, we simply cannot say anything about what God would be like without creation, if we are to stay within proper theological epistemic limits. In this way, apophaticism limits what we can say about God. However, since the doctrine of the essential Trinity does not seek to name or understand God as God would be considered apart from the world, this doctrine can say more about God than the traditional doctrine of the immanent Trinity could. Essential trinitarianism can say both that the divine essence *considered apart from the world* is inconceivable, and that we can know the divine essence *in relation to the world* as Love, Wisdom, and Universal Causality. By making this move, the wisdom tradition may be utilized only as it can be derived from the economy of salvation, in each stage of its unfolding. On this account, the Sophia tradition could emphasize Wisdom as a divine name by following Johnson's suggestion that Sophia should not be exclusively identified with the Logos tradition and Christology but could be more beneficially identified with the divine essence or *ousia*.[130]

A second difference between essential trinitarianism and the doctrine of the immanent Trinity, which could be a challenge for its adopters, is that Love, Wisdom, and Universal Causality do not correlate with the doctrine of the immanent Trinity's Father, Son, and Holy Spirit. A Schleiermacher-inspired doctrine of the essential Trinity must avoid such a correlation because a simple substitution of names would not address the problems within the doctrine of the immanent Trinity that Schleiermacher and contemporary theologians have identified. Relatedly, Schleiermacher's theology resists appropriating the three contours of the divine essence to the three phases of creation-redemption in the economy of salvation. All three contours of the divine essence are equally present and equally describe divine activity in each of the three phases of the economy of salvation. To show how this works in Schleiermacher's own thought, consider his description of Christ in relation to creation: "already Christ was also always coming into being,

---

130. Sophiology has a varied history that includes patriarchal uses of the "eternal feminine," which can be seen in some forms of Russian Orthodoxy, especially in the work of Vladimir Solov'ev and Sergius Bulgakov. See Brenda Meehan, "Wisdom/Sophia, Russian Identity, and Western Feminist Theology," *CrossCurrents* 46/2 (1996): 149–68; Judith Deutsch Kornblatt, *Divine Sophia: The Wisdom Writings of Vladimir Solovyov* (Ithaca, NY: Cornell University Press, 2009); Sergei Bulgakov, *Sophia: The Wisdom of God: An Outline of Sophiology* (Hudson, NY: Lindisfarne Press, 1993). However, Sophiology can also play a substantial role in feminist theologies, as is evident, for example, in Elizabeth Johnson's and Elisabeth Schüssler Fiorenza's work. See Johnson, *She Who Is*; and Fiorenza, *Jesus*.

even as a human person, at the same time as the world was coming into being."[131] By conceiving of creation Christomorphically, or of Christ as being knit together in and with creation as a whole, Schleiermacher makes it impossible to correlate Christ with Love apart from Wisdom and Universal Causality, or to correlate Universal Causality with the Creator apart from Wisdom and Love, or to correlate Wisdom with the Spirit of Christ apart from Love and Universal Causality. A Schleiermacher-inspired doctrine of the essential Trinity does not, therefore, include a doctrine of appropriation. These features of essential trinitarianism may be challenging simply insofar as they go against the grain of typical trinitarian thought. It can be difficult to break the habit of correlating, in this case, the three contours of the divine life from the three phases of creation-redemption.

What the doctrine of the essential Trinity has in common with the doctrine of the immanent Trinity, however, is that both doctrines go further than a mere affirmation of the doctrine of the economic Trinity. Rather than remaining content with a description of divine activity in creation, Christ, and the Spirit in Christian communities, the doctrine of the essential Trinity speaks about the three contours of the divine life that motivate, order, and actualize the economy of salvation. The doctrine of the essential Trinity maintains that the God who creates, redeems, and sanctifies does so because God is Love, Wisdom, and Universal Causality. Again, Schleiermacher does not name or develop this doctrine of the essential Trinity as another step in his reformulation of the doctrine of the Trinity, but as I read his *Christian Faith*, he very well could have. By drawing out these implicit features of his thought, I am constructively interpreting his work and showing how his "preliminary steps" are not so preliminary once his entire *Christian Faith* is read, back to front, as a trinitarian text.

The Liturgical Viability of Essential Trinitarianism
Essential trinitarianism quite clearly uses different words to speak of the triune God than is customary in Christian churches. Since the language of "Father, Son, and Holy Spirit" is deeply entrenched in most Christian traditions, in creedal statements, liturgies, and common ways of speaking, introducing new language would be difficult. However, the terms involved in essential trinitarianism have a rich history in Christian scripture and various theological traditions. Schleiermacher cites 1 Jn 4:16 when discussing the notion that God is love: "So we know and believe the love God has for us. God is love, and those who abide in love abide in God, and God abides in them." The notion that God is love has also been reiterated as a central claim in various strands of Christian traditions. Julian of Norwich, for instance, writes, "Know it well, love was his meaning. Who reveals it to you? Love. What did he reveal to you? Love. Why does he reveal it to you? For love. Remain in this, and you will know more of the same. But you will never know different, without end."[132] Wendy Farley cites this passage in Julian's work to argue

---

131. *CF*, §97.2, p. 595.

132. Julian of Norwich, *Showings*, trans. Edmund Colledge, OSA, and James Walsh, SJ, Classics of Western Spirituality (New York: Paulist Press, 1978), p. 342.

that for many on the underside, love is the one word of the gospel.[133] Likewise, Pamela Lightsey highlights love as the way she and other Black queer womanists know God from experience. She states,

> It is because we have experienced and know God as love that Black queer womanists must dismiss as heretical any theology that purports that God gives us up to the powers of evil, and leaves us to fend for ourselves. Bishop Yvette Flunder, African American lesbian, said it well, "Church encourages self-loathing." But our experience with God—rather than how homophobic Black preachers have interpreted the text—demonstrates over and over again that God loves us just as we are, in our self-identity and in our living out that identity.[134]

Love is here the primary way in which Black queer womanists like Lightsey experience and know God.

Lightsey also claims that "God as the first cause has been a source of hope for Black queer Christians."[135] She explains the importance of divine causality:

> To understand that this world ultimately does not belong to humanity but to somebody bigger than us has long been a source of hope for Black queer Christians. No matter how oppressive the sermons on Sunday morning, we take courage in the knowledge that our care, our wellbeing, is not dependent on human hands but on the providential care of God our Creator.[136]

Here the significance of humanity's absolute dependence on Universal Causality is highlighted in the language of the Creator's providential care. Janet Martin Soskice likewise draws together both Love and Universal Causality when she argues that "'Love' has good cause to be regarded as the supreme attribute of the Christian God or, as I would prefer to say, that Love is a supremely important divine 'name,' and 'Love' cannot be separated, in this respect, from the name 'Being Itself.'"[137] She argues that the combined insights of Schleiermacher, Aquinas, and Augustine are rich for understanding God not as "having" a number of particular attributes but as identified with at least two of these—Love and Being itself: "for it is not that God has Being Itself, but 'God is Being Itself,' and it is not that God has love, but 'God is love.'"[138] Many, including Schleiermacher, would conceive of the divine in terms

---

133. Farley, *Gathering Those Driven Away*, p. 8.
134. Pamela R. Lightsey, *Our Lives Matter: A Womanist Queer Theology* (Eugene, OR: Wipf and Stock, 2015), p. 39.
135. Ibid., p. 60.
136. Ibid.
137. Soskice, "Being and Love," p. 480.
138. Ibid., p. 489.

of activity rather than "Being Itself,"[139] but the basic idea remains, namely, that God is the source of all things.

In addition to Love and Universal Causality, others have emphasized divine wisdom; 1 Cor. 1:24 ("Christ the power of God and the wisdom of God") is often cited as scriptural precedent for such a move, where Christ is linked with divine wisdom. Elisabeth Schüssler Fiorenza argues that "while the Jesus movement, like John, understood Jesus as the messenger and prophet of divine Sophia, the wisdom Christology of the Christian missionary movement sees him as divine Sophia herself."[140] As another example, Elizabeth Johnson's trinitarian formula offered in *She Who Is*, mentioned above, draws out the wisdom tradition within scripture and classical Christian sources, and offers *Sophia* as a way to speak of the Triune divine *ousia* (essence). As these and other scholars have shown in their own book-length works, reflection on Love, Wisdom, and Universal Causality within Christian traditions is strong.

Despite these rich traditions, alternatives to the trinitarian formula of Father, Son, and Holy Spirit would be difficult for congregations and denominations to embrace even within communities that are open, at least in the abstract, to constructive forms of theology and inclusive language. In *Engendering Judaism*, Rachel Adler offers a model for remaking rituals in a Jewish context that could be instructive here. One of her influences is Barbara Myerhoff, who "observes that although ritual actually changes all the time, convincing rituals make us feel as if they have always been done this way."[141] In order to change a wedding ritual in her own Jewish context, for example, Adler retains as many of the elements of the traditional ceremony as she can. She then infuses traditions from other aspects of Jewish life, such as economic partnerships, into the ritual.[142] Learning from Adler's method, Christians could retain as much of the traditional trinitarian language as possible, while substituting words that would be traditional in other theological or liturgical contexts. "Love" and "Wisdom" might be familiar enough in Christian language, but "Universal Causality" is not a likely candidate for use in liturgical settings. To remedy this, trinitarian formulas could substitute "Life" or "Source of Life" for "Universal Causality."[143] Moreover, a trinitarian formula using words from the New Testament lexicon could use grammatically feminine, relatively

---

139. For a critique of envisioning God as Being, see Enrique Dussel's landmark text, *Ethics and the Theology of Liberation* (New York: Orbis, 1978).

140. Elizabeth Schüssler Fiorenza, *In Memory of Her: A Feminist Theological Reconstruction of Christian Origins* (New York: Crossroad, 1983), p. 89. Cited in Johnson, *She Who Is*, p. 95.

141. Adler, *Engendering Judaism*, p. 84. She cites Barbara G. Myerhoff, "Sanctifying Women's Lives Through Ritual" tape of workshop.

142. Adler, *Engendering Judaism*, pp. 197–8.

143. Schleiermacher himself prefers to call God "Living" when describing the divine being. See Julia A. Lamm, *The Living God: Schleiermacher's Theological Appropriation of Spinoza* (University Park, PA: Pennsylvania State University Press, 1996), pp. 199–228.

familiar terms for divine Life, Love, and Wisdom, namely, *Zoe*, *Agape*, and *Sophia*. By integrating these names for God into ecclesial liturgies, music, and imagery, traditional trinitarian language could be transformed such that kyriarchy is not woven into the minds and hearts of Christians during the very gathering times in which we aim to worship the Creator rather than creatures and to envision a life of just relationships.

***

In 2018–19, one of my undergraduate students completed a senior project for her Women's and Gender Studies major, which involved surveying a local United Methodist congregation regarding their views of adopting inclusive or expansive language in the church's services. On the heels of that project, I was invited to offer the congregation a four-week series on feminism and Christianity. During that series, I introduced participants to the Christian church's history of kyriarchy as well as theological critiques thereof, and some constructive alternatives to exclusively masculine language for the divine. Participants had mixed responses to this information over the course of the series, but most expressed their view that God is not male and that Christians should use inclusive language for the divine. Given this general perspective of the group, one of my goals for our sessions was to help participants see that their own ecclesial practices remain kyriarchal, even though they think of themselves as an inclusive and progressive community. In order to bring this to their awareness, I counted the times masculine names or pronouns were used for the divine during a few typical Sunday services. I did not count names and pronouns that referred to Jesus considered historically as male, but I did count references to the divine in any other form and context. On average over three typical services, masculine names and pronouns were used over one hundred times during one hour of worship in prayers, liturgical formulas, hymns, and sermons. Neutral and feminine references to the divine were negligible. When I presented this data, limited though it was, to the participants in my series on feminism and Christianity, they were astonished. Could it be that they, too, needed to integrate inclusive language into their services? When it came time to consider a few suggestions in that regard, the previously open tone of the group shifted. Many wanted to keep to tradition, insisting that because they know God is not male, they can keep using masculine language for the divine without that language having detrimental effects. Others thought referring to God as "she" or using feminine nouns for God might confuse the children in the congregation. These responses are not surprising, given the congregation's location in the deep South within a denomination struggling with gender and sexuality inclusion, and given the widespread use of masculine language for the divine in Christian communities more generally. In fact, the congregation is to be commended for allowing my student to carry out her senior project among them and then for inviting me to speak with them about the topic of feminist theology at all, wherein they entertained such ideas as the use of feminine pronouns for God or substituting non-kyriarchal trinitarian formulas for those currently used in their worship services. However, it is partially out of experiences like these that the present chapter is written.

If the androcentric trinitarian formula of Father, Son, and Holy Spirit along with exclusively masculine names for the divine are repeated each week over one hundred times in an hour, not to mention what may occur in Sunday School, Wednesday night, or small group studies, in the "*fellow*ship" hall, or in the kitchen, we should not be surprised when churches and societies influenced by Christianity remain kyriarchal. Schüssler Fiorenza writes that "education and religion are the primary institutions by which subjects are fashioned."[144] I would add at least the media and family to this list, but do not underestimate the important influence of religious communities and their lived theologies on the formation of individuals as persons. Our adults, young people, and children deserve better. We deserve to be formed in communities that are committed enough to avoiding idolatry and establishing social justice in order to accept the discomfort of changing liturgical elements and learning to speak in new ways. Without addressing the doctrine of the Trinity, which structures our ways of thinking, speaking, and being in the church, we should not expect to make much deep and lasting progress toward social justice.

Chief among the strengths of a Schleiermacher-inspired essential trinitarianism is that it is not androcentric and does not reinforce kyriarchal forms of church and society. At the heart of the divine life, we do not find Father, Son, and Holy Spirit. Rather, essential trinitarianism affirms the Christian understanding of the divine as Love, Wisdom, and Universal Causality or Life.[145] These divine names are grounded in the economy of salvation in each of its temporal unfoldings: in the person and work of Christ, Christ's ongoing Spirit in the church, and in all of creation. Naming the triune God as Love, Wisdom, and Life opens the door for Christians of all stripes and relationships—not just fathers and sons—to understand themselves as fully capable of participating in a community that is indwelt by and embodies the divine without having to participate in kyriarchal patterns of relationship. The triune naming of the divine as *Agape*, *Sophia*, and *Zoe* is compatible with theologies that emphasize the eradication of kyriarchy as part of the establishment of the divine reign on earth.

Because Love, Wisdom, and Universal Causality are not distinguished by relations of origin, the doctrine of the essential Trinity is also able to circumvent the specter of tritheism, on the one hand, and subordinationism on the other. Here God is not three persons, understood either as three centers of consciousness or three "I-do-not-know-whats."[146] Rather, Universal Causality, Love, and Wisdom are contours or structural features of the divine life. These are not mere attributes,

---

144. Fiorenza, *Jesus*, p. 5.

145. For a treatment of Schleiermacher's doctrine of God in relation to Spinoza's thought, wherein Schleiermacher highlights the livingness of God, see Lamm, *The Living God*.

146. Anselm of Canterbury, "Monologion," in *Anselm of Canterbury: The Major Works*, ed. Brian Davies and G. R. Evans (Oxford: Oxford University Press, 1998), p. 79: "One and a unity by virtue of the one essence, three and a Trinity by virtue of the three—three I-do-not-know-whats."

substitutable by others or alongside others. Rather, they are expressions of the very being of God as it is known through the economy of salvation, and each is interdependent on the others. Furthermore, the doctrine of the essential Trinity is clearly related to Christian faith. It is not speculatively conceived but results from reflection on divine self-communication in Christ and the Spirit. In fact, the doctrine of the essential Trinity and the doctrine of the economic Trinity work together, encouraging reflection back and forth between them. Because the doctrines of the economic and essential trinity are intimately intertwined and do not speculate about what God would be like apart from creation, the doctrine of the Trinity is directly relevant to Christian piety and worship.

Tonstad's postlude to *God and Difference*, where she makes her own debt to Schleiermacher clear, poignantly makes the case for a reconsideration of Schleiermacher's trinitarian thought and is worth reproducing at length:

> One of the significant, albeit subterranean, influences on this project has made only occasional appearances: Friedrich Schleiermacher, who is a target for most contemporary trinitarian theologians despite his successful attempt to secure the centrality of Christ for Christianity without a speculative trinitarian doctrine, and who—beyond almost any other theologian—considers humanity and creation intrinsically relational—intrinsically related to God, to each other, and to the world around—with no kenosis or fracturing needed. …
>
> Schleiermacher opens the door to a historical development and reformulation of doctrine in relation to the needs and dangers of a particular context—in a modern context, once the danger of heathenism is past, the strictures attached to theological "skewing" of pagan concepts might generate rather than protect against theological misunderstandings. … Immanent divine paternity and filiation first developed to counter categorical subordinationism. Now that such subordinationism has been vanquished in theory, paternity and filiation may advance subordination rather than counter it, or so I have argued. This is one of the many sites where trinitarian theologians need to be schooled by radical feminist, womanist, and queer thinkers. These discourses have taught us the futility of dislodging subordination and hierarchy by striking through the greater than sign and replacing it with the equals sign when the very relationship between the terms is constitutive inequality.[147]

Tonstad and I offer different constructive trinitarian proposals,[148] but there can be no doubt that our projects are aligned in the same direction not least because of

---

147. Tonstad, *God and Difference*, pp. 287–8.

148. The space of this chapter does not allow for a thorough examination and comparison of our proposals. However, an initial comparison suggests that we both find compelling Schleiermacher's argument regarding the subordinationism involved in distinguishing the persons of the immanent Trinity through relations of origin. In addition, both Tonstad and I reject an understanding of the triunity of God as including three centers of rational consciousness. Our proposals differ, however, in at least two important ways. Tonstad

the conversation partners to whom we are both indebted. Theologians working constructively today on trinitarian doctrine would be remiss to overlook the contribution and promise of Schleiermacher's own trinitarian thought.

retains a doctrine of the immanent Trinity, distinguishing the Father (or Name/Love), Son (or Glory), and Spirit (or Power) by means of intensification or gift (*God and Difference*, p. 228). In contrast, my proposal rejects the doctrine of the immanent Trinity and offers a doctrine of the essential Trinity, which distinguishes the three contours of the divine life by means of concepts (Love, Wisdom, and Universal Causality) that are related to one another in light of the economy of salvation. This difference between our proposals regarding whether to retain a doctrine of the immanent Trinity is integrally related to our differing use of trinitarian apophaticism. My proposal uses apophaticism to reject the doctrine of the immanent Trinity while retaining, through the doctrine of the essential Trinity, the ability to speak about the heart of the divine life in relation to the economy of salvation. Tonstad, in contrast, uses apophaticism within the doctrine of the immanent Trinity to highlight the incommunicability of the divine persons while simultaneously developing an account of their relations to one another and to the economy of salvation.

Chapter 2

CHRIST AND REDEMPTION

From Peter's response to Jesus himself (Mt. 6:13-20) to nineteenth- and twentieth-century quests for the historical Jesus, the identity of Jesus of Nazareth is elusive. That is appropriately so, since persons cannot be summed up or described comprehensively. At times, a story may capture a quintessential characteristic of a person or a certain way they move through the world, but a person can only be known as they are encountered in the flesh, and even then persons are more than we can grasp. Given the ineffability, materiality, and relationality of persons,[1] to know Jesus of Nazareth as the disciples did is impossible. For Schleiermacher, Christians now encounter Christ's Spirit as it is embodied in the church, that is, in Christ's Love that continues to live in Christian communities. This pneumatological framing of Christology means that although Jesus' person and work are soteriologically central and one's relation to God in and through Christ is of paramount importance for Schleiermacher, Christians only have access to Jesus through the Spirit of Christ that is embodied in contemporary Christian communities. This pneumatological framing of Christology is one of Schleiermacher's signal contributions to current feminist and womanist conversations about Christ. First, utilizing a pneumatological starting point for Christology places theologians working constructively on a different footing than those who begin with a consideration of Jesus' perceived maleness as the "God-man." It allows for the importance of Jesus' sex to be interpreted within a Christology that foregrounds the diversity of bodies in which Christ lives today. Second, Schleiermacher's Christology emphasizes the importance of learning about Jesus through a critical reception of the gospels and their interpretations. As a result, it can contribute to the decentering of traditional Christological doctrinal formulas, which are less adequate as a means of understanding the reality of a person than telling stories, reenacting events, and offering new applications of Jesus' life and ministry. From the perspective of a pneumatological Christology, a question of deep Christological importance is how Christian churches can carry on Christ's Spirit today, knowing that they can never know Christ fully or once and for all.

---

1. See Poe, *Essential Trinitarianism*, pp. 104-13.

A second significant contribution Schleiermacher's Christology makes to current theological discourse is an ontology of Christ that recovers the language of divine indwelling. By speaking of the union of the divine with human nature as divine indwelling, Schleiermacher offers contemporary theologians a way of signaling their commitment to understanding the special dignity and status of Jesus as the Child of God while also clearly affirming his humanity. In addition, since the language of divine indwelling applies to both the union of the divine with humanity in Christ and in Christian churches as they embody the Spirit of Christ, it contributes to a vision of Christ as our spiritual ancestor. This way of understanding the relationship between Christ and the church is congruent with a womanist emphasis on Christ as one with whom those on the underside of history can identify and whose Spirit can continue to empower Christians with compassion and resistance to injustice.

Third, by describing the divine indwelling in Christ and the church as the completion of human nature, Schleiermacher's pneumatologically framed Christology emphasizes that the work of Christ continues in the contemporary church. This way of speaking contributes to current conversation regarding a theology of risk, which does not allow Christians to simply sit back and rest assured in their reception of grace. Rather, Christian churches are envisioned as continuing the completion of human nature by advancing among their neighbors, friends, and enemies the Love that dwelt in Christ.

In this chapter, I present Schleiermacher's pneumatological Christology in conversation with contemporary constructive work in four sections. I first take a brief look at the history of feminist and womanist engagement with Christology, which has largely contended with Jesus' maleness in connection with the patriarchalization of Christology. I turn to Rosemary Radford Ruether, Kelly Brown Douglas, Delores Williams, Jacqueline Grant, and Monica Coleman, who offer arguments in support of the claim that Jesus' maleness is not ultimately, soteriologically important. They argue that who Jesus is as a person and what he does during his life and ministry are central. I both build on and diverge from these thinkers by suggesting that while Jesus' life and ministry should be put front and center instead of his sex, Jesus' perceived maleness nonetheless has soteriological import. I make this claim because, as Ruether and others have recognized, Jesus' sex has social symbolic importance as the "kenosis of patriarchy," and salvation is itself social. In this way, I uphold the limited salvific value of Jesus' perceived maleness insofar as his nonviolent message and life is a judgment against kyriarchy by someone who was privileged in certain respects within it. By signaling precisely how Jesus' perceived maleness is soteriologically important, his perceived sex can be interpreted as an important part of his work of redemption without endangering the dignity of women and non-binary people.

I also attend to the arguments of Douglas, A. Elaine Crawford, and Karen Baker-Fletcher, who claim that primary attention ought to be paid to the life of Jesus rather than the two-natures doctrine of Christ's person. Not only building on their criticism of the two-natures doctrine but also recognizing the theological need for an account of Jesus' being, I suggest in the second section of the chapter that Schleiermacher's Christology may provide an alternate ontology that is less problematic than those offered in traditional theological discourses. Schleiermacher affirms the divine being in Christ as well as Christ's humanity, while paying primary attention to the concrete life and ministry of Christ as the Wise fulfillment of Love within Universal Causality's progressive creation of humanity. In addition, I show how Schleiermacher's view dovetails with Christologies that emphasize the goodness of creation and the loving character of the divine-creaturely relationship. By speaking of the person of Christ in terms of divine indwelling and the completion of creation, Schleiermacher's Christology foregrounds natality, community, and loving activity.

In the third section of this chapter, I turn to Jesus' redemptive work, which is integrally connected to his person. I discuss Delores Williams's critique of substitutionary atonement, followed by a comparison with Schleiermacher's view of redemption. Schleiermacher offers a compelling soteriology that is congruent with Williams's thought. With Williams, he does not rely on substitutionary relationships and does not directly relate Jesus' suffering, in and of itself, to redemption. Instead, he foregrounds the goodness and in-progress nature of creation and the interdependent relationships therein. Drawing in the voices of Karen Baker-Fletcher, Traci West, and Jacqueline Grant, I argue that Schleiermacher's view could be a resource for those who do not want to single out Christ's physical suffering on the cross as having value for redemption but want to emphasize instead Jesus' identification with "the least of these" and his persistent resistance to injustice. Even so, I argue that Schleiermacher's Christology needs correction insofar as he tends to downplay Jesus' Jewish particularity. Drawing on James Cone, Jacquelyn Grant maintains that Jesus' Jewish particularity is what allows for his universal significance. I argue that Schleiermacher's view should be revised in accordance with this insight.

In the final section of the chapter, I describe a number of other ways Schleiermacher's theology coalesces with contemporary theologies aimed at gender, racial, and economic justice by returning to some of the soteriological themes briefly discussed at the close of this book's introductory chapter. I outline Schleiermacher's treatment of sin in the context of grace, arguing that his notion of sin is capacious enough to include a variety of human experiences, and that by treating "original perfection" prior to sin and evil, Schleiermacher's thought maps onto the anticipatory optimism involved in feminist discussions of sin. I also discuss Schleiermacher's understanding of sin as social and systemic, his emphasis on the body and affect as important for Christian life, and his emphasis on natality and joy in Christian community. However, in addition to these positive features of Schleiermacher's proposal, I also suggest that a modification to Schleiermacher's teleological view of redemption is needed that would bring it into line with religious pluralism. His reliance on a notion of an afterlife in order to bring all people into the Christian community both smacks of imperialism and goes against his otherwise consistent focus on the historical nature of the process of creation-redemption and the limits of theological knowledge. I argue that Schleiermacher's system of thought can go without a notion of the afterlife and simply affirm

Christian ignorance about God's relation to other religions while simultaneously maintaining the divine decree of blessedness for all.

My goal in this chapter is to introduce Schleiermacher's promise for constructive Christologies and soteriologies today, and to demonstrate that there is enough resonance between Schleiermacher's thought and contemporary constructive forms of theology to warrant further analysis and work in this direction. To accomplish this goal, I engage with a number of early womanists and feminists, since the basic ideas that they have introduced are still determinative for their fields today. It must also be admitted at the outset that I pull various strands of womanist and feminist thought into the conversation in somewhat truncated ways, as I regrettably do not have the space here to analyze the nuances and intricacies of each thinker's work. Despite these limitations, this chapter demonstrates that Schleiermacher's pneumatologically framed Christology and his theory of redemption are remarkably aligned with contemporary constructive work and hold great promise for those engaged in constructing Christologies and soteriologies with a view to establishing social justice.

Contemporary Challenges to Christology

At least two challenges have been brought forward by feminist and womanist voices to historically dominant Christologies, namely, androcentrism and a preoccupation with the two-natures doctrine. I survey them here in turn. In "Christology: Can a Male Savior Save Women?," Rosemary Radford Ruether argues that Christians have patriarchalized Christology through three historical steps.[2] At first, the spirit-filled community that followed Jesus and embodied his prophetic Spirit believed it was living in an apocalyptic age. The community believed that God would soon intervene to overthrow evil powers and principalities. However, as time went on, a portion of this original community took a second step. It began to develop institutional Christianity by installing bishops and closing divine revelation in the original apostolic community. In this institutional order, teachers became exclusively men. As a third step, Christianity became involved in the Roman Empire, and the Messiah was understood through kingship ideology. The result was that "the Christian emperor, with the Christian Patriarch on his right hand, now represents the establishment of Christ's reign upon the earth."[3] Within the Christian empire, so conceived, the King, who represents the divine Logos, governs women, slaves, barbarians, and religious minorities (the *a-logoi*, or mindless ones).[4] Within this theological and social order, Ruether explains, the

---

2. Rosemary Radford Ruether, *Sexism and God-Talk: Toward a Feminist Theology* (Boston, MA: Beacon, 1983), pp. 116–38. For a more detailed account, see also Rosemary Radford Ruether, "Sexism and Misogyny in the Christian Tradition: Liberating Alternatives," *Buddhist-Christian Studies* 34 (2014): 83–94.

3. Ruether, *Sexism and God-Talk*, p. 125.

4. Ibid.

Logos had to incarnate as male, and only men could represent Christ as priests.⁵ Although there were alternative Christologies in the early church, which Ruether identifies as "androgynous" and "spirit" Christologies, androgynous Christologies retained androcentrism, while spirit Christologies continued only in small factions of the church and looked outside of Christ for a new revelation of God.

In contrast to this history, Ruether maintains that after "the mythology about Jesus as Messiah or divine Logos, with its traditional masculine imagery, is stripped off, the Jesus of the synoptic Gospels can be recognized as a figure remarkably compatible with feminism," insofar as "the criticism of religious and social hierarchy characteristic of the early portrait of Jesus is remarkably parallel to feminist criticism."⁶ Ruether presents a Jesus for whom the last shall be first and the first shall be last, and in whose thought such a reversal is not simply a reimagining of who is on top, but is one in which "hierarchy and dominance are overcome as principles of social relations."⁷ For Ruether, what is ultimately important is not the maleness of Jesus but who he is as the Christ and what he does during his life and ministry. As such, she famously states,

> The maleness of Jesus has no ultimate significance. It has social symbolic significance in the framework of societies of patriarchal privilege. In this sense Jesus as the Christ, the representative of liberated humanity and the liberating Word of God, manifests the *kenosis of patriarchy*, the announcement of the new humanity through a lifestyle that discards hierarchical caste privilege and speaks on behalf of the lowly.⁸

Because Jesus' maleness is not intrinsic to his salvific role, Ruether maintains that "we can encounter Christ *in the form of our sister*."⁹ Christ is no longer exclusively tied to the male Jesus of Nazareth, but "goes ahead of us, calling us to yet incomplete dimensions of human liberation."¹⁰ In this way, Ruether answers her question whether a male savior can save women positively, on the condition that the history of the patriarchalization of Christ is not seen as essential to Christianity and in fact is understood as counterproductive to the true being of Christ as humanity's liberator.

In keeping with Ruether's view of the ultimate insignificance of Jesus' maleness, Kelly Brown Douglas maintains that "it was not who Jesus was, particularly as a male, that made him Christ, but what he did."¹¹ She criticizes the Nicene Creed and the Chalcedonian Definition as disembodied interpretations of the

---

5. Ibid., pp. 122–6.
6. Ibid., p. 135.
7. Ibid., p. 136.
8. Ibid., p. 137.
9. Ibid., p. 138. Emphasis in the original.
10. Ibid., p. 138.
11. Kelly Brown Douglas, *The Black Christ* (Maryknoll, NY: Orbis, 1994), p. 108. Compare Jacquelyn Grant, *White Women's Christ and Black Women's Jesus: Feminist Christology and*

incarnation because "by moving directly from the incarnation to the crucifixion and resurrection, this confession nullifies the importance of embodiment to God's revelation. The implication is that what took place between Jesus' birth and resurrection is unimportant to what it meant for him to be Christ."[12] Douglas attends to the actions and words of Jesus, which could be embodied by persons with any number of bodily characteristics that are different than those of Jesus of Nazareth. For example, one need not have brown hair, be born in Bethlehem, or speak Aramaic in order to be like Christ in the most significant respects. For Douglas, anyone who acts similarly to Christ can be an image of Christ. "To be like Christ," she explains, "requires living a life characterized by loving relationships, those that are liberating, healing, empowering, and life-sustaining."[13] For both Douglas and Ruether, we can, indeed, "encounter Christ in the form of our sister."

However, womanists rightfully hasten to further indicate who Christ is in the form of "our sister." There is, after all, no generic or universal woman. Delores Williams has criticized Ruether, specifically, for failing to take into account Black women's experiences in her early feminist theology. Williams writes that by failing to include racism and classism in her discussion of the future of feminist theology, Ruether and other white feminist theologians who follow suit "inadvertently reinforce another evil that continues to prevail in most theological academies: the evil of white supremacy."[14] Williams outlines a number of ways that white feminists need to raise their consciousness of racism. They need to:

1. understand the limitation of the feminist patriarchal critique for assessing the nature of Black women's oppression derived from Black women's *relation to white-male-white-female dominated social systems*,
2. recognize the need to assess the ethical significance of white feminists using "white patriarchal power" to gain privileges that benefit mostly white women,
3. realize that Black American women and white American women are apt to use different linguistic configurations to express the terms of their oppression. ...
4. consider women's liberation and family liberation as *inseparable goals*,
5. realize that the family (whether nuclear or extended) can be an effective unit for consciousness-raising with regard to gender, racial, and class oppression.[15]

Womanist Response. American Academy of Religion Series No. 64 (Atlanta, GA: Scholars Press, 1989), p. 220.

12. Kelly Brown Douglas, *Sexuality and the Black Church: A Womanist Perspective* (Maryknoll, NY: Orbis, 1999), p. 117.

13. Ibid., p. 118.

14. Delores Williams, "The Color of Feminism," *Christianity and Crisis* 45/7 (April 29, 1985): 164. Williams is criticizing Ruether's previous article in the same journal, "Feminist Theology in the Academy," *Christianity and Crisis* 45/3 (March 4, 1985): 57–62.

15. Delores Williams, "The Color of Feminism: Or Speaking in the Black Woman's Tongue," *The Journal of Religious Thought* 43/1 (1986): 55.

Consciousness-raising of this sort is needed, on Williams's view, because feminists have not reckoned with their own racism and privilege as white women.[16] The agendas for white feminists and Black womanists have therefore tended to be different. "White feminists," Williams explains, "struggle for women's liberation from male domination with regard for such priority issues as rape, domestic violence, women's work, female bonding, inclusive language, the gender of God, economic autonomy for women, and heterosexism."[17] These feminist priorities stand in contrast to that of "black women liberators," who prioritize

> physical survival and spiritual salvation of the family (with equality between males and females), the re-distribution of goods and services in the society (so that white families no longer get the lion's share of the economic, educational, political, and vocational resources available in every social class), encountering God as family (masculine and feminine, father, mother, and child), ending white supremacy, male supremacy (or any gender supremacy), and upper-class supremacy in all American institutions.[18]

In short, for Williams, white feminists tend to seek out white women's flourishing, while Black women liberators tend to be more focused on the survival and quality of life of the entire Black community.

Because of the different experiences and agendas of white and Black women, womanists beneficially specify who Christ is "in the form of our sister." For Jacqueline Grant, "Christ, found in the experiences of Black women, is a Black woman."[19] She argues that if Christ is to be identified with the lowly, then it is appropriate to identify the lowly not simply with women who are subjected to sexism but with Black women who bear the brunt of sexism, racism, and classism.[20] Other womanists make more expansive Christological moves. Douglas, for example, extends this image of Christ to all "Black people, men as well as women," wherever they "are struggling to bring the entire Black community to wholeness."[21] For her, God is incarnate not only in Jesus but also "in the lives of those who will accept the challenges of the risen Saviour the Christ."[22] Monica A. Coleman goes further, maintaining that "Christian womanist theologians can encourage the present generation to see Christ in the faces of the poor, blacks,

---

16. See also Ellen T. Armour, *Deconstruction, Feminist Theology, and the Problem of Difference: Subverting the Race/Gender Divide* (Chicago, IL: University of Chicago Press, 1999).
17. Ibid., p. 54.
18. Ibid.
19. Grant, *White Women's Christ and Black Women's Jesus*, p. 220.
20. Ibid., p. 202.
21. Douglas, *The Black Christ*, p. 109.
22. Grant, *White Women's Christ and Black Women's Jesus*, p. 220.

women, the elements, and the earth."[23] They can do so because of their focus on Jesus' humanity and creatureliness rather than his perceived maleness as having ultimate theological significance.

Elisabeth Schüssler Fiorenza offers two important comments on these features of feminist and womanist Christology. To begin, she emphasizes that Jesus' maleness should not be taken as an historical given. Rather, the constructed nature of secondary physical sex characteristics should be recognized. Fiorenza writes that "common sense has it that facial hair is a male physical secondary sex characteristic. This commonplace assumption conceals, however, that it is discursively constructed. In order to uphold this ostensibly male sex standard, a multibillion dollar cosmetic industry strives to eradicate all facial hair in women."[24] Of course, Jesus did not live at a time when that industry thrived. But Judith Butler's work also highlights the cultural ways of configuring bodies, noting that "'anatomy' and 'sex' are not without cultural framing (as the intersex movement has clearly shown)."[25] In addition, of course, masculinity is a constructed category that changes in each age and culture. As Butler writes,

> The very attribution of femininity to female bodies as if it were a natural or necessary property takes place within a normative framework in which the assignment of femininity to femaleness is one mechanism for the production of gender itself. Terms such as "masculine" and "feminine" are notoriously changeable; there are social histories for each term; their meanings change radically depending upon geopolitical boundaries and cultural constraints on who is imagining whom, and for what purpose.[26]

Schüssler Fiorenza and Butler are both pointing to the importance of remembering that what it means to be male, masculine, female, and/or feminine is not simply given. In the context of Christology, such a recognition requires the acknowledgment that contemporary Christians do not know whether Jesus had XY chromosomes and might not know exactly what it meant for Jesus to be perceived as male in first-century Israel.[27]

Schüssler Fiorenza also indicates that focusing on Jesus' "humanity" instead of his maleness will not solve the problem by itself. She writes about Ruether's position: "I wonder whether her positive articulation of Christ as 'liberated humanity' merely shifts the problem from masculine language for G*d and Christ to a masculine/male-defined notion of humanity."[28] One cannot simply focus on

---

23. Monica A. Coleman, *Making a Way Out of No Way: A Womanist Theology* (Minneapolis, MN: Fortress, 2008), p. 99.
24. Schüssler Fiorenza, *Jesus*, p. 40.
25. Judith Butler, *Undoing Gender* (New York: Routledge, 2004), p. 10.
26. Ibid.
27. For this reason, I refer in this chapter to Jesus' "perceived maleness."
28. Schüssler Fiorenza, *Jesus*, p. 160.

Jesus' humanity, then, without opening oneself up to the possibility that humanity itself might be conceived according to a masculine model. Schüssler Fiorenza is here highlighting the need to go beyond a simple focus on Jesus' humanity, so that the new focus on humanity is not simply co-opted by kyriarchal interests.

The same could also be said for a focus on Jesus' ministry, rather than his maleness. Emphasizing Jesus' ministry does not automatically rid Jesus' maleness of its significance. To see this in action, we might turn to Robert Goss's queer theology, which both emphasizes the activity of God in Christ as of the utmost significance and yet also views the maleness of Jesus as integral to his own relationship to God in Christ. He writes that "it is not Jesus' maleness that made him the Christ. It is his *basileia* practice of solidarity with the oppressed, his execution, God's identification with his crucifixion, and God's raising him from the dead that made Jesus the Christ."[29] At the same time, Goss also writes about his experience as a Jesuit priest: "I finally admitted to myself that I loved Jesus because he was a male and that it was OK to love Jesus passionately and erotically as a man."[30] It is clear from this example that an emphasis on Jesus' ministry does not preclude one from attributing significance to his maleness, and even making his maleness integral to one's own spirituality. For this reason, theologians working constructively today will need to go beyond an emphasis on Jesus' ministry in order to discuss the significance of Jesus' perceived maleness.

In fact, it is surprising that many who are otherwise convinced that attending to particularity is theologically important and that human persons are integrally bound up with human bodies would want to gloss over the particularity of Jesus' perceived maleness in favor of a general notion of humanity. While some of Jesus' particular characteristics are not likely to have been central to his experience as a human person, surely being perceived as male was significant biologically, socially, economically, politically, and religiously. As such, it is important to address the relationship between Jesus' perceived male body and his person, since human persons are inextricably bound up with their sociohistorically situated bodies. To deny that Jesus' sex was important for who he was as a human person would be to deny his true humanity. Going further, it is important to acknowledge that Jesus' perceived maleness did, in fact, have limited salvific import. Jesus' maleness does not have ultimate soteriological significance in the sense that maleness is more similar to the divine being than femaleness or being intersex. Jesus' life and ministry were not salvific simply or even primarily because he was male. Neither did his maleness allow him to represent the divine in a way females or intersex persons could not. I am not, therefore, suggesting that Jesus' perceived maleness reveals the divine ontology in any way.[31] Rather,

---

29. Robert E. Goss, *Queering Christ: Beyond Jesus Acted Up* (Eugene, OR: Wipf & Stock, originally published by Pilgrim Press, Cleveland, OH, 2002), p. 160.

30. Ibid., p. 17.

31. In Chapter 4, I explore the related idea of divine sovereignty and argue that for Schleiermacher and many contemporary theologians working constructively, the kind of "privilege" God has is qualitatively different than human forms of privilege, which are

I would suggest that the soteriological importance of Jesus' maleness should be exclusively tied to the sociohistorical importance of his perceived maleness. Ruether was right to say that Jesus' perceived maleness has social symbolic significance as the *kenosis* (self-emptying) of patriarchy. However, rather than distinguishing the *kenosis* of patriarchy from soteriology by claiming that Jesus' perceived maleness has *only* social symbolic significance, we would do well to recognize that the soteriological includes the social. In other words, the sociohistorical *kenosis* of patriarchy is part of the salvific establishment of the divine reign. It was precisely as a human person who was perceived to be male that Jesus, as Ruether says, lived "a lifestyle that discards hierarchical caste privilege and speaks on behalf of the lowly."[32] This fact does not change the ultimate message of salvation, which remains the same regardless of Jesus' perceived sex. Even so, Jesus manifests the *kenosis* of patriarchy, in Ruether's phrase, only because he was perceived to be male.[33]

While respecting Jesus' particularity as a person who was perceived to be male and the social importance of that privilege in his context, it is also important to recognize that many of his personal characteristics can be shared regardless of sex. A pneumatological Christology brings these characteristics to the fore in order to highlight the fact that many differently sexed bodies carry on Christ's Spirit. It is in this way that, as many feminist and womanist theologians have maintained, we can encounter Christ in the form of our Black, Latina, Asian, indigenous, lesbian, non-binary, poor, exploited, transgender, oppressed, and colonized sisters, brothers, and gender diverse people wherever they embody Love for the human community, the planet, and themselves. Indeed, Christ can be encountered in as many different forms as there are Christian communities who love God and neighbor as Jesus did. By looking to the Christian community's embodiment of Christ's Spirit of Love, pneumatologically constructed Christological accounts can recognize the importance of Jesus' perceived maleness in social terms, while simultaneously embracing the humanity and dignity of oppressed people in whom we can now encounter Christ.[34]

---

conceived in a competitive manner. Divine power is noncompetitive in the sense that it does not disempower but empowers others.

32. Ruether, *Sexism and God-Talk*, p. 137.

33. To claim that only privileged people should therefore preach, or that their preaching and ministry is more powerful than others, however, would be absurd. Giving ministerial privilege to men (either by exclusively ordaining men or by giving male ministers sociocultural, economic, or other religious privileges) and then asking them to preach the denial of their privilege while maintaining the privilege of their office would be absurd. Instead, once the anti-kyriarchal lesson has been learned from Jesus, the power of his message continues by enacting the content of Jesus' anti-kyriarchal message.

34. Rita Nakashima Brock centers her Christology on the community by using the term "Christa." See "Communities of the Cross: Christa and the Communal Nature of Redemption," *Feminist Theology* 14/1 (2015): 109–25.

2. Christ and Redemption

A second challenge brought especially by womanist theologians to traditional Christological formulations is their preoccupation with the ontological makeup of Christ as one person in two natures. As Douglas writes, "the enslaved crafters of the Black faith tradition did not refer to Jesus in the theological jargon of dominant Western culture as the 'word made flesh,' as the divine/human encounter, or as the incarnate one." They did, however, "witness in a clear-cut, theologically incisive manner to the radical uniqueness of Jesus and the oneness between Jesus and God."[35] More specifically, Douglas notes that "a womanist understanding of the Black Christ ... does not begin with abstract speculation of Jesus' metaphysical nature. Instead, it starts in history with Jesus' ministry as that is recorded in the Gospels."[36] Ontological statements about Christ's makeup might be made or assumed within various womanist theologies, but there tends to be less attention paid to strict adherence to orthodox formulas.[37] According to A. Elaine Crawford, "womanists employ a very 'high' Christology ... *in the African American sense*, indicating that Jesus has an integral place, a real consuming presence that empowers the life of the believer."[38] This is different than the "high Christology" of Chalcedonian theologians, for instance, who describe at some length a Christological grammar for speaking of Christ's two natures.[39] Karen Baker-Fletcher describes the importance of Jesus' work among Christian womanists and Black women:

> [They] identify Jesus by his work in the synoptic Gospels—laying on hands to heal, sharing food and wine, empathizing with the woman with the issue of blood, loving widows and orphans, forgiving women condemned by society, passing on wisdom as a teacher, listening to Mary and Martha, weeping over and healing Lazarus, conquering death and evil in his historical life and beyond.[40]

---

35. Douglas, *Sexuality and the Black Church*, p. 111.
36. Douglas, *The Black Christ*, p. 113.
37. Referring primarily to Grant and Williams, Monica A. Coleman writes, "Womanist theologians are broad and conflated in their language about God. Although Grant focuses on the humanity of Jesus, she still knows that black women understand Jesus as God. ... These womanist theologians use the term 'Jesus' to refer to all acts they consider divine" (Coleman, *Making a Way Out of No Way*, p. 37).
38. A. Elaine Crawford, "Womanist Christology: Where Have We Come from and Where Are We Going?" *Review and Expositor* 95 (1998): 376. Cited in Coleman, *Making a Way Out of No Way*, p. 37. My emphasis. See also chapter eight of Diana L. Hayes, *Standing in the Shoes My Mother Made: A Womanist Theology* (Minneapolis, MN: Fortress, 2011), pp. 135-60.
39. For an account of Schleiermacher's Christology that is framed in terms of "low" and "high" Christology, see Kevin W. Hector, "Actualism and Incarnation: The High Christology of Friedrich Schleiermacher," *International Journal of Systematic Theology* 8/3 (July 2006): 307-22.
40. Baker-Fletcher does explicate her understanding of Jesus as fully divine and fully human, and affirms the preexistence of the Logos. However, she emphasizes the concrete

This primary attention to the concrete life of Christ rather than preoccupation with a two-natures doctrine, along with a reinterpretation of Jesus' maleness as not ultimately significant, signals a marked divergence between feminist and womanist theologies, on the one hand, and historically dominant Christologies, on the other.

Schleiermacher's pneumatologically constructed Christology can provide support for this divergence in the form of avoiding a preoccupation with Jesus' maleness and focusing on the inseparability of Jesus' person and ministry, offering critical questions about the two-natures doctrine, and providing an alternate understanding of the ontological makeup of Christ that affirms both the divine being in Christ and Christ's humanity while paying primary attention to the concrete life and ministry of Christ.[41] In addition, Schleiermacher's understanding of the person and work of Christ highlights the goodness of creaturely natality and emphasizes loving activity in community. By foregrounding these notions, Schleiermacher's Christology offers itself as a beneficial resource for contemporary constructive work.

Schleiermacher's Christology

Avoiding the Chalcedonian Formula

In his *Christian Faith*, Schleiermacher uses the language of divine indwelling to describe the relationship of God and Christ.[42] He avoids the Chalcedonian formulation for three reasons.[43] First, as he understands them, Christologies that affirm the two-natures doctrine are "overladen with a mass of qualifications that

---

life and ministry of Christ even in so doing: "Jesus realizes the harmony of creation and Spirit in the actions associated with his life and work" (*My Sister, My Brother*, p. 87).

41. For a critique of ancient and modern Christologies on account of their inattention to the life of Christ, see James Cone, *God of the Oppressed* (New York: Orbis, 2003), pp. 106–9.

42. See Col. 2:9. A similar move is made by Eboni Marshall Turman, when she uses the historical Christological distinction between *kata sarka* (what happens to the flesh) and *en sarki* (what happens in the flesh) to structure her womanist ethic of incarnation. She writes,

> a womanist ethic of incarnation insists that the black church's parousia is possible only insofar as it remembers Jesus by looking to the bodies of black church women who, in their apparent brokenness, claim that God is not only *with* us in terms of God's presence in history on the side of the oppressed, but even more, that God is *in* us, namely, that God is *in* the flesh of even the "oppressed of the oppressed" (*Toward a Womanist Ethic of Incarnation: Black Bodies, the Black Church and the Council of Chalcedon* [Palgrave Macmillan, 2013], p. 172). Emphasis in the original.

43. For a treatment of Schleiermacher's relation to Chalcedon and early church writings, see Lori Pearson, "Schleiermacher and the Christologies behind Chalcedon," *Harvard Theological Review* 96/3 (July 2003): 349–67. She argues that

2. Christ and Redemption

stand in no relationship whatsoever to immediate Christian self-consciousness, except as traces of this mode of consciousness can be demonstrated through the history of doctrinal conflict."[44] In other words, the two-natures doctrine is so technical that it cannot have arisen immediately from Christian piety. Christian piety includes reverence for the special being and status of Christ, but it does not issue directly in a clear and detailed understanding of the two natures of Christ and how they interact to ensure that the natures are "without confusion, without change, without division, without separation."[45] These kinds of qualifications, for Schleiermacher, can only be connected to Christian piety insofar as they point to the piety that could have been behind the doctrinal history in which such distinctions were forged. While it is certainly appropriate for doctrines to develop within theological history, Schleiermacher objects to the "mass of qualification" that now stands attached to the two-natures doctrine, which is not clearly and directly relevant for Christian life.

Second, for Schleiermacher, the dominant Christological formulations of the church have produced theological conundrums that are not easily answerable. Referring to those formulations found in creeds such as the Augsburg Confession, the First and Second Helvetic Confessions, and the Nicene-Constantinopolitan Creed, Schleiermacher goes so far as to say that there is "almost nothing in the execution of it [i.e. of their 'presentation of the distinctive personal existence of the Redeemer'[46]] against which no protest would have to be lodged, whether we are inclined to look at the scientific quality of the expression or at its suitability for the church's use."[47] To give a typical example of reason for such protest: if the divine nature is all-powerful and all-knowing, but humanity is by nature limited in power and knowledge, then it would be difficult to sustain the idea that Jesus was both all-knowing and limited in knowledge at one and the same time while remaining one, integrated, human person. As Schleiermacher writes with regard to omniscience,

> Schleiermacher's Christology underscores the individual humanity and development of the Redeemer (a parallel to Theodore and Nestorius), while at the same time emphasizing the priority and dominance of the divine in the Redeemer, so that this divine element constitutes the center of who he is and the source of all that he does (a debt to Cyril, and behind him to Athanasius). (ibid., pp. 350–1)

44. *CF*, §95.1, p. 580.
45. Chalcedonian Definition, 451 CE.
46. *CF*, §96.1, p. 583.
47. Ibid. For Schleiermacher's use of Protestant confessions, see Walter E. Wyman, "The Role of the Protestant Confessions in Schleiermacher's The Christian Faith," *The Journal of Religion* 87/3 (July 2003): 355–85. He argues that Schleiermacher "denies that they have binding normative authority; they do not constitute a Protestant magisterium. Yet they must be taken seriously as initial statements of the distinctively Protestant perspective—a perspective that is subject to further development" (ibid., p. 357).

> If someone would want to deny this dependence of his [i.e., Christ's] development on those surroundings, then logically one would have to assume an empirical omniscience in Christ, by virtue of which all human ways of looking at things, hence languages too, would have been directly known to him and fluent in him. ... The Redeemer's true humanity, however, would also have been lost thereby.[48]

The problem, more generally, is that it would be impossible for "the unity of a person's life to endure with the duality of natures without the one yielding to the other when the one offers a larger and the other a narrower course of life, or, without the two natures blending into each other, in that the two systems of law and conduct actually become one in the one life."[49] In short, it is difficult to avoid either separating or confusing the natures.

Third, relating this problem to trinitarian doctrine, Schleiermacher is concerned that because of the use of the word "person" in both trinitarian and Christological contexts, the conundrums of classical Christology could lead to suspicions of tritheism. Schleiermacher explains, "either the three persons would have to be like human persons, wholly independent, self-standing individual beings, or Christ, viewed as a human being, would be no such thing, with which assertion the picture of Christ as a human being would then entirely dissolve into something docetic."[50] For Schleiermacher, then, the two-natures doctrine faces at least three problems. It is disconnected from immediate Christian piety, it runs the risk of either separating or confusing the natures, and if it is combined with the doctrine of the immanent Trinity then it reinforces the specter of tritheism.

The Person of Christ: Divine Indwelling and the Completion of Creation

Schleiermacher makes two basic Christological moves by which he avoids the problems he has identified with the two-natures doctrine and by which he provides the basic contours of an alternative account. First, in Schleiermacher's formulation, Jesus of Nazareth exists as a result of the union of the divine being (*Wesen*) and human nature, and this union continues to form Jesus' person and ministry. Schleiermacher writes about the union of the divine and human in terms of divine indwelling, and in so doing he emphasizes that what is salvific about Jesus is the divine activity by which he is formed and that he embodies and carries out. Here we notice that the person and work of Jesus are inseparable. Second, Schleiermacher conceives of Jesus as the divine completion of human nature, which is itself part of the whole interconnected process of nature. By speaking of the divine union with human nature as a whole in Jesus and by further identifying human nature as one part of the natural order of creation, Schleiermacher at once foregrounds the human creatureliness of Christ, establishes Christology's

---

48. *CF*, §93.3, p. 571.
49. Ibid., §96.1, p. 585.
50. Ibid., §97.2, p. 592.

connection to Christian piety, and links the activity of God in Christ to the activity of God in other temporal phases of the economy of salvation.

Taking Schleiermacher's link between Christology and the doctrine of creation first, we see that for him, the life of Christ is the completion of the creation of human nature.[51] Famously, Schleiermacher maintains that prior to Jesus' existence, the "strength of [human] God-consciousness" was weak and inconsistent,[52] and that Christ completes human nature through his strong and constant God-consciousness. In brief, Schleiermacher's notion of "God-consciousness" refers to a human being's immediate awareness of being in a relation of absolute dependence on God. The notion is first explicated in §4 of the *Glaubenslehre*, where he identifies the nature of piety as being "conscious of ourselves as absolutely dependent or, which intends the same meaning, as being in relation with God."[53] "God-consciousness" sums up Schleiermacher's understanding of the asymmetrical relationship between God and creation. The whole of creation is absolutely dependent upon God for its creation and preservation, and "God-consciousness" is an immediate awareness of this relationship.

In a fateful move, considering the history of interpretation, Schleiermacher describes God-consciousness as a "feeling" (*Gefühl*) of absolute dependence. It is important to note that for him, God-consciousness is neither an emotion nor an unconscious experience. Rather, Schleiermacher is using *Gefühl* technically in a Kantian sense to mean an effect of something upon a person.[54] Theodore Vial explains *Gefühl* as it is used in Schleiermacher's *On Religion: Speeches to Its Cultured Despisers*, where it first came to prominence: "[1] An object comes into contact with us, and [2] this has effects on us. The first is intuition, the second is feeling. They are two sides of the same coin of experience."[55] As Vial explains, intuition is the experience of perceiving an object through the senses. Feeling, on the other hand, is the modification of consciousness that results from the activity of an object upon a person in perception. As Schleiermacher states, "Every intuition is, by its very nature, connected with a feeling. Your senses mediate the connection between the object and yourselves; the same influence of the object, which reveals its existence to you, must stimulate them in various ways and produce a change in your inner consciousness."[56] *Gefühl* is, then, an immediate self-consciousness that arises in the subject as a result of the activity of an object upon her.

Schleiermacher explains that most of the time human self-consciousness, "viewed as a consciousness of our being in the world or as a consciousness of our coexistence with the world, exists as a series in which we have feelings [understood

---

51. Ibid., §92.1, p. 562.
52. Ibid., §93.2, p. 566.
53. Ibid., §4, p. 18.
54. For a full discussion of this feature of Schleiermacher's thought, see Vial, *Modern Religion, Modern Race*, pp. 55–92.
55. Vial, *Schleiermacher: A Guide for the Perplexed*, p. 69.
56. *OR*, p. 29.

in a Kantian sense] divided into those of dependence and freedom."[57] As part of the world, people are aware both that they are dependent on the world in some respects and are also free to influence it in other respects. However, people can never feel absolutely dependent on the universe or absolutely free within it, because they always both depend on other portions of the universe and simultaneously influence the universe, even if in subtle ways. Absolute dependence, for Schleiermacher, is only felt in relation to God, the "Whence" of all created existence.[58] As such, for him, "feeling oneself to be absolutely dependent and being conscious of oneself as in relation with God are one and the same thing."[59]

Before the existence of Christ, Schleiermacher thinks, this consciousness of one's relation to God was present in humanity in a weak and inconsistent fashion. People easily forget that they along with the entirety of creation depend upon God for their existence and preservation. Christ's particular "dignity," using Schleiermacher's terminology, is that in and through his person, which includes his powerful and constant God-consciousness, God completes human nature by implanting in it a uniquely strong consciousness of God. "The Redeemer is the same as all human beings by virtue of the selfsame character of human nature," Schleiermacher explains, "but he is distinguished from all other human beings by the steady strength of his God-consciousness, a strength that was an actual being of God in him."[60]

As we have seen, Schleiermacher conceives of the being of God "as pure activity."[61] Specifically, the divine activity or the "divine factor" in Christ is "the divine love in Christ, which love gave to human nature ... alignment of sense perceptions to the spiritual [or mental] states of human beings. By virtue of these sense perceptions and as a result of them, impulses leading to particular beneficial actions were then to develop in turn."[62] Three claims are being made here. First, the being of God in Jesus, originally identified as the steady strength of his consciousness of absolute dependence on God, is now further specified as what that God-consciousness allows, namely, the embodiment or indwelling of divine love. Second, divine love is said to align or unite Jesus' sense perceptions and mental states so that they work together with one another. That is, Jesus' bodily experience does not run counter to his spiritual life, but the two are united. Third, the result of indwelling divine love operative in Jesus is a human life characterized

---

57. *CF*, §4.2, p. 22.
58. Ibid., §4.4, p. 24.
59. Ibid., p. 26.
60. *CF*, §94, p. 574. As we will see, the completion of creation that occurs in Jesus' person is continued and carried on in the "moral person" formed within Christian communities. The union of the divine with humanity that occurs in Jesus of Nazareth completes human nature, but the efficaciousness of this completion grows over time as others are brought into Christian communities that cultivate in them a similarly powerful God-consciousness.
61. *CF*, §94.2, p. 576.
62. Ibid., §97.3, pp. 601–2.

by beneficial actions. For Schleiermacher, then, the indwelling of God in Jesus is enabled by his constant awareness of his relation to God, by which he embodies divine love, which in turn orders his life so that it results in beneficial activity. Christ's consciousness of his relation to God thereby determines "every element of his life steadily and exclusively."[63]

To ensure that the humanity of Jesus is not lost, Schleiermacher states that Jesus' God-consciousness unfolded gradually as he grew "in wisdom and stature."[64] On the other side, to rule out adoptionism, Schleiermacher maintains that the strength and power of Jesus' consciousness of being in relation to God "can be accounted for based only on … a creative divine act."[65] That is to say, the existence of Christ is part of the eternal divine decree.[66] In fact, God's Christological decree is "identical with God's decree of humanity's creation, and it is contained in that decree."[67] "Through the Redeemer that eternal decree is actualized in *one* point of space as well as in *one* period of time," Schleiermacher explains.[68] Simultaneously, it would be equally appropriate to say that "already Christ was also always coming into being, even as a human person, at the same time as the world was coming into being."[69] By claiming that Christ comes into existence alongside the world and that Christ is the actualization of the eternal decree at one place and time, Schleiermacher is emphasizing the interconnectedness of the process of nature and the continuity between God's decree of creation and redemption, even as he argues that the existence of Christ is a creative divine act.

An important aspect of Schleiermacher's thought to notice here in connection with its promise for constructive forms of theology is that his understanding of Christ's person is congruent with an emphasis on natality. While the claim that Jesus' person is the completion of human nature implicitly acknowledges the weakness of previous forms of human life, it is part of a fundamentally positive evaluation of human nature as a progressively completed life.[70] Schleiermacher's understanding of Christ as the one in whom God dwells, whose personal existence is the result of a creative union of the divine being and human nature, and whose existence completes human nature by infusing into human life a strong and constant sense of creation's dependence on a loving God, could contribute to constructive Christologies that emphasize the goodness of creation and the loving character of the divine-creaturely relationship.

The claim, however, that Christ is the completion of the creation of human nature may ring some alarm bells for feminist theologians in particular, who have

---

63. Ibid., §94.2, p. 578.
64. Ibid., §93.3, p. 570.
65. Ibid., §93.3, p. 569.
66. Ibid., §94.3, p. 580.
67. Ibid., §97.2, p. 594.
68. Ibid., p. 595.
69. Ibid.
70. See, for example, the introduction's discussion of original perfection.

critiqued Christologies that see Christ as an individualistic "hero," or "perfect man," who sweeps into history to save the day. This is a legitimate concern. With regard to Schleiermacher's thought, however, there are at least three things to keep in mind. First, by claiming that Christ was coming to be as a person simultaneously with the world itself, Schleiermacher is emphasizing how Christ's existence was not an interruption to the interconnected process of nature in an interventionist way. Rather, for him, the divine prepared for the existence of Christ from the beginning, and all things were created in relation to him from the outset. This means that for Schleiermacher, Jesus did not swoop in to save the day but was part of a continual process of creation. Second, Schleiermacher is not claiming that Jesus did not make any mistakes, or that he was somehow above the fray of natural human life. Rather, Schleiermacher emphasizes Jesus' strong and constant consciousness of his absolute dependence on God, which allowed him to leave an overall impression on the Christian community that highlights his life-affirming and life-giving ministry. Schleiermacher's account presents Christ as exhibiting wholeness of life through the integration of body, mind, and heart. This is not a "completion of creation" that would disrupt natural life but is the actualization of the potential that all humans have to live into the wholeness of natural life, as seen in Schleiermacher's doctrine of original perfection, to which I return in the final section of this chapter. Third, because Schleiermacher views the Holy Spirit as the Spirit of Christ who lives on in the Christian community, his Christology is pneumatologically and communally oriented. It is therefore coherent with accounts that place the "healing center of Christianity" in Christ's life within the community rather than in the historical Jesus.[71] I will return to this "center" in the third section and in Chapter 3.

The Work of Christ

Schleiermacher's understanding of the redeeming activity of Christ is tightly linked to his understanding of the person of Christ. The way he understands the redemptive activity of Christ could be especially significant for theologians who are interested in developing a doctrine of Christ and atonement that does not valorize suffering or require a bloody sacrifice to atone for sin, as we will see in the next section. For Schleiermacher, Christ's redeeming activity is that of taking persons of faith up into the strength of his God-consciousness.[72] In other words, Christ redeems by imparting to others the same constant and strong awareness of his relationship to God that enables him to embody Love and carry it out in relation to others.

---

71. See Nakashima Brock, *Journeys by Heart: A Christology of Erotic Power* (New York: Crossroad, 1988), p. 52. Schüssler Fiorenza notes Brock's view in this passage as representative of those who center feminist Christology in Christa/community rather than in Jesus as the heroic liberator. See Schüssler Fiorenza, *Jesus*, p. 52.

72. Ibid., §100, p. 621.

As Schleiermacher develops this idea, redemption is "an activity of creating. [It is] ... a creative engendering of the desire-to-take-him-up-into-oneself."[73] In this regard, the being of God in Christ is not different from the being of God in relation to the world prior to Christ. In both cases, the being of God is a creative activity of Love. Redemption occurs by Christ's communication of his consciousness of absolute dependence on God within the collective life of the church,[74] also called a "community of goodwill."[75] Linking Christ's person and work, Schleiermacher writes, "all activity of the Redeemer may also be considered to be a continuation of that person-forming divine influence on human nature."[76] As a result, just as the existence of the person of Christ creates a "new spiritual life" in human nature,[77] so too do Christians' personal self-consciousness and actions also become "something different" in community with Christ.[78] As such, for Schleiermacher, "the entire efficacious action of Christ is simply the continuation of God's creative activity, from which the person of Christ also came into being."[79] People receive salvation by becoming new creatures in the sense that their awareness of their relation to God, previously weak and inconsistent, becomes more powerful and constant. This occurs through community with Christ, which arises when "we are not conscious of our own individual life."[80] Instead, as Christ "gives us the impetus, we find that from which everything proceeds in him also to be the source of our activity—as a joint possession, so to speak."[81]

It is important here to note that although in the introduction to his *Christian Faith* it seems as though Schleiermacher is offering "the feeling of absolute dependence" from general experience, and in fact he does "borrow" material here from fields other than dogmatics in his effort to understand the concept of the Christian church, nonetheless the notion he provides here is of a piece with the reception of redemption in Christ. The integral link between the feeling of absolute dependence and redemption in Christ is gracious creative activity. Schleiermacher writes,

---

73. Ibid., §100.2, p. 623.
74. Ibid., §100.2, p. 623.
75. Ibid., §101.4, p. 636.
76. Ibid., §100.2, p. 624.
77. Ibid., §94.3, p. 579.
78. Ibid., §100.2, p. 624. For a treatment of the coherence and inseparability of Schleiermacher's dogmatics with his Christian ethics, see James Brandt, "Schleiermacher on Church and Christian Ethics," in *Schleiermacher and Sustainability: A Theology for Sustainable Living*, Columbia Series in Reformed Theology, ed. Shelli M. Poe (Louisville, KY: Westminster John Knox, 2018), pp. 7–27.
79. *CF*, §100.2, p. 625.
80. Ibid., §100.1, p. 622.
81. Ibid.

> The Redeemer takes up persons of faith into the strength of his God-consciousness, and this is his redeeming activity. By virtue of the teleological character of Christian piety, not only the arrested state of the higher life but also the furtherance of it ... appears in our self-consciousness as the very act of our own individual lives. However, the same furtherance is conceived as the act of the Redeemer by virtue of the distinctive character of Christianity in that selfsame self-consciousness. In this case, the two are able to combine in no way other than that this furtherance would be the act of the Redeemer become one's own act, and, accordingly, this is the clearest expression for the common element in Christian consciousness of divine grace. Consequently, if we proceed from this point, the distinctive work of the Redeemer would be ... this generating of an act in us. ... It is that activity by virtue of which he takes us up into this community of his activity and life, and the endurance of that activity subsequently constitutes the very nature of the state of grace.[82]

In this and the surrounding passages, Schleiermacher explains that Christians' experience of redemption depends on the existence within them of a strong consciousness of God, that is, a consciousness of their relationship to God as one of absolute dependence. Even though Christians experience this consciousness as their own, it is made possible only by the act of the Redeemer on them. The Redeemer's act is to take Christians up into his own activity, and that is a creative activity. When this is understood, it becomes clear that "the feeling of absolute dependence" is another way of talking about grace, that is, the fact that God gives unilaterally and without repayment or conditions to humanity in creation, redemption, and sanctification. The strength of Christians' feeling of absolute dependence, therefore, is itself dependent upon Christians' reception of redemption in and through Christ.[83]

Schleiermacher takes care to show that his account of Christ's work differs both from individualistic accounts and from those that see Christ simply as a teacher and exemplar. On the one hand, Christ's redemptive work cannot exist in a "magical" way, through the "immediate influence of Christ on individuals."[84] In Schleiermacher's view, if Christ could influence individuals immediately, either before or after his earthly life, then there would be little need for Christ to exist as a human person in the first place.[85] The seeds of Docetism could thereby be sown, which Schleiermacher guards against. In this connection, we note that because Schleiermacher rejects the doctrine of the immanent Trinity, Christ does not exist as the *Logos* prior to the incarnation and does not exist as the *Logos* after his earthly life ends. Jesus the Christ comes into existence with the creative act

---

82. *CF*, §100 (first sentence of the quoted material), and §100.1, pp. 621–2.

83. I return to divine grace in Chapter 4, where it is treated in the context of the relation of God and creation.

84. *CF*, §100.3, p. 627.

85. Ibid., p. 628.

of God that unites the divine being and human nature in his person. Likewise, after Christ dies an earthly death, he cannot have an immediate influence on individuals through some kind of intervention into creaturely life apart from the created order. Only if Jesus' person was not truly, fully human could he directly, immediately influence living people before his birth and after his death. Having rejected the doctrine of the immanent Trinity, then, Schleiermacher likewise does not hold that Christ currently acts immediately on individuals in the world. His ongoing activity is mediated by something natural, namely, the collective life of the church, which has been influenced by Christ and carries on Christ's Spirit. This is the pneumatological frame of Schleiermacher's Christology.

Nonetheless, for Schleiermacher, Christ's work is not simply "empirical," in the form of his teaching and example. If it were, Schleiermacher maintains that one would always be conscious of the guilt for sin that remains in an individual, no matter how well they attempted to follow Christ's example. The forgiveness of sin experienced in Christ's work of reconciliation is, for Schleiermacher, "the disappearance of any consciousness of meriting punishment."[86] It is not that one is to disregard or excuse sin, but simply that one is always aware of divine forgiveness of sin along with sin's existence.[87] As such, Christians with a powerful and strong consciousness of God do not view evil, which is any obstruction to life, as a punishment for their own sin but view everything that befalls them, including suffering and pain, as "solely related to the task of the new life."[88] Schleiermacher argues that forgiveness of sin is not "independent of being taken up into a common life with [Christ]."[89] In order to become conscious of God's forgiving love, one must enter the community of Christ, wherein one encounters and is influenced by Christ's life and ministry. In contrast to substitutionary forms of atonement, forgiveness is not the result of the suffering and death of Christ for humanity's sake. For Schleiermacher, "consciousness of deserving punishment" would not "cease simply because another has borne the punishment."[90] In fact, Schleiermacher himself points out that in his soteriology, "Christ's suffering is not mentioned at all."[91] He does not single out Christ's physical pain and suffering as having value for redemption. What is only secondarily important about Christ's suffering is not his suffering itself but the fact that he did not sin when he met resistance to his work, and he remained compassionate toward those inflicting pain upon him.[92] As Schleiermacher explains,

---

86. *CF*, §101.2, p. 631.
87. Ibid., p. 632.
88. *CF*, §101.2, p. 630. This is the person's "blessedness."
89. *CF*, §101.3, p. 633.
90. Ibid., pp. 633–4.
91. *CF*, §101.4, p. 634.
92. See ibid., p. 635.

> It is patent that his compassion regarding sin, as in a human sense that compassion existed within him and as that compassion was conditioned by what lay before him, had to have arisen to its greatest peak when the two chief classes of sinners were together arrayed against the sinless existence of his person. Just as this compassion in the face of human guilt and culpability was the initial occasion that motivated redemption, inasmuch as a distinct impression precedes every distinct human self-initiated activity, so too the greatest heightening of precisely this compassion was the direct inspiration that lay behind the greatest element in the work of redemption.[93]

Even unto death, then, Christ acted in accordance with Love. Christ's work is to take people up into community with himself, where their awareness of Love grows stronger and more consistent because of the influence of Christ in that community. Mary Streufert summarizes this well when she writes that for Schleiermacher, "Faith means not that we have accepted Christ as teacher and example; rather, it means that Christ lives in us. God's will is love, which becomes ours through Christ. '[N]ow Christ is in us', Schleiermacher writes, 'as the effective power of our life ... [A]nd everything else must relate to that purpose.'"[94] Drawing on Dawn DeVries' work, Streufert explains that Christ dwells in and recreates Christians in part through preaching, which re-presents Christ's person and work to the congregation.[95] "The impression we get from preaching," she explains, "is to be the same as that which the disciples received from Jesus Christ in his lifetime."[96] In that way, it is Christ's own activity through the Spirit in the church that recreates Christians, rather than, as Streufert notes, an individual's "ability or inability to follow Jesus' way of conversion and transformation."[97]

To summarize, Schleiermacher offers a way of understanding Christ as a human person within whom the very being of God dwells. On his account, however, the emphasis is not on intellectual conundrums generated by the combination of two natures in one person but on how Christ is related to the progressive creation of humanity and what sort of actions he undertakes and generates in relation to others. For Schleiermacher, Christ's redeeming activity consists of his influence in drawing people into his community of new life and his beneficial activity toward others. Because of his redeeming work, the members of the community's life are brought into Christ's own life of goodwill and beneficial activity.[98]

---

93. *CF*, §104.4, p. 660.

94. Mary Streufert, "Reclaiming Schleiermacher for Twenty-First Century Atonement Theory: The Human and the Divine in Feminist Christology," *Feminist Theology* 15/1 (2006): 101.

95. See Dawn DeVries, *Jesus Christ in the Preaching of Calvin and Schleiermacher* (Louisville, KY: Westminster John Knox, 1996).

96. Streufert, "Reclaiming Schleiermacher," p. 102.

97. Ibid., p. 116.

98. *CF*, §101.4, p. 637.

It is important to notice that in these moves, Schleiermacher does not place gender at the center of his understanding of Christ. Divine love, which is preached and lived in the Christian community, is not gendered. As Streufert notes,

> Schleiermacher emphasizes to no small degree the necessity of communion with Christ. If Christ is communicated in—incarnate in—the Word, this is without gender. Preaching is the genderless incarnation of Christ. To emphasize the genderless dimension embedded in Schleiermacher's argument, we see that Christ is doubly genderless in his argument about Christ's efficaciousness in the corporate Christian life, the locus of reconciliation, for the community is neither exclusively male nor exclusively female.[99]

Because, for Schleiermacher, redemption occurs by being drawn into the community of Christ through the preaching of Jesus' life and ministry, Christians need not foreground Jesus' maleness but the Love and Wisdom that were displayed in and through his life and work. Further, because the community of Christ consists of members who are diversely gendered and sexed, Love and Wisdom are displayed and carried on in multiply sexed and gendered ways.

Although a full description of Schleiermacher's Christology is outside the limited scope of this chapter, this account should be sufficient to show that Schleiermacher's Christology at least partially overlaps with the Christological ideas and aims of some contemporary theologians who are interested in social justice. Schleiermacher, as well as some prominent feminists and womanists whose thought has been briefly surveyed here, want to either downplay or remove the importance of the two-natures doctrine in exchange for a primary emphasis on the life and ministry of Christ. Likewise, Christ's words and actions, rather than his maleness, are the theologically significant criteria for Christ-likeness. Schleiermacher's understanding of the person and work of Christ could, therefore, be a resource for theologians who wish to maintain these emphases while also providing a description of the ontological makeup of Christ. His Christology foregrounds natality, community, and loving activity in its description of the indwelling of God within the person and redemptive work of Christ.

Womanist Atonement Theories and Schleiermacher's Soteriology

Picking up on the soteriological portions of the previous section, I turn to Delores Williams's argument against substitutionary atonement, highlighting the resonances of her and other womanists' views with Schleiermacher's position. At the most basic level, Schleiermacher's view is significant here because he recognizes that Jesus suffered unjustly and that his suffering was not of primary importance for redemption. Nonetheless, Schleiermacher's account includes flaws

---

99. Streufert, "Reclaiming Schleiermacher," p. 117.

that need to be corrected if it is to be helpful for contemporary constructive forms of theology: he downplays Jesus' Jewishness and does not go far enough in his advocacy for Jewish civil rights. To connect these features of his Christology and its political implications, I draw on Jacquelyn Grant, who argues along with James Cone that Jesus' particularity is key to his universal significance. I demonstrate that Schleiermacher's understanding of Christ's person and work remains compatible with an emphasis on Jesus' Jewish particularity, which highlights the significance of his life and work for oppressed peoples.

Womanist Critiques of Substitutionary Atonement

In her landmark book, *Sisters in the Wilderness*, Delores Williams argues that sacrificial and substitutionary atonement theories are detrimental to the well-being of Black women because they reify the surrogacy roles that Black women have filled since their enslavement in the United States. Drawing on decades of African American culture, Williams focuses on the biblical figure of Hagar, "a female slave of African descent who was forced to be a surrogate mother, reproducing a child by her slave master because the slave master's wife was barren."[100] As Williams describes it, the similarities between Hagar and African American women are many: both have African heritage and were enslaved peoples, large numbers of whom were brutalized and did not have control over their own bodies, were raped, and found themselves without survival resources.[101] At the same time, both Black American women and Hagar have histories of resistance featuring divine encounters along the way.[102] For these reasons, Williams uses the Hagar story as an "analogue for African-American women's historic experience."[103] In so doing, she identifies a "survival/quality-of-life tradition of African-American biblical appropriation."[104]

To lay the groundwork for this survival/quality-of-life tradition, Williams takes account of both coerced and voluntary forms of social-role surrogacy that Black women historically have filled. Coerced surrogacy roles during the antebellum period included taking care of white children's education and protection (e.g., "mammies"), doing "men's work" in fields or construction, governing the slave owner's household, and being treated as the slave owner's sexual object.[105]

---

100. Delores S. Williams, *Sisters in the Wilderness: The Challenge of Womanist God-Talk* (Maryknoll, NY: Orbis, 1993), p. 2.

101. See also Elsa Tamez's rereading of Hagar in "The Woman Who Complicated the History of Salvation," in *New Eyes for Reading: Biblical and Theological Reflections by Women in the Third World*, ed. John S. Pobee, Bärbel von Wartenberg-Potter (Bloomington, IN: Meyer Stone Books, 1986), pp. 5–17. I return to Hagar in Chapter 3.

102. Williams, *Sisters in the Wilderness*, p. 3.

103. Ibid., p. 4.

104. Ibid., p. 6.

105. Ibid., pp. 60–1.

2. Christ and Redemption

Although emancipation allowed Black women to refuse to engage in some of these previously forced surrogacy roles, "poverty and the nature of the work available, especially to southern black families, caused many black women to participate in some of the most strenuous areas of the work force" (e.g., sharecropping, farming, and industry work) and to continue in the role of mammy.[106] These historic social-surrogacy roles, Williams points out, have contributed to the stereotypical images of Black women today—as asexual mother figures, as masculine and physically strong, and/or as promiscuous and sexually passionate.[107]

The soteriological conclusion of Williams's analysis of Black women's surrogacy roles and its analogue in the biblical story of Hagar is a rejection of theories of atonement that emphasize Christ's redemption as a substitutionary work. In these theories, Christ's role, wherein he takes the place of sinful humanity on the cross, might be "coerced surrogacy (willed by the Father) or voluntary surrogacy (chosen by the Son) or both."[108] In any case, "a major theological problem here is the place of the cross in any theology significantly informed by African-American women's experience with surrogacy."[109] Such theologies implicitly encourage Black women to continue in their surrogacy roles, and their suffering is valorized as the means to salvation.

Rather than understanding redemption in the form of substitutionary atonement, Williams argues that Black women's redemption does not depend on surrogacy roles.[110] Instead, "their salvation is assured by Jesus' life of resistance and by the survival strategies he used to help people survive the death of identity caused by their exchange of inherited cultural meanings for a new identity shaped by the gospel ethics and world view."[111] In other words, Black women's redemption comes about in and through Jesus' life and ministry, which includes resistance and survival strategies, and by which he shapes their identity as Christians. For Williams, Jesus did not come to show "God's 'love' manifested in the death of God's innocent child on a cross erected by cruel, imperialistic, patriarchal power" but "to show humans life—to show redemption through a perfect ministerial vision of righting relations between body (individual and community), and mind (of

---

106. Ibid., p. 73. The latter reinforced patriarchal ideas and practices among Black families, which were, in turn, "reinforced by social, legal and economic customs of black men" (ibid., p. 78). As such, Williams writes that "the black woman in the protector role in the black community is not respected and is often critically labeled matriarch" (ibid., p. 80). See also Jacquelyn Grant, who highlights the ways in which "emancipation meant slavery without chains": Black women "were relegated in the labor market to the same service jobs and menial work which had been forced upon them during slavery" (Grant, *White Women's Christ and Black Women's Jesus*, p. 197).
107. Williams, *Sisters in the Wilderness*, p. 70.
108. Ibid., p. 162.
109. Ibid.
110. Ibid., p. 164.
111. Ibid.

humans and of tradition) and spirit."¹¹² The cross, for her, represents the attempt of evil within humanity to kill Jesus' ministerial vision of goodness. As such, she advises womanist theologians to avoid depending on Jesus' alleged surrogacy or substitution as a way to overcome sin and evil.¹¹³ For her, Jesus conquered sin and evil by resisting death and living his life with integrity.¹¹⁴

To understand Williams's soteriology further, it is important to see how it exemplifies a survival/quality-of-life tradition highlighted in the Black community's interpretation of the Bible. Williams illustrates such a tradition through her analysis of the story of Hagar found in Genesis. After Hagar births a child for Abram and Sarai at Sarai's request, Sarai treated Hagar "so badly that she ran away" (Gen. 16:6b). As such, Williams highlights the fact that Hagar is the first woman in the Bible to "liberate herself from oppressive power structures."¹¹⁵ God meets Hagar in the wilderness where she has fled but does not aid her in her journey toward Egypt. Instead, Yahweh tells her to go back to Sarai and submit to her. Critiquing dominant liberation narratives developed in Black theology, Williams is clear here that the "angel of Yahweh is, in this passage, no liberator God."¹¹⁶ Yahweh does, however, want Hagar to survive and have a better quality of life: "God apparently wants Hagar to secure her and her child's well-being by using the resources Abram has to offer."¹¹⁷ Although God is no liberator in this text, Hagar is promised multitudinous descendants, which gives her hope for future freedom.¹¹⁸ By emphasizing survival and quality of life over immediate liberation in this way, Williams focuses on resistance to oppression along with a long-term view of salvation. In this way, the survival/quality-of-life tradition coheres with a soteriology that emphasizes Jesus' life of resistance to sin and evil and his ministry of righting relationships, observed and enacted over a period of years rather than days.

Along with Williams, other womanists have also criticized a substitutionary theory of atonement. In *Disruptive Christian Ethics*, Traci C. West pointedly

---

112. Ibid., pp. 164-5.

113. Ibid., p. 165.

114. Ibid., p. 166. See also M. Shawn Copeland, who offers a womanist theology of suffering that "repels every tendency toward any *ersatz* spiritualization of evil and suffering, of pain and oppression" (M. Shawn Copeland, "Wading through Many Sorrows," in *Womanist Theological Ethics: A Reader*, ed. Katie Geneva Cannon, Emilie M. Townes, and Angela D. Sims [Louisville, KY: Westminster John Knox, 2011], p. 152). She explains, "a theology of suffering in womanist perspective is resistant. With motherwit, courage, sometimes their fists, and most often sass, Black women resisted the degradation of chattel slavery" and "dismantled the images that had been used to control and demean them" (ibid., p. 153).

115. Williams, *Sisters in the Wilderness*, p. 19.

116. Ibid., p. 21.

117. Ibid.

118. Ibid., p. 22.

questions substitutionary atonement theory by linking it to white liturgies of communion. She connects theological theories with practice because "our practices reveal our ethical commitments."[119] West asks,

> What does it mean for whites to repeatedly rehearse this ritual of giving thanks for the fact that Jesus suffered, sacrificed, and died to take away their sins? Does this ritual encourage whites in taking for granted the suffering of others, and maybe even the deaths that benefit them (whites)? To some degree, atonement theology expressed in church rituals like Communion could merge with and inform white people's sense of entitlement. It could teach them that reaping the benefits of forgiveness and absolution ... is due them because of God's intentional sacrifice of a person for their sake. Communion could function as a kind of liturgical reinscribing of the privileges of whiteness, possibly fostering a lack of concern for the systemic ways they may benefit from the sacrifice of the health, safety, and well-being of "alien others."[120]

West is highlighting the ways that substitutionary theories of atonement are not only believed but practiced. By drawing out the ethical implications of the repeated use of substitutionary atonement in the ritual of the Eucharist, she demonstrates how the theory could practically inform white people's sense of entitlement to others' suffering and feed into their apathy regarding the unjust systems from which they benefit.

Karen Baker-Fletcher also emphasizes the redemptive activity present in Jesus' life rather than a substitutionary understanding of his death. She writes that "it is vital for Christians to focus on the life and ministry of Jesus rather than his death because of the tendency to focus on the crucifixion in necrophilic ways."[121] She writes,

> If one reads the Pauline author of 1 Corinthians 1 and 2 further, it is evident that the purpose of preaching "Christ crucified" is not to glorify crucifixion but to reveal human limitations and sinfulness in relation to the power of God to resurrect and overcome evil through the Holy Spirit. The cross is a symbol of our capacity to sin—to abuse others and in the process defile that which is sacred. The resurrection is a symbol of the Spirit's power to re-create.[122]

---

119. Traci C. West, *Disruptive Christian Ethics: When Racism and Women's Lives Matter* (Louisville, KY: Westminster John Knox, 2006), p. 68.

120. Ibid., p. 124.

121. Karen Baker-Fletcher and Garth KASIMU Baker-Fletcher, *My Sister, My Brother: Womanist and Xodus God Talk* (Eugene, OR: Wipf & Stock, 2002; previously published by Orbis, 1997), p. 77.

122. Baker-Fletcher, *My Sister, My Brother*, p. 79.

The cross is not given symbolic power other than to remind humanity of its capacity of sin. It is the symbol of the resurrection that lifts up the ongoing creative power of God.

Somewhat in contrast, A. Elaine Crawford sees Jesus' resistance to sin and evil, in particular, as the important feature of his cross. Like Baker-Fletcher, she argues that the cross is an example and even the culmination of human evil and abuse, and "to deny the violence of the cross is to deny the reality of human violence in Jesus' life and ours." She continues, however, to raise the cross to awareness in the context of persecuted justice-seekers: "Jesus, like so many after him—Martin Luther King Jr, Malcolm X, Fannie Lou Hamer—was persecuted and killed because he risked all to stand for justice."[123] Crawford therefore sees the cross as mandating "a theology of risk."[124] As she writes,

> A theology of risk is the God consciousness and God confidence to risk all to fight against injustice and oppression, even if it means that one may be called upon to give one's life. A theology of risk employs a liberating message of the cross that breaks the cycle of violence in Black women's lives. The message of the cross is not one of resignation to violence or demands for revenge; rather, it is a passion for justice. It is an awareness of the Christ presence in one's life that empowers one to seize one's personal agency to act against, rather than acquiesce to, victimization and oppression.[125]

In this way, Crawford grants limited positive significance to the cross. However, that positive significance remains on the level of Jesus' nonviolent resistance to injustice, rather than attributing to the cross some form of atonement.

Other womanists draw on Black women and men's experience of Jesus "as the divine co-sufferer, who empowers them in situations of oppression."[126] Black women "identified with Jesus because they believed that Jesus identified with them. As Jesus was persecuted and made to suffer undeservedly, so were they."[127] As such, the cross of Jesus serves as a symbol of the suffering of Black people in the United States. "Yet the resurrection," Grant continues, "brings the hope that liberation from oppression is immanent."[128] Like Baker-Fletcher, Grant emphasizes the inseparability of Christ's crucifixion and resurrection in Black women's experience, such that suffering is not valorized but is resisted with the hope of being overcome.[129] This trend is also seen in Douglas's work, who links Jesus' crucifixion

---

123. A. Elaine Crawford, "Womanist Christology and the Wesleyan Tradition," *Black Theology: An International Journal* 2/2 (July 2004): 219.

124. Ibid., p. 210. See also Sharon Welch, *A Feminist Ethic of Risk* (Minneapolis, MN: Fortress, 1990).

125. Crawford, "Womanist Christology and the Wesleyan Tradition," p. 219.

126. Grant, *White Women's Christ and Black Women's Jesus*, p. 212.

127. Ibid.

128. Ibid., p. 216.

129. Ibid., p. 220.

with the resurrection: "His crucifixion indicates God's unwavering solidarity with the crucified peoples of the world, making it unmistakably clear that these lives matter to God. Even more, the crucified Jesus' resurrection reveals that it is only when the sacred dignity of those whose lives are most beset by crucifying violence is restored, that the justice of God can be realized."[130]

Moving even further toward a positive evaluation of Jesus' suffering and death, M. Shawn Copeland offers a womanist theology of suffering, which "repels every tendency toward any *ersatz* spiritualization of evil and suffering, of pain and oppression," but in which Black women make meaning of Jesus' suffering by comparing it to the ways that parents' suffering can contribute to the freedom of their children.[131] "By their very suffering and privation," Copeland writes, "Black women under chattel slavery freed the cross of Christ. Their steadfast commitment honored that cross and the One who died for all and redeemed it from Christianity's vulgar misuse."[132] Copeland recognizes how peoples' lives are intertwined such that one person's unjust suffering can contribute to others' liberation. She therefore does not want to avoid talking about Jesus' suffering. However, she wants to do so within the context of Black women's slavery in order to keep the use of the cross from valorizing suffering for its own sake and to honor the way Black women's suffering has allowed for the liberation of generations. It is important to notice here that Copeland does not interpret Black women's experience in light of Christ's cross but interprets Christ's cross in light of Black women's experience. This is of the utmost significance, because such a procedure does not make Christ's suffering worthy of Christian imitation. Rather, it stands in line with the practice of early Christians to make sense of Jesus' death by reference to their own experiences and frameworks of meaning. Schüssler Fiorenza notes just six of the many different early interpretations of Jesus' death that can be reconstructed from Pauline literature. These include the notions that (1) God's saving activity in the resurrection of Christ shows that Jesus was vindicated; (2) Jesus' death was likened to that of a friend dying for another friend, as in the Greek tradition; (3) what happened on the cross was reconciliation as a repair of the relationship between God and Israel; (4) in the cross, Christ ransomed "a people living under slavery or that of captives of war set free by the death of Christ";[133] (5) the cross fulfilled the promise that God had given Abraham in Gen. 22; and (6) God sent Jesus as a prophet who was rejected and killed.[134] In these and other ways, Schüssler Fiorenza indicates that "by borrowing from various contexts

---

130. Kelly Brown Douglas, "Introduction to 'A Womanist Looks at the Future,'" *Anglican Theological Review* 100/3 (2018): 582.

131. M. Shawn Copeland, "Wading through Many Sorrows," in *Womanist Theological Ethics: A Reader*, ed. Katie Geneva Cannon, Emilie M. Townes, and Angela D. Sims (Louisville, KY: Westminster John Knox, 2011), p. 152.

132. Ibid., p. 153.

133. Schüssler Fiorenza, *Jesus*, p. 115.

134. Ibid., pp. 111–19.

of meaning, early Christian wo/men in many different ways attempted to reflect upon the terrible experience of the crucifixion of their friend."[135] When womanists and others rethink the meaning of Jesus' suffering and death on the cross in light of their own experiences, like early followers of Jesus, they are not altering a fixed theological meaning of atonement but are standing in a long line of theologians and friends of Jesus who are making sense of his death vis-à-vis their own contexts and frameworks. The cross of Christ is not to be valorized, on Copeland's view, but can be given meaning if it is placed in relation to the ways that Black women's suffering contributed to their children's freedom.

As we have seen, womanists are not all of one mind on the Christological and soteriological questions under consideration here.[136] However, trends exist (1) to push Christ's suffering to the background in terms of its soteriological significance, (2) to emphasize the suffering of Christ as a way of identifying him with the "least of these" and/or with those who suffer in order to pave the way for generations to come, and (3) to link the cross to the resurrection, which provides hope and courage for empowerment and resistance. The womanists surveyed here are outlining some basic soteriological moves that would keep the cross of Christ from being interpreted in ways that could undermine the empowerment of those who are currently underprivileged not only with regard to sex and/or gender but also with regard to race and/or class.

Engaging Schleiermacher's Soteriology: Comparison and Evaluation

The Suffering of Christ

As we have seen above, Schleiermacher does not give the cross pride of place in his theory of redemption. In fact, Schleiermacher's initial account of redemption and reconciliation does not mention Christ's suffering on the cross. "The only conclusion to be drawn," he explains, "is that no basis existed to specify Christ's suffering as a primary feature."[137] For Schleiermacher, Christ's suffering is taken into account only secondarily and as it occurred in his whole life, rather than focusing on the point of his death. Schleiermacher holds that "all of Christ's suffering, altogether and viewed as *one*, can be thought of in this interconnection with his redeeming activity."[138] The connection of Christ's suffering with redemption occurs because Christ's "activity did not yield to any resistance, not even to that which was able to effect annihilation of his person."[139] For Schleiermacher, Christ's

---

135. Ibid., p. 119.

136. For a sacramental understanding of sacrifice, see JoAnne Marie Terrell, *Power in the Blood?: The Cross in the African American Experience* (Maryknoll, NY: Orbis, 1998), esp. 121–2. See also Diana L. Hayes, *Were You There? Stations of the Cross*, Art by Charles S. Ndege (Maryknoll, NY: Orbis, 2000).

137. *CF*, §101.4, p. 634.

138. Ibid., p. 636.

139. Ibid., p. 634.

suffering both throughout his life and at the point of death is significant insofar as his activity of Love did not yield to the resistance he encountered. Schleiermacher claims that Christ's "absolutely self-denying love is indeed manifested to us in his suffering unto death—itself evoked by his unfailing perseverance. Moreover, in this love we come to realize in utmost clarity how it was that God was in him reconciling the world to Godself."[140] It is important to notice here that Christ's suffering evokes Love not in and of itself but by Christ's perseverance. God was in Christ reconciling the world to Godself not through vicarious sacrifice to appease the justice, wrath, or honor of God but through Christ's persistence.

Schleiermacher explains the only sense in which he would consider Christ's or other people's suffering as "vicarious":

> The evil that he suffered was vicarious in that general sense in which one in whom human evil is not present is also not supposed to suffer, but if that person does nonetheless receive evil, that same person is thus struck by it in the place of those in whom human evil is present. Yet, in no way does this vicarious suffering make satisfaction.[141]

Schleiermacher could be joined by contemporary theologians in saying that both Jesus and all those on the underside of history—women of color, LGBT persons, Black men, white women, colonized peoples, economically disadvantaged peoples, and so on—have suffered unjustly. They do, indeed, suffer instead of others, and in this sense their suffering is "vicarious" but not redemptive. Indeed, at times their suffering comes about because of their willingness to engage an ethic of risk. The sinful forces of racism, sexism, classism, and heterosexism cause significant harm, but what is soteriologically significant is not the harm that one undergoes but the persistence one maintains in proclaiming and embodying the message of Love for each creature, including oneself. In this way, Schleiermacher's soteriology could be used in concert with those of contemporary theologians to claim that suffering is not redemptive in itself or reflective of Jesus' redemptive work.

Schleiermacher goes further in his renunciation of a substitutionary form of atonement when he claims that any notion of Christ "fulfilling the divine will in our place" is mistaken.[142] He claims that it would be against the Christian disposition to wish that Christians themselves would be excused from fulfilling God's will in any case, "since Christ's supreme accomplishment does indeed consist in his animating us in such a way that an ever-increasing satisfaction of the divine will would also proceed from us."[143] Genuine Christian faith does not want to be relieved of having to do God's will but wants to fulfill it ever more completely. In this way, Schleiermacher not only denies the surrogacy of Christ in his death

---

140. *CF*, §104.4, p. 661.
141. Ibid., p. 665.
142. *CF*, §104.3, p. 658.
143. Ibid.

and suffering but also denies that Christians may simply rely on what Jesus did in his life and ministry in a way that mitigates the need for Christians to carry on his life and ministry. Christians ought to make continued efforts toward establishing a just world.

Granted these substantial resonances with womanist positions, however, Schleiermacher's thought would have trouble with theologies that emphasize the co-suffering of God in Christ. First, such talk would be unduly anthropomorphic, for Schleiermacher. Speaking of the suffering of God would impute to the divine emotions that can only be meaningful when taken in conjunction with the human experience of the body. For instance, we know sorrow as a bodily feeling that may begin as a lump in the throat or a knot in the stomach, progress with the entire body becoming warm, and culminate in tears or sighs or deep breaths along with bodily heaviness. Our understanding of suffering is so closely intertwined with the human body that Schleiermacher thinks it would be inappropriate to attribute the same kind of feeling or process to God. Second, without the doctrine of the immanent Trinity to link the being of God in Christ to the being of God *in se*, there does not seem to be a compelling reason for Schleiermacher to conclude that God experiences human emotions or bodily experiences in some ontologically constituting way through the suffering of Christ that would be different than the way God knows the suffering of other creatures. Schleiermacher and theologians who wish to safeguard the divine from undue anthropomorphism could maintain that God cares for and loves creation, and divine activity aims to alleviate creaturely suffering and oppression through redemption. To take a further step, however, by attributing co-suffering to God, would be to humanize God inappropriately, from Schleiermacher's perspective.

In addition, Schleiermacher does not spend much time detailing Christ's suffering, for the reasons we have already surveyed. Streufert notes that Schleiermacher "distances himself and his grasp of Jesus from struggle, suffering, and body."[144] She argues,

> From a feminist perspective, this is highly problematic. Feminist valuation of the body and theological revaluation of struggle and suffering from the perspective of the oppressed helps to call Schleiermacher's theory of redemption back to incarnational thinking, bringing together body and spirit.[145]

Although Schleiermacher does not conceive of the Redeemer in terms of suffering, his theology is compatible with a further drawing out of the ways in which Jesus' historical subject position, in conjunction with his teachings about "the least of these," identifies him with the oppressed. Schleiermacher believes that Christ would not have thought of himself as lowly: "How can that person, who spoke of his relationship to God the Father in such a way that even his sitting at the

---

144. Streufert, "Reclaiming Schleiermacher," p. 110.
145. Ibid.

Father's right hand could not be regarded as an exaltation, have been conscious of a lowliness of his condition?"[146] Nonetheless, theologians who are interested in Schleiermacher's thought could draw out Jesus' identity with the oppressed as a statement about his position in his historical context. Jesus was the son of a Jewish woman and the stepson of a carpenter from Nazareth in Roman-occupied territory.[147] Furthermore, he was unjustly killed by Roman occupying powers in a gruesome manner. Jesus along with the poor, those who mourn, and the hungry and thirsty would not need to think of themselves as "lowly" in order to recognize their positionality in relation to social structures of their time. Rather, they may—with a strong and powerful consciousness of Love—resist the forces of human sinfulness that would seek to kill, enslave, or silence them. Their suffering, partially incurred because of the risks they are willing to take in the pursuit of justice and peace, is not valorized or made redemptive in any way. Rather, the pursuit of justice is lifted up as worthy of praise and imitation. The suffering of the oppressed thus stands as a testimony only to the power of oppressed people's personal and communal self-consciousness, which can include consciousness of their relation to God and which does not yield its integrity or debase itself in the face of unjust violence. By lifting up Jesus' positionality in this way, constructive forms of theology could build on scriptural references like Mt. 25:31–40:

> Then the righteous will answer him, "Lord, when was it that we saw you hungry and gave you food, or thirsty and gave you something to drink? And when was it that we saw you a stranger and welcomed you, or naked and gave you clothing? And when was it that we saw you sick or in prison and visited you?" And the king will answer them, "Truly I tell you, just as you did it to one of the least of these who are members of my family, you did it to me."

By drawing out the ways in which Christ is identified with "the least of these" and experienced suffering as they do, Schleiermacher's theology could be brought into line with contemporary insights about the power and significance of Christian compassion and resistance.[148]

---

146. *CF*, Postscript to §§92–105, p. 680.

147. Cf. Jn 1:46: "Nathanael said to him, 'Can anything good come out of Nazareth?' Philip said to him, 'Come and see.'"

148. See Pamela Ayo Yetunde, "Black Lesbians to the Rescue! A Brief Correction with Implications for Womanist Christian Theology and Womanist Buddhology," *Religions* 8/175 (2017): 10. She argues that the four-part concept of womanism set forth by Alice Walker and utilized by many Christian womanists needs to be contextualized by Walker's 1979 *Coming Apart*. Here, womanism is defined as

> the willingness on the part of women of all sexualities, to seek out wisdom from African American lesbians on how to create safe spaces for themselves, in the midst of threats to their emotional, mental, physical, and spiritual health, and take the risk of sharing that wisdom with their oppressor(s) in

Monica Coleman also importantly notes how reflection on Jesus' sacrifice, in tandem with reflections on Black women as working mothers, could help to "elevate the aspects of Jesus' life that involve self-care as critical to our understanding of soteriology."[149] She continues,

> Can we see fellowship with his friends as more than ministry to others, but perhaps, as food for his own soul, a way that his friends ministered to him? Can we see Jesus' times of solitude and prayer as the needed counterbalance to the public sacrificial aspects of his life? Are these activities more than lessons about prayer and ministry, but actually constitutive of what it means to be saved?[150]

Coleman's suggestion here would tip the scales to create more balance within Christian traditions where Jesus' suffering is emphasized. If it is important to recognize Jesus' suffering as a way of signifying that God is on the side of the oppressed and that systemic sin can be overcome, then it should be important also to recognize the ways Christ took care of himself throughout his life and ministry. By coupling Jesus' self-care with his self-sacrifice, the resulting theology may be less likely to valorize the sacrifice and suffering that underprivileged people endure.

The Particularity of Christ

Another area of Schleiermacher's Christology that needs attention and constructive rethinking is his emphasis on Christ's universality rather than Jesus' particularities. Schleiermacher tends to downplay the particularities of Christ in order to ensure that he has significance for all people. Before critiquing Schleiermacher's work, however, it is important to notice the limited ways in which he upholds Christ's particularity along with his emphasis on the capacity for God-consciousness that Christ shares with humanity as a whole.

As we have seen, for Schleiermacher, what is most important about Christ is "the strength of God-consciousness for giving impetus to all the elements of life and for determining them all."[151] He insists that Christ's God-consciousness develops in the same way as that of others:

> A way that does not harm the oppressor(s), with the intention to help the oppressor(s) awaken from ignorance and violence, and to be advocates for African American lesbians in the African American community. (4)

Without interpreting *Coming Apart* through a Black lesbian Buddhist lens, Yetunde asks "how would one know that the commitment to survival and wholeness also means practicing compassion for our oppressors?" (7). This focus on both compassion and resistance is also found in Schleiermacher's text.

149. Monica A. Coleman, "Sacrifice, Surrogacy, and Salvation," *Black Theology: An International Journal* 12/3 (2014): 210.
150. Ibid.
151. *CF*, §93.2, p. 566.

This God-consciousness would first have had to develop in him too, however, as in everyone, gradually in a human fashion up to the consciousness that was actually appearing in him. Earlier it would have existed only as a seed, though in a certain sense always as a force of some efficacy. Hence, also during this time of development, ever since it would have become a matter of consciousness, it also can have itself exerted its authority over sensory self-consciousness, but only to the degree that various functions of sensory self-consciousness would already have arisen.[152]

The idea here is that Christ's consciousness of God is like the capacity of other human beings, except that his God-consciousness grows at the same rate as his other human capacities, keeping pace with them. Like other human beings during the process of biological and psychological development, Schleiermacher recognizes that Christ was also influenced by his context:

He could have developed only in a certain affinity with his surroundings, thus in the general culture of his people. That is to say, first, his sensibility and intellect would have been nourished only based on this world surrounding him. Second, even his free, self-initiated activity would have had its distinct locus only in that specific world. Third, thus his God-consciousness would have been able, as at first the higher power of his sensibility and intellect would nevertheless also have been, to express and communicate itself only in notions that it had appropriated for itself from this domain, also in actions that were predetermined in this same domain [in] accordance with the possibility contained in those notions.[153]

In this passage, Schleiermacher recognizes that Jesus was Jewish, learned in his particular Jewish context, and expressed himself and acted within the horizons of his first-century world. Nevertheless, Schleiermacher does not extend the "prototypical" (*Urbild*) or "ideal" in Christ beyond the strength of his God-consciousness, which kept pace with his other human capacities and developed in his own specifically Jewish context. Schleiermacher imposes this limit in order to rule out Christ having to be "all knowing" or as having "all art and skill that develop in human society."[154] As we have already seen, Jesus was fully human and could not have been a prototypical human in all respects. As Ruth Jackson Ravenscroft writes, the "universalizing tendency in Schleiermacher does not in itself amount to a hegemonizing move, capable of collapsing difference. It is the condition of being bounded and limited, to be subject to change and decay, to be the recipient of one's existence rather than the author of it."[155] In these ways, "it

---

152. Ibid., §93.3, pp. 569–70.
153. Ibid., pp. 570–1.
154. *CF*, §93.2, p. 566.
155. Ruth Jackson Ravenscroft, *The Veiled God: Friedrich Schleiermacher's Theology of Finitude* (Leiden: Brill, 2019), p. 27.

was human dependence and our awareness of it that he established as the font and focus of the religious life."¹⁵⁶ Emphasizing Christ's capacity for God-consciousness as a shared aspect of human nature that developed "in the general culture of his people" makes Christ universally relevant, Schleiermacher thinks.

It also simultaneously allows Schleiermacher to consider many aspects of Jesus' life soteriologically irrelevant. Limiting Jesus' ideality to his God-consciousness means, for Schleiermacher, that Christians need not first become Jewish, religiously or culturally, in order to become Christian. Schleiermacher maintains that Jesus' Jewish characteristics "would in no way be the typus for his self-initiated activity but are only the typus for his receptivity to the self-initiated activity of spirit."¹⁵⁷ In Jesus, the characteristics of the Jewish people unite with a "most open and unclouded disposition toward everything else that is human and also with his recognition of the identity of nature and of spirit in all human forms."¹⁵⁸ In these ways, Schleiermacher recognizes Jesus' limited particularity, without making first-century Judaism (or maleness, for that matter) a prerequisite for Christian life.

Schleiermacher and Judaism

Even though Schleiermacher makes the basic acknowledgment that Jesus was Jewish, he generally tends to downplay the importance of Jesus' Jewishness for Christians. He rebuffs the idea that Christian faith requires assent to the claim that Jesus was the long-awaited Jewish Messiah and also has a negative attitude toward the Judaism of his day. In the following, I contextualize Schleiermacher's position, but in no way do I mean here to excuse him. It is important to recognize why Schleiermacher held the views he did, at the same time as it is crucial to renounce them and provide alternative positions.

In his *On Religion* (1799), Schleiermacher went so far as to call Judaism a "dead religion,"¹⁵⁹ and the 1830/1 edition of his *Christian Faith* does not offer a corrective to this view. To understand this perspective within Schleiermacher's context, we turn to his *Letters on the Occasion of the Political-Theological Task and the Open Letter of Jewish Householders* (1799).¹⁶⁰ At the time of its writing, Prussia was home to Ashkenazi Jews who were hopeful that they would be granted full civil rights sometime in the not too distant future, given that French Jews had been granted equality in 1791 and Friedrich Wilhelm III (1797–1840) had just come to power following the religious repression of Friedrich Wilhelm II (1786–97). In Berlin, most Jewish houses or salons were part of the Haskalah movement. As Richard Crouter describes those involved in that movement, "They wished to shake off the rigid religious tradition and ensure the possibility of cultural and

---

156. Ibid.
157. *CF*, §93.4, p. 573.
158. Ibid.
159. *OR*, pp. 113–14.
160. See also Vial, *Modern Religion Modern Race*, pp. 210–20.

political life for themselves and their children."¹⁶¹ Schleiermacher frequently visited the salon of Henriette Herz, who was a close lifelong friend with whom he openly communicated about Judaism and Christianity. In fact, he writes the *Letters* because of a promise he made to her to address the situation of Jewish emancipation. In this context, Crouter explains, "Schleiermacher's remark about Judaism being dead reflects a belief held by his acculturated Jewish friends—that Halakhic (or observant) Jewish practice and its accompanying ceremonial law were relics of antiquity and impossible to reconcile with modernity."¹⁶² Of course, it is one thing to criticize one's own religion and quite another to criticize someone else's religion. And yet, in light of the close relationship Schleiermacher shared with Herz and the prominence of the Haskalah movement in Berlin's Jewish salons, this context might allow Schleiermacher's readers to better understand his negative comments about the Judaism of his day.

It is in this context that David Friedländer (1750–1834), who was part of the Jewish elite and director of the Jewish Free School in Berlin after Moses Mendelssohn's death, wrote an *Open Letter* in 1799 to Wilhelm Abraham Teller, head of the Protestant Church in Berlin. Friedländer wrote the letter in order to argue for providing Jewish emancipation within Prussia through conversion to Protestantism. Schleiermacher's response to the anonymous *Political-Theological Task* and the *Open Letter* written by Friedländer came in six letters, which were also published anonymously by a fictional recipient of the letters.

Schleiermacher's basic position is that Jewish people should be able to become Prussian citizens without converting to Christianity. In the first letter, he writes that "reason demands that all should be citizens, but it does not require that all must be Christians, and thus it must be possible in many ways to be a citizen and a non-Christian."¹⁶³ His second letter protests against Friedländer's suggestion that Jews could convert to Christianity without assenting to the Christian doctrine that Jesus is the Son of God. "My God," Schleiermacher asks, "does the man know nothing about the ancient and modern history of Christianity and the weight which one has conferred ... on this dogma, and the opinions held about it for quite some time?"¹⁶⁴ He argues that Jews could not, without being hypocrites, interpret the phrase "Son of God" otherwise than Christians take it, in order to get around the doctrine. The third letter argues that if "educated and well-to-do persons, well versed in worldly matters" want to become citizens and would be required to do so by converting to Christianity, the Christian church would be harmed because it would see an influx of people who are motivated by their political gain and not by an interest in Christianity for its own sake.¹⁶⁵ More than

---

161. Richard Crouter, "Introduction," in *A Debate on Jewish Emancipation and Christian Theology in Old Berlin* (Indianapolis, IN: Hackett, 2004), p. 10.
162. Ibid.
163. *Letters*, p. 85.
164. Ibid., p. 93.
165. Ibid., p. 96.

that, Schleiermacher suggests that it is impossible for anyone who is truly engaged in a particular religion to give it up entirely and convert to another religion.[166] He therefore implores the church's official spokespersons to declare that "it would in no way consider itself wounded if in this matter the state, without showing the slightest consideration for religion, were to hit upon an arrangement that agrees with its insights and intentions."[167]

In the fourth letter, Schleiermacher makes it clear that he does not share the contemporary, widely held belief that Jews are morally corrupt. He reminds readers that his closest friends are Jewish and that he also wished in his third letter that most Christians would be thrust out of the church as well as any insincere converts to the religion. He then offers two requirements for Jewish Prussian citizenship: first, that Jewish people who wish to become citizens should subordinate ceremonial laws to state laws, and that they "officially and publicly renounce the hope for a messiah."[168] He calls for the establishment of a proto-Reform Judaism which would be composed of those who put into practice the requirements he offered.[169] Schleiermacher puts these requirements forward because he thinks it would be within the Prussian state's purview to deny full civil rights to those whose ultimate political allegiance would be to a Jewish nation rather than to the nation in which they reside. As Julie Klassen summarizes Schleiermacher's view, this "emphasis on Jews as an entity (a 'nation') with ultimate loyalties to a purported fatherland beyond the state only undermines the formation of civil loyalties and protracts their status as interim residents not eligible for citizenship, thereby making them eternal foreigners."[170] However, the state could recognize a proto-Reform Jewish sect and give to its members full civil rights. In the sixth and final letter, Schleiermacher makes some concluding statements. Crouter writes that reading between the lines of this letter, Schleiermacher is indicating to his readers that he "is more respectful of Jewish aspirations than were the majority of voices among Berlin clergy."[171]

Overall, Schleiermacher's point in the *Letters* is a positive one: that Jewish people should be given full citizenship in Prussia without requiring conversion to Christianity. However, he clearly does not go far enough when he calls for Jewish civil rights, since he would make Jewish citizenship dependent on membership within a new form of Judaism. In addition, in this and other texts including his *Christian Faith*, he interprets Judaism as a legalistic religion and gives Hebrew scriptures deuterocanonical status within Christianity.[172] In his own time and

166. Ibid., p. 97.
167. Ibid., p. 100.
168. Ibid., p. 103.
169. Ibid., p. 105, editorial footnote 49.
170. Julie Klassen, "A Postscript: Contemporary Parallels and Permutations," in *A Debate on Jewish Emancipation and Christian Theology in Old Berlin* (Indianapolis, IN: Hackett, 2004), p. 146.
171. Crouter, "Introduction," p. 24.
172. For my treatment, see *Essential Trinitarianism*, pp. 65–7.

place, however, it is still remarkable that, as Crouter and Klassen note, "he grasps the social-political situation of his Jewish contemporary with such empathy despite this aversion" to Orthodox Judaism and "Judaizing" tendencies within Christianity.[173] Joseph W. Pickle argues that "Schleiermacher's appreciative assessment of Judaism recognizes the uniqueness of Judaism and rejects attempts to treat it or the Old Testament as a *preparatio evangelii*. His critique of Judaism is best understood in the context of contemporary 'enlightened' Jewish criticism of the historical development of Judaism."[174] The result is a "coherent, but complex, attempt to deal with the Judaism of his day in a positive theological manner."[175]

Jesus and Messianic Faith
With this understanding of Schleiermacher's context in mind, we return to the account in his *Christian Faith* of Jesus' Jewishness as it relates to his birth and culture, and to his rejection of the claim that Christians must hold that Jesus was the Messiah for whom the Jewish people had been holding out hope. Schleiermacher writes that there are two ways of understanding the emergence of human life: "[1] as an event within the small circle of parentage and sociability, which it immediately inherits, and [2] as a fact of human nature in general."[176] For Schleiermacher, the beginning of Jesus' life is defined by the fact of human nature in general, rather than by his parents and society.[177] This claim might seem to deny what Schleiermacher has said above, regarding the influence of Jewish culture and life upon Jesus. However, in this passage, he is maintaining that Christ's unique existence was the result of "a new implanting of God-consciousness" within him.[178] In other words, the person of Christ is the result of the union of human nature and divine activity. Here, Schleiermacher especially wants to claim that in this union, Christ is "raised above every detrimental influence of his closest circle."[179] He is theologically motivated to do so by his concern to ensure that Christ's life is determined at every stage by his strong and constant God-consciousness rather than by any other factor.

Schleiermacher also wants to avoid requiring that Christians assent to the idea that Jesus is the Messiah based on the fulfillment of biblical prophecy. He does so, first, because he does not think that everyone would be capable of "a critical and scientific use of intellect," which would be required "to demonstrate the divine authority of Scripture purely on the grounds of reason."[180] The result would be

---

173. *Letters*, p. 98, editorial footnote 39.
174. Joseph W. Pickle, "Schleiermacher on Judaism," *The Journal of Religion* 60/2 (April 1980): 115.
175. Ibid., p. 116.
176. *CF*, §94.3, p. 578.
177. Ibid., p. 579.
178. Ibid.
179. Ibid.
180. *CF*, §128.1, p. 834.

an intellectual hierarchy within the church that "does not at all comport with the sense of equality among Christians that the Evangelical [i.e., Protestant] church declares."[181] Second, he rejects biblical argumentation as grounds for Christian faith. If biblical arguments could ground Christian faith, then "faith could exist even in persons who have no consciousness of a need for redemption at all, thus could also exist independently of repentance and change of mind, and thus … this faith would not actually be the true and vital faith."[182] We recall that for Schleiermacher, Christian piety is not a piece of knowledge or argumentation but a *Gefühl*, an immediate awareness of one's relationship to God as that of absolute dependence, which one receives through redemption in and through Christ. To support this view of Christian piety, Schleiermacher interprets the apostles' understanding of Jesus in a way that strains credulity. He writes, "although already at the outset of their relationship with Jesus, the apostles designated him as the one predicted by the prophets, this can in no way be understood as if they would have been brought to faith by studying these prophecies and comparing their content with what they saw in Jesus and heard from him."[183] The apostles, he explains, had faith because of "the immediate impression [of Christ] in their minds and hearts."[184] Their belief that Christ was the fulfillment of messianic prophecy was "simply an affirmation regarding this faith aroused by John the Baptist, itself tied to their faith in the prophets."[185] The prophets are cited, then, as confirmation of the impression of Christ that the apostles received from his ministry. Schleiermacher is mitigating Jesus' Jewish context here, in terms of apostolic claims that he is the Messiah, because he does not want Christian piety to be based on biblical arguments that are far removed from most Christians' expertise and even competency. As such, he creates an artificial separation between the apostles' messianic hopes and their faith in Christ as a result of the immediate impression he had on them. In reality, these two are not likely to have been neatly separated in the apostles' minds and hearts. Yet Schleiermacher wants to maintain such a distinction in order to safeguard Christian piety from depending on arguments regarding scriptural prophecy and its fulfillment in Jesus.

It is important to see, however, that in these arguments Schleiermacher is maintaining that Christianity and Judaism are two different religions rather than understanding Christianity as a Jewish reform movement. This is important because of the ways that talk of "renewal" or "reform" within the Judaism of Jesus' day has been used in anti-Jewish ways. Christians have a history of describing Judaism as in need of renewal, and that Jesus was offering a better form of Judaism than what was being preached and practiced during his time. This view easily leads to supersessionism, the claim that the religion of the followers of Jesus should

---

181. Ibid.
182. Ibid., pp. 834–5.
183. *CF*, §128.2, p. 835.
184. Ibid.
185. Ibid.

replace Judaism. As Schüssler Fiorenza notes, "Only if we explicitly acknowledge that Judaism and Christianity are two different religions, which have their roots in the Hebrew Bible and in the pluriform religious matrix of first-century Israel, can we avoid reading 'renewal movement' in a supersessionist fashion."[186] Though Schleiermacher was not consciously attempting to avoid supersessionism here and in fact maintains supersessionism in other passages, his view of the nature of Christian piety as a *Gefühl* that does not depend on biblical Messianic prophecy and fulfillment might actually help contemporary theologians to avoid supersessionism.

Even though Schleiermacher's motives may have been to ensure that there would be no intellectual hierarchy within the Protestant church, his downplaying of Jesus' Jewishness, his negative attitude toward the Judaism of his day, and his claim that Jesus' importance is separate from Jewish hopes for a Messiah are disconcerting, to say the least, to post-Second World War readers.

Correcting Schleiermacher on Jewish Particularity
Schleiermacher's motivations and claims about Jesus' Jewish particularity can be corrected in part by the work of Jacquelyn Grant, who agrees with James Cone that it is in and through Christ's particularity that he is universally significant. For Cone, Jesus' Christological or Messianic title "points to God's universal will to liberate particular oppressed people from inhumanity."[187] Likewise, Grant emphasizes Jesus' Jewishness in order to link him with those today who are oppressed, as the Jewish community was oppressed under Roman rule in the first century. Although Grant is clearly taking a different approach to Jesus' Jewishness and messianic title than Schleiermacher, it is important to notice that Schleiermacher and Grant's reasons for taking opposite approaches are not incompatible. One could uphold and even emphasize the particularity of Christ as a Jewish person and attribute to him a messianic title at the same time as one affirms his universal significance, without requiring that Christian faith be based on biblical argumentation regarding Jesus' fulfillment of messianic prophecy. Cone does this, as we have just seen, by interpreting the significance of the messianic title as referring to God's will to liberate oppressed people from inhumanity. Having drawn out the important aspect of Jesus' messianic title, Jesus' fulfillment of messianic hope is uncoupled from detailed scriptural argumentation regarding whether Jesus was the one Jewish people were waiting for or whether he might simply be the one in and through whom Jesus' followers find liberation.

To correct Schleiermacher's course, contemporary theologians can begin with an affirmation of Jesus' particularity as a Jewish person. Following Cone and Grant, we can highlight the fact that particularity does not oppose universality but supports it. Grant explains,

---

186. Schüssler Fiorenza, *Jesus*, p. 91.
187. James Cone, *God of the Oppressed* (New York: Seabury Press, 1975), p. 134. Grant cites this passage in her *White Women's Christ and Black Women's Jesus*, p. 216.

> In each of the three dynamics of oppression, Black women share in the reality of a broader community. They share race suffering with Black men; with White women and other Third World women, they are victims of sexism; and with poor Blacks and Whites, and other Third World peoples, especially women, they are disproportionately poor. To speak of Black women's tridimensional reality, therefore, is not to speak of Black women exclusively, for there is an implied universality which connects them with others.[188]

By using particularity to connect with others, Grant shows how the particular does not need to be mitigated in order to emphasize universality. The opposite is actually the case. If one focuses on the particular, one might see more clearly how one particularity connects to others. Cone illustrates this way of thinking when he claims that Jesus "*is* black because he *was* a Jew."[189] With Grant and Cone, then, one could say that Jesus' particularity as a Jew is what links him to the oppressed in all the world, no matter their ethnicity, gender, sex, sexual orientation, skin color, class, or religion. Further, Schleiermacher's focus on God-consciousness as that which is most theologically significant for his person and work is logically compatible with recognizing and even emphasizing Jesus' particularities in the service of demonstrating the significance of Christ's life and work for the oppressed.

I also find Susannah Heschel's playful understanding of the "transvestite Jesus" helpful here. Heschel attends to the history of Christian and Jewish scholarship about Jesus, noting that "modern Jewish and Christian scholars have struggled over Jesus as a figure on the boundary of the two religions, the Jew who was the first and greatest Christian, a Christian who actually lived and taught Judaism."[190] The figure of Jesus calls into question the self-understandings of both Christianity and Judaism. Drawing on Judith Butler's understanding of gender as performative, Heschel argues that "the idea of the transvestite offers a useful figure on which to position an argument," here regarding the boundary between Judaism and Christianity.[191] Figuratively speaking, "Jewish theologians dress him up as a rabbi; Christian scholars, even as they recognize his Jewishness, dress him as Christian."[192] Because Jesus is dressed up variously, situated as he is at the boundary of Judaism and Christianity, he becomes "that which signifies the undecidability of signification."[193] In this way, Jesus "queers" dominant ways of thinking about the boundary between these two traditions.[194] In keeping with Heschel's analysis,

---

188. Grant, *White Women's Christ and Black Women's Jesus*, p. 216.

189. James Cone, *God of the Oppressed*, rev. ed. (Maryknoll, NY: Orbis, 1997), p. 123.

190. Susannah Heschel, "Jesus as Theological Transvestite," in *Judaism Since Gender*, ed. Miriam Peskowitz and Laura Levitt (New York: Routledge, 1997), pp. 189-90.

191. Ibid., p. 191.

192. Ibid., p. 192.

193. Ibid., p. 194.

194. See also Robert E. Goss, *Queering Christ: Beyond Jesus Acted Up* (Cleveland: Pilgrim Press, 2002).

Jesus' queerness might be affirmed in order to remain conscious of the ways that descriptions of Jesus' identity are used within sociocultural and political systems of power. Jesus' queerness could also highlight the uncertainty that remains beyond futile attempts to uncover the historical Jesus and how best to represent him.[195] Nonetheless, it is important for theologians working constructively to be clear about their own interpretation and extension of Christ's message as condemning imperialism, xenophobia, anti-semitism, colonialism, and so forth. While Jesus' queerness vis-à-vis Judaism and Christianity might chasten historical efforts to pin down Jesus' identity as a religious figure, there need not be similar uncertainty about Jesus' message of divine love and its application with regard to the eradication of oppressive systems, policies, and actions.

Teleology and Theological Limits
Despite the ways Schleiermacher's theory of redemption might resonate with many contemporary constructive theologies, legitimate concerns may and should remain about the teleological character of his doctrine of God and creation. While many might agree that identifying a *telos* is important for efforts toward making the world more just, postcolonial thinkers, for instance, have also noted the way that teleology has been at work in colonial mindsets and actions. As I noted in the introductory chapter of this book, Theodore Vial has recently argued in *Modern Religion, Modern Race* that the teleological nature of Schleiermacher's work was itself bound up with a colonialism that saw religious others as needing to be brought up to the standard of Christianity.[196] Catherine Keller also notes that a linear understanding of time, which is typical of teleological accounts, is linked with racism.[197] Partly for this reason, Ivone Gebara even goes so far as to say that Christians should avoid saying "God's will," or the "divine plan," and should instead emphasize nonlinearity and the notion that God simply is.[198]

There can be no doubt that Schleiermacher understands Christianity as a teleological form of religion. In paragraph eleven of *Christian Faith*, he states, "Christianity is a monotheistic mode of faith belonging to the teleological bent of religion. It is distinguished essentially from other such modes of faith in that within Christianity everything is referred to the redemption accomplished through Jesus of Nazareth."[199] Even though Schleiermacher gives such a description, he notes the difficulty in offering a general description of Christianity, one that is neither

---

195. For an analysis of New Testament scholarship in nineteenth-century Germany, which suppresses Jesus' Jewishness, see Susannah Heschel, "The Image of Judaism in 19th Century Christian New Testament Scholarship in Germany," in *Jewish-Christian Encounter over the Centuries: Symbiosis, Prejudice, Holocaust, Dialogue*, ed. Marvin Perry and Frederick M. Schweitzer (New York: Peter Lang, 1994), pp. 215–40.

196. Vial, *Modern Religion, Modern Race*.

197. Keller, *Face of the Deep*, p. 23.

198. Ivone Gebara, *Longing for Running Water: Ecofeminism and Liberation*, trans. David Molineaux (Minneapolis, MN: Fortress, 1999), pp. 55–6, 117.

199. *CF*, §11, p. 79.

biased toward the perspective of the author nor attempts to account for all forms of religious life that are claimed to be Christian by any particular individual. The former is difficult to avoid, and the latter "confronts the danger of reaching a result far more meager and colorless in its contents" than would be beneficial for the study of the Christian religion.[200] Schleiermacher settles on the description of Christianity given in paragraph eleven because he thinks that "all Christians refer the community to which they belong back to Christ" and "the expression 'redemption' is also of a kind with which all Christians confess their faith ... in such a way that there is also something held in common that all have in mind, though each more closely defines it in a somewhat different manner."[201] In this paragraph, "redemption" is meant only to indicate "a crossing over from a wretched state ... into a better state," which involves "help rendered by another."[202]

In this context, Schleiermacher identifies "the teleological bent of piety" as implying that to whatever degree the "wretched state" might exist, even at its most extreme levels, redemption is still possible and is, in fact, the purpose or end of Christian life.[203] What is distinctive about Christianity, for Schleiermacher, is the essential significance of redemption to the religion and the fact that "redemption is posited as something generally and completely accomplished through Jesus of Nazareth."[204] Both factors must be involved, in his estimation, for a person to be considered Christian. He explains, "reference to redemption exists in every Christian religious consciousness only because the one who originated the Christian community is the Redeemer; and Jesus is the founder of a religious community only as those who are members of that community are becoming conscious of redemption through him."[205]

Schleiermacher makes these claims "only for Christians" and "strictly as a preliminary introduction," so that in the dogmatic material that follows the introduction, the reader might differentiate the Christian religious consciousness from the non-Christian religious consciousness and evaluate the reliability of expressions of the Christian religious consciousness.[206] Schleiermacher also renounces efforts at proving the truth or necessity of Christianity, since he holds that any Christian already has assurance of her piety.[207] For Schleiermacher, then, the teleological character of Christianity has to do primarily with an intrafaith movement from a worse state to a better state and does not hinge on an argument regarding the truth of Christianity over and above the rest of the world's religions.[208]

---

200. Ibid., §11.1, p. 81.
201. Ibid., §11.2, pp. 81–2.
202. *CF*, §11.2, p. 82.
203. Ibid., pp. 82–3.
204. Ibid., p. 84.
205. *CF*, §11.3, p. 85.
206. Ibid., §11.5, p. 89.
207. Ibid.
208. Schleiermacher states,

2. Christ and Redemption

However, Schleiermacher also makes the secondary claim that every Christian holds "the conviction of Christianity's exclusive excellence."[209] This does not imply, for him, that every other religion is entirely false whereas Christianity is entirely true. For him, "error never occurs anywhere in and of itself but always exists only in relation to what is true, and that error will never have been completely understood until one has found its connection with truth and with whatever that is true to which the error is affixed."[210] Even though Schleiermacher recognizes that other religions adhere to some truth, then, he nonetheless offers a categorization system for non-Christian and Christian forms of religious consciousness that affirms Christianity's more developed state in comparison to the rest. He states that "the various distinctly circumscribed religious communities that have gained some prominence in history are related to each other, in part, as different stages of development and, in part, as different kinds."[211] Schleiermacher first considers the different stages between, for example, "simple, isolated household worship" and religions that gain historical prominence.[212] Such development depends, he explains, on the "overall development of mental powers," including some form of 'scientific and artistic formation.'"[213]

Within the developmental series of religions, there are different kinds of religion as well, which are distinguished by their "internal differences."[214] Idol-worship, he claims, "marks out human beings' lowest state" because it does not separate the lower, sensory states of consciousness from the higher, more abstract states of consciousness in which the consciousness of absolute dependence appears.[215] Idolatry mixes up sensory and abstracting states of consciousness so that one "identifies oneself with only a tiny portion of finite being" and therefore

> That it is impossible to demonstrate the necessity for redemption to anyone is probably clear in and of itself. Moreover, on that account, one is not required to cite the many attempts to do so, which are always undertaken in vain. Rather, anyone who is able to obtain consolation through one's own effort will also always find a way to sidestep such attempts. Furthermore, once one's self-consciousness has been awakened in this regard, there can be no more possibility of demonstrating afterward that Christ is the only one who can bring about redemption than there was before that awakening. (*CF*, §14.2, p. 105)

The Christian simply knows herself to have moved from a worse to a better state only through her relation to Christ and Christian community (*CF*, §14.1, pp. 102–3; and postscript to §14).

209. *CF*, §7.3, p. 48.
210. Ibid., p. 49.
211. *CF*, §7, p. 45.
212. Ibid., §7.1, p. 46.
213. Ibid.
214. Ibid., p. 47.
215. *CF*, §8.2, p. 52.

feels dependent on an individual entity within the world, that is, an idol.[216] "In contrast," Schleiermacher writes,

> suppose that higher self-consciousness will have developed to the full in its differentiation from sensory self-consciousness. Then—to the extent that we are capable of being sensorily affected overall, that is, insofar as we are actually component parts of the world, thus inasmuch as we take up this being component parts of the world into our self-consciousness and extend it to the point of our being conscious of universal finitude—we will have become conscious of ourselves as absolutely dependent. Now, this latter form of self-consciousness can be exhibited only in monotheism.[217]

Monotheism, for Schleiermacher, requires a certain higher-level thinking that could identify the self not only with one's own particular locale or characteristics but with all finite existence as one world. Between idol-worship and monotheism, Schleiermacher places polytheism as an "amorphous middle stage."[218] It sometimes resembles idol-worship and at other times borders very closely on monotheism. The difference between these stages depends on the degree to which one identifies oneself with smaller or larger portions of the world:

> Having faith in one God, before which God the religious person positions oneself as a component part of the world and as absolutely dependent with this world, or having faith in a circle of gods, to which one stands in varied relations as they take part in dominion over the world, or, at bottom, having faith in particular idols, which are proper to a family or to a locale or to some particular occupation in which one has one's life.[219]

As such, Schleiermacher claims that "the various ways of forming a notion of that which is outside ourselves, to which the consciousness of absolute dependence is referred, is interconnected, in part, with how far self-consciousness can variously extend itself."[220]

Schleiermacher's explicit linkage of human development with the ways people conceive of themselves in relation to various regions of the world, either identifying the self with smaller or larger portions of the world, lends itself easily to racism. On his view, those groups of people who cannot or do not think of themselves as one finite part of a whole are less mentally developed than those groups of people who conceive of themselves in relation to the world as a totality. Moreover, the identification of the self with the whole, which Schleiermacher thinks is required

---

216. Ibid., p. 53.
217. Ibid., p. 52.
218. Ibid., p. 53.
219. Ibid., p. 52.
220. Ibid., p. 53.

for monotheism, could be easily translated into a colonial mindset whereby a person or nation places itself in relation to the whole in order to dominate others.

Complicating an assessment of this aspect of Schleiermacher's work, it will not have escaped the reader's notice that some of the ideas making an appearance here are bound up with those features of Schleiermacher's thought that are beneficial for ecotheology, namely, an awareness of the interconnection of all created things, and a sense that humanity is part of creation rather than separate from it. The challenge is to consider, first, whether Schleiermacher's notion of the interconnected process of nature (*Naturzusammenhang*) can be retained while avoiding the claim that those who do not think of themselves in relation to the whole but confine themselves to their own geographical region of the world are less mentally developed than monotheists; and second, whether Schleiermacher's understanding of the interconnected process of nature can be retained while mitigating colonial impulses that could be involved in linking the self with the whole of finite existence. To address these challenges, I briefly consider Schleiermacher's eschatology and recommend that Schleiermacher-inspired readers might cling to his own theological, epistemic limits more closely than he has in this arena.

When considering non-Christian religious traditions and the development of humanity over time, Schleiermacher claims that as the influence of Christ continues through time, "all other communities of faith are destined to pass over into Christianity."[221] That is, the "totality of the new creation [i.e., the corporate life that traces itself to the influence of Jesus] is simply equivalent to the total mass of humanity."[222] As we have seen, for Schleiermacher, the whole of creation is Christomorphic. That is, the whole is determined in relation to Christ, whose person and work ramify outward through time and space by the Spirit in the Church until all are brought within the Christian community of grace.

A key motivation for this claim is Schleiermacher's notion of humanity's species-consciousness along with his view that there is one divine decree of blessedness for all of humanity and creation.[223] For him, every individual human being co-constitutes the nature of humanity, and personal self-consciousness includes species-consciousness. In other words, humankind is constituted by each

---

221. *CF*, §117.1, p. 536.
222. *CF*, §119.3, p. 550. The bracketed text is a paraphrase based on p. 361.
223. For Schleiermacher's treatment of "species-consciousness," see *CF*, §60. For his discussion of the one election of all to blessedness, see *CF*, §109.3, pp. 718–19:

> There is only one eternal and general divine decree regarding justification of human beings for Christ's sake. This decree, in turn, is the same thing as Christ's mission; otherwise this mission would have to have been thought up and decided by God but without its intended effect. In addition, this decree, in turn, is also simply at one with that decree regarding creation of the human race, inasmuch as the human race first reaches its perfect end in Christ. ... Hence what we have to assume is simply one general divine act of justification in relation to redemption, one that is gradually realized in temporal fashion.

instance of being human, and humans think of themselves as part of humanity. Christians, in particular, have a robustly communal rather than individualistic understanding of their relation to others. A problem arises, for Christians, when to species-consciousness is added a recognition of the fact that all people are not brought within the Christian community before death. Schleiermacher explains, "the shared feeling of Christians is at ease with one or another person's being taken up into the community of redemption earlier or later; however, an irresolvable dissonance does remain if, on the presupposition that there is a continuing existence after death, we were to think of a portion of the human race as entirely excluded from this community."[224] He continues,

> All this gains a whole other perspective, as soon as we hold ourselves to be justified in assuming that this contrast is simply in the process of vanishing at every particular point, with the result that everyone who is now still outside this blessed community would at some time or other be within it, deeply touched by the workings of divine grace. This would be the case, for there would at that point be no bifurcation in our species-consciousness anymore, and for that consciousness the merely gradual transition of individuals into the full enjoyment of redemption would be entirely the same as the gradual progress of sanctification is for our personally-oriented self-consciousness. That is, it would simply be the natural form that divine activity would of necessity take on in its historical appearance, and, as was stated above, it would be the indispensable condition of all temporal efficacious action of the Word-become-flesh.[225]

In other words, thinking of humanity as fundamentally divided into two separated groups would disrupt Christians' species-consciousness and call into question the divine government of the world as one Christomorphic whole. Schleiermacher must, therefore, work out how to retain his understanding of divine government and species-consciousness in light of the fact that many people die apart from the Christian community. To create a coherent theological system of thought, he needs to retain divine omnipotence and omnibenevolence while avoiding divine arbitrariness and failure, and he must simultaneously present humanity as one co-referential and co-constituted organism. To do so, Schleiermacher seems to assume an afterlife, claiming that "the condition one would have at death would at that point be simply an intermediate one."[226] In an assumed afterlife, the divine would bring all individuals into the operations of grace through Christ.

By making this move, Schleiermacher seems to emphasize the individual within his soteriology in an uncharacteristically non-historical way. Here we find a "gradual transition of individuals into the full enjoyment of redemption" after death, apart from their historical location.[227] In this portion of the text,

224. *CF*, §118, p. 771.
225. Ibid., §118.1, p. 772.
226. Ibid., §119.3, p. 783.
227. Ibid., §118.1, p. 772.

Schleiermacher's organic, interdependent understanding of humanity curiously seems to drop out of view. While his theological anthropology emphasizes humanity's interconnectivity within the process of nature, his soteriology here treats the non-Christian human as an individual whose personal formation in community must be upended by an after-death transformation. There is no doubt that Schleiermacher tends toward this uncharacteristic claim, ironically perhaps, because of his deep affirmation of community, which is part and parcel of human species-consciousness. His understanding of the one divine decree of all to blessedness also pushes him to assert that the Christian community will become total.[228] However, because the transformation of the non-Christian person after death would occur outside the historical life of faith of an individual engaged with others, Schleiermacher here seems to prioritize the ahistorical individual in an uncharacteristic move.

By using Schleiermacher's characteristic concern for upholding properly Christian epistemic limits, theologians inspired by him may retain his Christomorphic understanding of the interdependent universe while avoiding his totalizing claims about Christianity in relation to other religions. They could do so by allowing for the possibility that enduring religious diversity is part of the divine election of humanity to blessedness. This would be an alternate way to cope with the "irresolveable dissonance" Schleiermacher identifies between the existence of non-Christian persons and the divine election of all to blessedness. What follows is a constructive proposal regarding Schleiermacher's system of doctrine that brings the flickering moment of ahistorical individualism in his ecclesiology and anthropology into line with his emphasis on the interconnected system of nature and brings the totalizing claim within his soteriology into line with his acknowledgment of the Christian's epistemic limitations.[229]

In order to deal with a potential cleavage in Christians' species-consciousness, Schleiermacher appeals to an ahistorical transformation of the individual in an afterlife. An afterlife, however, does not feature as an important theological focus in the rest of his *Christian Faith*. In fact, Schleiermacher states that, apart from belief in the unchanging character of the union of the divine essence with human nature in the person of Christ, a belief in the persistence of human personality after death "could not find any place within our account of Christian faith-doctrine."[230]

---

228. For analyses of Schleiermacher's doctrine of election, see Matthias Gockel, *Barth and Schleiermacher on the Doctrine of Election: A Systematic-Theological Comparison* (New York: Oxford University Press, 2006); Anette I. Hagan, *Eternal Blessedness for All? A Historical-Systematic Examination of Friedrich Schleiermacher's Reinterpretation of Predestination* (Cambridge: James Clarke, 2014); Sung-Sup Kim, *Deus Providebit: Calvin, Schleiermacher, and Barth on the Providence of God (Emerging Scholars Series)* (Minneapolis, MN: Fortress, 2014).

229. A version of this argument was originally published as Shelli M. Poe, "Friedrich Schleiermacher's Theology as a Resource for Ecological Economics," *Theology Today* 73/1 (2016): 9–23.

230. *CF*, §158.1, p. 967.

Indeed, only one paragraph—on the ascension of Christ—points in that direction, and that paragraph is not directly a doctrine of faith. This makes possible an embrace of the essential features of Christianity "even though we would have had no intimation of a state after death."[231] My interpretation of Schleiermacher's view on this point is corroborated by Albert Blackwell, who notes in his introduction to Schleiermacher's sermon at the grave of his 9-year-old son that Schleiermacher is "forthright in reinterpreting and rejecting traditional Christian views of death and life after death. Schleiermacher insists that religious piety, or 'God-consciousness' as he defines it, is not necessarily conditional upon belief in the immortality of the soul or the resurrection of the body."[232]

Given that an appeal to an afterlife is not integral to Schleiermacher's systematic theology, an alternative would be to emphasize at this point that diversity is a prerequisite for understanding creation as an interdependent whole. Diversity is not a problem to be overcome with time but is essential for the proper functioning of the interconnected process of nature.[233] Just as a diversity of plants, animals, minerals, and all the planet's constituents' activities are required for the healthy functioning of the whole, so too is humanity's religious diversity part of the divine decree of blessedness for all. Because every individual is created only in and with the whole of humanity and creation, Christians may come to appreciate the ways they are indebted to and dependent on others—historically, socially, and religiously—who are all sustained together by the divine activity.[234]

This alternative would clearly require a substantive change to Schleiermacher's system of doctrine, such that the total population would become Christian neither historically nor after death. Yet it is not altogether foreign to Schleiermacher's existing theology, since he already recognizes the interdependence of religious traditions and peoples. For example, as we have seen, Schleiermacher acknowledges that Jesus was born within the Jewish religion[235] and was influenced by his environment and developed in accord with the activities of other people around him: "he could have developed only in a certain affinity with his surroundings, thus in the general culture of his people."[236] Likewise, "Christ could hardly have been a complete human being if his personal existence had not been determined by characteristics of his people."[237] Even though Schleiermacher usually minimizes

---

231. Ibid., p. 968. In proposition 163, Schleiermacher also states, "We will remain forever uncertain as to how that state which comprises the supreme consummation of the church would ever be gained by the personal existence of individuals, viewed as rising into immortal life, or would ever be possessed in this form" (§163.2, p. 995). See also §161.3, pp. 985–6.

232. Albert L. Blackwell, "Schleiermacher's Sermon at Nathanael's Grave," *The Journal of Religion* 57/1 (January 1977): 68.

233. Compare *CF* §117, pp. 766–71.

234. There is no divine decree concerning the individual; *CF* §120.4, p. 793.

235. *CF*, §12.1, p. 90.

236. *CF*, §93.3, p. 570.

237. Ibid., §93.4, p. 573.

Jesus' Jewishness, he also says that Jesus could not be a human person without being materially constituted and situated in the context of Jewish people and culture.²³⁸ Thus, although Schleiermacher makes a number of quite regrettable statements (to say the least) about Judaism and the relation of Christianity to other religions, he nonetheless recognizes the historical character of religions. As Thomas Reynolds explains,

> Schleiermacher does not regard the religions as incommensurate and self-enclosed historical monads, each utterly relative to its own context. ... History is an open field of direct engagement between differences, differences that modify each other. Schleiermacher admits as much. There is no solitary community of discourse insulated from the experience of other communities and their modes of discourse.²³⁹

This indicates that Schleiermacher's existing system of doctrine is consistent with the acknowledgment that all of creation is interconnected not only as an ecologically organic whole but also as an historical life, including—at least to some degree—an historically interdependent religious life.²⁴⁰

It nonetheless remains the case that for Schleiermacher, the Christian speaks about Christ and Christ's Spirit in the Church as the way the divine determines the whole of interdependent creation. Schleiermacher does not build his dogmatics on a doctrine of creation or anthropology that is unconnected to the person and work of Jesus of Nazareth.²⁴¹ Dogmatics originates in the Church and it is intended for the Church. Moreover, as we have seen, "within Christianity everything is referred to the redemption accomplished through Jesus of Nazareth."²⁴² The Christian does not make claims about the divine, humanity, or creation on a universally discernable or mechanically reproducible basis. Rather, such claims arise out of piety in relation to the Redeemer. This means that Schleiermacher acknowledges—indeed, puts front and center—the idea that the Christian does not have unfiltered epistemic access to the divine activity. This way of putting it may sound too postmodern for Schleiermacher, but the point remains that his Christomorphism in relation to creation and humanity can neither entail nor provide warrant for any positive statements about the divine activity in relation to individuals or communities that are not Christian. Indeed, Schleiermacher himself states,

> From our standpoint, the term "passing over" is the most suitable one, because it says "no" to only a distinct action. It is not as if no divine activity, or no divine

---

238. Ibid., §161.1, p. 981.
239. Thomas Reynolds, "Schleiermacher and the Problem of Religious Diversity," *Journal of the American Academy of Religion* 73/1 (March 2005): 171–2.
240. Compare *CF*, §164.1, p. 999.
241. *CF*, §2.1, pp. 4–5.
242. Ibid., §11, p. 79.

decree for that matter, would have been implicated in relation to them. Rather, only as a consequence of the overall divine ordering of things is this divine activity so completely bound up in remote internal and external preparations that they merely seem to us to be passed over. ... Of those who do not evidence these workings we have no basis for declaring anything else but precisely this negation, and indeed only in their relation to the reign of God at a given time and the workings of grace that proceed from it.[243]

In this passage, Schleiermacher underscores Christians' epistemic limitations, Christomorphism, and his conviction that all are within the scope of divine activity and the decree of blessedness. As far as Christians are concerned, the entire scope of creation is included in the divine activity and foreordination to blessedness, and everything is related to Christ. These are claims made on the basis of Christians' pious reception of divine activity in Christ through the Spirit. At the same time, Christians have no grounds upon which to deny divine activity in relation to those who are not Christian. When considering those who appear to be "passed over," the appropriate Christian profession about the specific ways in which the divine operations of grace are present would seem to be ignorance, tempered by a robust sense of humanity's interconnectivity and the election of all to blessedness.[244] This is an alternative to making totalizing claims that do detriment to ecumenical relations and that cultivate an attitude about scale and domination that feed into a colonial mindset.

Schleiermacher's concept of the interconnected process of nature and his own theological limitations make possible a reconstructed version of his theology that would avoid these implications. Such a reconstruction foregrounds Christian agnosticism about how the divine election of humanity to blessedness is accomplished for each individual, while emphasizing diversity as an essential part of nature. It thereby puts into question Schleiermacher's totalizing claim regarding the Christian communion in relation to other religious faiths. In this way, it seems to me Schleiermacher's view could be modified to avoid racism and colonialism while retaining the beneficial features of his notion of the interconnected process of nature.

Further Benefits of Schleiermacher's Soteriology

We have now surveyed a number of problematic features of dominant Christologies and soteriologies, as identified by prominent womanists and feminists. We have also considered Schleiermacher's Christology and atonement theory, and have found that while Schleiermacher's thought resonates with feminist and womanist theologies in important ways, his thought nonetheless requires correction. After

---

243. Ibid., §119.2, p. 782.
244. Ibid.

Schleiermacher's Christology and theory of redemption have been criticized and corrected in at least the ways noted above—by emphasizing Jesus' identity with the oppressed, highlighting his Jewishness and its link to the oppressed of humanity, embracing his queerness as a figure on the boundary between Judaism and Christianity, and emphasizing the limits of theological knowledge in relation to non-Christians while simultaneously upholding the divine decree of blessedness for all—there are a number of features of his theology that commend themselves to contemporary theologians. In this final section, I return to some of the themes briefly discussed in the introductory chapter that illustrate how Schleiermacher's Christology and soteriology could further coalesce with contemporary constructive work. These include Schleiermacher's treatment of sin, his emphasis on body and affect as important for Christian life, and his emphasis on natality and joy in Christian community.

Sin

The Definition of Sin

Following Valerie Saiving Goldstein's early work, feminists have noted the prominence of theological understandings of sin as pride. Saiving writes that in such theologies, expressed, for example, in the work of Anders Nygren and Reinhold Niebuhr, "sin is the unjustified concern of the self for its own power and prestige; it is the imperialistic drive to close the gap between the individual, separate self and others by reducing those others to the status of mere objects which can then be treated as appendages of the self and manipulated accordingly."[245] The same theologians then define love, which is the opposite of sin and is redemptive, as

> completely self-giving, taking no thought for its own interests but seeking only the good of the other. Love makes no value judgments concerning the other's worth; it demands neither merit in the other nor recompense for itself but gives itself freely, fully, and without calculation. Love is unconditional forgiveness; … Love is personal; it is the concrete relatedness of an I to a Thou, in which the I casts aside all its particularities, all its self-affirmations, everything which separates it from the Thou, and becomes wholly receptive to the other.[246]

Saiving famously argues that such definitions of both sin and love ignore and invalidate the experience of women whose historical mode of sin has more often been a lack of self rather than an aggrandizement of the self. A woman learns, Saiving notes, that she "can give too much of herself, so that nothing remains of her own uniqueness; she can become merely an emptiness, almost a zero, without value to herself, to her fellow men, or, perhaps, even to God."[247]

---

245. Valerie Saiving Goldstein, "The Human Situation: A Feminine View," *The Journal of Religion* 40/2 (1960): 100.
246. Ibid., p. 101.
247. Ibid., p. 108.

In this situation, Saiving maintains that theologians should not continue to speak of sin as pride, because if "a woman believes the theologians, she will try to strangle those impulses" to be an individual.[248] Further, "she will believe that, having chosen marriage and children and thus being face to face with the needs of her family for love, refreshment, and forgiveness, she has no right to ask anything for herself but must submit without qualification to the strictly feminine role."[249] Although Saiving's perspective in this 1960 article contains much with which one may want to argue from a contemporary perspective, she nonetheless highlights an enduring point of contention within theological understandings of "the human situation": as we have seen with regard to womanists' critique of feminist views of "womanhood," what it means to be "human" cannot be defined solely in relation to one subset of humanity. Both of these categories need a heavy dose of particularity in order to adequately account for the reality of women's and humanity's varied experiences. Saiving's point is, therefore, still as relevant today as it was in the 1960s, as we continue to refine and rethink theology. She calls for theologians to "redefine its categories of sin and redemption" and to do so with women's as well as others' experiences in mind.[250] We see Cone and Douglas endeavoring to do just this when Cone writes that for Black people sin is "loss of identity" and when Douglas affirms that for Black people, "repentance requires an affirmation of their own blackness."[251]

Schleiermacher could be an ally in a redefinition of sin that is wide enough to account for various experiences of sin. He defines sin as "a hindering of spirit's determinative force, a hindering that is caused by autonomous activity of one's sensory functioning."[252] In other words, sin occurs when one's consciousness of God does not determine one's entire person and actions. Put more simply, for Schleiermacher, "sin exists when we desire what Christ holds in disregard, and vice versa."[253] On his account, different people manifest sin in different ways depending on their own tendencies and contexts. He considers, for example, a person inclined toward reflection, on the one hand, and a person of action, on the other:

> Those original differences in disposition continue to have an effect nonetheless, and in the first person awakening piety will more readily unite with thought, but modes of action will remain of a fleshly nature, whereas in the second person awakening into piety will be more readily resistant to understanding. As a result, sin will take a different shape in each of these persons.[254]

248. Ibid., p. 110.
249. Ibid.
250. Ibid., p. 111.
251. Douglas, *Sexuality and the Black Church*, p. 126.
252. *CF*, §67.2, p. 404.
253. Ibid. Desire is not the only human faculty involved. Schleiermacher treats immediate self-consciousness alongside understanding and will. Sin occurs wherever God-consciousness has not "evenly permeated our entire nature" (*CF*, §68.2, p. 411).
254. *CF*, §69.2, p. 415.

By defining sin as incompatibility with Christ's person and work, or a lack of consciousness of God powerful enough to consistently determine one's own person and activity, Schleiermacher leaves room for the different ways that sin could become apparent in any individual's life. One person might sin primarily through self-aggrandizing action, as in Niebuhr's understanding of sin as pride, but another person might sin primarily through inaction or passivity. As such, his notion of sin is capacious enough to include many different people's experience as human beings.[255] Importantly, it stands in line with liberation definitions of sin as "anything that subverts the liberation process and/or nurtures structures of oppression."[256]

The Placement of Sin
Schleiermacher's theological placement of sin is also helpful. We have seen in the introduction to this book that Serene Jones argues that sin ought to be seen "from the perspective of justification and sanctification." That is, one should approach sin "from the eschatological perspective of the woman who knows herself as sanctified and justified in faith."[257] Jones advocates this approach to sin so that theologies will not hurt women's developing sense of self. By beginning with justification and sanctification, "woman's dispersed and fragmented identity is pulled together and held in the 'envelope of God's grace,'" and "woman is pronounced a newly born agent and is called to live in just relation with others."[258] Only then can she hear a word about sin without the discussion working at cross-purposes with her own redemption. By speaking of sin within the framework of justification and sanctification, Jones "affirm[s] a present-day experience of transformation and a future horizon of flourishing." "This makes clear," Jones explains, "the anticipatory optimism of sin-talk in feminist perspective."[259]

Likewise, on Schleiermacher's view, one need not begin the redemption process with a recognition of one's own guilt. As he writes, "it is indeed not necessary that consciousness of sin precede entry into the sphere of the Redeemer. On the contrary, consciousness of sin can just as well first arise in the sphere of the Redeemer as an effect of the self-disclosure of the Redeemer, as, in any case, it first attains full clarity through perception of his sinless perfection."[260] For Schleiermacher, then, one needs to begin neither theologically nor experientially with guilt. Rather, one could begin, as Schleiermacher does in his *Christian Faith*, with "original perfection." As I noted in the introduction, he presents the "original perfection"

---

255. See also Kwok Pui-Lan's argument that sin and redemption should be conceived not so much as disobedience or egotism but as ideas and activities that have consequences, in "Ecology and Christology," *Feminist Theology* 15 (1997): 113–25.
256. Douglas, *Sexuality and the Black Church*, p. 125.
257. Serene Jones, *Feminist Theory and Christian Theology: Cartographies of Grace*, Guides to Theological Inquiry (Minneapolis, MN: Fortress, 2000), pp. 95–6.
258. Ibid., p. 112.
259. Ibid., p. 110.
260. *CF*, §100.2, p. 624.

of the world and humanity (§§59–61) before original and actual sin (§§70–74). "Original perfection" does not here refer to a historical state before the first sin of the first humans. Rather, it means that God has created the world and humanity in such a way that it is possible for redemption to occur. "The expression 'original perfection,'" he explains, "posits that inasmuch as all finite being codetermines our self-consciousness, this process can be traced back to eternal omnipotent causality."[261] In other words, the world and humanity within it are always already in a graced relationship with God. Accordingly, Schleiermacher writes that "consciousness of sin is conditioned by what is good, which must precede it and which is simply a result of that original perfection."[262] His insistence on treating the original perfection of the world and humanity as prior to sin and evil maps onto the anticipatory optimism involved in feminist sin-talk.[263] Schleiermacher explains that "in the soul of a Christian a consciousness of sin is never in place without consciousness of the force present in the process of redemption. ... Of itself alone, consciousness of sin simply represents a condition outside the domain in which redemption is the dominant force."[264] Further, he writes, "sin can have its place within us only at the same time as God-consciousness is present and also in relation to God-consciousness."[265] "Sin," therefore, "must be revealed only within some good that has already come into being and by virtue of that good; it is revealed to be sin simply as that which hinders future good."[266] For both Schleiermacher and Jones, then, the goodness of creation and the graced relationship of humanity with the divine is the framework within which one ought to speak of sin.

Sin as Social and Systemic
Jones also highlights the social and systemic nature of sin. She writes, "We are born into a nexus of oppressive social relations—institutional practices, cultural patterns, and habits of language—we can never completely escape."[267] While individual responsibility for sin is not dismissed, Jones highlights the fact that individuals do not exist outside of the social relationships that form them. Emilie Townes also foregrounds the systemic nature of sin. She not only recognizes the ways that individuals rely on relationships for their existence and formation, but also highlights "the systematic construction of truncated narratives designed to

261. Ibid., §57.1, p. 338.
262. Ibid., §68.2, p. 410.
263. Schleiermacher does treat sin before grace in Part Two, but he insists that in Christian consciousness the two cannot be properly separated: "Every Christian is indeed conscious of sin and of grace as well, but never in separation, rather always in relation to and along with each other" (*CF*, §64.1, p. 389). Furthermore, for Schleiermacher sin is always receding in Christian consciousness, while grace is becoming more prominent.
264. *CF*, §66.2, pp. 403–4.
265. Ibid., §67.1, p. 405.
266. Ibid., §68.2, p. 411.
267. Jones, *Feminist Theory and Christian Theology*, p. 123.

support and perpetuate structural inequities and forms of social oppression."[268] Jones and Townes here join the company of Gustavo Gutierrez, who explains,

> In the liberation approach sin is not considered as an individual, private, or merely interior reality—asserted just enough to necessitate "spiritual" redemption which does not challenge the order in which we live. Sin is regarded as a social, historical fact, the absence of fellowship and love in relationship among persons, the breach of friendship with God and other persons, and, therefore, an interior, personal fracture. When it is considered in this way, the collective dimensions of sin are rediscovered.[269]

For Gutierrez, sin is concretely manifested in the world in systems of injustice and oppression, within which individuals act and are implicated.

Schleiermacher, too, understands sin as social. For him, consciousness of sin is both grounded in individuals and "somewhere beyond our own individual existence."[270] This "somewhere beyond" is explained as the "dependence of a particular formation of individual life on some large type held in common" and the "dependence of later generations on earlier ones," such that "the sin of each individual has its source in an earlier existence above and beyond one's own existence."[271] Schleiermacher is here affirming the structural features of sin by talking about the sources of an individual's tendency to sin. While explicating his novel doctrine of original sin, Schleiermacher writes,

> If, on the one hand, the susceptibility to sin that precedes every deed is effected in each individual by the sin and susceptibility of sin of others, but if, at the same time, it is also both propagated in others and secured in them by each individual through one's own free actions, then sinfulness is of a thoroughly collective nature. ... In each individual susceptibility to sin is the work of all, and in all individuals it is the work of each. Indeed, susceptibility to sin is to be understood rightly and fully only in this commonality.[272]

Individuals are always set in the context of their social formation and therefore tend toward sin because of the sin of others. Schleiermacher understands the tendency to sin primarily in a corporate way as the result of social structures and

---

268. Emilie Townes, *Womanist Ethics and the Cultural Production of Evil* (New York: Palgrave Macmillan, 2006), p. 4.

269. Gustavo Gutierrez, *A Theology of Liberation: History, Politics, and Salvation*, trans. and ed. Sister Caridad Inda and John Eagleson (Maryknoll, NY: Orbis, [1971] 1988), pp. 102–3.

270. *CF*, §69, p. 413.

271. Ibid., §69.1, p. 414.

272. Ibid., §71.2, pp. 428–9.

practices that influence and shape individuals. As Kevin Vander Schel interprets Schleiermacher,

> The state of sin is not primarily a malformation of individual desiring, but a socially mediated and inherently collective condition that everywhere imprints and distorts communal human action. Accordingly, the consequences of sin also have a decidedly social cast. Beyond distortions in individual living, human sinfulness disfigures wider social institutions, cultural movements, and even the natural world.[273]

The hamartiological focus, for Schleiermacher as for Jones and Townes, is on social structures that reinforce and support injustice. Schleiermacher's understanding of redemption, as we have seen in this chapter, similarly focuses on the collective insofar as Schleiermacher understands redemption as requiring participation in a Christian community, which expands in beneficent activity outward toward all of humanity and creation.

Body and Affect

A second emphasis in constructive forms of theology that I would like to highlight is the importance of body and affect. Monica Coleman defines embodied theology as the notion that "our theologies are not simply or primarily rational constructions but rather rooted in the totality of our lives."[274] Schleiermacher's insistence that Christian piety is neither a knowing nor a doing but a *Gefühl*—an immediate consciousness or awareness—could be helpful for contemporary theologians who wish to emphasize the bodiliness of Christian faith, in spite of his own failure to emphasize Jesus' bodiliness. The density of his thought notwithstanding, Schleiermacher is not a theologian who could be appropriately accused of over-intellectualizing the Christian religion. Harkening back to the distinction between theology and religion sketched in the introduction, we recall that although Christian theology is a discipline that requires intellectual acumen, clarity, and precision, the Christian religion, or the practice of Christian piety, for Schleiermacher, is open to all. He does not make the ratiocinations of the scholarly community or arguments from scripture central to his understanding of religion, as we have seen in his treatment of messianic prophecy. Rather, Schleiermacher makes central Christians' reception of divine grace in and through Christ in the

---

273. Kevin Vander Schel, "Social Sin and the Cultivation of Nature," in *Schleiermacher and Sustainability: A Theology for Ecological Living*, ed. Shelli M. Poe (Louisville, KY: Westminster John Knox, 2018), p. 79.

274. Monica A. Coleman, "Speak Like Christ, Adorn Like Plaskow: Embodied Theologies," *Journal of Feminist Studies in Religion* 33/2 (2017): 105. Note, however, that because Coleman offers a version of process theology, her overall theological vision would not cohere with Schleiermacher's understanding of God's relationship to the world.

church, where they hear, see, and otherwise receive the self-presentation of Christ in sermons, gestures, dispositions, and communal actions.

Calli Micale draws out the bodiliness of Schleiermacher's theology in another way, showing how it could be used to construct a soteriology that includes people with profound intellectual disabilities. Honing in on Schleiermacher's understanding of God-consciousness as requiring awareness of self, she writes that "human persons with profound intellectual disability might be said to have self-awareness apart from theoretical knowledge of the self as a self. A basic self-awareness need only include an implicit differentiation between external and internal stimuli. This distinction is significant, because it both allows for participation without reflexive conceptual processing and emphasizes the activity of the divine agent."[275] Micale argues that those with intellectual disabilities may be included in the experience of redemption by receiving divine activity through participation in Christian community, even though they might not have theoretical self-knowledge.

Beyond an ability to receive the divine activity as external to the self, Micale argues that intellectually disabled people could also actively engage in the experience of redemption. She explains that, for Schleiermacher, individuals reproduce Christ's activity in the Christian community through loving actions. "The degree to which Christ's activity is replicated by the individual," however, "is effected by the mediation of the community. Her unique determination of Christ's activity is dependent upon her social and material possibilities and the situation in which she finds herself."[276] The community, then, conditions the way that individuals will replicate Christ's activity of love. Micale explains how such reproduction of Christ's loving activity in the church could apply to those with intellectual disabilities:

> Christ's activity can be "recognized" in the love expressed between humans apart from any "comprehension" of that activity as love. We might think of the content of this activity as transmitted through a mere touch. Genuine responsiveness towards Christ's love, as represented by the community of believers, contributes to the formation of the God-consciousness. This more capacious understanding of the communication of Christ's activity makes participation in the redeemed life possible for all humans. Redemption is socially mediated in the Church, and does not require reflexive conceptual processing by each participating member.[277]

---

275. Calli Micale, "A Schleiermacherian Solution: Eschatological Continuity, Disability, and Communication," Unpublished presentation offered at a session of the Schleiermacher Unit at the American Academy of Religion National Annual Meeting (Boston, MA, 2017), 3; used by permission of the author.
276. Ibid., p. 6.
277. Ibid., p. 10.

Micale's argument indicates a promising way forward in the use of Schleiermacher's theology to emphasize the bodiliness and affectivity involved in Christian life in ways that could coalesce with contemporary, constructive forms of theology.[278]

Natality and Joy

Finally, I want to emphasize how Schleiermacher's thought could contribute to theologies that focus on survival, living, or natality, and quality of life, joy, or thriving. As we have seen in the introduction, feminist philosopher Grace Jantzen has identified natality as a beneficial feminist mode of religious thought:

> Much of traditional philosophy of religion (and western culture generally) is preoccupied with violence, sacrifice, and death, and built upon mortality not only as a human fact but as a fundamental philosophical category. But what if we were to begin with birth, and with the hope and possibility and wonder implicit in it? How if we were to treat natality and the emergence of *this* life and *this* world with the same philosophical seriousness and respect which had traditionally been paid to mortality and the striving for other worlds?[279]

Jantzen offers a framework for considering these questions, posed not through the lens of death and despair but through the lens of life and transformation. Such an approach could cohere with attention to survival and quality of life among women of color, their families, communities, and planet. We have already briefly seen that Baker-Fletcher and Coleman prioritize the survival of creation alongside survival of the world's human inhabitants. Building on the work of Baker-Fletcher, Coleman writes, "a postmodern womanist theology talks about divine and creaturely agency. It will alert African Americans to ecological crises and the notion that the natural world, too, is and must be transformed into a higher quality of its own life."[280] The interconnections between communities of color, women, and ecological degradations are made visible by asking questions of survival or natality instead of being preoccupied with sacrifice, violence, and death. Ecological

---

278. Thandeka has also emphasized the bodiliness and affectivity involved in Schleiermacher's theology. In *The Embodied Self*, she argues that Schleiermacher "solved the problem of the gap in Kant's theory of the self," namely, the gap between thinking and being (Thandeka, *The Embodied Self: Friedrich Schleiermacher's Solution to Kant's Problem of the Empirical Self* [Albany, NY: SUNY, 1995], p. 83). While Thandeka is involved, here, in a complex argument regarding Schleiermacher's relationship to Kant, she is more basically highlighting the fact that Schleiermacher's understanding of piety is grounded in the notion of *Gefühl*—rather than thinking or doing. Schleiermacher's understanding of the essential character of piety as *Gefühl* could be utilized by those who wish to draw out the affective and bodily character of Christian life.

279. Jantzen, *Becoming Divine*, p. 2.

280. Coleman, *Making a Way Out of No Way*, p. 94.

2. Christ and Redemption

thinkers like Wendell Berry also ask the sort of questions Jantzen and womanists ask, with the hope that a focus on this life and world, rather than on technological innovations or religious themes that would allow humanity to escape it, would assist in creating a more just relationship with other human beings, animals, and the planet itself.[281] Sallie McFague, as another example, argues that focusing on survival, while it "might at first appear to be a minimalist view, reducing human beings to the physical (animal?!) level, it is precisely the minimum that those individuals and nations bloated with self, living the life of insatiable greed, refuse to recognize."[282] She argues that "the ecological view of sin refuses to raise its eyes above the minimalist view, insisting that justice among human beings means first of all adequate space for basic needs. It also means, for some, staying in their own proper, limited place."[283]

As we have seen with reference to his doctrine of original perfection and his creation-focused soteriology, Schleiermacher's theology, too, is heavily laden with an affirmation of created life. In addition to this natal theme, his theology also offers joy as a distinctive marker of Christian community.[284] In the introduction, I highlight Schleiermacher's natal and joyful themes in his *Christmas Dialogue* (1806), but his emphasis on joy permeates his theological corpus. For example, when Schleiermacher discusses conversion and regeneration in his *Christian Faith*, he writes,

> A wide range of relationships are also possible between the pain that is present in repentance and the joy that appears in one's consciousness of community of life with Christ. One of these relationships could be one in which a more glorious outburst of joy occurs quite adjacent to a faint state of sorrow, in which relationship the latter state can thereby become almost indiscernible. Actually, forms of conversion of this sort do undeniably exist, forms that are to be conceived simply as a blissful rescue from despondency. Likewise, forms also exist in which nothing whatsoever of a penitential struggle comes up. Instead, the person senses an almost pure blessing from on high, as it were, almost as

---

281. See, for instance, Wendell Berry, "Faustian Economics," *Harper's Magazine* (May 2008): 35–42. See also *Schleiermacher and Sustainability: A Theology for Ecological Living*, ed. Shelli M. Poe (Louisville, KY: Westminster John Knox, 2018).

282. Sallie McFague, *The Body of God: An Ecological Theology* (Minneapolis, MN: Fortress, 1993), p. 116.

283. Ibid.

284. For Schleiermacher, joy is one manifestation of feeling for others. When others are going through something painful, the manifestation is compassion, whereas when they are going through something pleasurable, the manifestation is joy (see editor's note 7 of *Christian Faith*, in the addendum on the Mercy of God). Joy can also be tinged with sadness or longing, when one considers the sin that exists in the world (see editor's note 20 of *Christian Faith*, in paragraph 110).

if what is painful in one's contrition can be rolled back, yet without its entirely disappearing.[285]

While Schleiermacher is clearly not dismissing an alternate account wherein conversion is marked by the pain of contrition and change of heart, in this passage he is foregrounding the joy that accompanies one's consciousness of community in life with Christ.

When he turns to justification, Schleiermacher prefers a "more positive feature"[286] within the doctrine than merely indicating the divine forgiveness of sin. He accomplishes this by saying that God recognizes "the person as a child of God."[287] For Schleiermacher, "faith, made active by love from its very emergence onward, is in thought one's consciousness of being a child in relation to God, viewed as the same consciousness as that of being in community of life with Christ."[288] The Christological force of this claim is evident, which Schleiermacher makes clear: "it is not possible for Christ to live in us unless the relationship he has to his Father is being formed within us as well. Consequently, we participate in Christ's relationship of Son to the Father, which by the impression Christ makes on us empowers us to be children of God."[289] Here again, the "positive feature" of Schleiermacher's thought comes to the fore. Rather than referring exclusively to the forgiveness of sin, he understands justification as including faith that issues from love in relationship, which results in joy. The joy that permeates Schleiermacher's theological thought can coalesce with contemporary calls for attention to the conditions that would create the flourishing of humanity. Bringing this focus into alignment with a framework of creation's goodness and natality could draw some feminists, womanists, ecotheologians, and others, along with Schleiermacher, into a circle of theological conversation partners for whom life and quality of life are chief concerns.

***

In this chapter, I have focused on the interconnections between Schleiermacher's Christology and soteriology and contemporary constructive forms of theology. Both Schleiermacher and the contemporary theologians surveyed here similarly emphasize that Christ's life and ministry are soteriologically central rather than his maleness, though I have argued that his perceived maleness too has its own limited soteriological significance. Further, the subject position and persistence in the face of injustice that Jesus displays throughout his life and in his death comports well with understandings of Christ as identifying with the "least of these." Schleiermacher along with Williams and others also reject a vicarious,

---

285. *CF*, §108.3, p. 700.
286. Ibid., §109.1, p. 711.
287. Ibid., §109, p. 710.
288. Ibid., §109.2, pp. 712–13.
289. Ibid., §109.2, p. 714.

substitutionary understanding of Jesus' death. They offer, instead, soteriologies that make room for the significance of suffering only secondarily and in such a way that suffering is not valorized. Using the insights of womanist theologians, Schleiermacher's Christology could be modified in order to better affirm the universality of Christ's significance for the oppressed without denying his particularity, especially as a Jewish person. Moreover, his soteriology could be modified using his own focus on epistemic limitations in order to avoid racism and imperialism. Even so, Schleiermacher's theology aligns with feminist calls to set theological presentations of sin in the context of justification. Schleiermacher treats sin as variously expressed in different circumstances, and as social and systemic in nature rather than individualistically. Moreover, he recognizes the importance of the body and affect for religious practice. Schleiermacher's thought is rich with resources for contemporary theologians who place an emphasis on natality and survival, along with quality of life and joy in community with Christ. In these ways, Schleiermacher's Christology and soteriology show significant promise for constructive forms of theology.

My own sense is that Schleiermacher makes three chief contributions to current conversations surrounding Christ and redemption. First, he frames his Christology pneumatologically, which means that current Christians only have access to Christ through his Spirit that is embodied and carried on in Christian churches. This puts Jesus' perceived maleness into the background and highlights instead the diversity of bodies in which Christ's Spirit lives today. It also draws to the fore the importance of a critical reception of Jesus' Spirit in the gospels, which is received and given in diversely gendered words and actions that carry on Jesus' ministry in new contexts. Second, Schleiermacher's Christology recovers the language of divine indwelling in order to offer an alternative ontology of Christ. His account of the person and work of Christ offers a way to communicate about who Jesus is as Christians' spiritual ancestor or sibling, who is not simply a teacher or example but whose Spirit continues to live in Christian communities that carry on Jesus' ministry. Jesus was convinced that he was God's child because of the Love that lived within him, and he believed that others could also become aware of their filial relationship to God and act in accordance with Love by becoming his spiritual siblings. This pneumatologically framed Christology embraces the natural transmission of communal ideas and values, emphasizes the depth of personal engagement involved in belonging to the Christian community, and harmonizes with the womanist and other liberation emphasis on Jesus' resistance to injustice as one with whom the oppressed can identify. Third, Schleiermacher's account contributes to the conversation by speaking of the indwelling of God in Christ as the completion of human nature, which both occurs in Christ and continues in the embodiment of Christ's Spirit in the church. This notion highlights the mission of the church today as being on the front lines of efforts toward social justice, in order to enact the beneficent Love of God.

Chapter 3

CHURCH AND SPIRIT

We have now considered Schleiermacher's approach to trinitarian doctrine, Christology, and soteriology in concert with contemporary theologies that are concerned with social justice. We have seen that Schleiermacher's work not only resonates with many of these but also sparks novel ways of approaching classical doctrines. This chapter turns to Schleiermacher's ecclesiology and pneumatology to demonstrate how his vision of church life—a life of joy rooted in Love, lived with diverse others in an interdependent community—can shape our responses to oppressive forces and help us to see how the beloved community might act. The chapter proceeds in two parts, both of which draw our contemporary context into the foreground.

In the first part, I contend that although joy is arguably an underdeveloped theme within Christian theologies, Schleiermacher's ecclesiology and pneumatology make it a basic feature of church life, which can aid oppressed persons as they persevere in the face of systemic forces of injustice. One of the tasks of a theologian working constructively is to speak critically against oppressive forces. Yet often when using the pen as a sword, theologians fail to take advantage of humor, laughter, and joy to unarm the oppressor while empowering the underprivileged. The extent to which joy features as a basic characteristic of the Christian community in Schleiermacher's work makes it a notable resource in what Wendy Farley calls "a counter-cultural practice of the reign of God."[1] To show how, I explore Schleiermacher's theology in his *Christmas Eve Celebration: A Dialogue* (1805, 1826) and *Christian Faith* (1830/1), wherein the common Spirit of the church is a shared love of Christ that gives rise to a dominant mood of joy within the community. I draw into the conversation Rachel Adler's analysis of the function of laughter as a response to sexism in particular.

The second part of the chapter is a constructive response to Schleiermacher's pneumatological ecclesiology. It does not directly draw on Schleiermacher's texts but illustrates one way of doing ecclesiology that is coherent with his work insofar as it prizes diversity, community, dignity, and interdependence and harmonizes with his organic understanding of humanity. I constructively gather four women figures who may be used to represent diverse demographics: Lilith, a religiously

---

1. Farley, *Gathering Those Driven Away*, p. 14.

"other" woman; Eve, a Protestant ideal; Hagar, a symbol for women of color; and Mary, a Catholic role model. Attending to the queer relations between these figures, I highlight what their presence with one another can elicit and evoke: women have striven against one another, misconceived the value of motherhood in socioeconomic terms, and struggled over the "ideal" family. Drawing on the work of Judith Plaskow, Phyllis Trible, Delores Williams, and Marcella Althaus-Reid, I argue that a queer community of this kind could aid the Christian imagination in embracing women's solidarity, upholding women's worth as subjects considered on their own terms, and attending to the complexity of human relationality.[2] Set in the context of this chapter on church and Spirit, the community of women figures I gather could inspire an understanding of how the Christian church today, indwelt by the Spirit of Christ, could embrace and celebrate women.

Joy and Laughter as Ecclesial Practices

It goes without saying that the Christian church has both perpetrated and resisted social injustices. From Constantinian uses of Christianity for imperial gain,[3] to the Confessing Church's resistance to the Nazi regime, to the Civil Rights movement within the United States, to the increased public visibility of racist, sexist, and heterosexist perspectives in the twenty-first century, Christians have been on the front lines of change—for good and ill. The struggle for social justice is part of Christian history, and for Prophetic Christianity that struggle is part of its basic existence. Cornel West notes that Constantinian and Prophetic forms of Christianity have been at war with one another since the beginning of Christian history. Constantinian Christianity originally arose with Constantine's conversion, which institutionalized "a terrible co-joining of church and state that has led to the suffering of the religion itself and its victims."[4] In short, Constantinian Christianity uses Christianity for "purposes of maintaining power."[5] Prophetic Christianity, on the other hand, critiques and resists imperialism and all forms of social injustice and is "a faith fundamentally based on tolerance and compassion."[6] Prophetic Christianity has much to speak against in the United States today, a

---

2. For a recent introduction to queer theology, see Linn Marie Tonstad, *Queer Theology: Beyond Apologetics* (Eugene, OR: Wipf & Stock, 2018). She understands queer theology to be "about visions of sociopolitical transformation that alter practices of distinction harming gender and sexual minorities as well as many other minoritized populations" (3).

3. See Cornel West, "The Crisis of Christian Identity in America," in *The Ethics of Citizenship: Liberal Democracy and Religious Convictions*, ed. J. Caleb Clanton (Waco, TX: Baylor University Press, 2009), pp. 293–310.

4. Ibid., p. 295.

5. Ibid.

6. Ibid.

task that is complicated by the fact that Christianity itself is being used to justify sexual assault,[7] racism,[8] and heterosexism,[9] to name just a few examples. As these injustices have been spoken against, some Americans have come to believe that Christianity itself is under attack, further fueling the protectionist stance of some right-wing Christians. An important task of the theologian, in this circumstance as in the rest of Christian history, is to denounce the powers that would threaten the well-being of any human person, to stand with and for the oppressed, and to demonstrate how the Christian *kerygma* is good news for those trampled by abuses of power. A number of contemporary theologians are living into their responsibilities as theologians and public intellectuals to condemn the powers of injustice at force in the world today.

At the same time, one might wonder at the complex task of the theologian in this context: how can she use her prophetic voice to speak against oppression without contributing to a further retrenchment of views? Further, how could the theologian empower the underprivileged at the same time as she denies coercive forms of activity and resists violent impulses? These are not easy questions, and I do not have sufficient answers. However, I do want to highlight a kind of theological and ecclesial response to injustice that seems to have been neglected in mainstream Christian history. I explore the possibility that joy, which issues in laughter, could go further than Christians have hitherto imagined as a lived practice in the stand against injustice.

In the consideration of joy as an ecclesial practice of resistance, I find Schleiermacher's theology beneficial because of how basic the mood of joy is to his understanding of Christian piety. Schleiermacher is most well-known, of course, as the founder of modern theology. His work addresses the historical appearance

---

7. Elaine Godfrey, "Roy Moore's Many Defenders," *The Atlantic* (November 10, 2017). http://www.theatlantic.com/politics/archive/2017/11/roy-moores-many-defenders/545609/?utm_source=eb. In the article, Alabama State Auditor Jim Zeigler is reported to have told the *Washington Examiner*, in defense of Alabama Republican Senate Candidate Roy Moore's alleged sexual encounter with an underage girl: "Take Mary and Joseph. Mary was a teenager and Joseph was an adult carpenter. They became parents of Jesus. … There's just nothing immoral or illegal here. Maybe just a little bit unusual."

8. As *The Washington Post* reports, Trump had to be "badgered to condemn neo-Nazis" because of the support he receives from white nationalist groups. It goes on to say, "Trump's dance with the racists is therefore inseparable from his agenda. A nativist, populist president without the support of the most extreme defenders of Christian white America would be an impossibility." Jennifer Rubin, "Why Trump Had to Be Badgered to Condemn Neo-Nazis," *Washington Post*, August 14, 2017. http://wapo.st/2w3vJZH?tid=ss_mail&utm_term=.c7ae566abc25.

9. The rise of "religious freedom" bills has direct ties to conservative Christian groups. See, for instance, Pete Madden, "Jeff Sessions Consulted Christian Right Legal Group on Religious Freedom Memo," *ABC News*, October 6, 2017. http://abcnews.go.com/Politics/jeff-sessions-consulted-christian-legal-group-religious-freedom/story?id=50336322.

of Newtonian science, Enlightenment and Romantic philosophies, the rise of the secular university, and all of the challenges that these present to theologians and the Christian church. However, Schleiermacher does more than show how Christians can engage with newly modern ways of thinking and transformations in the structures of society. He also developed a theology that can speak beyond its own context, enabling contemporary theologians to imagine an ecclesial body that could condemn social injustice forthrightly and unabashedly, without sharing in a spirit of divisiveness or hatred of the other.

In this section, I first introduce Schleiermacher's theological imagination and the large role that joy has to play there by examining his early Christmas Eve *Dialogue*. I then focus on Schleiermacher's Christological pneumatology in his *Christian Faith*, demonstrating how for him the loving spirit of Christ in the Christian community gives rise to joy. Finally, I turn to Rachel Adler, a contemporary Jewish feminist theologian, whose work brings laughter into the foreground. By bringing insights from these figures together, we might find an ecclesial practice that could help Christians work against social injustice.

Schleiermacher's Ecclesial Imagination

We have briefly encountered Schleiermacher's *Christmas Eve Celebration: A Dialogue* in the introduction. The dialogue was written quickly, primarily as a Christmas gift for his friends, but it accessibly illustrates ecclesial themes that are further theorized and made more precise in his mature work.[10] I will highlight just three of these themes: the celebration of embodiment, living harmoniously in community, and appreciation of the divine arrangement of the world. Although Christmas celebrations might not be the place where most people would think of mobilizing Christians to face social justice, it could be that the groundwork is laid within the Christian community's own celebrations and life for faithful responses to injustice.[11]

The setting of the *Dialogue* is Christmas Eve at the home of Eduard and Ernestine, who have a 10-year-old daughter, Sophie. They are joined by Friederike and Ernst, a young couple engaged to be married; Leonhardt, a non-Christian lawyer; Karoline, a single woman; Agnes, a pregnant mother of two boys (Anton and a younger sibling); and Josef, a friend. The predominant mood of the text is joyful celebration and its subject matter is the love of new creation. The story unfolds with Ernestine's arrangement of all the gifts her guests have brought for

---

10. Friedrich Schleiermacher, *Christmas Eve Celebration: A Dialogue*, rev. ed., ed. and trans. Terrence N. Tice (Eugene, OR: Cascade Books, 2010). Hereafter, cited as *CEC*.

11. Kurt Nowak notes that Christmas services were outlawed in the kingdom of Hannover since 1742 and in the duchy of Brunswick since 1762 because they had begun to take on the spirit of a New Year's Eve party. He points out that the *Dialogues* would benefit from analysis within this context. Kurt Nowack, *Schleiermacher: Leben, Werk, und Wirkung* (Göttingen: Vandenhoeck & Ruprecht, 2002), pp. 163–5.

one another. After she arranges the gifts, each guest must find their own present in the drawing room and then guess who has given it. Sophie's gift is to show the guests a panorama of the Christmas scene that she has constructed, replete with running water and fire. After enjoying the gifts, the women characters tell stories of Christmases past. They are interrupted by a group of visitors, who are welcomed and eat together briefly before they continue on their way. Then the men discuss, from varying points of view, the topic of Christmas. Their speeches cease with the arrival of Josef, who requests that Sophie return to the group if she is not already sleeping to see the gifts that have been given and to sing together.[12]

A celebration of embodiment is the first theme in the *Dialogue* I would like to highlight. At the outset of the story, family and friends are gathered to exchange gifts, sing, tell stories, eat, and talk with one another about the birth of Christ, the Redeemer. As a festival, it is all very sensual. The opening scene highlights Sophie's appetite for sweets, her love of music, and the smothering of her father with kisses in gratitude. Here is a celebration of life, which intermingles the artistic and the religious. Music, in particular, brings the guests' words of and about Christ alive by interpreting those words and lodging them deep within the hearers' hearts. Music and Christianity elevate and illuminate each other in the *Dialogue*. In part, the connection between these two is meant to show that although a variety of moods and feelings can be evoked through chords and lyrics, each feeling is accepted for itself when it is encountered in a Christmas spirit. As Sophie at one point exclaims, "I just like to be what I am."[13] Such childlike immediacy unites spontaneous play and reflective earnestness.[14] The Christmas festival thus includes strong voices that join breath and body in singing about the new life of the Christ child; acceptance of each feeling that is stirred in remembering past Christmases and experiencing the present; and communal eating, drinking, and exchanging handmade gifts. The festival is bodily, emotional, and material.

Sophie's gift is particularly sensual, combining what seem to be opposing elements: water and fire. Among the objects displayed within her panorama, one could find events within the history of Christianity—"the baptism of Christ, Golgotha and the mount of ascension, or the outpouring of the Spirit, the destruction of the temple, and Christians ranged in battle against the Saracens over the holy sepulcher."[15] The Christmas scene, however, is hidden within the panorama and has to be searched out, even as Madonna and child are recreated in person during the Christmas festival itself: Sophie's mother, standing behind her, beams about her child. The propriety of the recreation of the Christmas

---

12. For an analysis of gender in the *Dialogue*, see Dawn DeVries, "Schleiermacher's *Christmas Eve Dialogue*: Bourgeois Ideology or Feminist Theology?" *Journal of Religion* 69/2 (April 1989): 169–83.

13. *CEC*, p. 37.

14. These themes are also highlighted in Terrence N. Tice's introduction to *CEC*, pp. ix–xxvii.

15. *CEC*, p. 8.

nativity scene in this gathering—first as it is hidden in the panorama, and then clearly in the persons of Sophie and Ernestine—is voiced in Eduard's speech on Christmas: "What we celebrate is nothing other than ourselves as whole beings—that is, human nature, or whatever else you want to call it, viewed and known based on the divine principle."[16] Christmas is a celebration of the good-pleasure the divine takes in creation. As Ernestine takes pleasure in her daughter, so too does the divine delight in humanity. Human creatureliness—body and spirit, past and present—is good and to be enjoyed.

As a culmination of this attitude, the *Dialogue* ends with Josef's arrival at Ernestine and Eduard's home. He had been roaming from house to house all evening, celebrating the Christmas festival with many. He describes his roaming as "one long affectionate kiss that I have given to the world."[17] In Ernestine and Eduard's home, which had at that time been taken up by orations on Christmas, Josef returns the guests to a consideration of their Christmas gifts and to singing. What is celebrated in their festival is precisely divine wisdom given to the world as a tiny bundle of flesh, who assures that "life and pleasure will never more be lost to the world," though it may seem hidden in humble beginnings.[18] There is, here, no small celebration of embodiment, which joins seemingly opposed elements with the ease of a breath, a song, or a kiss.

Embodiment, however, is not celebrated in solitude. A second theme in the *Dialogue* is communal living. Relationships are celebrated by giving and receiving gifts, singing, and talking together as a harmonious group. For example, using music as an interpreter of social harmony, the narrator says of Sophie's piano playing that "she knew how to treat each note aright; her touch and phrasing made each chord sound forth with an attachment that can scarcely tear itself from the rest but that then stands forth in its own measured strength until it too, like a holy kiss, gives way to the next."[19] Each person within the community stands in her own strength and then turns to others, and the harmony belongs to "the music as a whole."[20] The enjoyment of life, which we find in the *Dialogue*'s celebration of embodiment, is here related to the whole community.

The community's high function in the text is also highlighted by a baptism story, told by Agnes, about her brother Ferdinand's first child. By way of introducing the hastily prepared baptism ceremony on a Christmas Eve past to those gathered, Ferdinand had proclaimed that when the Christian community welcomes an individual into itself, "the power of the higher life," which dwells in the community, "must stream out to him [i.e. the baptized child] from us all so that he may take it unto himself."[21] In other words, the community facilitates the indwelling of divine

16. Ibid., p. 81.
17. Ibid., p. 87.
18. Ibid., p. 9.
19. Ibid., p. 6.
20. Ibid., p. 7.
21. Ibid., p. 51.

wisdom and the love of Christ within each community member. Eduard develops the idea later in the *Dialogue*:

> For it is in community that whatever cognition is proper to our planet not only exists but develops. Only when a person sees humanity as a living community of individuals, cultivates humanity as a community, bears its spirit and consciousness in one's life, and within that community both loses one's isolated existence and finds it again in a new way—only then does that person have the higher life and peace of God within oneself.[22]

In baptism in particular, the fact that "a Christian child is welcomed with love and joy, and ever remains embraced by them, furnishes a guarantee that the Spirit of God will dwell in that child."[23] In this way, the individual is ever to be nurtured in communal life so that "the finest gift of all, Christ himself," may be received.[24] A celebration of the birth of Christ in the Christmas Eve festival here gives way to a remembrance of each person's own baptism by the community into new life.

Finally, a third theme in the *Dialogue* is taking joy in the divine arrangement of all things. For Schleiermacher, new life in Christ and the Christian community radiates "out again in every direction."[25] Indeed, from the beginning of the *Dialogue*, the harmonious setting of all things in their places is highlighted. Ernestine is the first character to be introduced, because it was she who thoughtfully arranged the drawing room with gifts. Like Sophie's panorama, "familiar things showed up clearly enough, but only by unhurried and close attention could one distinctly recognize and duly appreciate what was strange or new there."[26] Evoking a creation narrative, Schleiermacher writes that Ernestine was "grandly conjoining things that would look undistinguished by themselves. Now she had finished."[27] After making an arrangement of her guests' gifts, the narrator says that Ernestine was standing "half in the shadows, thinking to take delight, unnoticed, in her loved ones and their buoyant joy."[28] The arrangement was so beautifully done, however, that instead of clamoring to their own individual presents, all of her guests "gathered around her as though she had given them everything and they had already enjoyed it to the full."[29] Here, through deliberate arrangement and interconnection within a wider setting, each good gift is celebrated more robustly than it would be on its own.

22. Ibid., p. 83.
23. Ibid., p. 52.
24. Ibid.
25. Ibid.
26. Ibid., p. 1.
27. Ibid.
28. Ibid., p. 3.
29. Ibid.

When receiving their gifts, each individual in attendance expresses gratitude and love to those in the community. However, the love that emerges from being part of the community is also directed "toward something higher still."[30] Karoline explains that the childlike joy that is aroused and developed in contemplation of the Christ story and in the giving and receiving of gifts during the Christmas festival is basic to her existence. She says,

> In relation to the glorious salvation of the world, all love takes on a greater significance, as does everything good. … I mean, even with the deepest pain this joy can blossom within us unhindered, can cleanse and soothe the pain without being destroyed by it. That is how basic this joy is. That is how immediately rooted it is in an imperishable source.[31]

For Karoline, Christian joy is a balm even in the midst of pain and it is ever present because of its divine source. Although the *Dialogues* take place within a bourgeois home in nineteenth-century Prussia, Julia Lamm points out that the mood is

> a joy shared with intimate friends who have obviously also shared times of real grief. One of the points Schleiermacher returns to throughout is that the joy and serenity experienced that night are not passing states. Having their grounding in the gift of Christ in the incarnation, they are enduring states that define Christian piety through times of weal and woe.[32]

The divine arrangement of created things, which includes the salvific existence of Christ, gives greater significance to Karoline's individual life and loves, and roots her resulting joy in the divine source of all that is. In this way, Schleiermacher connects the Christ child to the community that receives him and wider still to the divine arrangement of all things.

Based on the portrait painted in the *Dialogue*, we can see that for Schleiermacher the Christian community is not a place for morose guilt-mongering, anger, or division. Rather, he envisions the Christian Spirit as loving, communal, material, embodied, and joyful. This venture into Schleiermacher's ecclesial imagination sets the scene for a fuller consideration of his Christological pneumatology in his *Christian Faith*. That tome is a drier, more precise, and systematic text, but—if infused with the spirit of Sophie—can nonetheless be seen as an intellectual

---

30. Ibid., p. 10.
31. Ibid., pp. 28–9.
32. Julia Lamm, *Schleiermacher: Christmas Dialogue, the Second Speech, and Other Selections*, ed. and trans. Julia Lamm (New York: Paulist Press, 2014), p. 27. Hereafter, cited as *SS*.

bulwark for ecclesial joy.³³ In turn, ecclesial joy could be the basis or lay the groundwork for Christian action in the face of injustice.

Schleiermacher's Christological Pneumatology

In paragraph 123 of his *Christian Faith*, Schleiermacher summarizes his pneumatology: "The Holy Spirit is the uniting of the divine being with human nature in the form of the common spirit that animates the collective life of faithful persons."³⁴ The common spirit that he refers to here is the love of Christ that one finds in the Christian church. This love of Christ does not simply dwell internally as a commonality shared among Christians. Rather, it impels Christians to outward actions that would conform them to the person and work of Christ. As Schleiermacher writes,

> The leading of the Holy Spirit in us is never anything other than the divine impetus to conformity with what Christ has been and done humanly by virtue of the existence of God in him. Moreover, the life of Christ in us is nothing other than efficacious action for the reign of God through the embrace of human beings in the love that proceeds from Christ—that is, the strength of the Christian common spirit.³⁵

For Schleiermacher, the doctrine of the Holy Spirit is intimately connected with both Christology and ecclesiology. The Holy Spirit is the continuation of the indwelling of God in humanity, which first occurred in and through Christ. By embodying the love of Christ, the Christian community extends Christ's action in the establishment of the reign of God on earth.

Although the indwelling of God in the Christian church is not a "person-forming union," as it was in Christ, it is nonetheless a genuine union of the divine essence and human nature. Indeed, Schleiermacher states in paragraph 125 that "the Christian church, being animated by the Holy Spirit, is formed as the perfect image of the Redeemer."³⁶ This image of Christ in the church—including both his person and work—has concrete implications in terms of its corporate life. With regard to the person of Christ, the corporate nature of the church is required because "only in the collectivity composed of all formations of spiritual life that are grounded in the variety of people's natural dispositions is the perfect likeness of Christ to be found."³⁷ By supplementing the weaknesses

---

33. As Lamm states, "Sofie very clearly is a product of that love and represents the early bud of Christian piety; and such love, according to Schleiermacher, necessarily creates a hospitable place of community and joy" (Lamm, SS, p. 27).
34. *CF*, §123, p. 807.
35. Ibid., §124.2, p. 816.
36. Ibid., §125, p. 818.
37. Ibid., §125.1, p. 820.

of one person with the strengths of another person, the image of Christ is able to be repeated in the church. Far from having a homogenizing effect, this kind of corporate spirit actually encourages diversity within the church, since each person needs many others—in and with their differences—to form the image of Christ within the church. Likewise, with regard to the work of Christ, Schleiermacher would "consider the church as an organic body equipped to be a collectivity of activities, a body in which the perfection of each expression of life is conditioned by the fullness brought by the various members."[38] The body of Christ, in this way, involves common activity: "everything in the church is a common deed and a common work, consequently a common merit and a common fault as well, but this commonality simply presents itself unevenly in different individuals."[39]

Taken with the Christmas Eve *Dialogue*, this brief account of Schleiermacher's Christological pneumatology in his *Christian Faith* demonstrates that he understands the church as intrinsically bound up with the person and work of Jesus of Nazareth; as an organic union of Christians, bound as they are by the love of Christ; and as a continuation of the existence of Christ on earth.[40] In the midst of these details of Schleiermacher's pneumatology and ecclesiology, it is important to notice the extent to which his understanding of Christ and the church is focused on the activity of creation, collective life, communion with God, and loving relationships. Schleiermacher's theology prioritizes embodied acts of love within a community that is reaching out to others. The result, as we have seen in the Christmas Eve *Dialogue*, is a predominant mood of joy. Indeed, these are marks of the church, for Schleiermacher: the Christian church ought to be known by its love, which issues forth into enjoyment of humanity and creation more widely, with confidence in the ongoing creative-redemptive work of God in history.

Feminist Laughter

All this might be well and good for those, like Schleiermacher, who lived before the tragedies of the First World War and the Second World War, the Vietnam War, and the continued threat of nuclear war.[41] Those who have lived after the Enlightenment and Romanticism and through the recent horrors of history have rightly come to question the modern optimism sometimes displayed in

---

38. Ibid., §125.1, p. 820.

39. Ibid., §125.2, p. 821.

40. For my understanding and a critique of Schleiermacher's eschatology as it relates to people outside the church, see Shelli Poe, "Friedrich Schleiermacher's Theology as a Resource for Ecological Economics," *Theology Today* 73/1 (2016): 9–23.

41. Of course, Schleiermacher himself was familiar with political invasions and structural injustice, having lived through Napoleonic invasions and having argued for the rights of Jewish citizens in Prussia. Two world wars and the hitherto unimaginable technological advances of the twentieth century, however, do tend to separate modern history into different phases of life that can seem quite distant from one another.

Schleiermacher's thought, with its confidence in the progress of humanity toward redemption. In the twenty-first century, we now see clearly that humanity is not on an upward trajectory, moving ever and consistently toward peace, love, and harmony. In the face of social injustices, including the persistence of sexism, racism, and heterosexism, which still plague humanity over two thousand years after the life of Jesus of Nazareth, and given the clearly tenuous and imperfect continuation of his Spirit in the church, what are contemporary theologians to say of Schleiermacher's theological imagination? How could Schleiermacher's vision of a loving and joyful Christian communion speak to the realities of contemporary life? Especially as Constantinian and Prophetic Christianity are at odds with one another, complicating the role of Christianity in the United States today, how are contemporary prophetic theologians to do their work of denouncing injustice without fueling hatred?

I turn to the work of Jewish feminist theologian, Rachel Adler, who offers the unintuitive practice of laughing in the face of injustice. In this practice, she reveals a kindred spirit to that of Schleiermacher insofar as for both of them, joy is a practice of empowerment and healing, which can erupt in redemptive laughter. By placing these figures together, I am boldly traversing the centuries that lie between them. I am also bounding over the gap between Judaism and Christianity, and do not provide any methodological or theological justification for doing so. My only defense and hope is that by placing the two next to one another in an imaginative conversation, theologians working constructively today might envision another beneficial way to stand against oppressive forces.

Adler writes about sexist Jewish texts and her goal is to restore these texts "by reframing them as comedies."[42] In this process, she thinks of a historical Jewish text being read to its original audience, which was composed of men and a few "eavesdropping women."[43] Gradually over the years, more women join the outer circle of listeners and eventually come to compose the inner circle along with men. "What happens to the story," Adler asks, "as the two circles become one, when all the hearers look into each other's faces? I imagine the shock of illumination in that moment issuing forth around the circle in a great flood of purifying laughter."[44] Laughter, for Adler, is the way "that our texts are redeemed and become redemptive."[45] She gives an example from her own life:

> When I first read these midrashim [from Midrash Aseret Ha-Dibrot], what startled me most was that I found them hilarious. ... But when I read a version of my analysis to a group, others also rocked with laughter. A classically trained male scholar said rather wistfully, "You know, I was taught these stories from

---

42. Rachel Adler, *Engendering Judaism: An Inclusive Theology and Ethics* (Boston, MA: Beacon Press, 1998), p. 2.
43. Ibid.
44. Ibid.
45. Ibid., p. 3.

childhood and, although I have long understood that they were misogynistic, I never found them funny before. Now, how will I ever read them again without laughing?" Then I understood at last: I told him, "That is a gift to you from feminist Torah."[46]

The laughter that Adler endorses is "not the laughter of separation and superiority, the laughter that says, 'I could not be a fool like you.' Not ungenerous laughter."[47] Instead, redemptive laughter is the kind that recognizes that "being human, none of us can see very far. Our choices in this predicament are to help one another to clearer vision and to discover a delight in the absurdity of our errors or to break our hearts alone in the darkness."[48] Adler, for her part, chooses "the hidden springs of laughter that well up once we are willing to relinquish the suffocating security of the dominator or the smoldering grudge of the victim."[49]

What Adler seems to be espousing here is a response to sexism that is born of the deeply felt conviction that those who currently hold sexist views are incorrect but need not be inherently evil. Primarily, such people are limited by their experiences in life, their upbringings, and their educations. They are not to be hated. Rather, we might see in them a trait we share by virtue of our common humanity, namely, our circumscribed perspectives. Granted, Adler was laughing at a text of the past, albeit one being read presently in community. Further, she was joined in laughter by a classically trained male scholar—an experience that many feminist scholars have yet to experience. The differences between Adler's interpreting texts of the past in a scholarly community and current, in-your-face experiences of oppression that sometimes have no witnesses are no small matter. Nonetheless, the experience of having two choices when responding to injustice seems quite familiar: to see the other as one who shares the human lot (and laugh) or to retreat into relative isolation (and either remain passive or attempt to achieve vengeance).

Adler's option for generous laughter issues from a recognition of the incongruity of the sexist content of the text with the interpreters who encircle it. While the text might portray women as inferior or unreasonable, the interpreters who surround it might be women who are scholars at the top of their fields. The incongruity between the text's message and the reality of those who look into each other's faces while reading it is enough to make the group erupt with laughter. The philosophical tradition that theorizes humor as arising from incongruity—whether logical, definitional, or context-based—arose from the work of Immanuel Kant and Arthur Schopenhauer. While scholars within the incongruity tradition all explain amusement as the result of an incongruity between two things, John Lippett explains that "recent writers in this tradition have disagreed as to whether what really causes amusement is the perception of incongruity itself, or

---

46. Ibid., p. 16.
47. Ibid., p. 18.
48. Ibid., p. 19.
49. Ibid.

the resolution of that incongruity: the fitting of an apparent anomaly into some conceptual schema."[50] In either case, Adler's experience of redemptive laughter seems to place her in the good company of a majority of theorists on humor who subscribe to some version of the incongruity thesis.

Adler's use of humor in incongruent situations also seems coherent with the biblical tradition itself. As J. William Whedbee summarizes his work in *The Bible and the Comic Vision*,

> Again and again we have beheld Genesis' generative drive toward new birth and fertility even amidst barrenness and death; Exodus' wedding of liberation and laughter in celebrating Yahweh's victory over the Egyptians and in founding a covenantal community; Esther's depiction of the collaboration of Mordecai and Esther in delivering a Jewish community from genocide and the resulting carnival celebration of Purim; Jonah's powerful punchline in the form of a question which affirms the sometimes capricious Creator's compassion for all creatures great and small; Job's song of creation in the carnival of morning stars and animals, a song that reveals a larger cosmic theater than Job's limited vision can perceive and leads to his re-vision of the universe which in turn results in his repentance and restoration; and finally, the Song of Songs' duet of two young lovers who delight in the wonders of wild gazelles and lush gardens as compelling images of their joyous participation in the spring-time of new love.[51]

Throughout the Bible, laughter is used subversively to pave the way for celebrations, liberation, and exulting in the senses. Moreover, on Whedbee's analysis, women in particular seem to have a knack for the humorous. He speculates that "perhaps the special powers of comedy are particularly invoked by those who are marginalized and subordinated. ... Standing on the margins of society, women are able to deconstruct the dominant power structures and to recharge the forces of life."[52]

Certainly, laughter alone is not an adequate response to injustice.[53] The hard work of organizing, raising awareness, registering people to vote, calling one's representatives, turning out at the polls, writing, reading, speaking, and agitating must be done. Even so, contemporary Christian theologians might find in laughter in response to sexist texts "a gift from feminist Torah." Schleiermacher's theological work in the *Christmas Eve Celebration* and the *Christian Faith* can

---

50. John Lippett, "Humor and Religion: Humor, Irony, and the Comic," in *Encyclopedia of Religion*, 2nd ed., ed. Lindsay Jones (Farmington Hills: Thomson Gale, 2005), vol. 6, p. 4221.

51. J. William Whedbee, *The Bible and the Cosmic Vision* (Cambridge: Cambridge University Press, 1998), pp. 280–1.

52. Ibid., pp. 282–3.

53. Laughter would also be inappropriate in many contexts, of course. For instance, I can see no plausible way to use laughter in response to clergy who have sexually abused children, or in response to genocide or murder.

add a distinctively Christian support to such a gift. The Christian church, as he understands it, is the place where joy arises as a fundamental mood of its members in response to the love of God in Christ. In the Christian community, persons are formed in such a way that they have deep confidence in the redemptive work of God in history. Christian joy is rooted in God's love of creation, illuminated by the life of Christ whose Spirit of love extends to the world. For Schleiermacher, creation and human bodiliness are good and to be enjoyed.[54] Accordingly, his telling of the Christmas festival exudes love, community life, and the pleasures of the body. When he then writes in his *Christian Faith* of Christ and the Holy Spirit in the church, he likewise emphasizes embodiment in a community united by love and freely extending the work of Christ in the world. Once personal formation within the Christian community has taken place, we might imagine Christians then going forth and encountering social injustice from a place of confidence in their own belovedness, despite what oppressors might say about them. Playful laughter might be one way of expressing the dynamic confidence involved in one's relation to the divine, others, and oneself. Perhaps in this way, laughter and joy could be used not as a blind refusal to reckon with the injustice that plagues individuals and societies throughout the centuries but as an empowering, playful, and redemptive resistance to oppressive forces.

The fundamental mood of joy that issues from Christian love—which can be found in Schleiermacher's theology as well as contemporary feminist theologies—might point one way forward as Christian theologians attempt to construct ecclesiologies in a time of social injustice. Reading and analyzing texts (written, visual, or aural) in a collective life, celebrating the good gifts of creation, recognizing the consistent need to become new persons: here might be some ways that the church might not lose its hope as it reckons with contemporary racism, sexism, heterosexism, classism, colonialism, and the degradation of the earth, but might find some redemption in the midst of its struggle against injustice. The redemptive power of joy within Christianity has not yet been fully tapped by prophetic theologians. Schleiermacher's Christological pneumatology, which understands love and joy to be the heart of Christian community, might be coupled with contemporary Jewish feminist thought to emphasize this initially unintuitive but potentially significant ecclesial practice.

Expanding the Imaginary: A Queer Community of Woman

I now turn to a constructive expansion of the ecclesial imagination that draws inspiration from Schleiermacher's ecclesiology and pneumatology but goes further to engage particular features of contemporary racism, sexism, heterosexism, and

---

54. There is a deep connection between one's view of humor or laughter and one's view of the body. For that history in Western theology and philosophy, see Lippett, "Humor and Religion," pp. 4218–19.

exclusivism. In this section, I imaginatively offer a "queer community of Woman" that could serve the church in its aim to establish a community that upholds the dignity and differences of its members while opening itself outward to all who wish to engage it.[55]

Feminist theologians recognize the power of imagery and metaphor for transforming Christianity in liberating directions. Nineteenth-century feminists, for example, used biblical criticism to form spiritual biographies of women who could serve as models for women of faith.[56] In the twentieth century, Janet Martin Soskice's *Metaphor and Religious Language*[57] and Sallie McFague's *Metaphorical Theology*[58] are particularly poignant examples of feminist theory that have updated and expanded the theme, going beyond spiritual biographies to explicit analysis and construction of imagery for feminist aims. In the current century, as theologians expand the Christian imaginary even further, I suggest that instead of focusing on singular individuals and raising them to our attention one after another, as has predominantly been the case in nineteenth- and twentieth-century feminist portrayals of female or woman-identified characters, theologians could expand their achievements by holding out for the imagination a community, in concert with Schleiermacher's ecclesial thought. A focus on individual women tends to create a narrative about women in relation to men—socioeconomically and personally. In contrast, putting women in cross-generational relationships within what I am calling a "queer community" allows the emergence of another narrative: one that is about Woman's homosocial relationality for social and economic survival and well-being. In constructing a homosocial community, I do not mean to suggest that the church should become exclusive to women. Rather, I am suggesting that this queer community of Woman could aid the Christian imagination in embracing an "otherwise" within the larger Christian community:[59] women's solidarity, upholding women's worth as subjects considered on their own terms, and attending to the complexity of human relationality. Further, this account could inspire theologians working constructively to embrace an updated version of Schleiermacher's ecclesiological focus on embodiment, diversity, joy, and community. Schleiermacher's understanding of human nature

---

55. There is a lively debate about the use of the category "woman" in feminist theory. For one view into the debate, see Hannah McCann, "Epistemology of the Subject: Queer Theory's Challenge to Feminist Sociology," *WSQ: Women's Studies Quarterly* 44/3 and 4 (Fall/Winter 2016): 224–43.

56. Rebecca Styler, "A Scripture of their own: Nineteenth-Century Bible Biography and Feminist Bible Criticism," *Christianity and Literature* 57/1 (2007): 65–85.

57. Janet Martin Soskice, *Metaphor and Religious Language* (New York: Oxford University Press, 1985).

58. Sallie McFague, *Metaphorical Theology* (Philadelphia, PA: Fortress, 1982).

59. Elizabeth A. Povinelli, "Geontologies of the Otherwise," Theorizing the Contemporary, *Cultural Anthropology* website, January 13, 2014. https://culanth.org/fieldsights/465-geontologies-of-the-otherwise.

as organic, interconnected, and unified in its diversity adds theoretical support to the queer community imagined here. In the final portion of this section, I draw on his organic understanding of human nature to offer an implicit critique of theologies that focus on the individual and demonstrate the potential of an ecumenical queer community of Woman for achieving social justice aims within the Christian church. Lilith, Eve, Hagar, and Mary, who I consider here, function not so much as four women but as representatives within a community of Woman, since they are and become who and what they are together. As such, my account of a queer community of Woman unfolds with each description adding another layer of complexity. Together, Lilith, Eve, Hagar, and Mary could intervene in theological thought to help Christians embrace their own multiple identities and gender constructions and to challenge them to be always open to other particular perspectives and concrete experiences.[60]

Before moving further, let me set out a few definitions of key terms and concepts that are employed here. I use the term "Woman" throughout to refer to an identity that, as Cathy J. Cohen states regarding any category, "includes multiple social positions and relations to dominant power."[61] "Woman" is not used in an essentialist mode but as an identity that is always shaped and being reshaped relationally within a community.[62] In the words of Marilyn Frye, this positive category might be conceived as "a plurality with internal structure whose elements are differentiated and differentiable and are in a significant variety of relations with each other."[63] That is to say, "Woman" is not an essentially defined category that includes a list of properties that each and every woman must possess. Instead, "Woman" is constituted by a community of different women who themselves are becoming as they remain in relation with one another.

This kind of use of the term can be seen in the work of Talia Mae Bettcher, who argues in the context of trans theory that gender identities ought to be forged outside of a "single-meaning position." In other words, a gendered term should not be conceived as having only one meaning. Using a "multiple-meaning position," she argues that trans women and trans men are women and men, respectively, not because they fit into dominant society's definitions. Rather, trans women and trans men are women and men, respectively, because the terms "trans woman"

---

60. A brief version of this portion of the chapter was presented to the Women, Gender, and Religion Group at the Southeastern Commission for the Study of Religion, a regional branch of the American Academy of Religion, under the title, "Expanding the Imaginary: A Queer Community for Feminist Ecumenism," in Raleigh, NC, on March 6, 2017.

61. Cathy J. Cohen, "Punks, Bulldaggers, and Welfare Queens: The Radical Potential of Queer Politics?" *GLQ* 3 (1997): 458.

62. For an argument that "women's experience" should not be constructed monolithically, see Mary McClintock Fulkerson, *Changing the Subject: Women's Discourses and Feminist Theology* (Minneapolis, MN: Fortress, 1994).

63. Marilyn Frye, "The Necessity of Differences: Constructing a Positive Category of Women," *Signs* 21/4 (Summer 1996): 1002.

and "trans man" are basic expressions.⁶⁴ Bettcher explains that this means, first, that trans persons are trans if they identify as such. Second, being a trans woman is a sufficient condition for being a woman, and being a trans man is a sufficient condition for being a man.⁶⁵ On this view, the dominant cultural model for understanding gender may simply be rejected and resistant cultural models accepted. "Put another way," Bettcher writes,

> there are actually two concepts and two meanings of "womanhood." [These include a dominant one and a resistant one.] The two concepts (and the two meanings) are related in that the latter is the result of changes performed on the former. One starts with a particular concept and then expands it, for example, to include something that wasn't included in it before.⁶⁶

Just in this way, I am using the term "Woman" without determining in advance what it means and will mean for all time. Rather, "Woman" is a concept that has multiple meanings that change and expand over time.

Following Annamarie Jagose's understanding, I am using "queer" as a "'a zone of possibilities,' always inflected by a sense of potentiality that it cannot yet articulate."⁶⁷ A queer community is one that celebrates unlikely alliances and solidarities, is open to the unexpected, and speaks honestly. "Broadly speaking," Jagose explains, "queer describes those gestures or analytical models which dramatize incoherencies in the allegedly stable relations between chromosomal sex, gender and sexual desire."⁶⁸ As such, "queer" is not to be exclusively identified with LGBT persons or communities, although it may be identified with the fluidity that many within the LGBT community have celebrated.⁶⁹ Although Jagose is now an historical rather than contemporary source in the development of queer theory, her basic claim remains useful. Though it has multiple uses, "queer" indicates a surprising surplus and points out instability. As Gerard Loughlin writes, "queer

---

64. Talia Mae Bettcher, "Trans Women and the Meaning of 'Woman,'" *Philosophy of Sex: Contemporary Readings*, 6th ed., ed. Nicholas Power, Raja Halwani, and Alan Soble (New York: Rowman & Littlefield, 2013), p. 240.

65. Ibid., p. 241.

66. Ibid., p. 244.

67. Annamarie Jagose, *Queer Theory: An Introduction* (Washington Square: New York University Press, 1996), p. 2. The quoted text is from Lee Edelman, *No Future: Queer Theory and the Death Drive* (Durham, NC: Duke University Press, 2004).

68. Ibid., p. 3.

69. In this way, I agree with Cathy J. Cohen, who argues that "queer" has been used dichotomously—queer vs. heterosexual—in unhelpful ways. When "queer" is used to distinguish LGBT persons from straight persons, the intersectionality of all such persons is ignored. What makes someone "queer" is their marginal relation to dominant power and their aim of transforming systems of oppression, including racial, economic, sexist, and heterosexist systems. See Cohen, "Punks, Bulldaggers, and Welfare Queens."

seeks to outwit identity. It serves those who find themselves and others to be other than the characters prescribed by an identity. It marks not by defining, but by taking up a distance from what is perceived as the normative. The term is deployed in order to mark, and to make, a difference, a divergence."[70] As I am using the term, then, "queer" is meant to highlight the undecidability, uncertainty, and surprises that stand in contrast to an unchanging rule that can or should be enforced. "Queer" therefore also indicates that the community has the potential to bring about an undoing of things as they stand.[71]

In *Gender Trouble*, Butler argues that feminists should not use "women" as a grounding category. By joining Woman with a queer community, I am using "queer" to acknowledge the limits of identity categories like "women." In this respect, my approach is similar to Jagose's description of Biddy Martin's endorsement of

> a rapprochement between feminist and queer theory. She urges that "we stop defining queerness as mobile and fluid in relation to what then gets construed as stagnant and ensnaring, and as associated with a maternal, anachronistic, and putatively puritanical feminism." She also advocates that we no longer "see queer theory and activism as disruptive of the potential solidarities and shared interests among women." (Martin 1994: 101)[72]

My approach similarly attempts to forge a synthesis between "women" and "queer" as signifiers, describing Woman (with a capital W) as a queer community. Joining the capitalized singular and the lowercase plural, I aim to integrate the benefits of identity with those of fluidity and diversity.

In this way, my approach sidesteps a lesbian feminist objection to using the word "queer," given by Philippa Bonwick: "Perhaps the most damaging aspect of the pervasive push to be queer is that it shrouds lesbians in an ever thicker cloak of invisibility ... Queer totally ignores the politics of gender. Using a generic term wipes out women again."[73] By joining Woman to a queer community, I take this critique seriously without forfeiting the productivity of queer theory.[74] E. Patrick Johnson recognizes a similar critique with respect to communities of color and suggests using "quare" instead of "queer" as a way to "critique stable notions

---

70. Gerard Loughlin, "Introduction: The End of Sex," in *Queer Theory: Rethinking the Western Body*, ed. Gerard Loughlin (Malden, MA: Blackwell, 2007), p. 9.

71. See Judith Butler, *Antigone's Claim: Kinship between Life and Death* (New York: Columbia University Press, 2000); Sara Ahmed, *The Promise of Happiness* (Durham, NC: Duke University Press, 2010); Sara Ahmed, *Queer Phenomenology: Orientations, Objects, Others* (Durham, NC: Duke University Press, 2006).

72. Jagose, *Queer Theory*, p. 124.

73. Ibid., p. 117. Quoted in Jagose: Philippa Bonwick, "It is Cool to Be Queer, but ..." *Brother Sister* (Melbourne, December 3, 1993): 10.

74. For further discussion of the relationship between "queer" and "feminist," see McCann, "Epistemology of the Subject," pp. 224–43.

of identity and, at the same time, to locate racialized and class knowledges."[75] Johnson explains: "I want to maintain the inclusivity and playful spirit of 'queer' that animates much of queer theory, but I also want to jettison its homogenizing tendencies. As a disciplinary expansion, then, I wish to 'quare' 'queer' such that ways of knowing are viewed both as discursively mediated and as historically situated and materially conditioned."[76] By joining "queer" to "Woman," I am attempting something similar: to maintain the many nuances of "queer" that have come out in the literature of the past decades and to retain an acknowledgment of the specific community that I have in mind, namely, women situated historically and materially in different ways.

Drawing on Elizabeth Johnson's work, a queer Christian community—with an emphasis on Christian, here—may be understood as a communion of the saints: a "cloud of witnesses, surrounding those who cry for justice with encouragement and blessing, lending the support of their own witness for personal and social transformation."[77] The queer community of Woman I gather in the pages that follow includes diverse women figures united by a love for justice and one another, and whose union has the potential for social transformation. I have selected four figures who may beneficially represent diverse demographics within ecclesial and religiously ecumenical relations: Lilith, a religiously "other" woman; Eve, a Protestant ideal; Hagar, a symbol for women of color; and Mary, a Catholic model. Of course, there are many other demographics that could and should be represented in a queer community. Further, it should be quite clear that differences remain within the demographics here depicted. These four figures, however, mark out some key religious, theological, and racial features that constructive forms of theology do well to keep in view. By creating a queer community of Woman through these four figures, I draw on Eve Kosofsky Sedgwick's understanding of queer as "the open mesh of possibilities, gaps, overlaps, dissonances and resonances, lapses and excesses of meaning where the constituent elements of anyone's gender, of anyone's sexuality aren't made (or can't be made) to signify monolithically."[78]

Lilith

Lilith is mentioned only once in the Hebrew Bible, in Isa. 34:14.[79] Her name, *lilit*, was translated as screech-owl, night-hag, vampire, witch, fury, or demon in the

---

75. E. Patrick Johnson, "'Quare' Studies, or (Almost) Everything I Know about Queer Studies I Learned from My Grandmother," *Text and Performance Quarterly* 21/1 (January 2001): 3.

76. Ibid., p. 3.

77. Elizabeth Johnson, *Friends of God and Prophets* (New York: Continuum, 1998), p. 180.

78. Eve Kosofsky Sedgwick, *Tendencies* (Durham, NC: Duke University Press, 1993), p. 8.

79. For an introduction to Lilith in biblical reception, see Shelli Poe, "Lilith, Christianity," in *Encyclopedia of Bible and Its Reception, vol. 16*, ed. Christine Helmer (Berlin: De Gruyter, pp. 665-6). Some of the material in this chapter is a revised version of that entry.

Septuagint (*Satyr*), Vulgate (*Lamia*), and English versions of the Hebrew Bible until the publication of the Catholic Jerusalem Bible (1966) and the New Revised Standard Version (1989).[80] In Isa. 34, Lilith takes up her abode in Edom after God has destroyed it. Jewish Lilith traditions, however, were first developed not in relation to this prophetic text but as an effort to explain the discrepancies between the two creation accounts in Gen. 1 and 2. In Gen. 1, God creates humankind in God's image, blesses humanity, and gives the earth to them as the place they will be "fruitful and multiply" (Gen. 1:28). In the next chapter, a different version of the story is offered, where God creates a male human being first and only subsequently creates a female from the rib of the male's body. To explain the discrepancies between the two creation accounts, medieval rabbis imagined that there were actually two women created, one in the first chapter of Genesis and the other in the second. Lilith was understood to be the first woman and stories about her were promulgated in midrashim and folklore.[81]

According to these narratives, Lilith refused to take the subordinate position in her relationship with Adam by laying on her back during sexual intercourse. Instead, she declared her equality with him, having been created simultaneously with him from the dust. When Adam did not respond favorably, Lilith pronounced the ineffable divine name and flew out of the Garden of Eden to the Red Sea, where she spawned demon children. In various traditions, Lilith seduced men, stole semen from men who slept alone, and strangled babies in their cribs. In answer to Adam's complaint that Lilith had left the Garden, God sent angels commanding Lilith to return. When she refused, the angels threatened to kill one hundred of her demon children each day. In reply, Lilith indicated that she would only be deterred from killing human babies if she saw an amulet bearing the names of the angels—Senoy, Sansenoy, and Semangeloff—when she approached an infant.

Even on this cursory treatment of Jewish Lilith traditions, it is clear that these stories do much more than explain a tension between the accounts of creation in Gen. 1 and 2. Howard Schwartz agrees that "Lilith is a projection of the negative fears and desires of the Rabbis who created her. If Lilith served no other purpose than to resolve the contradiction in the biblical text, such an extensive legend, with so many ramifications, would never have come into being."[82] Likewise, Raphael Patai claims,

---

80. Jerome's (347–419) early comment on Isaiah correlates Lilith with "furies," which may indicate his familiarity with Jewish "Erinyes" (cf. J. M. Tanja and E. van Staalduine-Sulman, "A Jewish Targum in a Remarkable Paratext," in *A Jewish Targum in a Christian World*, ed. A. Houtman, E. van Staalduine-Sulman, and Hans-Martin Kim [Boston, MA: Brill, 2014], pp. 179–82).

81. See, for example, *The Alphabet of Ben Sira*, and *The Zohar*.

82. Howard Schwartz, *Lilith's Cave: Jewish Tales of the Supernatural* (New York: Oxford University Press, 1988), p. 8.

There can be little doubt that a she-demon who accompanied mankind—or at least part of mankind—from earliest antiquity to the threshold of the Age of Enlightenment must be a projection, or objectification, of human fears and desires which, in a deeper sense, are identical with those of oft-mentioned "plagues of mankind" said in Kabbalistic literature to be the offspring of Lilith, but recognized by us as her psychogenic progenitors.[83]

To illuminate the psychological work that Lilith narratives perform, Patai brings Lilith into conversation with another female figure: Matronit, the goddess of the Kabbala. Patai believes that the meaning of Lilith traditions is illuminated by a comparison with Matronit because she is Lilith's opposite. Behind the opposing masks these goddesses wear—the evil mask of Lilith and the good mask of Matronit—"the numen, embodying man's fears and desires, is disconcertingly, yet reassuringly, the same."[84] Men think of these women as promiscuous and virgins, mothers and killers, wives and cut in two. "We thus recognize," Patai explains, "the ambivalence of religio-sexual experience. The same impulse or experience can, in the case of one man, be good, and in the case of the other, evil."[85] Patai is suggesting that in these sources, women are portrayed as mysterious and dangerous, and this portrayal can be used in the masculine imagination for multiple purposes, however contradictory. In part, Lilith traditions have been created to narrate fears about women and to inscribe a gender code within the Jewish tradition. As the ancient recitation found on amulets and incantation bowls puts it, "Adam and Eve, Out Lilith!"[86]

Most Christian reception of Lilith has also been indirectly related to the biblical text. Christian commentaries on Lilith in Isa. 34:14 are sparse. In the medieval period, popular Christianity was highly influenced by the association of deviant women with witchcraft, which led to the infamous witch hunts in Europe and North America during the twelfth to the sixteenth centuries. In the High Middle Ages, Christians explicitly used Lilith narratives to propagate anti-Semitism. They identified different hereditary lineages for Jews and Christians: Jews were the progeny of Lilith and Adam, while Christians were descendants of Adam and Eve.[87] Further, Renaissance humanist interest in returning to original sources (*ad fontes*) led to direct Christian contact with Jewish Lilith traditions. Works created by artists and authors from the Renaissance and Modern periods depict Lilith with

---

83. Raphael Patai, *The Hebrew Goddess* (Detroit, MI: Wayne State University Press, 1990), p. 252.

84. Ibid.

85. Ibid., p. 253.

86. This recitation has been found on amulets and was spoken at childbirth to keep Lilith away from vulnerable babies. Patai, *The Hebrew Goddess*, p. 238.

87. Irvin Resnick, *Marks of Distinction: Christian Perceptions of Jews in the High Middle Ages* (Washington, DC: Catholic University of America Press, 2012), p. 246.

Adam and Eve in the Garden of Eden, and associate her with witchcraft, seduction, demons, chaos, the night, and evil.[88]

With the New Revised Standard Version of the Bible, Christians in the contemporary period are reading the word "Lilith" directly in Isa. 34. Given the long tradition of demonizing Lilith, it is now an irony of interpretation history that scholars like John Sawyer suggest that Isa. 34 is intimating an overthrow of patriarchal society. In that text, once Lilith rests by taking her place in Edom, the owl will nest and gather her young and each kite will have a mate. It will be called "No Kingdom There," and its princes will be reduced to nothing.[89] A hermeneutic of Sawyer's kind would support a reinterpretation of Lilith, especially in relation to biblical reception history.

Most Christian feminists, however, are now familiar with Lilith because of Judith Plaskow's creative retelling of "The Coming of Lilith" (1972), first published in Rosemary Radford Ruether's *Religion and Sexism*.[90] Subsequently, feminists have used Lilith to question gender essentialism and kyriarchy, as well as construct new narratives for women's empowerment. Plaskow's retelling of the Lilith story was originally constructed after intensive conversation with three Christians: Karen Bloomquist, Margaret Early, and Elizabeth Farians. It was the product of an ecumenical imagination. In Plaskow's narrative, the scene is the Garden of Eden and the characters include Lilith, Eve, Adam, and God. The plot begins as Eve has been excluded from the close relationship between Adam and God in the Garden. Over time, Eve becomes curious about whether the stories she has been told about Lilith—allegedly a she-demon—are true. She suspects that Lilith is actually a woman like herself. One day, climbing over the wall that surrounds the Garden, she encounters Lilith and subsequently talks with her many more times. In fact, they forge a sisterhood: "They taught each other many things, and told each other stories, and laughed together, and cried, over and over, till the bond of sisterhood grew between them."[91] God and Adam then grow fearful as Eve and Lilith return to the Garden "to rebuild it together."[92] Plaskow explains, "Eve and Lilith by themselves are each isolated and powerless. Their ability to transform the garden and God results from their coming together; it is sisterhood that grows

---

88. See Michelangelo's Sistine Chapel ceiling (1508–1512); Rosetti's "Lady Lilith" (1864) and "Eden Bower" (1869); Robert Browning's "Adam, Lilith, and Eve" (1883); and George MacDonald's *Lilith* (1895).

89. John F. A. Sawyer, *The Fifth Gospel: Isaiah in the History of Christianity* (New York: Cambridge University Press, 1996), p. 218.

90. *Religion and Sexism: Images of Woman in the Jewish and Christian Traditions*, ed. Rosemary Radford Ruether (New York: Simon and Schuster, 1974).

91. Judith Plaskow, "Epilogue: The Coming of Lilith," in *Religion and Sexism: Images of Woman in the Jewish and Christian Traditions*, ed. R. Radford Ruether (New York: Simon and Schuster, 1974), p. 342.

92. Ibid., p. 343.

them into consciousness and action."⁹³ Reflecting on this retelling of the Lilith story twenty-three years later, Plaskow reiterates the judgment shared by Schwartz and Patai: "I came to see Lilith as a classic example of male projection. Lilith is not a demon; rather she is a woman named a demon by a tradition that does not know what to do with strong women."⁹⁴

In Lilith, the religiously "other" woman is appreciated and celebrated in her difference and strength. As part of a queer community, Lilith may remind us that solidarity in difference should include those some consider to be "other"— religiously, socially, economically, linguistically, and so forth—and who have been traditionally excluded.⁹⁵ In the queer community, Lilith may stand for all those who are misunderstood and excluded from a community because of people's fears. Lilith therefore challenges Christians to overcome false projections of themselves and others to see reality. By recognizing reality as well as the potential to create another world, the queer community has radical potential to undo the false projections and ideas that lie at the center of an exclusionary way of life.⁹⁶

Eve

Discussion of Lilith has already invited reflection on Eve, to which we now turn directly. With Eve, we return to the two creation accounts in Genesis. According to Phyllis Trible, in Gen. 1:26–31, one sexually undifferentiated human being is created (*hā-'ādām*). In Gen. 2, which accounts for human sin, the story is told again and this time God creates two sexually differentiated beings: *'iššâ and 'îš*.⁹⁷ The woman in the second creation account has been portrayed by many Christian interpreters as gullible, ignorant, and responsible for sin. As Trible understands the text, however, Eve is represented as the spokesperson for the couple and equal to Adam in creation.⁹⁸ As an example, when Eve speaks with the serpent, Trible explains that she is not in the process of being deceived but is engaging in standard midrash:

---

93. Judith Plaskow, "Lilith Revisited," in *Eve and Adam: Jewish, Christian, and Muslim Readings on Genesis and Gender*, ed. Kristen E. Kvam, Linda S. Schearing, and Valarie H. Ziegler (Bloomington: Indiana University Press, 1999), p. 428.

94. Ibid., p. 426.

95. See Chandra Talpade Mohanty, *Feminism without Borders: Decolonizing Theory, Practicing Solidarity* (Durham, NC: Duke University Press, 2003).

96. Judith Butler, *Undoing Gender* (London: Routledge, 2004); Lauren Berlant, *The Female Complaint: The Unfinished Business of Sentimentality in American Culture* (Durham, NC: Duke University Press, 2008).

97. Phyllis Trible, *God and the Rhetoric of Sexuality* (Minneapolis, MN: Fortress, 1978), p. 107.

98. Ibid., pp. 108–9.

The reference to touch [in 3:3] completes the appearance of the five senses in the story, and with these words the hermeneutical skills of the woman emerge. Not only can she relay the command of God; she can also interpret it faithfully. Her understanding guarantees obedience. If the tree is not touched, then its fruit cannot be eaten. Thus the woman builds "a fence around the Torah," a procedure that her rabbinical successors developed fully to protect the law of God and to insure obedience to it.[99]

Eve is, Trible shows, an intelligent "theologian, ethicist, hermeneut, [and] rabbi," who speaks "with clarity and authority."[100] So far from being ignorant and gullible, Eve is actually here displaying her intelligence.

On Trible's account, as Eve continues to discuss the tree of good and evil with the serpent, she acts independently of Adam. Adam is with her at all points, but she seeks "neither his permission nor his advice. … In the presence of the man she thinks and decides for herself."[101] This stands in contrast to Adam's character in the story; he simply eats from the tree without thinking. "This portrayal of his character in scene two," Trible explains, "contrasts with his ability in scene one to recognize sexuality, to speak sensitively of its delight, and then to decide the direction of his life by leaving father and mother and cleaving to his woman."[102] These opposing depictions of Adam in Gen. 2 are brought together to unite Adam and Eve in disobedience and to show that disobedience can come in both passive and active forms.[103] Whether passive or active, both character traits are compatible with disobedience. Interestingly, when Adam and Eve are questioned by God after they each disobey, Adam blames Eve and God, though he never says that Eve tempted him. Eve, on the other hand, blames neither God nor her companion.[104] Despite their different responses to God, for Trible, "the portrayals of the man and the woman in disobedience and defense equalize them in narrative stress and moral responsibility. Once again, opposite depictions have converged to unite this couple, ironically, in the brokenness of life."[105] In this way, the Adam and Eve story indicts the couple while highlighting their unity in brokenness.

Trible's depiction of Eve has been fresh air for many previously schooled in typical Protestant rhetoric about her. Negative portrayals of Eve are quite familiar and have been briefly noted above. However, even the "positive" portrayals of Eve within Protestant traditions—Eve as prototypical wife and mother, after she has been chastised and put in her place by God—are upset by Trible's account. If Eve is

---

99. Ibid., p. 110.
100. Ibid.
101. Ibid., p. 113.
102. Ibid.
103. Ibid., p. 114.
104. Ibid., p. 120.
105. Ibid., p. 122.

actually an intelligent rabbi who disobeys God as an individual but does not blame her companion for her error, and if God's pronouncements after the couple sins are not prescriptive but are descriptions of deplorable conditions, then Eve is neither the "embodiment of all that was wrong with the female sex" nor particularly useful for "arguments that marriage and motherhood were both natural and divinely ordained and that the domestic realm was the only sanctioned and legitimate place for the daughters of Eve."[106] Whereas Eve has been used within Protestant circles to teach women about their proper roles in society and the family, Trible's account of Eve presents a different image of this Protestant ideal.

A queer reading of Eve, which puts her in relation to Lilith, produces an even more radical image. Bringing Plaskow's depiction of Lilith into the conversation, we can see how for many, Lilith and Eve (like Lilith and Matronit) would be considered opposites—strong/weak, dominant/subordinate, active/passive, killing/nurturing. Plaskow, however, has identified these as false dichotomies, useful only as projections of some men's fears. These dichotomies have been used to divide women from one another, sapping their strength. They keep women from giving one another "a positive placement in the map of social relations."[107] In Plaskow's view, Lilith and Eve are able to build a world together only after they overcome the binaries and false projections that separated them.

By entering a queer community, Lilith and Eve begin to create Woman in a way that insists on multiplicity. She is strong, intelligent, faithful, disobedient, honest, and mature. She is all of these things and is becoming even more. Woman as queer community enables an understanding of how failure to be a "proper" woman according to traditional standards produces new, radical potential.[108] Trible's Eve and Plaskow's Lilith here join hands as part of a queer community to overcome false projections of themselves and to see the reality of the other's fragmented humanity and the complexity of being human. They also highlight the ways in which, as Cohen writes, "'nonnormative' procreation patterns and family structures of people who are labeled heterosexual have also been used to regulate and exclude *them*."[109] Lilith and Eve, routinely characterized as straight, are used to cultivate gender norms—the bad and the good, respectively. While Lilith is demonized for not submitting to Adam and Eve is held up as an ideal, submissive wife, if they come together in community to recognize and affirm one another's dissenting patterns and structures, then Lilith and Eve's relationship can be seen both as a powerful site of social action and also as holding possibilities that

---

106. Kathleen M. Crowther, *Adam and Eve in the Protestant Reformation* (New York: Cambridge University Press, 2010), p. 138.

107. Marilyn Frye, "Sisterhood Is Powerless," *Women's Review of Books* 19/8 (May 2002): 6.

108. See Jack Halberstam, *The Queer Art of Failure* (Durham, NC: Duke University Press, 2011).

109. Cohen, "Punks, Bulldaggers, and Welfare Queens," pp. 447–8.

are not clearly foreseeable.[110] Lilith and Eve might just be "straight queers."[111] Using Trible's image of Eve in concert with Plaskow's Lilith in this way draws together the first two women of the Jewish and Christian imaginations as an emerging Woman, a new kind of subject.

Hagar

We have already encountered Hagar in Chapter 2, where Delores Williams adopts her story as she responds to substitutionary atonement theories. Here we return to the story with an eye to the other details included in the biblical text. The story of Hagar, the Egyptian enslaved woman, is recorded in Gen. 16 and 21. In these chapters, Hagar is treated as Sarai's surrogate to produce a child for Abram. When Hagar becomes pregnant, Trible explains that Hagar begins to see Sarai as lowered. Hagar's pregnancy removes "hierarchical blinders," which had previously led her to consider Sarai as her superior.[112] As Hagar processes what her pregnancy could mean within her situation, "the exalted mistress decreases while the lowly maid increases."[113] Although this could be an opportunity for relative equalization of the relationship between Sarai and Hagar, Sarai takes pains to reestablish her perceived superiority by treating Hagar harshly. When Hagar flees to the wilderness, a messenger of Yahweh comes to speak with her, making her the first person to encounter God in the wilderness and the only woman in scripture to hear the divine promise to "so greatly multiply your descendants that they cannot be numbered for multitude" (Gen. 16:10, RSV).[114] In response to this promise concerning Ishmael, Hagar does what no other human being does in scripture. Reminiscent of Lilith, who utters the ineffable name before leaving the Garden of Eden, Hagar "calls the name of Yahweh who has spoken to her."[115] She then names God: "'You are a God of seeing'" (16:13b).[116] By this expression, Hagar "unites

---

110. Plaskow continues, "In a somewhat different vein, it was only when I came out as a lesbian more than a decade after writing the story that I first was struck by the potentially sexual nature of the energy between Eve and Lilith" (Plaskow, "Lilith Revisited," p. 426).

111. Cohen, "Punks, Bulldaggers, and Welfare Queens," p. 452.

112. Phyllis Trible, *Texts of Terror: Literary-Feminist Readings of Biblical Narratives* (Philadelphia, PA: Fortress, 1984), p. 12.

113. Ibid.

114. Rosalyn Murphy, "Sista-hoods: Revealing the Meaning in Hagar's Narrative," *Black Theology* 10/1 (2012): 85.

115. Trible, *Texts of Terror*, p. 18.

116. Murphy indicates the importance of this naming:

> In the ancient Near East, a great significance was placed on knowing the personal name of the god being worshipped. It was believed that the name of the god or goddess revealed their divine character, signified their existence, and gave the worshipper access to the deity's power. … Accordingly, Hagar's

the divine and human encounter: the God who sees and the God who is seen."[117] Even so, Trible notes that the messenger tells Hagar to return to Sarai and Abram. By chapter 21, she has been sent into exile again a second time and weeps over the possible death of her son, Ishmael. The wilderness "embodies for Hagar the polarities of life and death,"[118] even as it is the place where the divine and human encounter one another. As Trible interprets it, Hagar's story highlights oppression "in three familiar forms: nationality, class, and sex."[119]

Because of these features of this text, Williams explains, "The African-American community has taken Hagar's story unto itself. Hagar has 'spoken' to generation after generation of black women because her story has been validated as true by suffering black people."[120] In particular, Hagar stands with those women who have been subjected to multiple forms of oppression. In *Sisters in the Wilderness*, Williams shows that for the African American community, Hagar "began to represent both the positive antebellum black religious experience of meeting God in an isolated place and the negative postbellum experience of 'pioneering' in a wide world hostile to African-American social and economic advancement."[121] Black women are represented here in a different way than within "Anglo-American ideals about 'true womanhood.'"[122] Williams describes Black women on the model of Hagar's experience:

> This African-American notion affirms such qualities as defiance; risk-taking; independence; endurance when endurance gives no promise; the stamina to hold things together for the family (even without the help of a mate); the ability, in poverty, to make a way out of no way; the courage to initiate political action in the public arena; and a close personal relation with God.[123]

> naming of God elevates her to a status of interpersonal relationship with the divine, which certainly surpasses that of Sarai, but also that of Abram. (Murphy, "Sista-hoods," p. 86)

117. Trible, *Texts of Terror*, p. 18.
118. Ibid., p. 25.
119. Ibid., p. 28.
120. Delores Williams, *Sisters in the Wilderness: The Challenge of Womanist God-Talk* (Maryknoll, NY: Orbis, 1993), p. 33. See also Octavia Butler, *Kindred* (Boston, MA: Beacon, 1979); and Adam Clark, "Hagar the Egyptian: A Womanist Dialogue," *Western Journal of Black Studies* 36/1 (2012): 48–56. Clark argues that womanist theologians should also engage the tradition of Africana womanists in order to recover Hagar's role in highlighting Maat as an Egyptian goddess or divine feminine. He argues that Maat can do for pneumatology what Sophia can do for Christology (55).
121. Williams, *Sisters in the Wilderness*, p. 117.
122. Ibid., p. 122.
123. Ibid. Cf. Hortense Spillers's critique of the Moynihan report and African American kinship and gender in "Mama's Baby, Papa's Maybe: An American Grammar Book," *Diacritics* 17/2, Culture and Countermemory: The "American" Connection (Summer 1987): 64–81.

Rather than accepting the notion that women ought to be passive, dependent, and submissive, Hagar holds out the possibility that Woman is independent and innovatively active. Here, as in the imaginations of Plaskow and Trible, the woman-identified figure is strong, resilient, resourceful, intelligent, and trustworthy.

When Hagar joins Lilith and Eve in a queer community, the now doubled narrative about three persons in relation to one another—Lilith, Adam, and Eve, in the one case, and Hagar, Abram, and Sarai, in the other—provides encouragement for readers of their stories to honestly acknowledge another queer reality: in relationships, there are almost always more than two. Human beings are, on the whole, serial monogamists and polygamists. Adam tried to have sex with Lilith before Eve. Abram had sex with Hagar while married to Sarai, at Sarai's request. Because of the "more than two" of human relationships, at least three important themes come to light: women have striven against one another, misconceived the value of motherhood in socioeconomic terms, and have not sufficiently examined the "good" of motherhood. I will take each of these in turn as a way of analyzing what queer possibilities might emerge from the community of Lilith, Eve, and Hagar.

Recall the Jewish incantation, adopted by Christians as well: "Adam, Eve; Out Lilith." We could now easily add: "Abraham, Sarah; Out Hagar." In both cases, a division exists between individual women when one is favored over the other. Both Eve and Sarah are the currently favored women of Adam and Abraham, respectively; Lilith and Hagar are "out," even though they were the first of women and the first to bear descendants. In both cases, enmity between the women is fueled by the currently favored woman's desire for her own survival and security to be unhampered by the first woman's existence and/or actions: Lilith might kill Eve's children; likewise, Hagar's son might take away part of Sarah's son's inheritance. The "more than two" character of these stories highlights the socioeconomic dependence of women on men and the resulting androcentric view of the favored women involved. In these narratives, Eve and Sarah identify themselves socially and economically in relation to men. The woman currently favored by the man is afforded social privilege and economic benefit. In this situation, women are pitted against one another in competition for the man's favor.

Hagar's inclusion in the queer community being constructed here, however, may contribute to women's growing sense that the "more than two" of human relationships that evokes division and competition in a patriarchal context could evoke solidarity and mutual support in a context shed of androcentric relations. Putting women—Hagar, Lilith, and Eve—back into relation with one another creates a collective Woman whose life need not revolve around a man's favor. Hagar allows women to testify in the wilderness, "'Me and God stood up.'"[124] Although the divine is recorded as telling Hagar to go back to her oppressors and is thereby implicated in her oppression, Hagar and the divine nonetheless see one another in a context bereft of men. Like Lilith before her, Hagar is in a desolate place named

---

124. Williams, *Sisters in the Wilderness*, p. 139.

"No Kingdom There." Shedding the androcentrism so familiar to women in a patriarchal society, Hagar and Lilith may help Eve to identify herself not always or primarily in relation to men, but as a person who stands in a direct relation to God and who has the power to name the divine: the One who sees. By naming the divine, women may mold themselves into a community of Woman, come to support one another as persons who have been oppressed by kyriarchal actions, and work toward making women's socioeconomic status less dependent on men.

These narratives about Hagar, Lilith, and Eve also illuminate misplaced confidence in the benefits attached to motherhood. Biblical texts make clear that women are seen as useful for their child-bearing capacities, making motherhood a woman's primary identity. As a result, some women have believed that motherhood therefore grants them some measure of financial security or social status. Hagar's story suggests that such a belief is manifestly untrue. When Hagar was not yet a mother, she spoke with the divine and received a promise of divine blessing. After giving birth, as Trible explains, "Hagar decreases as Ishmael increases. ... The narrator depicts the woman serving the [male] child, as God has decreed."[125] African American women's experiences likewise confirm that women are not materially valued as mothers, and Althaus-Reid notes the same in a Latin American context:

> Motherhood supposedly gives a Latin American the highest investment rate in terms of status in church and society. However, the bank of historical reality has never paid any interest on these promises of respect and status made in romantic Christian literature. On the contrary, motherhood is the most devalued position for women in Latin America in real value terms.[126]

Whereas Eve might not previously have seen that motherhood is underappreciated—she being the symbolic mother of all humankind—Hagar's presence in the queer community could motivate the queer community of Woman to work for social change such that current mothers are given the support they need for survival and an increased quality of life. Through relationship with Hagar, Eve might come to acknowledge the way her image has been used as a symbol of romanticized motherhood; to speak the truth about the real experiences and needs of mothers; and to stand with other women who have found themselves decreased and devalued as mothers, all while receiving lip service to their motherhood, paid as a bribe to keep them quiet. Eve, with Hagar and Lilith as her sisters, might call for the "bank of historical reality" to materially value her labor.[127]

---

125. Trible, *Texts of Terror*, p. 26.
126. Marcella Althaus-Reid, *Indecent Theology: Theological Perversions in Sex, Gender and Politics* (London: Routledge, 2000), p. 51.
127. See Eva Feder Kittay, *Love's Labor: Essays on Women, Equality, and Dependency* (New York: Routledge, 1999).

Furthermore, Hagar's presence in the queer community could motivate Woman to question the primary bases on which mothers are praised in current society, namely, self-sacrifice and other-centeredness. If a mother's value is in denying her own needs and desires to support the growing life of another, then the theoretical seeds for her destruction as a person in her own right are already planted. Hagar's story prods women to consider whether in reifying the "mother" in theological language without questioning whether and/or on what bases she ought to be praised, theologians have unwittingly contributed to women's oppression. Motherhood, the raped and enslaved Hagar might say, is not a good in itself, but is a good only when it is chosen by a woman whose existence and quality of life would become fuller in her own estimation as a result, and whose offspring would be raised with the support they need to survive and thrive.

Mary

Finally, another layer of theological imagery is added with the introduction of Mary to the discussion. The literature on Mary, as on Eve, is vast. Most basically, however, we might begin by recognizing that in the string of women figures that feature within the traditional imagination, Lilith (bad) and Eve (good) are surpassed by Mary (even better). Here is the ultimate woman. Especially for Roman Catholic Christians, Mary restores to womanhood what was lost in the fall of humankind: she is obedient and submissive where Eve was disobedient and rebellious.[128] Further, in contrast to the naked and ashamed, sinful Eve, Mary is beautifully adorned. As Marcella Althaus-Reid describes the fantasy, Mary is never indecent, but wears long, impenetrable dresses. She is perpetually young, fair-skinned, and attractive. She does not speak or walk; she is an appearance, the object of another's gaze. Above all, Mary is the impossible: a Virgin Mother.

Althaus-Reid critiques Mariology of this sort incisively. She argues that this Mary is not recognizable as a historical or contextual person. She does not have genitals, she does not lust, she does not procreate like other humans, and her motherhood is materially valued. As these characteristics have not been actualized historically, Mary has become an object rather than a subject: "Women have become things in life and the divine pantheon alike, and male ideas (including Christian gods) have become people."[129] The ideal woman, as it turns out, is no woman at all.[130] Drawing this thought out to its logical boundaries, Althaus-Reid says that "if the Virgin Mary had paws instead of hands and her vagina was in

---

128. For a discussion of Mary as coredeemer in Asian feminist theology, see Chung Hyun Kyung, *Struggle to Be the Sun Again: Introducing Asian Women's Theology* (Maryknoll, NY: Orbis, 1990), pp. 74–84. See also Ivone Gebara and Maria Clara Bingemer, *Mary: Mother of God, Mother of the Poor* (Maryknoll, NY: Orbis, 1989).

129. Althaus-Reid, *Indecent Theology*, p. 39.

130. Ibid., p. 100.

her ear, thus making it easier for the Word of God, the Logos, to 'say its Word' and penetrate her, it would not make any theological difference. Mary is in the realm of the fantastic and phantasmagorical."[131] As Althaus-Reid describes her, the traditional Mary is an idea used for patriarchal gain and currently has very little other use within Christianity.

As such, if Mary is to be part of a queer configuration of Woman, according to Althaus-Reid, theologians will need to abandon Mariology for Mujeriology, "in order to stop subordinating women's political experiences to ghostly talks of apparitions of Virgins in the Hills."[132] Althaus-Reid's mujeriology speaks of Mary as a real woman.[133] She is the "Queer of Heaven": someone who lusts and receives clitoral pleasure, is not a virgin, and whose power is in her womanhood rather than her reproductive capabilities.[134] Mary, Queer of Heaven, is the woman who cannot be made into a statue, sealing off further possibilities for what it means to be herself.[135] A queer Mary would be a human being with whom women could converse and relate in a political discussion.

According to Althaus-Reid, the first thing that must go is Mary's virginity. She makes this claim about Mary not to denigrate virginity as such but to acknowledge that most Latin American women do not have the luxury to choose to remain virgins. Their history includes poverty, violence, and coerced pregnancy:

> Poor women are seldom virgins, because poverty in Latin America means crowded conditions of violence and promiscuity, where girls get raped before puberty or married as adolescents as part of the few available economic transactions on offer, except for several forms of prostitution and sexual bondage. Women thus get pregnant before they know what their own sexuality is.[136]

As such, Mary cannot be a virgin if she is to be a real human being with whom most Latin American women and other women living at the intersection of poverty and violence can relate. By denying the reality of women's sexual exploitation, the

---

131. Ibid., p. 39.

132. Ibid., p. 46.

133. For a book-length discussion of the "unreal" uses of Eve, see also Gale A. Yee, *Poor Banished Children of Eve: Woman as Evil in the Hebrew Bible* (Minneapolis, MN: Fortress, 2003).

134. Althaus-Reid, *Indecent Theology*, pp. 51, 71. See also Brittney Cooper, "How Sarah Got Her Groove Back, or Notes toward a Black Feminist Theology of Pleasure," *Black Theology* 16/3 (2018): 195–206. She uses Sarah's response to the idea that she would have a child in old age ("Shall I have pleasure?" Gen. 18:12) as an entrance into thinking about Black women's sexual pleasure. See also Phillis I. Sheppard, *Self, Culture, and Other in Womanist Practical Theology* (New York: Palgrave Macmillan, 2011), esp. chapter 9. She highlights the "black and beautiful" woman in the *Song of Songs* as a model for Black womanhood (176).

135. Althaus-Reid, *Indecent Theology*, p. 64.

136. Ibid., p. 49.

Virgin Mary is denied her power as a symbol for real women. She becomes an apparition.

Looking at Mary's virginity from Lilith's point of view, however, a queer community of Woman might also see Mary's virginity as the refusal to be in sexual relation to men. Mary's "virginity" might allow her to be open to other forms of relation. In that case, Mary's "virginity" could point not to a denial of sexuality but to a sexuality that is not circumscribed within heterosexual penetrative relationships. Indeed, as Althaus-Reid states, "unless Mary can stand with her fantasies in front of us, then she excludes the historicity of our sexuality."[137]

If Mary cannot be a virgin, as that term is understood by androcentric cultures that exploit women, especially those who are poor and vulnerable, then, for Althaus-Reid, neither can she be a mother whose exclusive or primary residence is within the private home. Rather, she is a woman who engages in radical political subversion.[138] For Althaus-Reid, a fitting image of Mary is, therefore, not a pregnant woman or the often-depicted mother with child. The focus ought to be on Mary's vulva instead of her uterus. It is Mary's boldness in pursuing her own pleasure that aptly symbolizes women's political engagement. This indecent Mary is a proper symbol for the justice that is to be established at the "Second Coming." Mary thus enters the queer community, standing and agitating as a liberatory symbol for Roman Catholic women in particular.

Because the indecent Mary of Althaus-Reid's work draws on Latin American women's experiences, Mary and Hagar might have an immediate affinity for one another. Women of color may find in Hagar a woman who defies stereotypes in order to survive and whose "ain't I a woman?" challenges white feminists to expand their imaginary. Women of color may also join with those who reject "Vanilla" (hetero)sexuality as normative, to find in Mary a real woman who is as passionate about justice as she is about love.

Along with Hagar, Lilith, and Eve, Mary may also have a queering effect on families. Although the Mary and Joseph story has been used to normalize a two-parent, patriarchal family whose focus is a male child, the story is, in fact, much more complicated. Mary's story troubles the ideal of the nuclear family as consisting of two parents and their biological children. The "holy family" comes about through the conception of Jesus within Mary quite apart from Joseph. Jesus' subsequent rearing then occurs in a family composed of his biological mother and his stepfather, alongside his half brothers and half sisters. The reality is that human relationships and families are complicated and interwoven. Families are constituted, broken, and put together again in creative and unforeseen ways. Lilith, Eve, Hagar, and Mary can all attest to this reality. With Mary, Queer of Heaven, the community of Woman could boldly recognize that the idyllic vision of family held out to women, which is focused on one biological mother and one biological father, is often unreal. The political subversion that an indecent Mary

---

137. Ibid., p. 75.
138. Ibid., p. 51.

might inspire thereafter could include agitation for the rights of persons within families that are "nontraditional."

Schleiermacher and a Queer Community of Woman

As I have described them here, Lilith, Eve, Hagar, and Mary could be particularly important woman-identified figures for the Christian theological imagination. Lilith may be particularly important for women who have been demonized as "other," both within and outside of Christian communities. A reconstruction of Eve may be significant for Protestant women who have been encouraged to be proper helpmates for their husbands and mothers to all. Hagar may stand with African American women who have been subjected to slavery, rape, and left for dead; women who continue to survive and enact their vision of right relations. Finally, Roman Catholic women may find in the Queer Mary a real, indecent woman, whose clitoral pleasure brings together love and justice. For all their power in various communities considered separately, these figures are even more formidable in the Christian imaginary as a queer community of Woman. With Elizabeth Johnson, I hope to have shown that "as women connect with this great historical company, we do not try to erase differences."[139] Instead, we put them in tension and relation to one another. Johnson continues, "The category of solidarity in difference works to prevent memory from making women of old into merely mirror images of ourselves, as well as to promote appreciation rather than rejection of the otherness of their ways."[140] The intersectionality of the queer community I have constructed here might unfold further possibilities for transforming Christian imaginations, especially ecclesiologies.

We have seen that Lilith and Eve can help Woman overcome false binaries used to divide them. Hagar, joining the community, checks faulty assumptions about "true womanhood." In addition, with Hagar, Sarah, and Abraham, a pattern emerges in relation to Lilith, Eve, and Adam: we see that human relations often include more than two. This complexity of human relations and relationships, in turn, can lead Woman to homosocial solidarity and a rejection of androcentrism. Hagar, in particular, highlights Woman as making a way out of no way, with God at her side. The stories of the threesomes we have encountered have also raised Woman's consciousness of the neutrality of motherhood, which can become a moral good or evil depending on whether Woman's dignity and freedom have been respected in the choice to reproduce, and whether her life as a mother is supported in socioeconomic material terms. Finally, when Mary is added to the queer community of Woman, unchanging monuments to femininity are broken. She becomes Mary, Queer of Heaven, uniting love and justice in radical subversion that prioritizes the vulva rather than the uterus. The threesome we encounter in the holy family—Mary, the Holy Spirit, and Joseph—add to the existing pattern

---

139. Johnson, *Friends of God and Prophets*, p. 179.
140. Ibid.

of relationships and sanctify the "nontraditional" family. By offering the Christian imagination this queer community of Woman, theologians working constructively may advance social transformation, political subversion, and religious ecumenism.

Briefly, I want to turn to Schleiermacher's understanding of human nature as a potentially fruitful theoretical underpinning for the foregoing work—particularly my use of "Woman" as signifying a community of women who are raising one another up, challenging one another to work for justice, embracing one another in solidarity, and becoming who they are together. For Schleiermacher, humanity is an organism, which is part of the interconnected process of nature. As he writes while explaining the relation between Christ and humanity, "the being of God dwelling in Christ has to relate to human nature taken as a whole in the same way as the prior innermost core of a human being related to the human organism taken as a whole. This analogy has already run through the entire presentation up to now, though not explicitly stated."[141] In other words, the being of God that is in Christ is not simply in Christ as an individual, extending no further. Instead, because Schleiermacher conceives of humanity as one organism and because the impacts of his life ripple out to the interconnected process of nature, humanity and creation are changed by his existence. In and through the existence of Christ, in whom God dwells, human nature is completed through the implantation of a strong and constant awareness of its relation to God, and through the effects of that awareness on human and creaturely life.

This completion happens not as a result of a divine intervention but as part of the divinely intended process of creation. Schleiermacher explains,

> Christ had come to be determined in the way he was only because and insofar as the whole given interconnection of things was also determined in a certain fashion, and, in reverse, the whole given interconnection of things would have been determined in the way it was only because and insofar as Christ too would have been determined in a certain fashion.[142]

The organic nature of humanity set within an interdependent world means that humans depend upon one another, influence one another, and carry one another's spirits on in repeated words, gestures, and habits. As Schleiermacher writes with respect to Christian individuals and community,

> Each individual is, in turn, moved by Christ to present the power of Christ that is efficacious within oneself just as Christ has presented himself, which process does indeed happen through all the good works of the regenerate. Still less, however, is the other aspect, the cooperative one, ever in process of fading away. Rather, this aspect can be made easier and progress only in the same measure as the new life gains strength in each individual. Moreover, manifestly, each one

---

141. *CF*, §97.4, pp. 605–6.
142. Ibid., §120.3, p. 790.

must also lay claim to related powers and must do so to the degree that one's will for the reign of God, which is simultaneously grounded in a vital faith in Christ, is more definitely formed in oneself and develops within an interconnected body of functions.[143]

Christian personhood is, in this way, overlapping, creating an interlocking web of human persons who remain distinct, yet are also appropriately understood as one family or one community. This kind of diverse community is highlighted by Copeland when she discusses the flesh of the church. She writes,

> If my sister's mark of sexuality must be obscured, if my brother's mark of race must be disguised, if my sister's mark of culture must be repressed, then we are not the flesh of Christ. ... The thankful living manifestation of God's image through particularly marked flesh, demand the vigorous display of difference in race and culture and tongue, gender and sex and sexuality.[144]

She cites Gregory of Nyssa to bolster her claim: "The establishment of the Church is re-creation of the world. But it is only in the union of all the particular members that the beauty of Christ's Body is complete."[145]

In just this way, the community of Woman I have been envisioning here is not an essentialized understanding of Womanhood but a recognition of the interdependent connective tissue that binds woman to woman, just as it binds together humanity as a whole. Women are distinct persons, but they are in relationships with one another that deeply influence and change them. When Lilith, Eve, Hagar, and Mary come together, Woman is evolving and becoming in powerful ways that cannot be fully known in advance. This is a queer community wherein Woman is being redefined as each woman is added to her community. In this queer community, Woman loves herself, accepts each part of herself, orients herself by looking to other women, makes a way with the God who sees, and in her own dignity and freedom makes choices regarding her reproductive life. She is politically subversive and radically joins love and justice. Schleiermacher's understanding of humanity as an organism that is diverse and changing, and which can be radically changed with the existence of each new human being, could dovetail with such a theological imagination to bolster constructive accounts like this one that aim to provide a new way of thinking, feeling, and acting in Christian community and in relation to others.

***

---

143. Ibid., §121.1, p. 798.
144. M. Shawn Copeland, *Enfleshing Freedom: Body, Race, and Being* (Minneapolis, MN: Fortress, 2010), p. 82.
145. Ibid. Gregory of Nyssa, "On the Making of Man," in *Gregory of Nyssa, Dogmatic Treatises*, ed. Philip Schaff and Henry Wace (Grand Rapids, MI: Eerdmans, 1979), p. 13.

In this chapter, I have joined two related projects: First, to highlight the implications that Schleiermacher's bodily and joyful ecclesiology and pneumatology might have for contemporary churches' resistance to social injustices; and second, to illuminate how a theological imagination informed by Schleiermacher's emphases on diversity and community in the formation of human persons could play out with specifically ecumenical, feminist, womanist, and mujerista concerns in mind. Townes writes that "to recover the record of Black women, children, and men as communities rather than as autonomous experiences is a part of the work of womanist ethics."[146] I have demonstrated here how Schleiermacher's ecclesial imagination, transported to the contemporary context and in conversation with Christian texts and traditions, could coalesce with this womanist goal, hand in hand with feminist and other constructive aims. Schleiermacher envisions church life as a life of joy rooted in love, which is lived with diverse others in an interdependent community. It can shape our responses to oppressive forces and help us recognize the beloved community.

---

146. Emilie Townes, *Womanist Ethics and the Cultural Production of Evil* (New York: Palgrave Macmillan, 2006), p. 149.

Chapter 4

GOD AND CREATION

The notion of divine sovereignty, bound up as it is with the concept of domination and a history of gendered authoritarianism, has come under scrutiny in many contemporary theologies. The concern is that if God is affirmed as standing in a dominant relation to creation (including humanity), then because of the gendered character of much of Christian theology and life, those on the underside of history (including the earth and nonhuman animals) will have their oppression theologically legitimized rather than eradicated. Theologians working constructively thus seek to develop notions of divine sovereignty that take into account the implications of that doctrine for the underprivileged, including people of color, women, poor people, LGBT individuals, and creation.

In this chapter, I attend to this concern from both sides of the relationship of God and creation, first treating relevant aspects of Schleiermacher's doctrine of God and then turning to the creaturely side by developing a Schleiermacherian form of Christian prayer in conversation with R. Marie Griffith, Sarah Coakley, and Delores Williams. I argue that Schleiermacher's understanding of the asymmetrical relationship between God and creation aligns with the aims of contemporary ecotheologies insofar as it offers a noncompetitive relation between God and creatures, rejects a premodern understanding of divine intervention within the order of nature, and offers a communal rather than individualistic understanding of creation. I also argue that by affirming that God is responsible for sin and evil, Schleiermacher's perspective is congruent with the insight of Williams, who takes the existence and experiences of enslaved women of color as evidence that God is not always and immediately a liberator. I return to Williams's considerations of atonement and Schleiermacher's understanding of prayer to develop "incarnational submission" as a way to acknowledge the value of prayerful submission while avoiding its potentially oppressive features. The two sides of the relationship between God and creation are linked together by attending especially to the ways in which divine causality enables and encourages humanity to actively resist systems of oppression.

In the first section of the chapter, I circle back to Schleiermacher's trinitarian thought to further explore his understanding of God as absolute or Universal Causality. I treat Schleiermacher's understanding of divine aseity, human self-initiated activity, and divine omnipotence, highlighting the benefits of these notions for ecotheologies. I then describe Schleiermacher's view as a form of "radical monotheism," wherein sin and evil are not attributed to any entity that is independent of God. By acknowledging God's complicity in sin and evil, Schleiermacher's view aligns with Williams's insight that God is simply not a liberator of all people immediately. Instead, sin and evil are placed in the schema of creation–redemption, which is a progressive unfolding of divine activity that unceasingly works to eradicate sin. In the second section of the chapter, I turn to the Christian practice of prayer, which exemplifies the relation between God and creation. Here I analyze an ongoing debate regarding the use of "submission" in feminist Christian theologies. I trace the conversations that have arisen around the idea of adopting "submission" vis-à-vis the Christian notion of *kenosis* (self-emptying; Phil. 2:5–8), attending particularly to the work of R. Marie Griffith and Sarah Coakley. I turn the conversation in a new direction by arguing that Coakley's apophatically cruciform understanding of submission in contemplative prayer contrasts with Williams's womanist approach, and that feminist approaches that do not take account of prominent womanist perspectives are not adequate. "Incarnational submission," as I am referring to it, is a Schleiermacherian understanding of prayer that accords with Williams's perspective by urging Christian submission not to God considered in and of Godself but to God in relation to creation: Love that unites, Wisdom that perfectly orders the working of Love, and Universal Causality that is responsible for the whole of creation taken together, in which Love and Wisdom are manifested. Doing so foregrounds creaturely interdependence along with divine communion with humanity through Christ and his Spirit in the church, and places "submission" most properly in a liturgical celebration of Christmas rather than in the apophatic lacuna of Holy Saturday. The difference this makes, I argue, is vital for understanding divine sovereignty in life-giving rather than oppressive ways.

Absolute Causality and Divine Sovereignty

Beginning most poignantly with Freud and Marx and continuing in a number of contemporary theologies, the notion of divine sovereignty has come under scrutiny for perpetuating Christian immaturity and passivity, which allows for systems of oppression to exist without resistance. If God is conceived as a mighty being who is in control of the universe, then Christians might be encouraged to simply wait with childlike trust that everything will come out okay. This kind of Christian passivity is actively opposed in theologies concerned with social justice, which highlight the need for human agency by using notions like co-creation, co-determination, and democratic relationship to describe the relation of God and creation. For instance, Wendy Farley criticizes forms of theology that insist on divine power in terms of physical interventions and that understand divine sovereignty as total control. She writes that "the gospel is not about a power that dissolves the efficacy of might."¹ Instead, she emphasizes the anti-imperialist aspects of the gospel by indicating the qualitatively different power of the gospel. For Farley, the gospel's power

> is conjured through laws of contradiction that use Augustus Caesar's titles (Son of God, Savior, Prince of Peace) to describe the significance of a tortured criminal. Crazy, amoral stories linger in the air about sheep and seeds and widows and fathers and kings who behave in ways no patriarchal authority would ever behave. A meal gathers strangers and abolishes their social standing. When they slip out they are slaves again, women subject to the paterfamilias. But for a moment, like slaves in American hush arbors, they bore the full luminosity of their divine image. The incarnation of Wisdom in Jesus of Nazareth is announced in an impenetrable interplay of success and failure, victory and defeat.²

Divine power is here understood not as the power of might but the power that is manifest in jarring juxtapositions, countercultural stories, and meals together. Ivone Gebara applies a similar critique to dominant understandings of the God-world relation by attending to gendered patterns of domination: "Patriarchal theology, and especially creation theology, legitimized both the oppression and domination of nature and the existence of hierarchical relations among all beings. ... God stands above nature as creator and lawgiver. Nature is somehow subject to the divine will. In this sense, it is by divine command that nature gives us what we need in order to live."³ In addition to providing for human needs, however, Gebara notes that the relationship between God and nature has been gendered such that it resembles "the relationship of domination between men and women."⁴ In this way, the sovereignty of God implies human submission, and within the created order the gendered repetition of sovereignty requires especially the submission of women. Kwok Pui-Lan raises a similar objection against divine hierarchy and authoritarianism in her introduction to *Postcolonial Imagination and Feminist Theology*. She outlines the various ways in which ancient, medieval, modern, and contemporary forms of Christianity have utilized patriarchal notions and political structures to oppress, enslave, and kill indigenous people, people of color, and women. For her, the God who stands at the apex of a patriarchal Christian theology is one that postcolonial feminist theologians simply cannot embrace.⁵

---

1. Farley, *Gathering Those Driven Away*, p. 6.
2. Ibid., pp. 6–7.
3. Ivone Gebara, *Longing for Running Water: Ecofeminism and Liberation*, trans. David Molineaux (Minneapolis, MN: Fortress, 1999), pp. 16–17.
4. Ibid., p. 17.
5. Kwok Pui-Lan, *Postcolonial Imagination and Feminist Theology* (Louisville, KY: Westminster John Knox, 2005), chapter 5.

Divine Aseity, Human Self-Initiated Activity, and Divine Omnipotence

Divine aseity, in particular, is a prime candidate for criticism along these lines within many doctrines of God. Aseity is the divine attribute by which Christians indicate the independence and autonomy of God's being in and for Godself. To affirm divine aseity is to claim that God is self-existent and dependent upon no one except Godself. Once such an understanding of God is gendered, it is susceptible to criticism as supporting a kind of masculinity that is not beneficial to humanity's well-being. God is viewed as independent of others, self-sufficient, and, in some immanent Trinitarian accounts, perfect in "his" perpetual love of "himself" without regard for others.

Even though Schleiermacher does not embrace language that reinforces such intra-divine love within a doctrine of the immanent Trinity, his notion of divine sovereignty should still face scrutiny because he quite clearly affirms that there is no "real" relation between God and creation, understood in the technical Thomistic sense that God does not depend on creation in any way. Schleiermacher himself does not highlight divine aseity or independence as a special attribute in addition to divine omnipotence, since aseity is merely a negative attribute. He treats divine aseity only in a postscript to the doctrine of omnipotence and defines it as follows: "for any given thing in God no ground of determination outside God is to be posited."[6] Schleiermacher affirms divine aseity as an implied notion within his understanding of divine omnipotence because for him, as we have already seen, one of the basic meanings of the word "God" is the "Whence" of creation.[7] Absolute or Universal Causality cannot depend on finite causalities without destroying the very notion of God itself within Christian piety. For Schleiermacher, we recall, "the world exists only in absolute dependence on God."[8] Thus, even if Schleiermacher does not highlight divine independence as a special attribute, he clearly exhibits a strong sense of divine sovereignty: "nothing—no point in space and no point in time—is to be excluded from that sovereignty over all."[9]

Despite the thoroughgoingness of the scope of divine sovereignty, for Schleiermacher, the absoluteness of Universal Causality does not mean that humanity is devoid of self-initiated activity. Self-initiated activity, or voluntary human decisions and actions, do not in any way hinder the absolute dependence of creatures on God. Rather, the human "freedom" that Schleiermacher is concerned to avoid is the ability to determine who God is or what God does.[10] Although humanity acts on the basis of its own deliberations and choices, these finite causalities do not determine divine activity. In other words, human beings

---

6. *CF*, Postscript to §54, p. 316.
7. Ibid., §4.4, p. 24.
8. Ibid., §36, p. 205.
9. Ibid., §37.1, p. 209.
10. It is worth noting that Schleiermacher thinks God is beyond the contrast between freedom and necessity, so that this notion of "freedom" does not apply to God any more than it applies to creatures.

make their own voluntary decisions in accordance with their human nature, and even when their self-initiated activity is at its most unhampered, this neither diminishes their absolute dependence upon God nor God's unconditioned being. Schleiermacher explains,

> In relation to God there is no immediate feeling of freedom, nor can there be even the slightest feeling of dependence in relation to God such that a feeling of freedom could be attached to it as its counterpart. Rather, even at the highest level of Christian piety and given the clearest consciousness of having the most unhampered self-initiated activity, the absoluteness of the feeling of dependence would still remain undiminished in relation to God.[11]

What Schleiermacher is outlining here is a noncompetitive relation between Universal Causality and finite causalities within the interconnected process of nature.[12] Universal Causality enables finite beings and activities rather than competing with them. The universality involved in "Universal Causality" means that divine omnipotence applies to the *Naturzusammenhang*, or the interconnected process of nature as a whole, rather than to particular entities considered in and of themselves. Schleiermacher explains, "Everything is and comes to be entirely through the interconnected process of nature, with the result that each part persists by means of all and everything persists entirely by divine omnipotence, in such a way that everything persists indivisibly by that 'One' source."[13] Because each thing is dependent on each other thing in an interdependent web of existence, "it can be said regarding all particulars that the fact that it exists and how it exists God wills only conditionally because everything is conditioned by something else."[14] Even so, "it is all absolutely willed by God."[15] God is responsible for the whole interconnected process of nature, within which each finite thing is conditioned by and conditions other finite things through their own self-initiated activities. Universal Causality and finite causalities do not compete because they have entirely different scopes and qualities. Further, on Schleiermacher's view, God does not intervene within the process to make any changes to it. "In no way," he explains, "could divine omnipotence step in the place of natural causes as a supplement to them, as it were, in that at that point divine omnipotence would also have to work temporally and spatially, in the same fashion as natural causes

---

11. *CF*, §32.2, pp. 189–90. Note that for Schleiermacher, the feeling of absolute dependence points to or refers back to absolute or divine causality (*CF*, §51, p. 289).

12. For a treatment of the relation of God and creation, see Daniel Pedersen, *The Eternal Covenant: Schleiermacher on God and Natural Science* (Berlin: Walter de Gruyter, 2017); and Andrew Dole, *Schleiermacher on Religion and the Natural Order* (Oxford: Oxford University Press, 2010).

13. *CF*, §54.1, pp. 306–7.

14. Ibid., §54.4, p. 311.

15. Ibid., §54.4, p. 312.

do."[16] For Schleiermacher, each particular thing is codetermined as part of the entire web of existence, which proceeds according to the order of creation without divine intervention. Schleiermacher's view encourages Christians to break free from individualistic understandings of their existence and preservation in relation to God.

Going further, for Schleiermacher, humanity is not set apart from but is part of the interconnected web of existence: "we are placed within a general interconnected process of nature. ... we are conscious of ourselves as part of the world."[17] Humanity, therefore, is no exception to the laws of science and nature, but acts and lives as other created organisms do, each according to their own natures. As such, "God-consciousness is not in an inverse relation with consciousness regarding the interconnectedness of nature."[18] One can have consciousness of God and consciousness of the regularities of the system of nature at the same time because they do not compete. In fact, Schleiermacher states that "no Christian religious stirring is imaginable ... in which we would not find ourselves to be placed in some interconnectedness of nature."[19]

Schleiermacher's anti-individualism and anti-exceptionalism comports well with the insights of a number of contemporary theologians who are working constructively. As Karen Baker-Fletcher writes, "Humankind is not separate from nature but is a part of it."[20] She emphasizes how Jesus' life and ministry encourage such a notion when she writes that "Jesus as Immanuel feels with us. Jesus not only sustains us but teaches us to feel anew the interconnectedness of life. Feeling such interconnectedness moves people out of prisons of individualism to relearn compassion."[21] While Schleiermacher's doctrine of creation is explicated in different language, the idea is similar. For Schleiermacher, Christian religious stirrings that understanding the self as interconnected with nature "occur more frequently when a given mind and heart ... is in community with Christ."[22]

Schleiermacher maintains his particular understanding of God's omnipotence in order to safeguard the Christian reception of divine grace.[23] As he explains,

16. Ibid., §54.1, p. 306.
17. Ibid., §34, p. 198.
18. Ibid., §35.2, p. 200.
19. Ibid., §35.3, p. 201.
20. Baker-Fletcher, *My Sister, My Brother*, p. 85.
21. Ibid., p. 91.
22. *CF*, §35.3, p. 201.
23. See Poe, *Essential Trinitarianism*, chapters 5–7, pp. 115–70. Another route is to use process theology to radically reimagine divine sovereignty. For instance, see Carter Heyward, *The Redemption of God: A Theology of Mutual Relation* (Eugene, OR: Wipf and Stock, 2010; previously published by University Press of America, 1982). She imagines God as "a transpersonal spirit, power in relation, which depends upon humanity for making good/making justice/making love/making God incarnate in the world. To do so is to un-do evil. The doing of good and un-doing of evil is a human act, a human responsibility. God is our power to do this" (ibid., p. 159).

"we term the mighty power of God-consciousness in our souls 'grace,' precisely because we are not conscious of grace as our own deed."[24] The Christian's powerful awareness of their own absolute dependence upon God comes to them from without, as a gift received. We recall that it does so, for Schleiermacher, in and through the creating-redeeming work of God in Christ and Christ's Spirit in the church. Schleiermacher can only account for the Christian reception of grace by understanding creation-redemption as the sole and unconditioned work of God. For that reason, he claims that creation-redemption is a gift of God, which is not merited or conditioned in any way by or on creatures. This being the case, Schleiermacher's notion of divine omnipotence is decidedly not about ensuring the perfection of God's loving gaze upon "himself" before the creation of the world and for all eternity in an immanent Trinity. What God might be like apart from creation, we recall, is not a matter of significance to Schleiermacher: "the question as to whether a being of God can or must be imagined without creatures, is in any case of no concern whatsoever to what the feeling of absolute dependence immediately contains, and therefore it is, in and of itself, a matter of indifference."[25] Divine aseity, as implied within Schleiermacher's treatment of divine omnipotence, ought, therefore, to be understood in the context of the Christian reception of divine grace in and through Christ and Christ's Spirit. All things depend upon God for their existence and preservation, but the "unreal" relationship between God and creatures does not mean that God is aloof, self-absorbed, and/or indifferent to others. In fact, divine omnipotence actually ensures the constant relation of God to all things: "the entire interconnected process of nature, encompassing all spaces and times, is grounded in divine causality."[26] This, in turn, safeguards the Christian reception of divine grace.

The other side of the coin for Schleiermacher is that "divine causality ... is completely presented in the totality of finite being."[27] Schleiermacher explains,

> Just as little can we also think God's willing of Godself and God's willing of the world to be separated from each other. This is so, for if God wills Godself, God also wills Godself to be Creator and Preserver, with the result that God's willing of the world is already included in God's willing-of-Godself. Likewise, if God wills the world, God also wills in the world God's eternal omnipresent omnipotence, wherein God's willing of Godself is thus included.[28]

What Schleiermacher is saying here is that the only God Christians know is the Creator and Preserver, who redeems through progressive creative activity in creation, Christ, and Christ's Spirit. God does not will Godself to be without

---

24. *CF*, §80.1, p. 491.
25. Ibid., §41.2, p. 226.
26. Ibid., §54, p. 305.
27. Ibid., §54, p. 305.
28. Ibid., §54.4, p. 313.

creation. To consider whether God could have willed to be God without creation would be speculative, and therefore a matter of indifference to Christian piety. As soon as Christians think of God, they think of God in relation to the world. Schleiermacher states this idea more provocatively in *On Religion*, where he says, "you can have no God without the world."[29] The thoroughgoingness of Schleiermacher's account of the absolute dependence of the universe upon God is, therefore, matched by an account of divine causality as fully presented in the totality of finite existence. Because of this, Schleiermacher's doctrine of God is not an appropriate target for critiques of the notion that God is a perfectly independent, preexistent being who could have been God without creation.

Instead, his view is consonant with feminist and mujerista theologies that see God and world as intimately related. For instance, despite vast differences in their language and metaphysics, Schleiermacher, Catherine Keller, and Ivone Gebara would all affirm that one should not invoke divine aseity in order to try to think of God apart from creation. In the first chapter of her theology of becoming, Catherine Keller affirms Ivone Gebara's thought: "'*We no longer think of God first and creation later, because this sort of gap between atemporality in God and temporality in creation does not make sense to us.*' (That may be all I'm hoping to say.)"[30] The passage from Gebara's work continues by saying that "we no longer speak of the presence or absence of God, but, basically, of presence. It is a presence that is hard to speak of in traditional terms. Traditional discourse on God referred to a separate, preexistent being who could be invoked in all life's joyful and difficult circumstances."[31] What Gebara and Keller are after, instead, is an understanding of God that is never separated, in thought or in activity, from creation. Keller "looks neither for Creator nor for the human creature outside of the ecosocial web of all life."[32] Rather, "only in relation to what we call *creation* can what we call *Creator* be signified, i.e. be imagined to exist."[33] For Keller, the Creator is creativity itself, which "does not become; *it makes becoming possible.*"[34] While Gebara and Keller are doubtless writing in different contexts, with different metaphysics, and in different theological registers than Schleiermacher, they nonetheless think of God and creation together rather than imagining a God "before" or considered apart from the world. Schleiermacher, Keller, and Gebara all think of God as intimately involved in creaturely life, inconceivable without creation, and as that which makes creaturely life possible. Each of these features of their theologies is compatible with further ecotheological thought that aims at planetary justice.

---

29. *OR*, p. 53.
30. Catherine Keller, *Face of the Deep: A Theology of Becoming* (London: Routledge, 2003), p. 22. Gebara, *Longing for Running Water*, p. 105; Keller's emphasis.
31. Gebara, *Longing for Running Water*, p. 105.
32. Keller, *Face of the Deep*, p. 191.
33. Ibid., p. 181.
34. Ibid.

Radical Monotheism and Sin and Evil

Schleiermacher's view of divine sovereignty is, however, not yet cleared of the charge that God here holds an oppressive form of authority in relation to others. Of such an oppressive form of sovereignty, Keller writes that "when faith is most urgently needed, the logic of omnipotence lays upon naked suffering the added burden of godforsakenness."[35] For her, "the theogram of central Power who controls all the outcomes," exhibited in the Markan and Matthean accounts of the crucifixion "encrypt a crisis and contradiction that will beset innumerable Jews and Christians at *their* worst moments."[36] Further analysis of Schleiermacher's understanding of divine omnipotence, specifically with regard to sin and evil, is needed in order to assess whether his view of God's relation to creation is oppressive or could be beneficial to constructive forms of contemporary theology.

As we have seen above, Schleiermacher describes divine omnipotence as a two-pronged concept: first, that all of creation "is grounded in divine causality" and second, that "everything for which there is a causality in God also comes to be realized and does occur."[37] In other words, there is no remainder on either the creaturely or divine sides when accounting for reality. Every creaturely thing is grounded in divine activity, and all divine activity is realized in creation. That being the case, "whatever has not become actual ... is also not possible in relation to God."[38] For Schleiermacher, omnipotence is not an affirmation that God can do anything that is materially possible or logically non-contradictory. Rather, omnipotence means that everything that is the case is grounded in divine causality and that there is no divine causality that does not come to be realized in creation. The contrast between the possible and the actual is not to be applied to God, for Schleiermacher, because that distinction would make the divine into a creature. Omnipotence, in short, means "the one all-encompassing divine will."[39]

This account certainly seems susceptible to the charge of being an oppressive form of divine sovereignty insofar as it is a "power who controls all the outcomes" and those outcomes include all sorts of worldly atrocities and horrors. In response, as it were, Schleiermacher admits that God is responsible for sin to the extent that the divine activity of creating-redeeming is a process that develops over time, during which sin arises, and that God ordained collective punishment, or evil, as a consequence for collective sin.[40] Schleiermacher writes, "We are conscious of sin as the force and work of a time when the bent toward God-consciousness had not

---

35. Ibid., p. 215.
36. Ibid.
37. *CF*, §54, p. 305.
38. Ibid., §54.2, p. 307.
39. Ibid., §54.4, p. 314.
40. Ibid., §84, pp. 522–34. For an insightful account of Schleiermacher's notion of sin, see Kevin M. Vander Schel, *Embedded Grace: Christ, History, and the Reign of God in Schleiermacher's Dogmatics* (Minneapolis, MN: Fortress, 2013), pp. 134–7.

yet come to the fore within us."[41] Sin occurs when one knows what one ought to do but does not do it. Although this unevenness between understanding and force of will is part of what it means to be human apart from Christ, Schleiermacher does not characterize it as simply part of human nature. Rather, because he conceives of human nature Christomorphically (i.e., in relation to Christ), Schleiermacher says that sin is a "distortion of nature."[42] "Complete knowledge of sin comes to us only in and through the Redeemer's utter lack of sinfulness and his absolute strength of spirit," Schleiermacher explains.[43] Likewise, sin appears to us as a distortion of nature because "the possibility presents itself to us that … God-consciousness could have developed steadily from the first human being right on up to the pure and holy state it had in the Redeemer."[44] God is responsible for the fact that humanity's God-consciousness did not develop steadily in all human beings as it did in Christ.

Likewise, God is responsible for evil, which he describes as "causes that hinder one's life"[45] and therefore "destroys the original harmony between the world and human beings."[46] For Schleiermacher, evil does not include "natural death and any bodily hinderances to life in the form of illness or disability that preceded death."[47] Such things can be viewed as "stimuli toward an unfolding of the human spirit."[48] Rather, evil is that which diminishes "the fullness of stimuli through which the development of the human being would be advanced" or which limits "the world's adaptiveness by means of human activity."[49] "Natural evil," therefore, "issues in the evils of being in more or less dire need and deficiency [*Dürftigkeit und Mangel*, e.g. poverty], and social evil issues in the evils of being in more or less dire hardship and adversity [*Druck*, e.g. political oppression, *und Widerstand*, e.g. mutually damaging conflict]."[50] Schleiermacher conceives of social evil as a direct punishment for collective sin, while natural evil is only indirectly a punishment for collective sin. The collectivity involved here is of the utmost importance, for Schleiermacher: "On no account may the evils that affect an individual be referred to that individual's sin as their cause."[51] Sin is correctly conceived only as the "collective act of the human species."[52] As such, evil can only be understood as a

41. *CF*, §67, p. 405.
42. Ibid., §68, p. 407.
43. Ibid., §68.3, p. 413.
44. Ibid.
45. Ibid., §75, p. 473.
46. Ibid., §75.1, p. 473.
47. Ibid., p. 474.
48. Ibid., §76.2, p. 481.
49. Ibid., §75.2, p. 476.
50. Ibid. The examples given for the German nouns are offered in editorial note 16 on pages 476–7.
51. *CF*, §77, p. 483.
52. *CF*, §77.1, p. 483.

collective consequence of that collective act. By this he means that "in whatever degree sin increases within the human species as a whole, evil must also increase—except that since the effect of sin naturally sets in only gradually, often the children and grandchildren first suffer and make amends for the sins of the fathers—but likewise, as sin decreases, evil would also decrease."[53] The connection here between sin and evil is a result of divine causality. Schleiermacher's theology is therefore consonant with the thought of those in the Reformed tradition who acknowledge that if one is to affirm "radical monotheism," which avoids all forms and hints of Manicheanism and Pelagianism, then one must also acknowledge that God is responsible for sin and evil.[54]

I am using "radical monotheism" here because Schleiermacher's position reminds me of the work of H. Richard Niebuhr in *Radical Monotheism and Western Culture*.[55] Niebuhr defines radical monotheism as

> reliance on the source of all being for the significance of the self and of all that exists. It is the assurance that because I am, I am valued, and because you are, you are beloved, and because whatever is has being, therefore it is worthy of love. It is the confidence that whatever is, is good, because it exists as one thing among the many which all have their origin and their being, in the One—the principle of being which is also the principle of value.[56]

Niebuhr is affirming here that the God who creates is the God of grace, and the two cannot be separated.[57] I do not think that Schleiermacher's theology accords in all respects with Niebuhr's theology (or vice versa); there are clearly wide differences between them. However, there is also great resonance between Niebuhr's work and Schleiermacher's own commitment to identifying the God of creation and redemption. Evidence that this is the case even with regard to God's responsibility for sin and evil might be found in Niebuhr's supplementary essay, "Faith in Gods and in God."[58] There he draws on Alfred North Whitehead's language in order to write of the coming to be and passing away of all things:

> By whatever name we call it, this law of things, this reality, this way things are, is something with which we all must reckon. We may not be able to give a name to it, calling it only the "void" out of which everything comes and to which

---

53. Ibid., §77.1, p. 483.
54. Ibid., §98.2, p. 612.
55. H. Richard Niebuhr, *Radical Monotheism and Western Culture* (Louisville, KY: Westminster John Knox, 1960).
56. Ibid., p. 32.
57. Ibid. To see how radical monotheism as Niebuhr conceives of it is not at odds with trinitarianism, see Christoph Schwöbel, "Radical Monotheism and the Trinity," *Neue Zeitschrift für systematische Theologie und Religionsphilosophie* 43/1 (2001): 54-74.
58. Niebuhr, *Radical Monotheism*, pp. 114-26.

everything returns, though that is also a name. But it is there—the last shadowy and vague reality, the secret existence by virtue of which things come into being, are what they are, and pass away. Against it there is no defense. This reality, this nature of things, abides when all else passes. It is the source of all things and the end of all.[59]

Niebuhr writes that the strange thing is that we have been able to affirm this reality, the source and end of all things. We can say, "Though it slay us yet we will trust it."[60] This "slaying" includes God's responsibility not only for ordaining death as part of the natural order but also for creating progressively such that sin and evil are part of humanity's life. When asking how an individual comes to have faith in this kind of God, Niebuhr says that it does not happen without experience of "the great social catastrophes" and "recognition of the unworthiness both of our transgressions and our obediences to our moral laws."[61] But it also does not usually, Niebuhr says, occur outside of a concrete meeting with Jesus Christ and with others who have already received faith in God through Christ. For Niebuhr, "we confront in the event of Jesus Christ the presence of that last power which brings to apparent nothingness the life of the most loyal man. Here we confront the slayer, and here we become aware that this slayer is the life-giver."[62] Niebuhr is focusing on death here in a way that Schleiermacher would not, since Schleiermacher views death neither as an evil that results from sin nor as a hindrance to faith. However, it remains that for both thinkers God is responsible not only for giving creatures the good parts of life but also for progressively creating in such a way that sin and evil are part of human experience.

If we are to understand something about Schleiermacher's perspective by reading it in light of Niebuhr's radical monotheism, we must at this point say that for Schleiermacher God ordains sin and evil differently than God ordains goodness and redemption. God ordains sin and evil only in relation to redemption, which is the ultimate *telos* of creation, and God ordains that sin and evil diminish as redemption increases over time. In this way, Schleiermacher relativizes sin and evil by placing them in the context of the process of creation-redemption. We come to love God as the "slayer and life-giver," but these descriptions are not equal in significance. God is this "slayer and life-giver," ordainer of both goodness and evil, sin and redemption, but when we encounter Christ we receive with him a trust and confidence in God as Love, Wisdom, and Life. In and through Christ, we come to trust the divine source and end of all things even though we hate the sin and evil that God wills as part of the process of creation-redemption, because we see divine activity moving progressively toward a fuller completion of redemption.

59. Ibid., p. 122.
60. Ibid.
61. Ibid., p. 124.
62. Ibid., pp. 124–5.

Set in the context of the challenges for the concept of divine sovereignty with which this chapter began, we can now see that Schleiermacher's view would be more aptly construed as promulgating divine weakness rather than divine capriciousness or child abuse. For it is not the case that Schleiermacher imagines a two-faced God (loving and wrathful) or a God who enjoys making creatures suffer as a result of sin and evil. Rather, for Schleiermacher, God simply cannot do otherwise. Of course, Schleiermacher would not call this "weakness" and would balk at such a characterization, because naming it as such would be to imagine that "power" means having the ability to do anything one wishes, conceived anthropomorphically. For Schleiermacher, however, we do not know what divine power should look like apart from the self-communication of God in Christ, where it is best construed as "almighty love." For that reason, Schleiermacher does not think the existence of sin and evil is to be blamed on divine weakness. Rather, he simply claims that things are the way they are because God is the way God is. He points to the divine being rather than offering a defense of progressive creation-redemption because he conceives of divine activity only in relation to creation, without speculation about God considered apart from creation. He does not want to entertain the notion that God existed prior to creation, considered the options, and then chose this world rather than another. Such speculation would divorce God and creation, on the one hand, and anthropomorphize God, on the other.[63] For Schleiermacher, God does not choose a plan of action after deliberating, but God simply acts in accord with the divine being. Again, we have the kind of world we have, he would say, because we have the kind of God we have. Schleiermacher offers as an analogy the image of an artist, "in a state of inspired discovery," who "would think of nothing else, nor would anything else be offered, than what this artist is actually bringing forth."[64] The heart of this divine "artist," however, is not decisively revealed in the artist's creation of nature or history or reason by themselves; Schleiermacher does not offer a form of natural theology in his dogmatics. For Schleiermacher, the heart of the divine life is decisively revealed by divine self-communication in and through the person of Christ and his Spirit in the church, as we have seen in Chapter 2. And as we have seen in Chapter 1, since God communicates Godself as Love in the person and work of Christ, Universal Causality is understood together with Love and Wisdom. Schleiermacher's notion of divine sovereignty, therefore, includes a strong sense of divine omnipotence in relation to creation as a whole, but divine omnipotence is not to be understood simply as divine Might within a vacuum. For him, divine omnipotence is best understood as Mighty Love and Mighty Wisdom, communicated in and through Christ and Christ's Spirit. What this means for Schleiermacher's account of God's responsibility for sin and evil is that there is no explanation for the fact that reality includes horrors, small and great. There is only the dual acknowledgment, first, that God has ordained this world in accordance with who God is, and second, that

---

63. *CF*, §55.2, p. 326.
64. Ibid.

God is ever active in reducing and eradicating sin and evil through preparation for and then the union of the divine and humanity in Christ and in Christ's Spirit in the church.

Schleiermacher's acknowledgment that God is responsible for sin and evil even as God is always working to reduce and remove it accords with the realism involved in Williams's criticism of Black liberation theology for not recognizing the fact that God simply is not a liberator of all people at the same time. God does not liberate Hagar when she cries out to the divine in the wilderness, for example. Instead, God tells her to go back to her oppressors. For Williams, this narrative does not reveal God's disregard for oppressed people, but God's concern first that oppressed people survive using whatever resources are at hand. This perspective "preaches" by simultaneously recognizing the realities of human tragedy, legitimizing grief and lament, maintaining trust in the overall goodness of God's creative-redemptive activity, and motivating human activity in the quest to establish the reign of God on earth in whatever ways Christians are able.

Difficult as this perspective may be, I would argue that the notion of divine omnipotence at work here is quite different than and less susceptible to misuse than the idea that God can do whatever is logically possible and sometimes does intervene within the world's natural order. On an interventionist view, the question legitimately arises why God sometimes liberates and sometimes does not in particular circumstances. If God controls each of the world's outcomes in a particular and interventionist way and has inscrutable reasons for liberating some people while allowing others to suffer, then God could easily be construed as a despot or tyrant wielding "his" power unjustly. On Schleiermacher's view, in contrast, individual cases drop out of view and a different question arises: why or how is this entire order of creation better than other possible worlds God could have created? To this question, as we have seen, Schleiermacher has no reply other than to state that God creates in accord with God's being, which I have argued is essentially Love, Wisdom, and Universal Causality. Given who God is, there is no other world God could have created: "God's willing of the world is already included in God's willing-of-Godself."[65] Schleiermacher never sought to do apologetics in his dogmatics. He simply offers doctrines of God and creation that take Christian piety for granted. Christians, because of their reception of Love and Wisdom in Christ and Christ's Spirit in the church simply have a sense that this world, despite its atrocities, is God's world, that the horrors God's creatures endure are not individual punishments for individual sins, and that the world is still worth inhabiting as it comes to fuller redemption over time. Sin and evil notwithstanding, created life and the divine who brought it forth are yet good.

In summary, we have seen thus far that Schleiermacher maintains the total determination of creation by God, by which all things considered as a whole are subject to the divine will. He affirms divine aseity within his doctrine of divine omnipotence, by which he claims that God is not dependent upon others. At the

---

65. *CF*, §54.5, p. 313.

same time, Schleiermacher respects human self-initiated activity. He upholds both claims by conceiving of the activity of God and creatures in a noncompetitive manner. Divine omnipotence applies to the whole of nature, rather than to individuals considered by themselves. In addition, divine intervention into the nature system is ruled out of court. This has the effect of highlighting the interconnected web of existence within which humanity is a part and safeguarding divine grace so that the feeling of absolute dependence that is communicated to Christians in the reception of redemption by Christ is upheld. These features of Schleiermacher's thought are consonant with the aims of ecotheologians, who want to affirm the goodness of creation, respect its integrity as a system and humanity's own part within it, and limit human activity such that the health and integrity of the ecosystem are not jeopardized.[66] He offers a non-interventionist God that maintains the integrity of the process of nature, and he turns Christian thought away from individualistic accounts of the relation of creation and God.

The opposite side of the coin is also upheld within Schleiermacher's doctrine of divine omnipotence: just as everything that exists depends upon God for its existence and preservation, so is divine activity completely presented in the totality of finite existence. That is to say, Christians are not to speculate about who God is or what God could have done if God had not done what God did do. Schleiermacher maintains this "radical monotheism" even to the point of claiming that sin and evil do not come from any other source than God. God is responsible for sin, which arises due to the weak consciousness of God that characterizes humanity apart from Christ. Likewise, God is responsible for evil as a collective consequence of collective sin. However, Schleiermacher maintains that God ordains sin and evil only in relation to God's ultimate purpose of redemption, in which sin and evil are progressively eliminated. Why God creates-redeems in this progressive way, Christians do not know—not because it is God's prerogative to do whatever God wills without explanation, but because there are no counterfactuals of divine freedom. God is who God is and therefore does what God does, and Christian piety cannot get any further than simply trusting its own reception of divine grace in the self-communication of God as Love and Wisdom in Christ. By recognizing the reality of sin and evil, however, Schleiermacher's view accords with Williams's perspective that theologians need to reckon with the ways in which God is not a liberator immediately for all people. By claiming that God is responsible for sin and evil within the schema of creation-redemption, Schleiermacher recognizes the realities of the world, legitimizes lament, trusts in God as Love, Wisdom, and Universal Causality, and motivates human activity to resist sin and evil.

In the next section, I turn our focus to the question of how Christian prayer practices might simultaneously encourage resistance to sin and evil and recognize the need for Christians to submit to God upon whom everything depends. Only if this is possible can Schleiermacher's view of divine sovereignty avoid the challenge

---

66. For a full explication of how this is the case, see *Schleiermacher and Sustainability*, ed. Poe.

presented at the outset of this chapter: that divine sovereignty inculcates passivity in Christians that keeps them in an infantile state, rather than encouraging human activities that would help to eradicate systems of oppression.

Divine Sovereignty and Prayerful Submission

Here we enter the debate about how to properly conceive divine sovereignty by considering the practice of Christian prayer. In prayer, Christians enact and embody their conceptions of their relatedness to God. It is, therefore, a valuable site for exploring how Christians understand their relation to God and how these ideas might be developed in ways that are not likely to reinforce sexism and/or other oppressive practices like racism, classism, and colonialism. To complicate matters, R. Marie Griffith argues that in explorations of this type feminists ought to pay attention to the lives and thought of evangelical women.[67] She contends that part of the lack of sympathy between feminist liberals and evangelical women has been motivated by socioeconomic difference. Feminists' "general hostility toward religious and cultural 'backwardness,'" she states, "is fuelled by interests that are profoundly class-based."[68] Griffith argues that if feminists are genuinely concerned about oppressed and marginalized women, then they ought to listen to the voiced experiences of evangelical women, including their experiences of the "power of submission." Going further in another context, Sarah Coakley argues that Christian feminists might beneficially reclaim "submission" in prayer practices. Through prayerful contemplation, or "regular, silent waiting on the divine,"[69] she explains that Christians may enter a practice that is "not the silence of being silenced. Rather, it is the voluntary silence of attention, transformation, mysterious interconnection, and (in violent, abusive, or oppressive contexts) rightful and divinely empowered resistance."[70] Coakley maintains that this "power-in-vulnerability" is compatible with Christian feminism.[71] Both Coakley

---

67. A version of this portion of the chapter was originally published as Shelli M. Poe, "Locating Prayerful Submission for Feminist Ecumenism: Holy Saturday or Incarnate Life?" *Feminist Theology* 26/2 (2018): 171–84.

68. R. Marie Griffith, *God's Daughters: Evangelical Women and the Power of Submission* (Berkeley: University of California Press, 1997), p. 205. I do not intend to defend this claim. The situation is undoubtedly complex and changing over time. Reducing the division between liberals and evangelicals to economic disparity would be simplistic. However, it is also the case that historically, discourses in feminist thought have been disconnected from and rejected by those who are not among the intelligentsia, and that being part of the intelligentsia has typically corresponded to some socioeconomic privilege.

69. Sarah Coakley, *God, Sexuality, and the Self* (New York: Cambridge University Press, 2014), p. 340.

70. Coakley, *God, Sexuality, and the Self*, p. 84. Cf. Sarah Coakley, *Powers and Submissions: Spirituality, Philosophy and Gender* (Malden, MA: Blackwell, 2002).

71. Coakley, *God, Sexuality, and the Self*, p. 343.

and Griffith suggest in different modes, then, that practices of submission are powerful in ways feminists have not acknowledged, and both present fieldwork on charismatics as they construct their arguments.

Womanist approaches, however, are not included in these assessments of the value of "powers and submissions" in ecumenical Christian feminism. My concern is that without womanist perspectives, the conversation might make progress by bridging class-based differences with evangelical women only to ignore racially inflected differences. Of course, there is a liberal-evangelical divide among Black communities as well; not all African American women agree with womanist perspectives, and womanists themselves have various projects and proposals. What I am suggesting is simply that if womanist voices are not a prominent part of the discussion, then feminists may make significant missteps when attempting to forge a more inclusive type of feminist ecumenism. I argue that a focus on prayerful submission is likely to be more beneficial for women within various communities if it is incarnational rather than apophatically cruciform. Given Schleiermacher's emphasis on creation's absolute dependence upon the divine, which we have seen above, and the centrality of the incarnation for his soteriology, which we have seen in Chapter 2, his work is well suited as a conversation partner in theorizing an incarnational understanding of submission. I begin by tracing the feminist conversation about submission thus far and then turn to Williams and Schleiermacher to move the conversation in a new direction.

Feminist Ecumenism and Purgative Submission

Griffith aims to avoid stereotypical and dismissive descriptions of non- or anti-feminist evangelical women because such descriptions "betray a rude gap" in what she believes is "a central feminist task: focusing with thorough mindfulness on women previously ignored or hidden from view, including—perhaps especially—those who challenge prior assumptions within feminist thought or who patently reject feminist tenets altogether."[72] By focusing on this task, Griffith raises her readers' awareness of the "internal challenges and debates over whom feminism can speak for," which have "perpetually tested the limits of feminist solidarity and inclusion."[73] Underlying Griffith's descriptive ethnographic work are meta-feminist

72. Griffith, *God's Daughters*, p. 204.
73. Ibid. Cf. Esther Byle Bruland, "Evangelical and Feminist Ethics: Complex Solidarities," *Journal of Religious Ethics* 17/2 (September 1989): 139–60; Kelly H. Chong, "Coping with Conflict, Confronting Resistance: Fieldwork Emotions and Identity Management in a South Korean Evangelical Community," *Qualitative Sociology* 31/4 (December 2008): 369–90; Pamela Cochran, *Evangelical Feminism: A History* (New York: New York University Press, 2005); Julie Ingersoll, *Evangelical Christian Women: War Stories in the Gender Battles* (New York: New York University Press, 2003); Sally K. Gallagher, "The Marginalization of Evangelical Feminism," *Sociology of Religion* 65/3 (2004): 215–37; Sally K. Gallagher, "Where Are the Antifeminist Evangelicals? Evangelical Identity, Subcultural Location, and Attitudes toward Feminism," *Gender & Society* 18/4 (August 2004): 451–72; Gaye M.

concerns: What does it mean to be feminist? Who ought to be included in feminist discourse? What boundaries ought the feminist community draw around a faithful interpretation of their central concerns? Griffith highlights the complexity of these questions by drawing attention to the paradoxical relationship of power and submission within evangelical women's narratives. Her ethnographic research subjects are the women who participate in Women's Aglow Fellowship International—an interdenominational parachurch organization involved in the charismatic renewal movement. Griffith argues that recognizing the nuances of these evangelical women's lives allows for the possibility of counting them as friends in the pursuit of women's well-being. The goal, she explains, is "not to turn evangelical women into feminists (or feminists into anonymous or crypto-Christians) but rather to realize what is shared by these distinctive yet overlapping female cultures."[74]

One commonality between these cultures is the recognition by those on both ends of the spectrum that freedom must be contained within limits.[75] Griffith shows that although Aglow women draw boundaries around their actions differently than feminists, both groups recognize the importance of bounded freedom for the well-being of women. For feminists, the limits in question are chiefly those of justice. People should not do whatever they wish but should act in accord with their responsibilities to preserve and respect all persons' dignity and well-being. For anti-feminists, the limits of freedom are found, more particularly, in patriarchal orderings of family, church, and society. Such bounded freedom is presented as liberating, since it protects evangelical women from the confusion, unhappiness, and sinfulness that would occur if they were to forsake the God-given limits of their place in society and the home. For instance, Griffith describes an evangelical perspective offered to women in unhappy marriages:

> Their lives seem isolated and they fail at their wifely roles because they wish for their husbands to be, in Dorothy's words, "someone different." To be healed, they must repent of their error and realize the "deception" behind it, taking full responsibility for their unhappiness and accepting their husbands without

---

Bammert, "Narrating the Church: Protestant Women Pastors Challenge Nostalgic Desire," *Journal of Feminist Studies in Religion* 26/2 (2010): 153–74; Kelly H. Chong, "Negotiating Patriarchy: South Korean Evangelical Women and the Politics of Gender," *Gender & Society* 20/6 (December 2006): 697–724; Carol Virginia Pohli, "Church Closets and Back Doors: A Feminist View of Moral Majority Women," *Feminist Studies* 9/3 (Autumn 1983): 529–58.

74. Griffith, *God's Daughters*, p. 208. Some evangelicals have attempted to do this as well; see, for instance, *Tamar's Tears: Evangelical Engagements with Feminist Old Testament Hermeneutics*, ed. Andrew Sloane (Eugene, OR: Pickwick, 2012). Cf. Orit Avishai, Lynne Gerber, and Jennifer Randles, "The Feminist Ethnographer's Dilemma: Reconciling Progressive Research Agendas with Fieldwork Realities," *Journal of Contemporary Ethnography* 42 (August 2013): 394–426.

75. Griffith, *God's Daughters*, p. 211.

expecting them to change. Giving up all hopes or expectations of marital satisfaction and simply accepting the duties bestowed by their supposedly God-given role of wife as helpmeet, these women describe the pleasant surprise of discovering greater happiness that is the reward for this sacrificial obedience, some finding their husbands to be "the man I had always longed for."[76]

Clearly, this is not a message that feminists would find empowering for women or conducive to their well-being. While many feminists may agree with Aglow members that people in healthy relationships should not try to change each other, they would likely also suggest both that it is healthy to communicate one's expectations for a satisfying partnership and that it is one's responsibility to carefully consider the actions one might need to take on one's own behalf in order to maintain one's integrity and honor others' agency. This example illustrates that without downplaying monumental differences in the ways feminists and the women of Aglow variously define the limits of freedom, it is nonetheless the case that for both, true liberty occurs within boundaries for right action.

Another central commonality between feminists and evangelicals, for Griffith, is that both have a concern for women's well-being at their core. Griffith herself became more attuned to this feature of Aglow women's narratives as her ethnographic research developed over time. Her original theme of female submission, "though still significant, receded somewhat in importance as motifs more often evoked in women's narratives—intimacy, healing and transformation, for instance—moved to the centre."[77] In the core chapters of her book, Griffith highlights Aglow women's pursuit of their own well-being. In particular, she focuses on Aglow women's practices of prayer: "Aglow prayer narratives hinge on moments when the possibility for a new identity are conceived, and it is in surrendering to such possibilities that new selves may be born."[78] Griffith acknowledges that "the ritual sense that these women share, forged in a symbolic world that allows them to redefine themselves as healed, delivered, and set free, produces and reinforces power relationships in crucial ways."[79] At the same time, she believes that "this sense also opens up possibilities for new worlds to be imagined and lived and thus may open the way for vital transformations of another, more concrete, and

---

76. Ibid., p. 173. Similar advice is given in, for example, *Recovering Biblical Manhood & Womanhood: A Response to Evangelical Feminism*, ed. John Piper and Wayne Grudem (Wheaton, IL: Crossway, 2006). Compare to Kristin Aune, "Marriage in a British Evangelical Congregation: Practicing Postfeminist Partnership?" *Sociological Review* 54/4 (2006): 638–57; John Bartkowski, *Remaking the Godly Marriage: Gender Negotiation in Evangelical Families* (New Brunswick, NJ: Rutgers University Press, 2001).

77. Griffith, *God's Daughters*, p. 5. A similar suggestion is made in a Chinese evangelical context: Yi-Jung Pan, "Chinese Women's Spiritual Formation in Evangelical Churches: A Reflection," *Asia Journal of Theology* 27/2 (October 2013): 226–42.

78. Griffith, *God's Daughters*, p. 213.

79. Ibid., p. 79.

potentially more radical, order."[80] Thus, Aglow women have this in common with feminists as well: imagining new possibilities and personal transformations that might facilitate women's well-being. While these similarities should not be overemphasized, they do provide commonalities that might be used to forge a feminist ecumenism that attends to evangelical women's experiences.

Coakley, like Griffith, also turns her attention to prayer practices as a site for exploring appropriate powers and submissions in forging a Christian way of life that will support and advance women's well-being. Generally speaking, Coakley's theological project is to draw upon the resources of Gregory of Nyssa and pseudo-Dionysius the Areopagite, among others, to make an "apophatic turn" within feminist Christian thought by advancing a kenotic form of Christianity. Within this project, Coakley argues that the repression of "vulnerability" in feminist Christianity is detrimental to it. For her, vulnerability, submission, and feminist subversion go hand in hand because in Jesus' humanity, "weakness, passivity, or vulnerability (all traditionally demerits for the 'male', but manifestly present in Jesus' passion)" are presented as normative for humans or even revelatory of the divine.[81] As such, Coakley's project is heavily influenced by her understanding of the kenotic character of Jesus' cross. Her work is also partially influenced by her brief fieldwork on charismatics in a university town in northern England. Partially in light of her engagement with charismatics, Coakley concludes that "we cannot get this vision of powers and submissions right by political or theological manipulation or fiat; we can only get it right by *right* primary submission to the Spirit, with all the purgative costliness that involves."[82] She ultimately recommends a profusion of metaphors for God, nuanced theological and philosophical understandings of creedal trinitarianism, and contemplative prayer. I focus on the latter, which she describes as involving "purgative kneeling before the blankness of the darkness which nonetheless dazzles."[83] In prayerful submission before the divine, Coakley believes that Christian feminists can learn how to rightly call God "Father"—the ultimate source of tenderness and joy.[84] Christian feminists must above all call God "Father," she holds, because they "do the kneeling work that ultimately slays patriarchy at its root."[85] In this way, Coakley links a posture of vulnerability and submission with both Christian feminism and evangelical God-talk.[86]

80. Ibid.
81. Coakley, *Powers and Submissions*, p. 25. Her chapter in *Powers and Submissions* was originally published as "*Kenosis* and Subversion: On the Repression of 'Vulnerability' in Christian Feminist Writing," in *Swallowing a Fishbone? Feminist Theologians Debate Christianity* (London: SPCK, 1996), pp. 82–111.
82. Coakley, *God, Sexuality, and the Self*, p. 322.
83. Ibid., p. 325.
84. Ibid., p. 326.
85. Ibid., p. 327.
86. For an insightful critique of Coakley on these points, see Linn Marie Tonstad's third chapter, "Speaking 'Father' Rightly: Kenotic Reformation into Sonship in Sarah

4. God and Creation

What if, Coakley asks, "true divine 'empowerment' occurs most unimpededly in the context of a special form of human 'vulnerability'?"[87] This special form of vulnerability may be experienced in the waiting of contemplative prayer, which "marks one's willed engagement in the pattern of cross and resurrection."[88] By repeating this pattern, the one who prays is perpetually placed within Holy Saturday, submitting to death and awaiting the display of divine power. The methods used in contemplative prayer can vary. Such prayer may "use a repeated phrase to ward off distractions, or be wholly silent; it may be simple Quaker attentiveness, or take a charismatic expression (such as the use of quiet rhythmic 'tongues')."[89] In any case, the one who prays exhibits a posture of vulnerability and submission: self-purgative kneeling while making space for the divine presence and power. Coakley admits that such a posture is open to abuses. Since there is "so much self-deception, and so much bewilderment and uncertainty" in contemplative prayer, she suggests that it "might only be able to be adequately evaluated by its results."[90]

For Coakley, contemplative prayer of this kind repeats the sort of kenosis Jesus powerfully exhibited on the cross and in the tomb. Kenosis, she says, is "a choosing *never to have* 'worldly' forms of power."[91] Bullying is offered as an example of a form of power that Jesus never took up. Coakley explains the relationship between Christ's kenosis and contemplative prayer: "What Christ on this view instantiates is the very 'mind' that we ourselves enact, or enter into, in prayer: the unique intersection of vulnerable, 'non-grasping' humanity and authentic divine power, itself 'made perfect in weakness.'"[92] Contemplative prayer is a kenotic practice insofar as it is a denial of a certain type of self, one which Jesus never instantiated in the first place but of which others may need to purge themselves to enact the mind of Christ. Notice, however, that cruciform kenosis is not simply the denial of a particular set of characteristics like fear, revenge, bullying, or grasping of power-over. The liturgical location of the practice is theologically significant because it patterns the Christian life symbolically and concretely. Cruciform kenotic prayer is a repetition of Good Friday's death and Holy Saturday's empty waiting with the hope of resurrection Sunday.

Coakley's view has generated a lively discussion among scholars.[93] The conversation began in the 1990s between Coakley and Daphne Hampson. It has

Coakley," in *God and Difference: The Trinity, Sexuality, and the Transformation of Finitude* (New York: Routledge, 2016), pp. 98–132.

87. Coakley, *Powers and Submissions*, p. 32.
88. Ibid., p. 35.
89. Ibid.
90. Ibid., p. 38.
91. Ibid., p. 31.
92. Ibid., p. 38.
93. See Daphne Hampson, "On Power and Gender," *Modern Theology* 4/3 (April 1988); 234–50; and Daphne Hampson, *Theology and Feminism* (Oxford: Basil Blackwell, 1990). Coakley rejected Hampson's view in "*Kenosis* and Subversion: On the Repression of 'Vulnerability' in Christian Feminist Writing," in *Swallowing a Fishbone? Feminist*

been extended into the present by Aristotle Papanikolaou, Carolyn Chau, Michelle Gonzalez, Anna Mercedes, Jennifer Newsome Martin, and Linn Marie Tonstad. In many of these continued discussions, even authors generally sympathetic to Coakley's view nonetheless suggest modifications to her portrayal of kenotic submission. Take, for example, Chau's response to Papanikolaou's extension of Coakley's view. Papanikolaou contends that kenosis is present in the healing process of trauma victims as they empty themselves of fear and submit themselves to a therapeutic relationship. It is a "giving over of oneself for the sake of self."[94] In response, Chau recalls Hampson as an early interlocutor with Coakley:

> While Papanikolaou analyses the movements of healing in terms of self-giving, it could be argued by Hampson that the abused person who seeks healing does so precisely because she chooses to "resist" and to claim herself as a self. To advise the abused person to "give herself away," Hampson may say, would not have brought her to begin the path of healing through therapy: she had no self to give! Her healing is, rather, a result of her choice to become "mature," "responsible," "autonomous" and her courage to define herself rather than allow her abuser to define who she is.[95]

The criticism here is that Papanikolaou's extension of Coakley's view is misplaced because what happens in therapy is not self-emptying but self-building. Chau ultimately finds this critique unsatisfactory because it does not hold out the possibility that the divine could allow the traumatized person, even in a state of emptiness, to give of herself in a kenotic relationship.[96] In brief, Chau repeats Coakley's view that divine empowerment is made perfect in human weakness. Nonetheless, Chau seems ultimately to conclude that the apophatic inflection of kenosis is out of place in a discussion of healing. She attempts to

---

Theologians Debate Christianity (London: SPCK, 1996), pp. 82–111. The conversation was continued with Aristotle Papanikolaou's article, "Person, Kenosis and Abuse: Hans Urs von Balthasar and Feminist Theologies in Conversation," *Modern Theology* 19/1 (January 2003): 41–65. The thread was picked up once more by Michelle A. Gonzalez, "Hans Urs von Balthasar and Contemporary Feminist Theology," *Theological Studies* 65 (2004): 566–95; Carolyn A. Chau "'What Could Possibly Be Given?': Towards an Exploration of Kenosis as Forgiveness—Continuing the Conversation between Coakley, Hampson, and Papanikolaou," *Modern Theology* 28/1 (January 2012): 1–24; Jennifer Newsome Martin, "The 'Whence' and the 'Whither' of Balthasar's Gendered Theology: Rehabilitating Kenosis for Feminist Theology," *Modern Theology* 13/2 (April 2015): 211–34; and Linn Marie Tonstad, *God and Difference: The Trinity, Sexuality, and the Transformation of Finitude* (New York: Routledge, 2016), Chapter 3.

94. Aristotle Papanikolaou, "Person, Kenosis and Abuse: Hans Urs von Balthasar and Feminist Theologies in Conversation," *Modern Theology* 19/1 (January 2003): 56.

95. Chau, "'What Could Possibly Be Given?,'" p. 10.

96. Ibid., p. 11.

refine Papanikolaou's view by offering "forgiveness" as a way of understanding therapeutic *kenosis*, because it "resonates less as negation and more as donation."[97] By denying the apophatic inflection of healing, Chau takes a different path than Coakley even as she is sympathetic to Coakley's view. The conversation about submission surveyed here reveals that, in multiple modes of thought, feminists are forging an ecumenism that attempts at least to attend to evangelical women's voices (Griffith) and at most to include some insights of evangelicals within feminist theologies (Coakley). More particularly, some are turning their attention to kenotic submission as a potentially feminist theological commitment and practice in various practical contexts (e.g., Papanikolaou, Chau).

Linn Marie Tonstad's devastating criticism of Coakley's work goes against this grain and offers corroboration for my view that a different kind of prayerful submission than Coakley offers is needed. Tonstad notes that Coakley interprets dependence upon God as vulnerability and "construes the God-world relation in dangerously competitive ways for someone committed to classical transcendence."[98] By envisioning contemplative prayer as space-making and purgative, so that God might create the pray-er "anew by the power of the Spirit so as to bring her to the Father in the form of the crucified Son,"[99]

> Coakley fails to recognize that the difference between God and creation is not a binary difference. Binaries entail the definition of one term by the exclusion of the other. Making the difference between God and creation a binary difference of that sort produces a bad infinity, as it would define (and so limit) the divine by its opposition to the finite, negating transcendence.[100]

Moreover, the "Sonship" into which the Spirit forges the pray-er "once more becomes sacrificial, for the content of the Son's person just is cruciformity."[101] Tonstad explains that the most frequent depiction of the suffering of Christ that a person is brought into through contemplative prayer is "a loss of noetic certainty and of idolatrous assumptions of control. Why these amount to *suffering* is never quite explained."[102] Nonetheless, it is clear that for Coakley, "true human freedom is 'submission' to God. Submission to God means freely willing what God wills through alignment of divine and human desire."[103] Combined with Coakley's focus on suffering in purgative, contemplative prayer, this means that "all of creation may, through its bodied and suffering existence, return to God, but only by affirming its existence as suffering and through suffering."[104]

---

97. Ibid., p. 15.
98. Tonstad, *God and Difference*, p. 99.
99. Ibid., p. 109.
100. Ibid., p. 107.
101. Ibid., p. 111.
102. Ibid., p. 109.
103. Ibid., p. 112.
104. Ibid., p. 118.

Coakley's use of ethnographic fieldwork in coming to this position is also suspect. As Tonstad notes, in the eighteen interviews Coakley conducted in northern England during the mid-1980s,

> Nearly all her informants think the Spirit's activity of praying in the pray-er leads to joy and an uplifted affect, for instance. Coakley strongly believes, to the contrary, that mature contemplative prayer entails pain and participation in "genuinely Christlike dereliction." The decision whether to consider such dereliction and pain either a Spirit-willed condition or a sign of the Spirit's absence or "inactivity" becomes the "theological crux" of the maturation and true Spirit-directedness (the orthodoxy) of her informants. When congregants insist on "joyousness" as the "norm," Coakley presses them until they admit "phases of dryness themselves."[105]

As for whether contemplative prayer results in resistance and empowerment, Tonstad looks to Coakley's second set of enthnographic subjects: jailed prisoners in the Boston area with whom Coakley "spent an hour a week for a semester teaching the practice of silent prayer."[106] Tonstad explains,

> Coakley enthusiastically describes the transformative effects of silent prayer on the prisoners in prayer's production of "[g]entleness, poise, peace and solidarity," but she fails to reckon too with a deeper challenge the experience poses to her thesis regarding sociopolitical transformation. The prisoners reportedly become calmer and less resistant as a result of their contemplative activities—a desirable transformation, perhaps, in the context of a just order. But the prison system in the United States is, as Coakley comes to recognize, decidedly not a just order.[107]

With Tonstad, I question Coakley's competitive view of the God-world relation, in which dependence upon God is understood as vulnerability and suffering. As we have seen above, Schleiermacher conceives of the relation between God and creation as noncompetitive, wherein dependence upon God enables human self-initiated activity. Although his account recognizes that suffering is part of reality, which God is responsible for, it nonetheless stands against quietism and passivity in relation to that suffering. Just as God is consistently working to reduce and eliminate sin, so too ought the Christian to resist sociopolitical oppression. Prayer ought to help her do so.

Incarnational Submission

I want to change the direction of the conversation surrounding the theological location and inflection of prayerful submission by drawing in womanist

105. Ibid., p. 119.
106. Ibid.
107. Ibid., p. 120.

perspectives. As Coakley herself notes, womanists have been bold in facing issues of submission head-on. However, when Coakley speaks of kenotic submission in contemplative prayer as creating space for the divine by participating in the pattern of cross and resurrection, her view is at odds with Williams's understanding of the cross and its implications for Black women's lives. Submission understood within the theological locus of Holy Saturday is out of sync with a womanist focus on living an active life of healing and justice through resistance. As such, if "submission" is to gain currency in a feminist ecumenism that keeps faith with both evangelical women and womanist perspectives like that of Williams, I contend that it ought to be an incarnational rather than an apophatically cruciform type of submission. By drawing in Schleiermacher's work as well, I aim to connect a particular understanding of "submission" with a correlating prayer practice that could advance the ecumenical conversation among evangelicals, feminists, and womanists regarding the relation of God to creation. This constitutes not only a break with Coakley's apophatic and cruciform approach but also serious support for the project of feminist ecumenism of which Coakley's work is a part.

In *Sisters in the Wilderness*, Williams surveys a number of historical theories of atonement, including ransom, satisfaction, substitution, and moral theories. She argues against each of these theories but retains a common strategy of those who proffered them, namely, rendering Christian symbols accessible to a particular audience by using the language and sociopolitical thought of their time. As we have seen in Chapter 2, Williams reflects on the cross within the context of Black women's experience of surrogacy roles in the pre- and post-civil war periods. Black women have a history of substituting for white people by, for instance, working their fields, taking care of their children, being used for sexual gratification, and cleaning their homes. Williams uses and critiques both liberation and feminist thought to construct "a Christian understanding of redemption that speaks meaningfully to black women, given their historic experience with surrogacy."[108] According to Williams, Jesus' purpose was not to die a self-sacrificial death in order to ransom humanity from the devil, satisfy God's wrath, substitute for humanity's sin, or reveal divine love through suffering. None of these interpretations of the cross is good news for Black women, who would thereby be glorified when they perform surrogacy roles rather than delivered from those roles. As we have seen in Chapter 2, in Williams's account, the cross is the gory suffering of a human being who ran afoul of those with political power. The cross is a sign of human sinfulness and "represents historical evil trying to defeat good."[109] Theological importance attaches to the cross only as a reminder of human sinfulness and an opportunity for solidarity with sufferers. For Williams, the gospel is primarily about living and living well in community with others: "the spirit of God in Jesus came to show

---

108. Delores S. Williams, "Black Women's Surrogacy Experience and the Christian Notion of Redemption," in *Cross Examinations: Readings on the Meaning of the Cross Today*, ed. Marit Trelstad (Minneapolis, MN: Fortress, 2006), p. 11.
109. Ibid.

humans life – to show redemption through a perfect ministerial vision of righting relationships."[110] Jesus does not become the victor over sin and death through the cross. Instead, Williams explains,

> Jesus conquers the sin of temptation in the wilderness (Mt 4:1–11) by resistance—by resisting the temptation to value the material over the spiritual ("Man shall not live by bread alone"); by resisting death (not attempting suicide; "if you are the son of God, throw yourself down"); by resisting the greedy urge of monopolistic ownership ("He showed him all the kingdoms of the world and the glory of them; and he said to him, 'All these I will give you, if you will fall down and worship me'"). Jesus therefore conquered sin in life, not in death.[111]

There are definite similarities between Coakley's understanding of kenosis and Williams's description of resisting temptations here. By refusing inappropriate priorities, death, and greed, Jesus never took up sinful forms of power. However, by emphasizing life and not death, resistance and not waiting, Williams takes a different theological approach than Coakley, who highlights the passion narrative as the theological location of submission in prayer. Williams strives, rather, to promote a culture of resistance, survival, and increasing quality of life.[112]

Schleiermacher could be a valuable partner in this discussion, now set in the context of the relation of God and creation. His emphasis on creation's absolute dependence upon the divine may be used to reconstruct Christian "submission" in a way that further resonates across the theological spectrum. As we have seen, Schleiermacher holds that creatures are wholly dependent on the divine for their existence and preservation. Paying special attention to the concerns outlined at the beginning of this chapter, Anna Mercedes highlights a legitimate criticism of focusing on creation's absolute dependence upon the divine. This focus seems to hold out "a cosmic contrast between power and vulnerability."[113] Indeed, both absolute dependence upon the divine and Coakley's portrayal of "contemplative space-making" still call to mind, Mercedes explains, "an old-fashioned heterosexual coupling between a male (God) and a female (humanity): the submissive one makes space to willingly receive the potency of her divine lover. Consensual and nonviolent, yes—but not a transformation of gender norms."[114] Tonstad concurs that by using Coakley's "readings of gender fluidity, valorization of 'vulnerability' and 'submission' to God, and hypersexualized trinitarian theology, she strengthens rather than weakens the symbolic-theological order of gender that trinitarian theology helps hold in place" (104).

---

110. Ibid.
111. Ibid., p. 12.
112. Williams, *Sisters in the Wilderness*, pp. 205–6.
113. Anna Mercedes, *Power For: Feminism and Christ's Self-Giving* (New York: T&T Clark, 2011), p. 37.
114. Ibid., p. 36.

One response to this critique might be similar to Coakley's early reply to Hampson on the same issue: submission to the divine is a problem for feminist thought only if it retains gender stereotypes. However, these stereotypes are, in part, what feminists seek to abolish.[115] If the divine is not associated with the male and masculine, then there is no danger of reinforcing sex-stereotypes in the relation of absolute dependence of humanity on the divine. This response is logically compelling. Unfortunately, however, the present condition of human life, including Christian life, is still very much marked by sexism, where the divine is, in fact, associated with the male and masculinity. Whatever is the case logically, emphasizing the relation of absolute dependence on the divine without further comment in the current context does evoke and reinforce kyriarchy, including the sex-stereotypes and gender prescriptions kyriarchy involves. Furthermore, as we have seen and as Tonstad explains, for Coakley, "the Father remains marked as masculine even 'after' the purgative success of contemplative prayer in that the pray-er must know that, when she says Father, what she does not mean is specifically *father*, rather than anything else. Speaking Father rightly in this way retains rather than undoes a relation to human fatherhood."[116]

One beneficial way forward, which both retains prayerful submission to the divine and avoids reinforcing sex-stereotypes, is to focus attention away from submission to the divine considered in and for Godself (e.g., in the immanent Trinity) and to focus attention instead on submission to Love and Wisdom who creates the world with its web of interrelations.[117] This is, in fact, a much more accurate understanding of Schleiermacher's notion of absolute dependence as well. As we have seen in Chapter 1, for him, there is no divine in general or God considered apart from the world, but only Universal Causality in Love and Wisdom as communicated in Christ, the church's Spirit of Christ, and creation. For Schleiermacher, the divine should not be considered apart from the world, as if Christians could understand what God might be like apart from God's Christomorphic relation to creation. In what follows, I explore how prayerful submission to the triune God in relation to creation and in the context of the incarnation has advantages over prayerful submission to God considered in the abstract and within the context of the cross and Holy Saturday.

Schleiermacher's 1801 sermon, "The Power of Prayer in Relation to Outward Circumstances," offers resources for constructing an incarnational form of submission that takes its cues from the person of Christ. The sermon's scriptural basis is Mt. 26:36–46, where Jesus prays in the garden of Gethsemane before his arrest. Schleiermacher takes Christ's prayer here as a model for developing a properly Christian practice of prayer. As he defines it,

---

115. Coakley, *Powers and Submissions*, p. 32.
116. Tonstad, *God and Difference*, p. 102.
117. Cf. *OR*, esp. the Second Speech, pp. 18–54.

> To join the thought of God with every thought of any importance that occurs to us; in all our admiration of external nature, to regard it as the work of His wisdom; to take counsel with God about all our plans, that we may be able to carry them out in His name; and even in our most mirthful hours to remember His all-seeing eye; this is the prayer without ceasing to which we are called.[118]

For Schleiermacher, prayer without ceasing is not to be identified with petitionary prayer and an attendant belief in the effectiveness of such prayer to change outward circumstances.[119] Such a belief would set "limits to the reasonableness of our wishes, and even to the humility of our hearts!"[120] Using Christ's prayer in Gethsemane and its results as a paradigm case, Schleiermacher concludes that any apparent granting of petitions requested in prayer cannot be attributed to the divine's pleasure with the petitioner, the petitioner's need of special help, or the nature of that which was requested.[121] If any petition seems to be answered, what was requested was simply already part of the divinely ordained interdependent web of creation rather than being the result of divine intervention within the created order.

The purpose of prayer, Schleiermacher explains, is not to change the course of events but to "lift us up out of the helplessness into which we are brought by fear and passion, and bring us to the consciousness and full use of our powers that so we may be able in all circumstances to conduct ourselves as it becomes those who remember that they are living and acting under the eye and the protection of the Most High."[122] Prayer is meant to empower the Christian to live as one in right relation to the divine—the unchangeable, ineffable, Only Wise, and Kind One. When divine Wisdom and kindness or Love are rightly understood, then in prayer,

> We are occupied with something else than our feelings; with the question, What will be required of me should this or that befall? What kind of powers shall I employ? What kind of stand shall I make against it? What acts of thoughtlessness must I avoid? And if we find that it always depends on those same qualities which we have often exercised and studied over; that the whole of what we may be able to accomplish consists of single acts which we have often before performed with good results; then the soul that had shrunk in fear comes

---

118. Friedrich Schleiermacher, "The Power of Prayer in Relation to Outward Circumstances," in *Selected Sermons of Schleiermacher*, ed. W. Robertson Nicoll, trans. Mary F. Wilson (Eugene, OR: Wipf & Stock, 2004), p. 38. Hereafter, cited as *PP*.

119. Petitionary prayer, incidentally, is ubiquitous among Pentecostal and charismatic individuals, though Griffith and Coakley do not focus on this form of prayer in their fieldwork. Cf. Amos Yong, *Spirit of Love: A Trinitarian Theology of Grace* (Waco, TX: Baylor, 2012), pp. 52–3.

120. *PP*, p. 39.

121. Ibid.

122. Ibid., p. 44.

back to the consciousness of its powers; then we feel ourselves strong enough to walk in the way that God has traced out for us, strong enough to comfort those who are sad on our account and more disheartened than ourselves; and if the hour comes when the evil does befall, we can say, with a mind composed and at peace, Let us rise and go to meet it.[123]

This passage from Schleiermacher's work is reminiscent of Williams's emphases on overcoming sin in creaturely life rather than in death, actively living well, and resisting injustice until the end. It also sidesteps the problem Mercedes raises about reinforcing sex-stereotypes in submission to the divine, since Schleiermacher denies the contrast between divine power and human weakness, seeing divine and human action as noncompetitive. For him, human weakness is not required for divine power to be made manifest; likewise, human agency does not negate divine activity. Schleiermacher explains that when such a contrast between these two is at the center of Christian prayer, it tends to be used manipulatively:

For why is it, after all, that our prayer takes the form of entreaty? When we desire something that we ourselves cannot accomplish, and at the same time remember God; then it occurs to us first of all the thought of His almighty power in contrast to our weakness, and we would like to try to make that power favourable to us. That is prayer as dictated by the weak human heart. But there lies at the bottom of this a defective idea of God.[124]

Schleiermacher continues: "He who is chiefly aroused to the thought of God by a sense of dependence certainly does not think really of Him at all, and the true Christian spirit is utterly wanting in him."[125] Of course, Schleiermacher wholeheartedly maintains the absolute dependence of all things in creation on Universal Causality, Love, and Wisdom. What he is insisting on here is that right prayer is not motivated by a desire to use divine causality to fill a gap created by a mismatch between human weakness and desires. Likewise, the relation of the divine to the world is not an interventionist one. Instead of a contrast between divine power and human vulnerability and the notion that the divine intermittently acts in the world, Schleiermacher understands true prayer, again, as

a heart-stirring thought of the Creator, when our eye rests on His works, out of the quiet delight which we take in his creation; a thought of the Ruler of the world, checking our false estimates, amidst our talk of the fortunes and undertakings of men; a sense of Him whose image becomes manifest in us when we feel ourselves overflowing with love and good-will, amidst the social

---

123. Ibid., p. 46.
124. Ibid., p. 49.
125. Ibid., p. 50.

enjoyment of those noble human feelings; a glad sense of His love when we are enjoying His gifts; when we succeed in some good work, a thankful sense of His support; when we meditate on his commandments, the great hope that He wishes to raise us to His own likeness; this is true prayer.[126]

True prayer is the constant remembrance, sense of, and trust in the divine in relation to all matters of importance in life. It is, therefore, decidedly present amidst day-to-day activities. Prayer without ceasing occurs while delighting in creation, conversing about business, enjoying others' company, appreciating divinely given gifts, walking, working, loving, and contemplating. This kind of prayer is embodied and particular. It is also cognizant of ongoing divine creation, sovereignty, presence, love, support, and goodwill in everyday life.

Prayer without ceasing, as conceived by Schleiermacher, shares with Coakley's view an emphasis on non-grasping humility and submission to the divine activity. In contrast to apophatic submission, however, his understanding of submission is theologically located not in Holy Saturday, within a repetition of the passion narrative, but in the bodily particularities of a life variously characterized by challenges, tragedies, and delights. It is consonant with the work of Emilie Townes, who suggests that there is a need for theologians to become "very particular about the particular."[127] "Incarnational submission" means living and living well in relation to others through attunement to the divine activity in all things, and submission to both Love, Wisdom, and Universal Causality and to the creaturely interdependence that is divinely ordained. In incarnational submission, one submits to God not through space-making or self-purgation before the divine "blankness" but to Love and Wisdom in creating the web of interrelations in which creatures live and in which redemption in and through Christ and Christ's Spirit occurs.

Incarnational submission is therefore in keeping with womanist theologies that aim to avoid repeating oppressive patterns of self-negation and passivity and emphasize instead the interdependence of creation. Traci West's description of liturgical practices that highlight the interdependence of creation bring the conversation to a point:

> Christians need worship rituals that destabilize rituals of white dominance and confront its entangled religious and political veneer. Especially for predominantly white faith communities, liturgical acknowledgment of dependence upon both God *and* upon other people could lead to an awakening, instigating a cognizance of the rituals of white dominance in the broader community in which they also participate.[128]

---

126. Ibid., pp. 50–1.
127. Townes, *Womanist Ethics and the Cultural Production of Evil*, p. 2. Cf. Althaus-Reid, *Indecent Theology*.
128. Traci West, *Disruptive Christian Ethics: When Racism and Women's Lives Matter* (Louisville, KY: Westminster John Knox, 2006), p. 127.

By emphasizing submission to God and the divinely created web of existence within which humans live and move, which includes dependence upon other persons for both joy and justice, liturgical practices could be developed that disrupt classism, racism, and sexism.[129] In this way, "incarnational submission" could expand feminist ecumenism so that it takes into account women with different socioeconomic and racial experiences.

Before concluding, I want to return to the commonalities between evangelical women, feminists, and womanists that can be discerned within Griffith's account of Aglow women, namely, their focus on the need for boundaries of freedom and their pursuit of women's well-being. These commonalities are repeated in incarnational submission's focus on creaturely dependence and interdependence. Women may enjoy well-being by submitting to Love, Wisdom, and Universal Causality as it is communicated in and through Christ and his Spirit (which illuminates creation), and by accepting their creaturely interdependence. Importantly, incarnational submission shifts the focus from hierarchical boundaries to the complex and multidirectional limitations of interdependence set by Love and Wisdom in Universal Causality. By shifting the framework for understanding human boundedness in this way—focusing on human life and its always already existent and complex interdependent relationships rather than on entering a holy death and holding open a negative space for divine power—incarnational submission could shift the conversation within which evangelicals, feminists, and womanists might begin to imagine women's well-being together.

Finally, turning back to the debate about divine sovereignty and human submission, incarnational submission also brings content and context to the notion of divine sovereignty. "Sovereignty" here does not mean acquiescing to oppressive kyriarchal domination. Rather, divine activity empowers creaturely activity. This noncompetitive way of understanding the relationship between Universal Causality and finite causalities allows the Christian to trust in Wisdom and Love who creates-redeems progressively and to recognize her freedom to resist oppression within the interconnected web of divinely created existence. When Christians submit to the divine will—that is, to reality taken in its entire compass—they acknowledge their important part in a large, complex set of relations, interactions, and processes; and they view themselves not as exceptional individuals to be liberated quite apart from others but as part of a whole that is coming to redemption. In short, this way of thinking keeps Christians humble while motivating liberating actions on behalf of all people and creatures.

***

I have argued that Schleiermacher's theology holds promise for constructive theologies in at least three ways. First, his understanding of the asymmetrical relation between God and creation, which I have outlined with reference to his doctrine of divine omnipotence, aligns with contemporary ecotheologies insofar

---

129. Ibid., pp. 139–40.

as it establishes a noncompetitive God-world relation, rejects a premodern view of divine intervention that would disturb the integrity of nature, and encourages a communally focused understanding of creation rather than an individualistic one. Second, by affirming that God is responsible for sin and evil, Schleiermacher's thought is congruent with that of Williams, who recognizes that God is not always and immediately a liberator. By affirming "radical monotheism," which is a rejection of attributing sin and evil to a source independent of God, Schleiermacher maintains his non-speculative manner of theologizing in order to recognize the realities of life, legitimize grief and lament, and motivate human activity all while trusting in God's continual, progressive work of creation-redemption. Third, Schleiermacher's theology can be used along with Williams's work to develop an understanding of prayer as "incarnational submission," which acknowledges the value of recognizing one's absolute dependence upon God while also avoiding the potentially oppressive features of that claim. In contrast to Coakley's apophatic and cruciform understanding of contemplative prayer, "incarnational submission" emphasizes active forms of relation to God that empower women, men, and children and recognizes the complex relationships to others that are involved in each action taken by individuals. Taken together, these features of Schleiermacher's theology set his understanding of divine sovereignty apart from those that might appropriately be the target of concerns regarding accounts of omnipotence that only reinforce passivity in response to oppression. Schleiermacher's notion of divine sovereignty at once retains a strong sense of divine omnipotence while empowering Christian resistance to systemic injustice.

CONCLUSION

In 2018, I had the opportunity to travel with a small group of grassroots activists, pastors, and students to Hawai'i to learn about *aloha 'aina*, or love of the earth.[1] By meeting with farmers, activists, and spiritual practitioners, we explored Hawaiian practices of agriculture and land stewardship, reflecting theologically to recognize the deep connection between land and spirit. At the end of the trip, we stayed at Kahumana Retreat Center in the Lualualei Valley on the west side of O'ahu. Kahumana began in 1974 as an alternative community grounded in the values of mindfulness, empathy, and working together. Today, this nonprofit organization celebrates Hawai'i's natural and cultural resources and works to address some of its pressing needs. In addition to its retreat center, Kahumana provides a certified organic farm, a farm-to-table café, a day program for adults with developmental disabilities, and housing and services for families transitioning out of homelessness.

The Retreat Center also includes a small chapel, called the Chapel of the Holy Sophia.[2] When we visited, it featured a statue of the Hawaiian Madonna in the front and central position within the sanctuary. To the side, a triptych of Sophia, Wisdom of God, stood in a separate worship area. The icon is of the Novgorod type, so named after the Russian city in which an icon like this first appeared in the fifteenth century. Sophia is fiery and winged, seated on a throne, crowned, and holding a scepter. She is flanked by Mary on the left and John the Forerunner (the Baptist) on the right, both of whom are winged. Mary is holding an icon of Emmanuel. Above her is the moon. John holds a scroll inscribed with the words from Jn 1:29: "Behold the Lamb of God" in one hand, and a censer holding a small Christ child in the other. Above him is the sun. Jesus appears above Sophia, at

---

1. The Eco-stewards Program (https://ecostewardsprogram.wordpress.com/) is sponsored by Presbyterians for Earth Care (https://presbyearthcare.org/eco-stewards/).

2. Under the guidance of Father Philip Harmon, M.Div. OOSJ., a priest of the Ukrainian Greek Catholic Archeparch of Lviv, Ukraine, the chapel was constructed in 1982. The chapel was reconsecrated in 2015 to Holy Sophia under the direction of Father Philip Harmon, who had resigned his position as the pastor of the Ukrainian Community in 2008 and who had begun an independent ministry under the blessing of His Grace Kyr Alexander, Bishop of the American Orthodox Catholic Church.

half-length. Above Jesus is an empty throne, which is flanked by three angels on either side.[3]

When I entered the chapel, I was drawn to the icon of Sophia because of the connection of Sophia/Wisdom traditions with feminist theology and because of the simple worship space offered in the chapel for contemplating the icon. As I now look back at the experience of those few moments in front of the icon of Sophia, the Wisdom of God—in a small chapel within an alternative community providing for the needs of vulnerable people on an island in the middle of the Pacific—I wonder what it would be like if future generations were to grow up with images of Sophia in their churches, instead of a proliferation of crosses. I wonder how they would view relationships—personal, familial, societal—if they recited the divine names of Love, Wisdom, and Life on Sundays rather than Father, Son, and Holy Spirit. I wonder how they would respond to systemic injustices if they consistently identified Christ with the "least of these" and understood sin as a social condition. How would they treat one another and make policy if they believed that salvation was a healing salve of wholeness and integrity extended to all through communities of care? I wonder how our children and grandchildren would view the world if they saw Lilith, Hagar, Mary, Eve, and the many other female figures who are part of the consciousness of those working toward racial, economic, gender, and ecological justice on their church's stained glass windows. What if they prayed with a sense of absolute dependence on the divine, coupled with a sense of the interdependence of creation within which they live? I wonder how the next generations would view themselves and their communities, identify their values, prioritize their goals, and love their neighbors, families, friends, and enemies if they were to imbibe images and stories and liturgies that included female figures and feminine pronouns as pointing to the very essence of the divine being. I can imagine it would be a different world altogether.

It is this world that I have been imagining and working toward in the chapters of this book. Even though Schleiermacher's thought needs correction on a number of points, I have suggested that his work is remarkably in step with what some leading theologians are calling for today. My aim has been to entice those working constructively to take another look at Schleiermacher and to find in him much more than an emphasis on religious experience, important though that may be, and to see him as much more than a foil for the work of Karl Barth, as important as Barth's work may be. Schleiermacher's mature theology offers insight into and opportunities for development of each of the major loci of Christian doctrine.

As we have seen, the doctrine of the Trinity has been fraught with general and community-specific challenges from the early church to the contemporary period. In conversation with Elizabeth Johnson, Grace Jantzen, and Linn Marie Tonstad,

---

3. For an account of Sophia and her relation to both Russian sophiology of the nineteenth and twentieth centuries and Western feminist theology, see Brenda Meehan, "Wisdom/Sophia, Russian Identity, and Western Feminist Theology," *CrossCurrents* 46/2 (1996): 149–68.

we have seen that Schleiermacher's theology offers a way of thinking about God that is trinitarian but is not focused on androcentric, hierarchical, logically elusive, death-centric eternal hypostases. In Schleiermacher's theology, we find potential for constructing a doctrine of the essential Trinity that is relevant because it is tethered to the economy of grace, and it is a mystery of faith not because it is intellectually baffling but simply because there are no cognitive reasons one can provide to explain why God, in God's wisdom, loves creation. In a Schleiermacher-inspired doctrine of the essential Trinity, the divine is self-communicated as Love, Wisdom, and Universal Causality through Christ and his Spirit in the church, who illuminates the entirety of creation. A Schleiermacherian doctrine of the essential Trinity leaves to history the androcentric, patriarchal language of Father, Son, and Holy Spirit and affirms instead the three basic contours of the divine life, which are related to one another conceptually in light of the economy of salvation. This development of Schleiermacher's trinitarian thought emphases divine names that have already been lauded by contemporary theologians like Janet Martin Soskice, Wendy Farley, and Pamela Lightsey. In conversation with Farley, Marcella Althaus-Reid, and Elisabeth Schüssler Fiorenza, I have argued that to be implemented successfully, the doctrine of the essential Trinity needs further elaboration from contemporary theologians in terms of specific activities that qualify as loving, to be derived from analyses of the gospels along with the experiences of marginalized and oppressed people today. The doctrine of the essential Trinity, and especially its treatment of divine causality, also needs to be translated into contemporary liturgical settings so that non-oppressive trinitarian language and thought can be integrated into the fabric of Christian life. I have utilized the work of Rachel Adler to offer liturgical suggestions of this kind. A circumscribed form of apophaticism that insists on avoiding speculation about God *in se*, such as is being recovered, for example, in some feminist and queer theologies today, needs to be lifted up from the Christian tradition in order to successfully weave the doctrine of the essential Trinity into Christian thought. If these projects are undertaken, the doctrine of the essential Trinity could be a non-androcentric, non-hierarchical, life-focused understanding of the triune God that advances both Christian doctrine and social justice.

In Chapter 2, we surveyed the work of theologians like Rosemary Radford Ruether, Kelly Brown Douglas, Delores Williams, Jacqueline Grant, and Monica Coleman, who have challenged dominant forms of Christology and soteriology to emphasize the words and actions of Christ instead of his maleness, to focus on Christ's life rather than his constitutional makeup, and to avoid substitutionary theories of atonement that valorize suffering and uphold oppressed people's continued surrogacy roles. In conversation with Schüssler Fiorenza, I argued for a recognition that insofar as Jesus' life was a *kenosis* of patriarchy, his maleness has soteriological import because the eradication of patriarchy is sociohistorically salvific. We then saw how Schleiermacher presents a Christology that makes Christ's ministry central for salvation. In Schleiermacher's view, Christians are redeemed by being taken up into the strength of Christ's own ministerial vision and there becoming indwelt by God in and through Christ's Spirit. Not only, therefore, does Schleiermacher foreground the possibility for persons of many genders and sexualities to be united with the divine by embodying the Spirit of Christ. In line with the calls of A. Elaine Crawford and Karen Baker-Fletcher, Schleiermacher also critiques the Chalcedonian two-natures doctrine and constructs an alternative that highlights the life and work of Christ. Moreover, with Delores Williams and Traci West, Schleiermacher's thought gives substitutionary atonement no place but advances a creation-affirming soteriology that understands redemption as the completion of a process of human becoming. His soteriology also sets its discussion of sin in the context of original perfection, in alignment with Serene Jones's call for anticipatory optimism about sin that would enclose women and other oppressed persons in an envelope of God's grace before calling for repentance. Further, echoing Valerie Saiving Goldstein, Schleiermacher understands sin as varied in nature, which accommodates different modes of sin as they are expressed in differently gendered persons. With Emilie Townes, he treats sin in social and systemic ways rather than focusing on the individual. Schleiermacher's Christology and soteriology recognize the importance of the body and affect for the Christian religion and emphasize, with Grace Jantzen and Sallie McFague, natality and joy as distinctive markers of community with Christ. In these ways, Schleiermacher's theology is rich with potential for bolstering similarly constructed contemporary theologies. Nonetheless, I have also argued that Schleiermacher's soteriology needs revision where he relies on an afterlife to bring all into the Christian community. By holding Schleiermacher to his own understanding of the limits of theological knowledge and his own celebration of creaturely interdependence, his teleological view of salvation can coexist with a commitment to religious pluralism.

Chapter 3 detailed the prominent place joy occupies in Schleiermacher's ecclesiology and pneumatology. In conversation with Rachel Adler's work, I have shown how this can be used in constructive forms of theology operating in contemporary times of social injustice. Joy, which arises from a focus on love in the Christian church, is an underdeveloped ecclesial practice of resistance. Schleiermacher's *Christmas Eve Celebration* demonstrates this practice of love by celebrating embodiment, communal living, and gratefulness for creation and the divine arrangement of the world. While an initially unintuitive mode of social mobilization against injustice, the habits practiced during Christmas's natal celebrations might allow Christians to laugh in the face of injustice instead of seeking vengeance, isolation, or becoming apathetic. The chapter then built on Schleiermacher's communally focused theology to offer a queer community of Woman that might expand the ecclesial imaginary with particular injustices in mind. To frame this endeavor, I engaged the work of Talia Mae Bettcher, Anna Marie Jagose, Gerard Loughlin, E. Patrick Johnson, Philippa Bonwick, Elizabeth Johnson, and Eve Kosofsky. Lilith, Eve, Hagar, and Mary were then drawn together to create an organically constructed, diverse understanding of Woman that could playfully and powerfully transform the Christian ecclesial imagination to practical effect for religiously "other" women, Protestant white women, women of color, and Roman Catholic women both in developed and developing nations. I have drawn on the work of Raphael Patai, Judith Plaskow, Phyllis Trible, Delores

Williams, and Marcella Althaus-Reid to discuss these four figures together as a growing community. Rather than perpetuating kyriarchal notions, I have shown how this community of Woman can emphasize the diversity of women's lives and experiences, encourage solidarity with women, support women's efforts toward their own liberation from injustice, and empower Christian women to embrace their bodies, desires, and relationships as they are actually found in real women's lives. While this constructed community goes beyond Schleiermacher's thought, it draws on his organic understanding of humanity and his focus on Christian community to demonstrate one way to bring his theological impulses into conversation with contemporary theology. Christ lives on in the church, Schleiermacher writes, not by making everyone the same but by drawing together and celebrating the diversity of each of its members.

Finally, we have seen in Chapter 4 that Schleiermacher's theology offers a way to relate to both creation as a whole and to God through a recognition of creaturely interdependence and a grateful appreciation of all things' absolute dependence on the divine. Theologians like Wendy Farley and Kwok Pui-Lan have challenged the notion of divine sovereignty as infantilizing Christians and supporting oppressive forms of power. We entered the discussion by considering Absolute Causality and divine omnipotence within Schleiermacher's theology, noting how he upholds both the absolute dependence of all things upon God and also respects human self-initiated activity. His understanding of the God-world relation is noncompetitive, non-interventionist, and relational. In addition, he maintains the non-speculative view that divine causality is completely presented in the totality of finite existence. These features of his thought combine such that, in Schleiermacher's view, although God is not dependent on creation in any way, neither is God to be considered as "separate" from creation. For these reasons, even though he is working on a different metaphysical basis, his work is remarkably consonant with that of Catherine Keller and Ivone Gebara on the issue of the God-world relationship. Furthermore, we have seen that by forthrightly acknowledging that God is responsible for sin and evil as part of the process of creation-redemption, Schleiermacher's work aligns with Delores Williams's insight that God simply is not always and immediately a liberator. Here is no Pollyanna view of God as a protector who will take care of each of us as individuals if we only trust and obey. Instead, we find a stark recognition of the imperfection of humanity, which leads to sin and evil on a collective level and manifesting itself in systemic ways. Humanity depends on God, recognizing that all is not well and that God is responsible, as are we ourselves. And yet Schleiermacher's vision gives hope, rooted in the incarnation of Love and Wisdom, that structures Christians' view of the entire world: Love will continue to be embodied among us, and we can work in concert with divine activity to resist sin and abolish systems of oppression. In the second part of the chapter, I entered the discussion from another direction, by way of an analysis and critique of cruciform kenosis as an adequate prayer practice for feminists involved in ecumenical efforts. I first traced the conversation about kenotic submission begun by Sarah Coakley and continued with Daphne Hampson, Karen Baker-Fletcher, Aristotle Papanikolaou, Carolyn Chau, and Linn Marie Tonstad. I then drew Williams into the conversation again, arguing that with an analysis of Schleiermacher's sermon on the power of prayer, "incarnational submission" could be developed as a way of recognizing the importance of the notion of divine sovereignty within Christian theology and practice, without advancing the infantilization or imperialism that can result from affirming authoritarian forms of divine sovereignty.

We have seen that although Schleiermacher is not part of the traditions of feminism, womanism, postcolonialism, queer theology, ecotheology, ecumenical theology, and so on, about which he and other theologians of previous centuries could never have known or imagined, his theology dovetails with these approaches in significant ways that advance current conversations around the doctrine of the Trinity, Christ and redemption, church and Spirit, and the relation of God and creation. Schleiermacher thinks in novel ways about nearly all of the major doctrinal loci of the Christian faith. By drawing on Schleiermacher's insights—forthrightly chastened by contemporary corrections—we continue the work of dismantling and reconstructing dominant theologies. As theologians who work constructively know, this is a task of paramount importance if we want to live in a world that is not characterized by kyriarchy, with its racism, sexism, patriarchy, classism, colonialism, imperialism, heterosexism, transphobia, and other instances and systems of oppression. The theologies that are preached from the pulpit, embodied in Christian communities and their leaders, displayed in stained glass windows and paintings, and otherwise expressed have supported these systems of oppression for millennia. It is our responsibility to dismantle and reconstruct them in ways that support social justice instead.

BIBLIOGRAPHY

Adler, Rachel. *Engendering Judaism: An Inclusive Theology and Ethics*. Boston, MA: Beacon Press, 1998.
Ahmed, Sara. *The Promise of Happiness*. Durham, NC: Duke University Press, 2010.
Ahmed, Sara. *Queer Phenomenology: Orientations, Objects, Others*. Durham, NC: Duke University Press, 2006.
Ain't I a Womanist Too? Third Wave Womanist Religious Thought. Edited by Monica A. Coleman. Minneapolis, MN: Fortress, 2013.
Althaus-Reid, Marcella. *Indecent Theology: Theological Perversions in Sex, Gender and Politics*. London: Routledge, 2000.
Anselm of Canterbury. "Monologion." In *Anselm of Canterbury: The Major Works*. Edited by Brian Davies and G. R. Evans. New York: Oxford University Press, 1998, pp. 5–81.
Armour, Ellen T. *Deconstruction, Feminist Theology, and the Problem of Difference: Subverting the Race/Gender Divide*. Chicago, IL: University of Chicago Press, 1999.
A Theology for Ecological Living: Schleiermacher and Sustainability. Edited by Shelli M. Poe. Louisville, KY: Westminster John Knox, 2018.
Aune, Kristin. "Marriage in a British Evangelical Congregation: Practicing Postfeminist Partnership?" *Sociological Review* 54/4 (2006): 638–57.
Avishai, Orit, Lynne Gerber, and Jennifer Randles. "The Feminist Ethnographer's Dilemma: Reconciling Progressive Research Agendas with Fieldwork Realities." *Journal of Contemporary Ethnography* 42 (August 2013): 394–426.
Awake to the Moment: An Introduction to Theology. Edited by Laurel C. Schneider and Stephen G. Ray, Jr. Louisville, KY: Westminster John Knox, 2016.
Baker-Fletcher, Karen. *Dancing with God: The Trinity from a Womanist Perspective*. St. Louis, MO: Chalice, 2006.
Baker-Fletcher, Karen, and Garth Kasimu Baker-Fletcher. *My Sister, My Brother: Womanist and Xodus God Talk*. Eugene, OR: Wipf & Stock, 2002; previously published by Orbis, 1997.
Bammert, Gaye M. "Narrating the Church: Protestant Women Pastors Challenge Nostalgic Desire." *Journal of Feminist Studies in Religion* 26/2 (2010): 153–74.
Barth, Karl. *The Theology of Schleiermacher: Lectures at Göttingen, Winter Semester of 1923–24*. Grand Rapids, MI: Eerdmans, 1982.
Bartkowski, John. *Remaking the Godly Marriage: Gender Negotiation in Evangelical Families*. New Brunswick, NJ: Rutgers University Press, 2001.
Bediako, Kwame. *Christianity in Africa: The Renewal of a Non-Western Religion*. Maryknoll, NY: Orbis, 1995.
Bediako, Kwame. *Jesus in Africa: The Christian Gospel in African History and Experience*. Selangor, Malaysia: Editions Clé and Regnum Africa, 2000.
Berlant, Lauren. *The Female Complaint: The Unfinished Business of Sentimentality in American Culture*. Durham, NC: Duke University Press, 2008.
Berry, Wendell. "Faustian Economics." *Harper's Magazine* (May 2008): 35–42.

Bettcher, Talia Mae. "Trans Women and the Meaning of 'Woman.'" In *The Philosophy of Sex: Contemporary Readings*, 6th ed. Edited by Nicholas Power, Raja Halwani, and Alan Soble. New York: Rowman & Littlefield, 2013, pp. 233–50.

Blackwell, Albert L. "Schleiermacher's Sermon at Nathanael's Grave." *Journal of Religion* 57/1 (January 1977): 64–75.

Bonwick, Philippa. "It Is Cool to Be Queer, but ..." *Brother Sister* (December 3, 1993): 10.

Brandt, James. "Schleiermacher on Church and Christian Ethics." In *Schleiermacher and Sustainability: A Theology for Sustainable Living*. Columbia Series in Reformed Theology. Edited by Shelli M. Poe. Louisville, KY: Westminster John Knox, 2018, pp. 7–27.

Brock, Rita N. "Communities of the Cross: Christa and the Communal Nature of Redemption." *Feminist Theology* 14/1 (2015): 109–25.

Brock, Rita N. "The Feminist Redemption of Christ." In *Christian Feminism: Visions of a New Humanity*. Edited by Judith Weidman. New York: Harper and Row, 1984, pp. 55–74.

Bruland, Esther Byle. "Evangelical and Feminist Ethics: Complex Solidarities." *Journal of Religious Ethics* 17/2 (September 1989): 139–60.

Butler, Judith. *Antigone's Claim: Kinship between Life and Death*. New York: Columbia University Press, 2000.

Butler, Judith. *Undoing Gender*. London: Routledge, 2004.

Butler, Octavia E. *Kindred*. Boston, MA: Beacon, 1979.

Calvin, John. *Institutes of the Christian Religion*. Edited by John T. McNeill. Translated by Ford Lewis Battles. Philadelphia, PA: Westminster, 1960.

Chau, Carolyn A. "'What Could Possibly Be Given?': Towards an Exploration of Kenosis as Forgiveness—Continuing the Conversation between Coakley, Hampson, and Papanikolaou." *Modern Theology* 28/1 (January 2012): 1–24.

Chong, Kelly H. "Coping with Conflict, Confronting Resistance: Fieldwork Emotions and Identity Management in a South Korean Evangelical Community." *Qualitative Sociology* 31/4 (December 2008): 369–90.

Chong, Kelly H. "Negotiating Patriarchy: South Korean Evangelical Women and the Politics of Gender." *Gender & Society* 20/6 (December 2006): 697–724.

Clark, Adam. "Hagar the Egyptian: A Womanist Dialogue." *Western Journal of Black Studies* 36/1 (2012): 48–56.

Coakley, Sarah. *God, Sexuality, and the Self*. New York: Cambridge University Press, 2014.

Coakley, Sarah. "*Kenosis* and Subversion: On the Repression of 'Vulnerability' in Christian Feminist Writing." In *Swallowing a Fishbone? Feminist Theologians Debate Christianity*. Edited by Daphne Hampson. London: SPCK, 1996, pp. 82–111.

Coakley, Sarah. *Powers and Submissions: Spirituality, Philosophy and Gender*. Malden, MA: Blackwell, 2002.

Cochran, Pamela. *Evangelical Feminism: A History*. New York: New York University Press, 2005.

Cohen, Cathy. "Punks, Bulldaggers, and Welfare Queens." *GLQ* 3 (1997): 437–65.

Coleman, Monica A. *Making a Way Out of No Way: A Womanist Theology*. Minneapolis, MN: Fortress, 2008.

Coleman, Monica A. "Sacrifice, Surrogacy, and Salvation." *Black Theology: An International Journal* 12/3 (2014): 200–14.

Collins, Paul M. *The Trinity: A Guide for the Perplexed*. London: T&T Clark, 2008.

Cone, James. *The Cross and the Lynching Tree*. Maryknoll, NY: Orbis, 2011.

Cone, James. *God of the Oppressed*. New York: Seabury Press, 1975.
Cone, James. *God of the Oppressed*, rev. ed. Maryknoll, NY: Orbis, 1997.
Constructive Theology: A Contemporary Approach to Classic Themes. Edited by Paul Lakeland and Serene Jones. Minneapolis, MN: Fortress, 2005.
Cooper, Brittney. "How Sarah Got Her Groove Back, or Notes Toward a Black Feminist Theology of Pleasure." *Black Theology* 16/3 (2018): 195–206.
Copeland, M. Shawn. *Enfleshing Freedom: Body, Race, and Being*. Minneapolis, MN: Fortress, 2010.
Copeland, M. Shawn. "Wading through Many Sorrows." In *Womanist Theological Ethics: A Reader*. Edited by Katie Geneva Cannon, Emilie M. Townes, and Angela D. Sims. Louisville, KY: Westminster John Knox, 2011, pp. 135–54.
Cornwall, Susannah. *Controversies in Queer Theology*. London: SCM, 2011.
Crawford, A. Elaine. "Womanist Christology: Where Have We Come from and Where Are We Going?" *Review and Expositor* 95 (1998): 367–82.
Crawford, A. Elaine. "Womanist Christology and the Wesleyan Tradition." *Black Theology: An International Journal* 2/2 (July 2004): 213–20.
The Creeds of Christendom: With a History and Critical Notes. Vol. III: The Greek and Latin Creeds with Translations. Edited by Philip Schaff. Revised by David S. Schaff. Grand Rapids, MI: Baker, 2007.
Cross, Richard. "Medieval Trinitarianism and Modern Theology." In *Rethinking Trinitarian Theology: Disputed Questions and Contemporary Issues in Trinitarian Theology*. Edited by Robert J. Wozniak and Giulio Maspero. New York: T&T Clark, 2012, pp. 26–43.
Crouter, Richard. "Introduction." In *A Debate on Jewish Emancipation and Christian Theology in Old Berlin*. Edited and translated by Richard Crouter and Julie Klassen. Indianapolis, IN: Hackett, 2004, pp. 1–29.
Crouter, Richard. Introduction to *On Religion: Speeches to Its Cultured Despisers*. Cambridge Texts in the History of Philosophy. Edited by Richard Crouter. Cambridge: Cambridge University Press, 1996, pp. xi–xxxix.
Crowther, Kathleen M. *Adam and Eve in the Protestant Reformation*. New York: Cambridge University Press, 2010.
Daly, Mary. *Beyond God the Father: Toward a Philosophy of Women's Liberation*. Boston, MA: Beacon, 1973.
Dawson, Jerry. *Schleiermacher; The Evolution of a Nationalist*. Austin: University of Texas, 1966.
Day, Keri. "Doctrine of God in African American Theology." In *The Oxford Handbook of African American Theology*. Edited by Anthony B. Pinn and Katie G. Cannon. Oxford: Oxford University Press, 2014, pp. 139–52.
DeHart, Paul. "Ter mundus accipit infinitum: The Dogmatic Coordinates of Schleiermacher's Trinitarian Treatise." *Neue Zeitschrift für Systematische Theologie und Religionsphilosophie* 52 (2010): 17–39.
DeVries, Dawn. *Jesus Christ in the Preaching of Calvin and Schleiermacher*. Louisville, KY: Westminster John Knox, 1996.
DeVries, Dawn. "Schleiermacher's Christmas Eve Dialogue: Bourgeois Ideology or Feminist Theology?" *Journal of Religion* 69/2 (April 1989): 169–83.
Dole, Andrew. *Schleiermacher on Religion and the Natural Order*. Oxford: Oxford University Press, 2010.
Douglas, Kelly Brown. *The Black Christ*. Maryknoll, NY: Orbis, 1994.

Douglas, Kelly Brown. "Introduction to 'A Womanist Looks at the Future.'" *Anglican Theological Review* 100/3 (2018): 581–2.
Douglas, Kelly Brown. *Sexuality and the Black Church*. Maryknoll, NY: Orbis, 1999.
Duck, Ruth C. *Flames of the Spirit: Resources for Worship*. New York: Pilgrim, 1985.
Duck, Ruth C., and Patricia Wilson-Kastner. *Praising God: The Trinity in Christian Worship*. Louisville, KY: Westminster John Knox, 1999.
Edelman, Lee. *No Future: Queer Theory and the Death Drive*. Durham, NC: Duke University Press, 2004.
Farley, Wendy. *Gathering Those Driven Away*. Louisville, KY: Westminster John Knox, 2011.
Fiorenza, Elisabeth Schüssler. *In Memory of Her: A Feminist Theological Reconstruction of Christian Origins*. New York: Crossroad, 1983.
Fiorenza, Francis Schüssler. "Understanding God as Triune." In *The Cambridge Companion to Friedrich Schleiermacher*. Edited by Jacqueline Mariña. Cambridge: Cambridge University Press, 2005, pp. 171–88.
Frye, Marilyn. "The Necessity of Differences: Constructing a Positive Category of Women." *Signs* 21/4 (Summer 1996): 991–1010.
Frye, Marilyn. "Sisterhood Is Powerless." *The Women's Review of Books* 19/8 (May 2002): 6–7.
Fulkerson, Mary McClintock. *Changing the Subject: Women's Discourses and Feminist Theology*. Minneapolis, MN: Fortress, 1994.
Fulkerson, Mary McClintock. *Places of Redemption: Theology for a Worldly Church*. New York: Oxford University Press, 2007.
Gallagher, Sally K. "The Marginalization of Evangelical Feminism." *Sociology of Religion* 65/3 (2004): 215–37.
Gallagher, Sally K. "Where Are the Antifeminist Evangelicals? Evangelical Identity, Subcultural Location, and Attitudes toward Feminism." *Gender & Society* 18/4 (August 2004): 451–72.
Gebara, Ivone. *Longing for Running Water: Ecofeminism and Liberation*. Translated by David Molineaux. Minneapolis, MN: Fortress, 1999.
Gebara, Ivone, and Maria Clara Bingemer. *Mary: Mother of God, Mother of the Poor*. Maryknoll, NY: Orbis, 1989.
Gerrish, Brian A. *A Prince of the Church: Schleiermacher and the Beginnings of Modern Theology*. Eugene, OR: Wipf & Stock, 2001; previously published by Augsburg Fortress, 1984.
Gockel, Matthias. *Barth and Schleiermacher on the Doctrine of Election: A Systematic-Theological Comparison*. Oxford: Oxford University Press, 2006.
Godfrey, Elaine. "Roy Moore's Many Defenders." *The Atlantic* (November 10, 2017): http://www.theatlantic.com/politics/archive/2017/11/roy-moores-many-defenders/545609/?utm_source=eb.
Gonzalez, Michelle A. "Hans Urs von Balthasar and Contemporary Feminist Theology." *Theological Studies* 65 (2004): 566–95.
Goss, Robert E. *Queering Christ: Beyond Jesus Acted Up*. Eugene, OR: Wipf & Stock, 2006; originally published by Pilgrim Press, 2002.
Grant, Jacquelyn. *White Women's Christ and Black Women's Jesus: Feminist Christology and Womanist Response*. American Academy of Religion Series No. 64. Atlanta, GA: Scholars Press, 1989.

Gregory of Nyssa. "Concerning We Should Think of Saying That There Are Not Three Gods, to Ablabius." In *The Trinitarian Controversy*. Edited and translated by William G. Rusch. Philadelphia, PA: Fortress, 1980, 149–61.

Griffiths, R. Marie. *God's Daughters: Evangelical Women and the Power of Submission*. Berkeley: University of California, 1997.

Guenther-Gleason, Patricia E. *On Schleiermacher and Gender Politics*. Harvard Theological Studies. Harrisburg, PA: Trinity Press International, 1997.

Guth, Karen V. "Doing Justice to the Complex Legacy of John Howard Yoder: Restorative Justice Resources in Witness and Feminist Ethics." *Journal of the Society of Christian Ethics* 35/2 (2015): 119–39.

Guth, Karen V. "Moral Injury, Feminist and Womanist Ethics, and Tainted Legacies." *Journal of the Society of Christian Ethics* 38/1 (2018): 167–86.

Gutierrez, Gustavo. *A Theology of Liberation: History, Politics, and Salvation*. Translated and edited by Sister Caridad Inda and John Eagleson. Maryknoll, NY: Orbis, [1971] 1988.

Hagan, Anette I. *Eternal Blessedness for All? A Historical-Systematic Examination of Friedrich Schleiermacher's Reinterpretation of Predestination*. Cambridge: James Clarke, 2014.

Halberstam, Jack. *The Queer Art of Failure*. Durham, NC: Duke University Press, 2011.

Hampson, Daphne. "On Power and Gender." *Modern Theology* 4/3 (April 1988): 234–50.

Hampson, Daphne. *Theology and Feminism*. Oxford: Basil Blackwell, 1990.

Harvey, Van A. "A Word in Defense of Schleiermacher's Theological Method." *Journal of Religion* 42/3 (1962): 151–70.

Hayes, Diana L. *Standing in the Shoes My Mother Made: A Womanist Theology*. Minneapolis, MN: Fortress, 2011.

Hayes, Diana L. *Were You There? Stations of the Cross*. Art by Charles S. Ndege. Maryknoll, NY: Orbis, 2000.

Hector, Kevin W. "Actualism and Incarnation: The High Christology of Friedrich Schleiermacher." *International Journal of Systematic Theology* 8/3 (July 2006): 307–22.

Hector, Kevin W. *Theology without Metaphysics: God, Language, and the Spirit of Recognition*. Cambridge: Cambridge University Press, 2011.

Helmer, Christine. *Theology and the End of Doctrine*. Louisville, KY: Westminster John Knox, 2014.

Heschel, Susannah. "Jesus as Theological Transvestite." In *Judaism since Gender*. Edited by Miriam Peskowitz and Laura Levitt. New York: Routledge, 1997, pp. 188–99.

Heschel, Susannah. "The Image of Judaism in 19th Century Christian New Testament Scholarship in Germany." In *Jewish-Christian Encounter over the Centuries: Symbiosis, Prejudice, Holocaust, Dialogue*. Edited by Marvin Perry and Frederick M. Schweitzer. New York: Peter Lang, 1994, pp. 215–40.

Heyward, Carter. *The Redemption of God: A Theology of Mutual Relation*. Eugene, OR: Wipf and Stock, 2010, previously published by University Press of America, 1982.

Hickman, Hoyt L. *Holy Communion: A Service Book for Use by the Minister*. Nashville, TN: Abingdon, 1987.

Isherwood, Lisa, and Marcella Althaus-Reid. "Queering Theology." In *The Sexual Theologian: Essays on Sex, God, and Politics*. Edited by Marcella Althaus-Reid and Lisa Isherwood. New York: T&T Clark, 2004, pp. 1–15.

Jagose, Annamarie. *Queer Theory: An Introduction*. Washington Square: New York University Press, 1996.

Janzten, Grace M. *Becoming Divine: Towards a Feminist Philosophy of Religion*. Bloomington: Indiana University Press, 1999.

Johnson, Elizabeth. "The Living God in Women's Voices." *Sewannee Theological Review* 48/3 (2005): 287–300.

Johnson, Elizabeth. *She Who Is: The Mystery of God in Feminist Theological Discourse*, 10th anniversary ed. New York: Crossroad, 2002.

Johnson, Elizabeth. *Friends of God and Prophets: A Feminist Theological Reading of the Communion of Saints*. New York: Continuum, 1998.

Jones, Serene. *Feminist Theory and Christian Theology: Cartographies of Grace*. Guides to Theological Inquiry. Minneapolis, MN: Fortress, 2000.

Julian of Norwich, *Revelations of Divine Love*. Translated by Elizabeth Spearing. London: Penguin, 1998.

Julian of Norwich. *Showings*. Translated by Edmund Colledge, OSA, and James Walsh, SJ. Classics of Western Spirituality. New York: Paulist Press, 1978.

Jungkeit, Steven R. *Spaces of Modern Theology: Geography and Power in Schleiermacher's World*. New Approaches to Religion and Power. New York: Palgrave Macmillan, 2012.

Keller, Catherine. *Face of the Deep: A Theology of Becoming*. London: Routledge, 2003.

Kim, Sung-Sup. *Deus Providebit: Calvin, Schleiermacher, and Barth on the Providence of God*. Minneapolis, MN: Fortress, 2014.

Kittay, Eva Feder. *Love's Labor: Essays on Women, Equality, and Dependency*. New York: Routledge, 1999.

Kornblatt, Judith Deutsch. *Divine Sophia: The Wisdom Writings of Vladimir Solovyov*. Ithaca, NY: Cornell University Press, 2009.

Kwok, Pui-Lan. "Ecology and Christology." *Feminist Theology* 15 (1997): 113–25.

Kwok, Pui-Lan. *Postcolonial Imagination and Feminist Theology*. Louisville, KY: Westminster John Knox, 2005.

Kyung, Chung Hyun. *Struggle to Be the Sun Again: Introducing Asian Women's Theology*. Maryknoll, NY: Orbis, 1990.

LaCugna, Catherine Mowry. *God for Us: The Trinity and Christian Life*. New York: HarperOne, 1991.

Lamm, Julia A. *The Living God: Schleiermacher's Theological Appropriation of Spinoza*. University Park, PA: Pennsylvania State University Press, 1996.

Lamm, Julia A. *Schleiermacher: Christmas Dialogue, The Second Speech, and Other Selections*. Edited, translated, and with an introduction by Julia Lamm. Mahwah, NJ: Paulist Press, 2014.

Lightsey, Pamela R. *Our Lives Matter: A Womanist Queer Theology*. Eugene, OR: Wipf and Stock, 2015.

Lippett, John. "Humor and Religion: Humor, Irony, and the Comic." In *Encyclopedia of Religion*, vol. 6, 2nd ed. Edited by Lindsay Jones. Farmington Hills: Thomson Gale, 2005, 4218–23.

Loughlin, Gerard. "Introduction: The End of Sex." In *Queer Theory: Rethinking the Western Body*. Edited by Gerard Loughlin. Malden, MA: Blackwell, 2007, 1–34.

Madden, Pete. "Jeff Sessions Consulted Christian Right Legal Group on religious Freedom Memo." *ABC News*. October 6, 2017. http://abcnews.go.com/Politics/jeff-sessions-consulted-christian-legal-group-religious-freedom/story?id=50336322.

Marmion, Declan, and Rik Van Nieuwenhove. *An Introduction to the Trinity*. Cambridge: Cambridge University Press, 2011.

Martin, Biddy. "Extraordinary Homsexuals and the Fear of Being Ordinary," *differences: A Journal of Feminist Cultural Studies* 6/2–3 (1994): 100–25.

Martin, Jennifer Newsome. "The 'Whence' and the 'Whither' of Balthasar's Gendered Theology: Rehabilitating Kenosis for Feminist Theology." *Modern Theology* 13/2 (April 2015): 211–34.

McCale, Calli. "A Schleiermacherian Solution: Eschatological Continuity, Disability, and Communication." Unpublished Presentation offered at a session of the Schleiermacher Unit at the American Academy of Religion National Annual Meeting. Boston, MA, 2017.

McCann, Hannah. "Epistemology of the Subject: Queer Theory's Challenge to Feminist Sociology." *WSQ: Women's Studies Quarterly* 44/3&4 (Fall/Winter 2016): 224–43.

McCann, Hannah, and Whitney Monaghan. *Queer Theory Now: From Foundations to Futures*. London: Macmillan International and Red Globe Press, 2020.

McFague, Sallie. *The Body of God: An Ecological Theology*. Minneapolis, MN: Fortress, 1993.

McFague, Sallie. *Metaphorical Theology*. Philadelphia, PA: Fortress, 1982.

McFague, Sallie. *Models of God: Theology for an Ecological, Nuclear Age*. Philadelphia, PA: Fortress, 1987.

Meehan, "Brenda. Wisdom/Sophia, Russian Identity, and Western Feminist Theology." *CrossCurrents* 46/2 (1996): 149–68.

Mercedes, Anna. *Power For: Feminism and Christ's Self-Giving*. New York: T&T Clark, 2011.

Mohanty, Chandra Talpade. *Feminism without Borders: Decolonizing Theory, Practicing Solidarity*. Durham, NC: Duke University, 2003.

Murphy, Rosalyn. "Sista-hoods: Revealing the Meaning in Hagar's Narrative." *Black Theology* 10/1 (2012): 77–92.

Myerhoff, Barbara G. "Sanctifying Women's Lives Through Ritual." Tape of workshop.

Niebuhr, H. Richard. *Radical Monotheism and Western Culture*. Louisville, KY: Westminster John Knox, 1960.

Nowack, Kurt. *Schleiermacher: Leben, Werk, und Wirkung*. Göttingen: Vandenhoeck & Ruprecht, 2002.

Pan, Yi-Jung. "Chinese Women's Spiritual Formation in Evangelical Churches: A Reflection." *Asia Journal of Theology* 27/2 (October 2013): 226–42.

Papanikolaou, Aristotle. "Person, Kenosis and Abuse: Hans Urs von Balthasar and Feminist Theologies in Conversation." *Modern Theology* 19/1 (January 2003): 41–65.

Patai, Raphael. *The Hebrew Goddess*. Detroit, MI: Wayne State University Press, 1990.

Pearson, Lori. "Schleiermacher and the Christologies behind Chalcedon." *Harvard Theological Review* 96/3 (July 2003): 349–67.

Pedersen, Daniel. *The Eternal Covenant: Schleiermacher on God and Natural Science*. Berlin: Walter de Gruyter, 2017.

Phan, Peter C. *Christianity with an Asian Face: Asian American Theology in the Making*. Maryknoll, NY: Orbis, 2003.

Pickle, Joseph W. "Schleiermacher on Judaism." *Journal of Religion* 60/2 (April 1980): 115–37.

Plaskow, Judith. "The Coming of Lilith: Toward a Feminist Theology." In *Eve and Adam: Jewish, Christian, and Muslim Readings on Genesis and Gender*. Edited by Kristen E. Kvam, Linda S. Schearing, and Valarie H. Ziegler. Bloomington, IN: Indiana University, 1999, 422–5.

Plaskow, Judith. "Epilogue: The Coming of Lilith." In *Religion and Sexism*. Edited by R. Radford Ruether. New York: Simon and Schuster, 1974, pp. 341–3 (republished by Wipf and Stock, Eugene, OR in 1998).

Plaskow, Judith. "Lilith Revisited." In *Eve and Adam: Jewish, Christian, and Muslim Readings on Genesis and Gender*. Edited by Kristen E. Kvam, Linda S. Schearing, and Valarie H. Ziegler. Bloomington, IN: Indiana University, 1999, pp. 425–30.

Poe, Shelli M. *Essential Trinitarianism: Schleiermacher as Essential Trinitarianism*. T&T Clark Explorations in Reformed Theology. London: Bloomsbury, 2017.

Poe, Shelli M. "Friedrich Schleiermacher's Theology as a Resource for Ecological Economics." *Theology Today* 73/1 (2016): 9–23.

Poe, Shelli M. "Lilith, Christianity." In *Encyclopedia of Bible and its Reception*, vol. 16. Edited by Christine Helmer. Berlin: De Gruyter, 2018, pp. 665–6.

Poe, Shelli M. "Locating Prayerful Submission for Feminist Ecumenism: Holy Saturday or Incarnate Life?" *Feminist Theology* 26/2 (2018): 171–84.

Poe, Shelli M. "Friedrich Schleiermacher's Christian Faith." In *Oxford Handbook of Reformed Theology*. Edited by Michael Allen and Scott Swain. Oxford: Oxford University Press, 2020, pp. 312–27.

Pohli, Carol Virginia. "Church Closets and Back Doors: A Feminist View of Moral Majority Women." *Feminist Studies* 9/3 (Autumn 1983): 529–58.

Povinelli, Elizabeth A. "Geontologies of the Otherwise." Theorizing the Contemporary, *Cultural Anthropology* website, January 13, 2014. https://culanth.org/fieldsights/465-geontologies-of-the-otherwise.

Powell, Samuel M. *The Trinity in German Thought*. Cambridge: Cambridge University Press, 2001.

Purvis, Zachary. *Theology and the University in Nineteenth-Century Germany*. Oxford: Oxford University Press, 2016.

Rahner, Karl. *The Trinity*. Translated by Catherine Mowry LaCugna. New York: Crossroad, 2005.

Ravenscroft, Ruth Jackson. *The Veiled God: Friedrich Schleiermacher's Theology of Finitude*. Leiden: Brill, 2019.

Recovering Biblical Manhood & Womanhood: A Response to Evangelical Feminism. Edited by John Piper and Wayne Grudem. Wheaton, IL: Crossway, 2006.

Religion and Sexism: Images of Woman in the Jewish and Christian Traditions. Edited by Rosemary Radford Ruether. New York: Simon and Schuster, 1974.

Resnick, Irvin. *Marks of Distinction: Christian Perceptions of Jews in the High Middle Ages*. Washington, DC: Catholic University of America Press, 2012.

Rethinking Trinitarian Theology: Disputed Questions and Contemporary Issues in Trinitarian Theology. Edited by Robert J. Wozniak and Giulio Maspero. New York: T&T Clark, 2012.

Reynolds, Thomas. "Reconsidering Schleiermacher and the Problem of Religious Diversity: Toward a Dialectical Pluralism." *Journal of the American Academy of Religion* 73/1 (March 2005): 151–81.

Reynolds, Thomas. "Schleiermacher and the Problem of Religious Diversity." *Journal of the American Academy of Religion* 73/1 (March 2005): 151–81.

Rieger, Joerg. "Friedrich Schleiermacher." In *Empire and the Christian Tradition: New Readings of Classical Theologians*. Edited by Kwok Pui-lan, Don H. Compier, and Joerg Rieger. Minneapolis, MN: Fortress, 2007, pp. 271–82.

Rubin, Jennifer. "Why Trump Had to Be Badgered to Condemn Neo-Nazis." *Washington Post*. August 14, 2017. http://wapo.st/2w3vJZH?tid=ss_mail&utm_term=.c7ae566abc25.

Ruether, Rosemary Radford. "Feminist Theology in the Academy." *Christianity and Crisis* 45/3 (March 4, 1985): 57–62.

Ruether, Rosemary Radford. *Sexism and God-Talk: Toward a Feminist Theology*. Boston, MA: Beacon, 1983.

Ruether, Rosemary Radford. "Sexism and Misogyny in the Christian Tradition: Liberating Alternatives." *Buddhist-Christian Studies* 34 (2014): 83–94.

Said, Edward. *Orientalism*. New York: Vintage Books, 1979.

Sawyer, John F. A. *The Fifth Gospel: Isaiah in the History of Christianity*. New York: Cambridge University Press, 1996.

Schippert, Claudia. "Too Much Trouble? Negotiating Feminist and Queer Approaches in Religion." *Theology and Sexuality* 11 (1999): 44–63.

Schleiermacher and Feminism: Sources, Evaluations, and Responses. Schleiermacher: Studies and Translations, vol. 12. Edited by Iain Nicol. Lewiston, NY: Edwin Mellen, 1992.

Schleiermacher and Sustainability: A Theology for Ecological Living. Edited by Shelli M. Poe. Louisville, KY: Westminster John Knox, 2018.

Schleiermacher, Friedrich. *Brief Outline of the Study of Theology*. Translated by William Farrer. Eugene, OR: Wipf & Stock, 2007.

Schleiermacher, Friedrich. *Christian Faith: A New Translation and Critical Edition*, 2 Vols. Translated by Terrence Tice, Catherine Kelsey, and Edwina Lawyer. Edited by Catherine Kelsey and Terrence Tice. Louisville, KY: Westminster John Knox, 2016.

Schleiermacher, Friedrich. *The Christian Faith*. Edited by H. R. Mackintosh and J. S. Stewart. Edinburgh: T&T Clark, 1986.

Schleiermacher, Friedrich. *The Christian Household: A Sermonic Treatise*. Translated by Dietrich Seidel and Terrence N. Tice. Lewiston, NY: Mellen, 1991.

Schleiermacher, Friedrich. *Christmas Eve Celebration: A Dialogue*, rev. ed. Edited and translated by Terrence N. Tice. Eugene, OR: Cascade Books, 2010.

Schleiermacher, Friedrich. *Die Christliche Sitte nach den Grundsätzen der evangelischen Kirche im Zusammenhang dargestellt*. Waltrop: Spenner, 1999.

Schleiermacher, Friedrich. *On Freedom*. Translated with an introduction by Albert L. Blackwell. Lewiston, NY: Mellen, 1992.

Schleiermacher, Friedrich. *Friedrich Schleiermacher und die Trinitätslehre*. Edited by Martin Tezt, Texte zur Kirchen- und Theologiegeschichte, vol. XI. Gütersloh: Gütersloher Verlagshaus Gerd Mohn, 1969.

Schleiermacher, Friedrich. "Gelegentliche Gedanken über Universitäten in deutschem Sinn, nebst einem Anhang über eine neu zu errichtende." *Kritische Gesamtausgabe*. Edited by Dirk Schmidt and Hermann Fischer, i/6, pp. 15–100.

Schleiermacher, Friedrich. *Kritische Gesamtausgabe*, vol. 1.1, *Jugendschriften 1787-96*. Edited by Günter Meckenstock. Berlin: De Gruyter, 1983.

Schleiermacher, Friedrich. "Letter to Georg Reimer (30 April 1802)." In *Aus Schleiermacher's Leben. In Briefen. I-IV*. Edited by Ludwig Jonas and Wilhelm Dilthey. Berlin: Georg Reimer, 1860-3. pp. 294–5 (subsequently published by De Gruyter in Berlin in 1974).

Schleiermacher, Friedrich. "Letters on the Occasion of the Political-Theological Task and the Open Letter of Jewish Householders." In *A Debate on Jewish Emancipation and Christian Theology in Old Berlin*. Edited and translated by Richard Crouter and Julie Klassen. Indianapolis, IN: Hackett, 2004.

Schleiermacher, Friedrich. "On the Discrepancy between the Sabellian and Athanasian Method of Representing the Doctrine of a Trinity in the Godhead (Part One)." Translated by Moses Stuart. *Biblical Repository and Quarterly Observer* 5/18 (April 1835): 265–353.

Schleiermacher, Friedrich. "On the Discrepancy between the Sabellian and Athanasian Method of Representing the Doctrine of a Trinity in the Godhead (Part Two)." Translated by Moses Stuart. *Biblical Repository and Quarterly Observer* 6/19 (July 1835): 1–116.

Schleiermacher, Friedrich. *On Religion: Speeches to Its Cultured Despisers*. Cambridge Texts in the History of Philosophy. Edited by Richard Crouter. Cambridge: Cambridge University Press, 1996.

Schleiermacher, Friedrich. *Schleiermacher: Christmas Dialogue, the Second Speech, and Other Selections*. Edited and translated with an introduction by Julia A. Lamm. Mahwah, NJ: Paulist Press, 2014.

Schleiermacher, Friedrich. "To Jacobi. Berlin, March 30, 1818." In *Schleiermacher: Christmas Dialogue, the Second Speech, and Other Selections*. The Classics of Western Spirituality. Edited, translated, and with an introduction by Julia Lamm. Mahwah, NJ: Paulist Press, 2014, pp. 260–6.

Schleiermacher, Friedrich. "The Power of Prayer in Relation to Outward Circumstances." In *Selected Sermons of Schleiermacher*. Translated by Mary F. Wilson. Edited by W. Robertson Nicoll. Eugene, OR: Wipf & Stock, 2004, pp. 38–51.

Schwartz, Howard. *Lilith's Cave: Jewish Tales of the Supernatural*. New York: Oxford University Press, 1988.

Schwöbel, Christoph. "Radical Monotheism and the Trinity." *Neue Zeitschrift für systematische Theologie und Religionsphilosophie* 43/1 (2001): 54–74.

Sedgwick, Eve Kosofsky. *Tendencies*. Durham, NC: Duke University Press, 1993.

Sheppard, Phillis Isabelle. *Self, Culture, and Other in Womanist Practical Theology*. New York: Palgrave Macmillan, 2011.

Sonderegger, Katherine. "On the Holy Name of God." *Theology Today* 58/3 (October 2001): 384–98.

Soskice, Janet Martin. "Being and Love: Schleiermacher, Aquinas and Augustine." *Modern Theology* 34/3 (2018): 481–91.

Soskice, Janet Martin. *The Kindness of God: Metaphor, Gender, and Religious Language*. Oxford: Oxford University Press, 2007.

Soskice, Janet Martin. *Metaphor and Religious Language*. New York: Oxford University Press, 1985.

Spillers, Hortense. "Mama's Baby, Papa's Maybe: An American Grammar Book." *Diacritics* 17/2. Culture and Countermemory: The "American" Connection (Summer 1987): 64–81.

Streufert, Mary J. "Reclaiming Schleiermacher for Twenty-first Century Atonement Theory: The Human and the Divine in Feminist Christology." *Feminist Theology* 15/1 (2006): 98–120.

Styler, Rebecca. "A Scripture of Their Own: Nineteenth-Century Bible Biography and Feminist Bible Criticism." *Christianity and Literature* 57/1 (2007): 65–85.

Tamar's Tears: Evangelical Engagements with Feminist Old Testament Hermeneutics. Edited by Andrew Sloane. Eugene, OR: Pickwick, 2012.

Tamez, Elsa. "The Woman Who Complicated the History of Salvation." In *New Eyes for Reading: Biblical and Theological Reflections by Women in the Third World*. Edited by John S. Pobee and Bärbel von Wartenberg-Potter. Bloomington, IN: Meyer Stone Books, 1986, pp. 5–17.

Tanja, Johanna M., and Eveline van Staalduine-Sulman. "A Jewish Targum in a Remarkable Paratext." In *A Jewish Targum in a Christian World*. Edited by Alberdina

Houtman, E. van Staalduine-Sulman, and Hans-Martin Kim. Boston, MA: Brill, 2014, 179–82.
Tanner, Kathryn. *Christ the Key*. Cambridge: Cambridge University Press, 2010.
Tanner, Kathryn. *Jesus, Humanity, and the Trinity: A Brief Systematic Theology*. Minneapolis, MN: Fortress, 2001.
Tanner, Kathryn. "Social Theory Concerning the 'New Social Movements' and the Practice of Feminist Theology." In *Horizons in Feminist Theology: Identity, Tradition, and Norms*. Edited by Rebecca S. Chopp and Sheila Greeve Davaney. Minneapolis, MN: Fortress, 1997, pp. 179–97.
Terrell, JoAnne Marie. *Power in the Blood?: The Cross in the African American Experience*. Maryknoll, NY: Orbis, 1998.
Thandeka. *The Embodied Self: Friedrich Schleiermacher's Solution to Kant's Problem of the Empirical Self*. Albany, NY: SUNY, 1995.
Thandeka. "Schleiermacher, Feminism, and Liberation Theologies: A Key." In *The Cambridge Companion to Friedrich Schleiermacher*. Edited by Jacqueline Mariña. Cambridge: Cambridge University, 2005.
The Anglican Church in Aotearoa, New Zealand, and Polynesia, *A New Zealand Prayer Book / He Karakai Mihinare o Aotearoa*. San Francisco, CA: Harper and Row, [1989] 1997.
The New Companion to the Breviary with Seasonal Supplement. Indianapolis, IN: Carmelites of Indianapolis, 1988.
Tice, Terrence N. Introduction to *Christmas Eve Celebration: A Dialogue*, rev. ed. Edited and translated by Terrence N. Tice. Eugene, OR: Cascade Books, 2010, pp. ix–xxvii.
Tinker, George. "Jesus, Corn Mother, and Conquest: Christology and Colonialism." In *Native American Religious Identity: Unforgotten Gods*. Edited by Jace Weaver. Maryknoll, NY: Orbis, 1998, pp. 134–54.
Tonstad, Linn Marie. "Ambivalent Loves: Christian Theologies, Queer Theologies." *Literature & Theology* 31/4 (December 2017): 472–89.
Tonstad, Linn Marie. *God and Difference: The Trinity, Sexuality, and the Transformation of Finitude*. New York: Routledge, 2016.
Touch Holiness: Resources for Worship. Edited by Ruth C. Duck and Maren C. Tirabassi. New York: Pilgrim, 1990.
Townes, Emilie. *Womanist Ethics and the Cultural Production of Evil*. New York: Palgrave Macmillan, 2006.
Trible, Phyllis. *God and the Rhetoric of Sexuality*. Philadelphia, PA: Fortress, 1978.
Trible, Phyllis. *Texts of Terror: Literary-Feminist Readings of Biblical Narratives*. Philadelphia, PA: Fortress, 1984.
Turman, Eboni Marshall. *Toward a Womanist Ethic of Incarnation: Black Bodies, the Black Church and the Council of Chalcedon*. New York: Palgrave Macmillan, 2013.
Vander Schel, Kevin. *Embedded Grace: Christ, History, and the Reign of God in Schleiermacher's Dogmatics*. Minneapolis, MN: Fortress, 2013.
Vander Schel, Kevin. "Social Sin and the Cultivation of Nature." In *Schleiermacher and Sustainability: A Theology for Ecological Living*. Edited by Shelli M. Poe. Louisville, KY: Westminster John Knox, 2018, pp. 78–93.
Van Wyk, Tanya. "An Unfinished Reformation: The Persistence of Gender-Exclusive Language in Theology and the Maintenance of a Patriarchal Church Culture." *Verbum et Ecclesia* 39/1 (2018): 7 pages.
Vial, Theodore. *Modern Religion, Modern Race*. Oxford: Oxford University Press, 2016.

Vial, Theodore. *Schleiermacher: A Guide for the Perplexed*. T&T Clark. New York: Bloomsbury, 2013.
Welch, Sharon. *A Feminist Ethic of Risk*. Minneapolis, MN: Fortress, 1990.
West, Cornel. "The Crisis of Christian Identity in America." In *The Ethics of Citizenship: Liberal Democracy and Religious Convictions*. Edited by J. Caleb Clanton. Waco, TX: Baylor University Press, 2009, pp. 293–310.
West, Traci C. *Disruptive Christian Ethics: When Racism and Women's Lives Matter*. Louisville, KY: Westminster John Knox, 2006.
What Is Constructive Theology? Histories, Methodologies, and Perspectives. Edited by Marion Grau and Jason Wyman. New York: Bloomsbury, 2020.
Whedbee, J. William. *The Bible and the Cosmic Vision*. Cambridge: Cambridge University Press, 1998.
Wiegman, Robyn, and Elizabeth A. Wilson. "Introduction: Antinormativity's Queer Conventions." *differences: A Journal of Feminist Cultural Studies* 26/1 (2015): 1–25.
Williams, Delores S. "Black Women's Surrogacy Experience and the Christian Notion of Redemption." In *Cross Examinations: Readings on the Meaning of the Cross Today*. Edited by Marit Trelstad. Minneapolis, MN: Fortress, 2006, pp. 19–32.
Williams, Delores S. "The Color of Feminism." *Christianity and Crisis* 45/7 (April 29, 1985): 164–5.
Williams, Delores S. "The Color of Feminism: Or Speaking in the Black Woman's Tongue." *Journal of Religious Thought* 43/1 (1986): 42–58.
Williams, Delores S. *Sisters in the Wilderness: The Challenge of Womanist God-Talk*. Maryknoll, NY: Orbis, 1993.
Wilson-Kastner, Patricia. *Imagery for Preaching*. Minneapolis, MN: Fortress, 1989.
Wyman, Jason A. *Constructing Constructive Theology: An Introductory Sketch*. Minneapolis, MN: Fortress, 2017.
Wyman, Walter E. "The Role of the Protestant Confessions in Schleiermacher's The Christian Faith." *Journal of Religion* 87/3 (July 2003): 355–85.
Yee, Gale A. *Poor Banished Children of Eve: Woman as Evil in the Hebrew Bible*. Minneapolis, MN: Fortress, 2003.
Yetunde, Pamela Ayo. "Black Lesbians to the Rescue! A Brief Correction with Implications for Womanist Christian Theology and Womanist Buddhology." *Religions* 8/175 (2017): 10 pages.
Yong, Amos. *Spirit of Love: A Trinitarian Theology of Grace*. Waco, TX: Baylor, 2012.
Zachhuber, Johannes. *Theology as Science in Nineteenth-Century Germany: From F.C. Baur to Ernst Troeltsch*. Oxford: Oxford University Press, 2013.

INDEX

absolute dependence, 62, 72, 93–8, 118, 123–4, 182–6, 193, 204–205, 207, 212
Adler, Rachel, 50 n.49, 73, 153–5
Althaus-Reid, Marcella, 6 n.11, 66, 171–4
androcentrism, 1–2, 33, 39, 50–1, 75, 82–3, 170–1, 175
apophaticism, 69–70, 76–7 n.148, 129–30, 198–201, 208

Baker-Fletcher, Karen, 45 n.31, 89 n.40, 105–6, 138, 184
Bible (*see* scripture)
Butler, Judith, 86, 120, 160, 165 n.96

Calvin, John, 5, 28, 56
Christ
  as brother/ancestor, 4 n.7, 80, 141
  as completion of creation, 57, 80–1, 92–6, 176–7
  as indwelt by God, 34, 56, 59–60, 65, 79–81, 90–2, 94–5, 100–1, 141
  and Judaism (*see* Judaism)
  and messianic faith, 82–3, 114, 116–19, 136
  the particularity of, 81, 87–8, 102, 112–14, 119–21, 141
  the suffering of, 52, 81, 96, 99, 101–12, 201–3
church, 2, 4–5, 9, 13–16, 22, 30, 39, 43–5, 49, 54–60, 66–8, 74–5, 80, 88 n.34, 97–101, 122, 125–6, 129, 137, 140, 143–52, 156–8, 175, 177
Coakley, Sarah, 39–40, 194, 198–205
Coleman, Monica A., 85–6, 89 n.37, 112, 136, 138
colonialism (*see* postcolonial theology)
community (*see* church)
Cone, James, 65, 90 n.41, 119–20, 132
Copeland, M. Shawn, 104 n.114, 107–8, 177
Crawford, A. Elaine, 89, 106

creation, 8–9, 44, 49, 54, 55–8, 61 n.96, 62–3, 70–1, 92–6, 125, 128–30, 139–40, 148–50, 162, 165, 176, 182–7, 191–3, 207–8

DeVries, Dawn, 100, 147 n.12
diversity, 2–3, 8, 23–4, 30, 46 n.33, 79, 127–8, 151–2, 160
Douglas, Kelly Brown, 83–5, 89, 106–7, 132–3

ecclesiology (*see* church)
ecological theology, 31, 66 n.112, 125–9, 138–40, 184–6
eschatology, 10, 28, 125–30

Farley, Wendy, 66, 71–2, 180–1
feminist theology, 6–7, 28–31, 51, 69–70, 84–5, 95–6, 110, 131–4, 138, 152–5, 157–65, 186, 194–8, 201, 203, 205

Gebara, Ivone, 121, 181, 186
God-consciousness, 60–3, 93–9, 106, 111–14, 117, 120, 123–4, 128, 133–4, 137, 140, 184–5, 187–8, 193
Grant, Jacquelyn, 85, 89 n.37, 103 n.106, 106, 119–20
Griffith, R. Marie, 30, 194–8, 201, 209

Hagar, 102–4, 168–72
Heschel, Susannah, 120–1
heterosexism, 17–20, 52–3, 64, 85, 145
Holy Spirit, 39–40, 45, 47–9, 54–7, 79–80, 88, 96, 99, 105, 141, 151–2, 169 n.120

interdependence, 19, 128, 208–9

Jantzen, Grace, 31, 51–2, 138
Johnson, Elizabeth, 39, 50–1, 65 n.108, 70, 73, 161, 175
Jones, Serene, 28–30, 133–6

joy, 11, 19, 31, 138–40, 143–51, 155–6
Judaism, 26, 53, 114–21, 128–9
Julian of Norwich, 39, 71
justice, 135–6, 139–41, 144–6, 153–6, 161, 174, 196, 209

Kant, Immanuel, 19, 24–5, 93–4, 154
Keller, Catherine, 121, 186–7
Kwok, Pui-Lan, 7, 133 n.255, 181
kyriarchy, 1, 39, 50–3, 74–5, 82–3, 181, 205, 209

love, 11, 19, 57–72, 94–7, 100–1, 109, 131, 137, 141, 150–2, 156, 180, 182, 191

McFague, Sallie, 40 n.10, 139, 157
mujerista theology, 172–4

natality, 31–2, 51–2, 95, 138–40, 147–8

original perfection, 28–9, 133–4
orthodoxy, 15, 49, 89, 202

particularity, 30, 87–8, 102, 112–14, 119–20
Plaskow, Judith, 164–8
pneumatology (*see* Holy Spirit)
postcolonial theology, 4 n.7, 7, 20–4, 27, 66 n.112, 69 n.128, 121–5, 180–1

queer theology, 6n.11, 66–7, 72, 87, 120–1, 157–61, 167–8, 170–2

racism, 24–7, 84–5, 121, 124, 145
Ravenscroft, Ruth Jackson, 18 n.77, 24 n.118, 113
redemption, 9, 56–9, 61, 96–101, 103, 108, 110, 118, 121–3, 133–4, 137, 190, 203–4
Reformed theology, 5, 8, 9, 22, 43–4, 57, 189
religion, 10–13, 17–18, 23–6, 30, 121–4, 129, 136

resistance, 23, 99, 102–4, 106, 108–9, 111, 112 n.148, 193, 202–4
Rieger, Joerg, 20–6, 66 n.112
Ruether, Rosemary Radford, 82–4, 86, 88, 164

Sabellianism, 41, 48–9, 53–7
Schüssler Fiorenza, Elisabeth, 1 n.1, 69 n.128, 70 n.130, 73, 75, 86–7, 96 n.71, 107–8, 119
science, 9, 13–14, 30, 44, 184
scripture, 5, 8, 15, 43, 45–6, 66, 71, 116–18, 136, 153–5
sexism, 17–20, 32, 50–3, 120, 154–6, 205
sin, 28–30, 99–100, 104–6, 131–6, 144–5, 165–7, 180, 187–93
Sophia (*see* wisdom)
Soskice, Janet Martin, 39, 69, 72, 157
soteriology (*see* redemption)
Streufert, Mary, 100–1, 110
Substitutionary atonement, 1, 8, 99–109, 203–4

Tanner, Kathryn, 6–8, 27, 40 n.10
Tonstad, Linn Marie, 40, 49 n.44, 51–2, 67 n.113, 76–7, 144 n.2, 198 n.86, 201–2, 204–5
Townes, Emilie, 30, 134–6, 178, 208
Trible, Phyllis, 165–71
Trinity, 92, 98, 99, 110, 185

universal causality, 61 n.96, 62–4, 68–73, 75, 134, 182–7, 191, 205, 207, 213

Vial, Theodore, 5, 8 n.18, 24–6, 93, 121

West, Traci C., 104–5, 208–9
Williams, Delores, 84–5, 89 n.37, 102–4, 169, 192, 203–4, 207
wisdom, 40, 58 n.80, 59–63, 68–74, 148, 181, 206, 211–12
womanist theology, 30, 72, 80, 84–5, 89–90, 101–10, 111 n.148, 138, 168–70, 192, 195, 202–3, 208

www.ingramcontent.com/pod-product-compliance
Lightning Source LLC
Chambersburg PA
CBHW072149290426
44111CB00012B/2012